HOW TO READ
T. F. TORRANCE

UNDERSTANDING
HIS TRINITARIAN
& SCIENTIFIC
THEOLOGY

ELMER M. COLYER

P. 70

129
₽₮₿

InterVarsity Press
Downers Grove, Illinois

InterVarsity Press
P.O. Box 1400, Downers Grove, IL 60515-1426
World Wide Web: www.ivpress.com
E-mail: mail@ivpress.com

InterVarsity Press® is the book-publishing division of InterVarsity Christian Fellowship/USA®, a student movement active on campus at hundreds of universities, colleges and schools of nursing in the United States of America, and a member movement of the International Fellowship of Evangelical Students. For information about local and regional activities, write Public Relations Dept., InterVarsity Christian Fellowship/USA, 6400 Schroeder Rd., P.O. Box 7895, Madison, WI 53707-7895.

All Scripture quotations, unless otherwise noted, are the author's translation.

ISBN 0-8308-1554-6

Printed in the United States of America ∞

Library of Congress Cataloging-in-Publication Data

Colyer, Elmer M., 1956-
*   How to read T. F. Torrance: understanding his Trinitarian & scientific theology / Elmer*
M. Colyer.
*   p. cm.*
*   Includes bibliographical references and indexes.*
*   ISBN 0-8308-1554-6 (pbk.: alk. paper)*
*   1. Torrance, Thomas Forsyth, 1913- I. Title.*

BX4827.T67 C65 2001
230'044'092—dc21

00-054443

20	19	18	17	16	15	14	13	12	11	10	9	8	7	6	5	4	3	2	1
17	16	15	1'4	13	12	11	10	09	08	07	06	05	04	03	02	01			

Preface

There is a growing consensus that Thomas F. Torrance is one of the pre-mier theologians in the second half of the twentieth century. No one can deny that Torrance is a scholar's scholar, a true theological heavy-weight.

Reading Torrance without a guide is a bit like entering a labyrinth. You just have to wander around for awhile, often retracing your steps, until you learn to find your way through his many books and articles to the theological vision he has pursued throughout his career. The purpose of my book is to facilitate an intelligent reading of the immense body of literature (well over six hundred items) that has flowed from Torrance's pen over the past sixty years. The chapters that follow are a kind of blueprint or guide on how to read the scientific trinitarian theology of T. F. Torrance.

While Torrance is a theologian's theologian, he is also a humble and godly disciple of Jesus Christ, deeply committed to the gospel and the church, and deserving of the appellation *evangelical*. Readers will find a thoroughly evangelical and christocentric theology in the pages that follow—one that is intellectually rigorous, yet rooted in a passionate encounter with and concern for the gospel. Torrance's theology arises out of the evangelical and doxological life of the church, but uncovers the theological deep-structures that inform Christian life and worship and thereby enriches and deepens the church's life and worship.

I am especially hopeful that evangelicals, among others within the great tradition of classical Christian faith, will read this book and begin to examine Torrance's theology, since I am convinced that they will find it especially fruitful. If my book encourages others to read Torrance's work and stimulates a much broader conversation about his theology, I will consider the effort in writing what you are about to read well worthwhile. The writing of this book has been an extremely beneficial exercise for me personally, for it is impossible to seriously read a theologian of Torrance's caliber without undergoing a kind of transformation into a new depth of theological reflection.

I am especially grateful to Geoffrey Green and T & T Clark for permission to utilize quotations from two of Torrance's books published by T & T Clark, *The Trinitarian Faith: The Evangelical Theology of the Ancient Catholic Church* (1988) and *The Christian Doctrine of God, One Being Three Persons* (1996). I also want to thank Donald Simpson and Helmers & Howard Publishers for permission to use extensive quotations from Torrance's book *The Mediation of Christ* (Helmers & Howard, 1992). Dr. Green and Mr. Simpson have been extraordinarily gracious in all of my contacts with them.

There are a number of people who have contributed significantly to the writing of this book. I want to thank Jeffrey F. Bullock, president of the University of Dubuque; Bradley J. Longfield, dean of the University of Dubuque Theological Seminary; and the Board of Trustees of the University of Dubuque, who provided me a sabbatical to complete the book. Several colleagues (Donald G. Bloesch, Alan Crandall and David Moessner) read the manuscript at various stages and provided helpful comments. Mark Achtemeier saved my book (at least it seemed like it) more than once by solving all manner of computer problems I encountered along the way.

Several generations of student research assistants (Brian Boyd, James Dauer, Realff Ottesen and Greg Schrimpf) handled various mundane details that are part of the publication process, as did Lu LeConte, our talented and gracious faculty secretary.

I also wish to thank the Wabash Center for Teaching and Learning in Theology and Religion, Raymond B. Williams (director) and Lucinda A. Huffaker for providing a Wabash Center Summer Grant (funded by the Lilly Endowment) which enabled me to devote two summers to my research for this book. The Wabash Center is a wonderful resource for teachers and scholars beginning their careers in the field of theology and religion.

I am grateful to Tom Torrance for graciously answering a number of questions concerning his theology and for providing various materials that I needed for the research and writing of this monograph. David

Torrance provided important information for the biographical chapter.

Four other people have contributed more to this book than anyone else. As you will discover in later chapters, Torrance argues for an "onto-relational concept of person" in which the relations between persons are deeply formative of the persons in those relations. Once when asked in an interview what was his greatest achievement and what has given him the most satisfaction in life, Torrance responded that it was getting married and having a family.[1]

That is true for me as well. My wife, Natalee, and our three sons, Josh, Jon and David, are a part of this book, both in the love of God I have learned from them, and also in the sacrifices they have made so that this book could find its way to publication. So I dedicate this book to them in gratitude and love.

---

[1]See Torrance's interview with Michael Bauman in Bauman's *Roundtable: Conversations with European Theologians* (Grand Rapids, Mich.: Eerdmans, 1990), p. 117.

INTRODUCTION

I would claim that it [the heart of my theology] is deeply Nicene
and doxological (theology and worship going inextricably together),
with its immediate focus on Jesus Christ as Mediator,
and its ultimate focus on the Holy Trinity.
THOMAS F. TORRANCE,
INTERVIEWED BY R. D. KERNOHAN

Thomas F. Torrance is considered by many to be the most outstanding living Reformed theologian in the Anglo-Saxon world. One of the leading theologians in the dialogue between theology and philosophy of science, he was awarded the Templeton Foundation Prize for Progress in Religion in 1978. His *Theological Science* received the first Collins Award in Britain for the best work in theology, ethics and sociology relevant to Christianity for 1967-1969. Torrance started the *Scottish Journal of Theology*, which he edited for over thirty years; founded the "Scottish Church Theological Society"; and served as Moderator of the Church of Scotland in 1976-77. He has written over thirty books and several hundred articles.

Yet despite the fact that Torrance is a world-class scholar and theologian, his work has not had the impact one might expect. There are several reasons for this lacuna which form the rationale for the publication of this book. Torrance is a theological heavyweight whose writing style can be dense to the point of obscurity. Critics, even friendly ones, have repeatedly commented on his enigmatic prose and overly compressed composition.[1] Torrance acknowledges this as a weakness of his theology,[2] though he also claims that the density of his style "is sometimes due to the difficulty of the subject matter."[3]

This problem of obscurity is exacerbated by the somewhat unorganized character of Torrance's publications. Most of his books are published lectures and collections of essays with overlapping content, but without an overarching architectonic that structures his theological vision. Nowhere in his publications does Torrance really systematize the various themes of his theology and method, though I suspect that he is probably a bit like Ernst Troeltsch who said, "I keep one [a system] in the back of my head . . . but only to correct it constantly."[4] Torrance had planned, though never wrote, a three-volume dogmatics which would have helped considerably.[5] But at the present time, the only way to fully grasp the contours of Torrance's theology is to read through his major works, a formidable task.

Two other factors contribute to the difficulty and the neglect of Torrance's work. In light of his encounter with natural science and philosophy of science (Maxwell, Einstein and Polanyi), Torrance operates with a rigorous and refined notion of science. This conditions his theological vision and leads to a distinctive orientation that is quite frankly incongruent with much of the theological world today.[6]

The second factor that complicates Torrance's theology is his *holism*. It

---

[1]Daniel Hardy, "Thomas F. Torrance," in *The Modern Theologians: An Introduction to Christian Theology in the Twentieth Century*, ed. David Ford (Oxford: Basil Blackwell, 1989), 1:86. In my research on Torrance I have discovered that the terse elucidation of his own views and those of others is often a capsule summary of an entire previously published essay on the subject.

[2]See Michael Bauman, *Roundtable: Conversations with European Theologians* (Grand Rapids, Mich.: Eerdmans, 1990), pp. 117-18.

[3]Thomas F. Torrance, *The Christian Doctrine of God, One Being Three Persons* (Edinburgh: T & T Clark, 1996), p. xi.

[4]See Ernst Troeltsch, "Meine Bücher" in *Gesammelte Schriften* (Tubingen: J. C. B. Mohr, 1925), 4:4.

[5]See I. John Hesselink, "A Pilgrimage in the School of Christ—An Interview with T. F. Torrance," *Reformed Review* 38, no. 1 (Autumn 1984): 61.

[6]On the novelty of Torrance's relational thinking, see Thomas F. Torrance, *The Ground and Grammar of Theology* (Charlottesville, Va.: University Press of Virginia, 1980), pp. 174-78. Also see Thomas F. Torrance, *Transformation and Convergence in the Frame of Knowledge: Explorations in the Interrelations of Scientific and Theological Enterprise* (Grand Rapids, Mich.: Eerdmans, 1984), p. 195.

is one of the difficult, yet intriguing, features of his thought. The integrative character of Torrance's theological vision is rooted in his conviction that analytical, deductive, discursive and linear forms of thought tend to break up the dynamic interrelationality of reality (divine and created), and are therefore inadequate.[7] Not only must Torrance's readers reconstruct his overall position by studying all of his important works, that overall position is itself *holistic*: the whole that can only be grasped by simultaneous subsidiary attention to the parts.[8] This is also part of the reason for the extreme length and intricate structure of sentences one regularly encounters in Torrance's prose. The interrelations between method and content are especially perplexing because Torrance's publications tend to focus on either one or the other rather than on the relations between the two.

The consequences of these characteristics of Torrance's position and publications are that his theology is repeatedly misunderstood,[9] and his work has not influenced the church and the theological community as significantly as it should.

My Encounter with Torrance's Theology

This book arises out of my encounter with Torrance's theology over the past two decades and my use of his work in the seminary classroom. My interest in Thomas F. Torrance's theology goes back to my early years in seminary. Even before that, in undergraduate studies, I encountered the problems posed for Christian faith by the intellectual history from Descartes and Newton through Hume and Kant to Nietzsche, Sartre and Heidegger, including developments within theology and historical/critical biblical studies in reaction to this history. I found my evangelical friends turning to a concept of verbal inspiration guaranteeing an infallible and inerrant Bible as the foundation on which to build theology and

---

[7]Robert J. Palma has Torrance right on this point. See Palma's "Thomas F. Torrance's Reformed Theology," *Reformed Review* 38, no. 1 (autumn 1984): 24-25. Palma's article is an excellent brief overview of Torrance's theology. Daniel Hardy's article "Thomas F. Torrance" is more insightful.

[8]See Torrance, *Christian Doctrine,* p. xi.

[9]A classic example of this is the case of Ronald Thiemann's discussion of Torrance's understanding of intuitive knowledge and his charge that Torrance is a foundationalist. See Ronald Thiemann, *Revelation and Theology: The Gospel as Narrated Promise* (Notre Dame, Ind.: University of Notre Dame Press, 1985), pp. 32-45. Part of Thiemann's problem is his highly selective reading of Torrance. See pp. 343-44, endnote 97, below for an in-depth discussion of Thiemann's work.

circumvent these historical/critical and epistemological problems. In spite of my respect for this approach, I found it to be inadequate.

My first encounter with Thomas F. Torrance's theology was not pleasant nor was I overly appreciative. I had to write a précis of *Reality and Evangelical Theology*[10] for a course in pastoral care, and Torrance's complex prose and over-compressed exposition made the experience frustrating. However, he at least was addressing what I perceived to be the right questions, and every so often the fog would lift for a moment in the course of my reading and an astonishing theological and spiritual panorama would come into view. At times, quite frankly, I found myself on my knees in praise and thanksgiving to God as I began to understand Torrance's rigorous trinitarian theological vision in a way that deepened and clarified my faith and my theological apprehension of the gospel. Much of the book, however, remained submerged in the fog.

Toward the end of seminary, when I decided to pursue doctoral studies, I knew that I wanted to work on Torrance's theology because this would take me into the epistemic and methodological problems posed for Christian faith by modern philosophy, science and critical biblical studies which those on the theological left and on the right tried to address from within their divergent perspectives. This study of Torrance's work throughout a graduate program reinforced my earlier impressions of his theology.

The difficulty and obscurity of Torrance's theology was frustrating, yet I repeatedly found myself coming to understand what I had always tacitly believed as a Christian in a way that deepened my faith and clarified my grasp of the theological structure of the gospel. This is not to say that I agree with all of Torrance's theology. But overall I have found his work extremely illuminating and beneficial, opening new possibilities for developing a rigorous trinitarian evangelical theology.

This has also been my experience as a seminary professor, guiding students into Torrance's theology. After teaching theology for a number of years, I have found that many students find Torrance's work (once they understand it) to be extraordinarily helpful (personally and pastorally) in preparing for ministry. I have witnessed seminarians' Christian lives and visions for ministry remarkably transformed by reading Torrance's work,

---

[10]Thomas F. Torrance, *Reality and Evangelical Theology* (Philadelphia: Westminster Press, 1982).

though not without frustration due to the difficult character of his publications for seminary students.

All of this has deepened my respect for Torrance and his theology. In the spiritual and pastoral wasteland of too much of modern academic theology, the rigorous yet evangelical and doxological character of Torrance's christocentric and trinitarian theology is a welcome relief, despite the difficulty of his work.

The Purpose of This Book

My book is designed to help overcome the difficulties in reading and interpreting Torrance's writings, and the resultant misunderstanding and unfortunate neglect of his work. The book can be viewed as an exercise in "local hermeneutics" in which I provide readers with the perspective, knowledge and tools necessary for productive reading of Torrance's publications. It is a book on how to read Thomas F. Torrance.

The following chapters address multiple issues in order to facilitate assimilation of Torrance's thought. Together the chapters provide a comprehensive overview of the salient themes of Torrance's theology and therefore a framework within which to read his work. The biographical essay (chapter one) situates Torrance's publications and theology within his life history. The footnotes, the selected bibliography and especially the suggestions for further reading for each chapter (found at the end of the book) all direct the reader to primary and secondary material for further research. Together this information provides a map to Torrance's diverse publications and their interrelations.

At various points in the text I deal with areas of Torrance's thought that require clarification, for example, his understanding (and rejection) of dualism and his views on natural theology. Throughout the book, especially in the notes, I interact with secondary literature and dispel a series of misunderstandings of Torrance's position.

In order to accomplish all of this, it was necessary to impose certain limits on my book. While I have read virtually everything he has written, I analyze only Torrance's mature positions, without sketching the development of his thought.[11] The reader will find indications of formative influences on Tor-

---

[11] On the development of Torrance's thought, see the outstanding work by Alister McGrath, *T. F. Torrance: An Intellectual Biography* (Edinburgh: T & T Clark, 1999). McGrath's book deals more with Torrance's intellectual development and the basic "contours" of Torrance's "scientific theology." Our books are quite different. McGrath focuses much more

rance's theology, but I do not thoroughly investigate his sources or trace his dependence on John Calvin, Karl Barth, Athanasius, Scottish realism, John Macmurray, Albert Einstein or Michael Polanyi.[12] Nor do I generally compare Torrance's work with that of other prominent theologians.

The book is also primarily descriptive, rather than critical. I do not assess the adequacy of Torrance's historical generalizations or his interpretation of other theologians.[13] Nor do I evaluate Torrance's theological contributions. As David Ford has correctly noted, it would be an enormous task to adequately assess Torrance's thought and it is unlikely that any individual scholar could do so.[14]

What follows is based on a careful reading of Torrance's published writings over many years. Except for a few exceptions I do not deal with Torrance's unpublished lectures, manuscripts or letters, or with unpublished dissertations on his theology. Priority is given to Torrance's later publications (post-1980), though supplemented by his earlier work at certain points.

The depth, breadth and integration of Torrance's theology can only be captured in an extensive analysis. Curtailing exposition in favor of these other activities, although they are indeed important, would prove detrimental to careful and comprehensive delineation of Torrance's theological vision. As such, my book is a prelude to many of these other activities.

Indeed, there is no way for the academy and the church to assess the fruitfulness of Torrance's work or appropriate his contributions without

---

on Torrance's intellectual development and offers a brief treatment of a number of key themes in Torrance's theology. My book outlines Torrance's mature theological position, but deals with very little of his life and theological development. The books actually complement one another nicely and together provide a comprehensive picture of Torrance's life, intellectual development and mature theological perspective.

[12]Anyone even faintly familiar with Karl Barth's work will see parallels in Torrance's theology in the chapters that follow.

[13]Torrance's readers cannot but feel a little cautious about his interpretations of a variety of theologians in the history of the church when those interpretations seem to closely approximate Torrance's own position; however, this is in large measure due to the creative dialectic Torrance employs between historical investigation and his own constructive theological perspective, as we will see in chapter nine.

[14]See Ford's review of Thomas F. Torrance, *Reality and Scientific Theology* (Edinburgh: Scottish Academic Press, 1985), in the *Scottish Journal of Theology* 41, no. 2 (July 1988): 277. The reason for this is that Torrance's work spans so vast a horizon. He has contributed substantially to Greek patristic scholarship, Reformation studies, hermeneutics and the doctrine of the Trinity. He is an authority on Karl Barth and is virtually unique among theologians in his understanding of philosophy of science. Torrance is best known for his work on theological method and the dialogue between theology and natural science, but he has written on nearly every theme in theology.

an informed conversation about his work. This conversation cannot take place without a carefully crafted blueprint on how to read his theology, and this is the *raison d'être* of my book.

Torrance's Theological Vision

There are several crucial autobiographical essays that reveal Torrance's theological orientation and provide pivotal clues concerning how to read his work,[15] especially with regard to the architectonics of his theological vision. I have developed the basic structure and content of this book in light of this material.

Already in his undergraduate studies Torrance had encountered Schleiermacher's *The Christian Faith* in English translation. While "captivated by the architectonic form and beauty of Schleiermacher's method and his arrangement of dogmatics into a scientific system of Christian doctrine,"[16] Torrance thought that the whole conception was quite wrong. Schleiermacher's fundamental presuppositions were, in Torrance's mind, incompatible with the nature and content of the gospel, and the categorical structure Schleiermacher imposed on Christian consciousness seemed to Torrance to have no basis in a realist scientific objectivity.[17]

Theology, if it is to be truly "scientific," needed another more adequate way of fulfilling Schleiermacher's intent, and Torrance recounts that, he was "determined from then on to make it one of. . . [his] primary objectives."[18] Thus, Torrance's goal early on has been the development of a methodologically and architectonically rigorous scientific theology true to the nature and content of the gospel. But what exactly constitutes a "scientific" theology? Readers who operate with a preconceived notion of science, one that is universally applicable *(scientia universalis)*, and then read

---

[15]See Torrance's essay "My Interaction with Karl Barth" in *How Karl Barth Changed My Mind*, ed. Donald K. McKim (Grand Rapids, Mich.: Eerdmans, 1986), p. 52. This essay also appears in Thomas F. Torrance, *Karl Barth: Biblical and Evangelical Theologian* (Edinburgh: T & T Clark, 1990), pp. 121-35. This book is primarily a collection of Torrance's previously published essays on Barth and is especially illuminating of Torrance's relationship to Barth. Also see Hesselink, "A Pilgrimage," pp. 51-64. This interview provides an autobiographical overview of Torrance's entire life, especially his career as a pastor, professor and scholar. For this study, what is significant in these autobiographical essays is Torrance's overall theological vision, not what the essays may (or may not) disclose concerning the development of this vision.

[16]See Torrance, "My Interaction," p. 52.

[17]Ibid.

[18]Ibid.

Torrance in light of it will completely miss his intent.

A theology is scientific *not* when it conforms to the presuppositions or procedures of a universal science (there is no universal science in Torrance's perspective),[19] or even of other special sciences *(scientiae speciales)* such as natural science. Rather, in Torrance's mind, theological science, like every special science, *has its own particular scientific requirements and material procedures determined by the unique nature of its object or subject matter.*[20]

In fact, for Torrance, there are only particular special sciences with certain formal similarities (for instance, the method of any particular science has to be determined by the nature of its object) as human inquiries within the same space-time universe. Those similarities constitute general science *(scientia generalis)* which has no independent reality at all without the existence of the special sciences. While special sciences can, of course, learn from one another (as Torrance has from the natural sciences), each individual science must allow the nature of its object to be the controlling factor of every aspect of that science.

Thus theology can be scientific *if* God is knowable and *when* theology proceeds in accordance with the nature of its object—when it allows actual knowledge of God to determine the appropriate mode of knowing, to disclose the inherent relations in that knowledge and to generate the conceptual structures and their interrelations (and even the form of life) appropriate to that knowledge. So, for Torrance, a scientific theology is simply a theology governed from beginning to end by the nature of a knowable God.[21]

---

[19]For Torrance, there is no *scientia universalis* at all, despite the claims of certain philosophies. See Thomas F. Torrance, *Theological Science* (Oxford: Oxford University Press, 1969); reprint (Edinburgh: T & T Clark, 1996), pp. 106-40.

[20]Ibid., pp. 112-14. See ibid., pp. 106-40 for an extended discussion of the scientific character of theology.

[21]This is a point that George Hunsinger seems to have missed in his otherwise stunning book on Karl Barth. Hunsinger warns of Torrance's one-sided emphasis on "revelation objectivism" in which "perhaps entirely too much of the atmosphere of the physics lab hangs subtly over the account." Hunsinger is criticizing Torrance's early work, *Karl Barth: An Introduction to His Early Theology* (London: SCM Press, 1962). See George Hunsinger, *How To Read Karl Barth: The Shape of His Theology* (Oxford: Oxford University Press, 1991), p. 11. Or it may be that Hunsinger fails to realize that what Torrance finds especially interesting in Barth is the possibility of a "scientific" theology, a point which is pivotal in understanding Torrance's relation to (and appropriation of) Barth. Hunsinger's comments seem to imply that Torrance appropriates his understanding of science from physics and applies it to theological science. This is a common misreading of what Torrance has in mind.

With these convictions Torrance began a serious study of the theology of Karl Barth (Barth's *Church Dogmatics* I/1) while on the divinity faculty at New College under H. R. Mackintosh.[22] It was clear to Torrance at this early stage in his theological reflection "that any rigorous scientific approach to Christian theology must allow actual knowledge of God, reached through his self-revelation to us in Christ and in his Spirit, to call into question all alien presuppositions and antecedently reached conceptual frameworks, for form and subject matter, structure and material content, must not be separated from each other."[23] This implied the development of a rigorous epistemology, conceptuality and architectonic governed from beginning to end by the nature of the object or subject matter, God in God's self-revelation.[24]

While Torrance appreciated Barth's own understanding of dogmatics (*Church Dogmatics* I/1) as a critical science testing the dogmas (doctrinal formulations) of the church, in light of the objective *datum* or *the dogma* of God's self-revelation (Jesus Christ himself), "it appeared to be little more than a formal science and fell somewhat short" of what Torrance had in mind.[25]

When Torrance studied the second chapter on the revelation of the triune God (*Church Dogmatics* I/1.2), he began to find what he was looking for "in the doctrines of the *hypostatic union* between the divine and human natures in Christ, and the *consubstantial communion* between the Persons of the Holy Trinity."[26] Here Torrance felt he was "probing into the essential connections embodied in the material content of our knowledge of God and his relation to us in creation and redemption and that it might be possible to develop a coherent and consistent account of Christian theology as an organic whole in a rigorously scientific way in terms of its objective truth and inner logic, that is to say, as a dogmatic science pursued on its

---

[22]See Hesselink, "A Pilgrimage," p. 53.

[23]Torrance, "My Interaction," p. 53.

[24]Ibid.

[25]Ibid. What Torrance means by *formal* science is that Barth defined theology as a formal process of critically testing the church's doctrine in light of Jesus Christ, the objective *datum* of God's revelation. Torrance thinks that theological science is first and foremost about bringing the realities and inherent relations in God's self-revelation to articulation. It is those realities and their interconnections that determine the character of theology as a special science, not its formal characteristics such as critically testing the church's doctrinal formulations.

[26]Ibid., p. 54.

own ground and in its own right."[27]

Another point of some significance for Torrance was the doctrine of grace he learned from H. R. Mackintosh and H. A. A. Kennedy at New College, since it plays a pivotal role in understanding the relationship between divine and human agency throughout Torrance's soteriology.[28] So the nature of grace along with the "hypostatic" union and the internal relations of the Trinity provides the basis for a scientific account of theology "from its Christological and soteriological centre and in light of its constitutive trinitarian structure,"[29] a theology "deeply Nicene and doxological (theology and worship going inextricably together), with its immediate focus on Jesus Christ as Mediator, and its ultimate focus on the Holy Trinity."[30] The "concept of grace together with the internal structure of the Trinity and Christology" gave Torrance a "grasp of theology in its inner scientific relations."[31]

Part of Torrance's goal in all of this was to "isolate the core of basic and central theological concepts and relations, as few in number as possible . . . in order to grasp something of its [theology's] inner coherence and unity, and then use it as an instrument with which to comb through the whole corpus of accumulated beliefs and doctrines in the service of clarification and simplification."[32] This kind of scientific activity promotes a "penetrating grasp of the organic structure of our knowledge of God," and thereby enables theology to cut through the confusing and disorienting fragmentation of the church.[33]

---

[27]Ibid.

[28]See Hesselink, "A Pilgrimage," p. 53. Torrance later encountered and appropriated Barth's use of the *anhypostasis-enhypostasis* couplet to bring the nature of grace to expression (see Torrance, "My Encounter," p. 54).

[29]Torrance, "My Encounter," p. 54. Also see Hesselink, "A Pilgrimage," p. 53. These autobiographical accounts are decisive for understanding not only the genesis but also the structure and content of Torrance's theological vision. They also reveal that while Torrance has been influenced by Barth, he is no simple repeater of Barth.

[30]R. D. Kernohan, "Tom Torrance: The Man and Reputation," *Life and Work* 32, no. 5 (1976): 14. Also see Torrance, *Christian Doctrine*, p. 146.

[31]Hesselink, "A Pilgrimage," p. 53. I am not convinced that Hunsinger has properly understood Torrance's overall theological vision. When Torrance speaks of "a theology of the Word. . . a positive Christian dogmatics centered in Jesus Christ" (a citation by Hunsinger), all of the themes of Torrance's theological vision are implied. Once this point is clear, Hunsinger's criticism of Torrance's "revelational objectivism" when interpreting Barth misses the mark. See Hunsinger, *Karl Barth*, pp. 9-12.

[32]Thomas F. Torrance, *Reality and Scientific Theology* (Edinburgh: Scottish Academic Press, 1985), p. 156.

[33]Ibid., pp. 150-57. There is also a distinctively ecumenical motive behind this kind of clarification and simplification, since Torrance believes that many of the divisions among

Thus Torrance's early encounter with Barth played a formative role in the development of his vision for a scientific theology, and these autobiographical reflections provide clues to his overall theological vision and its architectonics. The immediate focus of Torrance's theology is on Jesus Christ as Mediator (the soteriological/christocentric center); Torrance's theology is fundamentally evangelical and christocentric. The ultimate focus is on the Trinity, whereas the movement from the economic Trinity to the ontological Trinity provides Torrance's theology with its constitutive trinitarian structure. Since theology and worship are intertwined throughout Torrance's work, his theology is also inherently doxological; theology is one aspect of the church's response to grace in obedience and worship.[34]

A Guide to the Chapters That Follow
The structure and important features of this book. So what exactly will this scientific theology look like? The answer to that question, of course, would have been Torrance's projected three-volume dogmatics. But even without his definitive synthesis, any serious interpreter of Torrance's theology must ask and answer the question, presumptuous as that may be. Anything less can be little more than a summary or interpretation of *themes* in Torrance's theology, which falls short of the architectonic holism (especially with reference to coinherence of form, content and method) intrinsic to Torrance's actual theological vision.

This book attempts to answer the question on the basis of Torrance's published writings in light of the autobiographical clues to his theology vision. Chapters two through nine elaborate the architectonic, content and method implicit in the compressed descriptions of Torrance's theological vision cited above. The initial focus is on Christology and soteriology (the mediation of Christ, chapters two and three). The overall organization of the chapters is trinitarian (see parts I-III in the table of contents). However, Part IV (chapters eight and nine) should not be viewed as an addendum

---

churches are due to "locally and temporally derived doctrines" that become the center of focus when they are really only of contextual and peripheral significance. This is Torrance's motive in focusing the dialogue between Reformed and Orthodox churches on the doctrine of the Trinity as a way to cut behind the divisions between East and West.

[34]Torrance sees theology not as a collection of abstract propositions, but as embodied truth in which faith, worship, discipleship and rigorous knowledge of God interpenetrate one another. See Torrance, *The Trinitarian Faith: The Evangelical Theology of the Ancient Catholic Church* (Edinburgh: T & T Clark, 1988), p. 6.

separate from the previous chapters. Rather, these chapters, on the Trinity and Torrance's theological method, thematize and develop content and method from chapters two through seven and thereby transpose the reading of those earlier chapters.

This means that the reader may need to review the material in chapters two through seven while reading chapters eight and nine (or even read the book twice) in order to grasp Torrance's holism, which only comes into view when one understands the whole with subsidiary attention to the parts. In order to adequately express Torrance's holism, key themes will appear in several contexts so as to emphasize the interconnections constituting his holism. Yet in order to keep repetition to a minimum, these themes will not be developed at length in every context. There are, therefore, numerous cross-references throughout the book so that readers can access in depth discussions of themes and more easily assimilate Torrance's holism.

Thus the structure of this book is not that of a progressive, sequential argument. Rather the chapters that follow discuss different facets of an integrated whole. Only by seeing how the elements of Torrance's thought interpenetrate one another will his theological holism gradually come into view.

Each chapter will build on those that precede it as the discussion progresses from one aspect of Torrance's theology to another. The chapters generally become progressively more difficult and presuppose mastery of the earlier chapters where basic themes in Torrance's theology are developed at an elementary level.[35] The order of the chapters could have been different (I might have started with "The Love of God the Father Almighty"), though the sequence used here has certain strengths over others.[36]

---

[35]The progressive difficulty of the chapters of this book is my attempt to strike a balance between providing an introduction to Torrance's theology that is accessible for pastors and upper-level seminarians, yet faithful to the subtlety and complexity of Torrance's holism.

[36]Consider, for example, a crucial statement of this sequence from the beginning of what is arguably Torrance's magnum opus, *The Christian Doctrine of God* (p. 2):

> The doctrine or the Trinity enshrines the essentially Christian conception of God: it constitutes the ultimate evangelical expression of *the Grace of the Lord Jesus Christ* who though he was rich for our sakes became poor that we through his poverty might become rich, of *the Love of God* who did not spare his own Son but delivered him up for us all, for it is in that personal sacrifice of the Father to which everything in the gospel goes back, and of *the Communion of the Holy Spirit* through whom and in whom we are made to participate in the eternal Communion of the Father and the Son and are united with one another in the redeemed life of the people of God.

There are three additional features of this book designed to aid readers. The first is that at points the footnotes contain further elaboration of themes for readers who are less well-versed in theology, philosophy and science. The table of contents provides an outline of each chapter with page references so that readers can easily locate discussions of particular topics within chapters and between chapters (for example, discussions of Torrance's view of Scripture are found in several chapters). Finally there is a detailed index that includes key concepts of Torrance's theology. The page numbers in the index that appear in bold indicate where the reader will find the crucial discussions of that concept which function in lieu of a formal definition of the concept.[37]

The bibliography for each chapter, found at the end of the book, provides a guide for reading Torrance's work on the subject matter covered in each chapter. The order of items in each bibliography indicates my suggestion for the most helpful sequence for reading Torrance's publication on a particular theme. The selected bibliography at the end of the book is a chronological list of what I consider to be the most important primary literature for understanding Torrance's mature theology, and the significant

---

Also see ibid., pp. 50-67. Elsewhere Torrance says that "the Grace of the Lord Jesus Christ, the Love of God and the Communion of the Holy Spirit constitute the trinitarian structure of all Christian faith and life." See Thomas F. Torrance, "Crisis in the Kirk," in *St. Andrews Rock: The State of the Church in Scotland,* ed. Stewart Lamont (London: Bellows Publishing, 1992), pp. 21-22.

In his book on the theology of the Nicene-Constantinopolitan Creed, Torrance follows the pattern of that creed. He begins with God the Father Almighty and then deals with "The Incarnate Saviour" followed by "The Eternal Spirit." See Torrance, *Trinitarian Faith,* pp. 76, 146, 191. Torrance also points out that in the liturgy of the church, the Father often comes first, as in the case of the baptismal formula. Yet in the benediction and in the evangelical witness of the church, the Son is mentioned first, since faith in God the Father and faith in the Holy Spirit are included in and arise out of faith in Jesus Christ as our Lord and Savior (see p. 197). The structure of this book follows this latter pattern in order to emphasize the evangelical and christocentric character of Torrance's trinitarian theology.

Also see Torrance, *Christian Doctrine,* pp. 136-37, where he discusses the relation between the *ordo cognoscendi* and the *ordo essendi.* Note that Torrance acknowledges the diversity of order in the New Testament which underscores the fact that the order used in no way detracts from the full equality of the three persons.

[37]One aspect of Torrance's *critical* realism is his emphasis on thinking *realities* through concepts, rather than simply thinking *concepts.* This is an important point and it is the reason Torrance is wary of rigid, formal definitions of terms and concepts, and prefers a more dynamic use of concepts and terms rooted in the intricate informal connection between concepts and the tacit, participatory context within which concepts ultimately bear upon reality and vice versa. This is why I have avoided using a glossary of terms in favor of a detailed index so that readers can assimilate the meaning of concepts and terms from the contexts in Torrance's theology within which they are embedded.

secondary literature on Torrance's theology published to date.

An overview of the content of the book. The incarnation constitutes the
ontological ground of knowledge of God, since for Torrance what God reveals to us is not mere information but rather a Self-revelation and Self-
communication. To know God through Jesus Christ, the incarnate Son
who is of the same being *(homoousios)* as God the Father, is to know God in
strict accordance with God's nature.[38] For Torrance, *homoousios* is the epistemological and ontological linchpin of revelation and reconciliation, and
therefore of Christian theology.[39]

Since there is no inherent isomorphism between human thought/life
and knowledge of God, revelation has to be a revealing of *God* by *God* that
is nevertheless actualized within the structures of *our* creaturely, historical
existence, including the media of human thought and speech. This means
that for Torrance, revelation is dynamic *and* ontological on both the divine
and human poles. The mediation of revelation is intimately bound up with
the nation of Israel, the incarnation, and the apostolic foundation of the
church. It is neither simply an event nor merely the inspired text of Scripture. God's self-revelation includes Scripture (though it cannot be reduced
to Scripture), but in a far more embodied and historical manner than is often recognized within evangelical circles.

Yet to really know a personal God in an intimate way demands that we
enter into an intensely personal and saving relationship with God through
Jesus Christ. Revelation and reconciliation are inseparable in Torrance's
theology. We cannot know God in an impersonal manner or apart from
God's purposes for our lives. Theology can never be more than a refinement and extension of the knowledge of God that arises at the evangelical
and doxological level of our living personal relationship with God
through Jesus Christ in the Holy Spirit.[40] Here Torrance emphasizes the

---

[38]See Torrance, *Trinitarian Faith*, p. 3.

[39]Torrance argues that "it is the incarnation of the Word [in Jesus Christ] which prescribes to
dogmatic theology both its proper matter and its method, so that whether in its activity as
a whole or in the formulation of a doctrine in any part, it is the Christology pattern that
will be made to appear." Thomas F. Torrance, *Theology in Reconstruction* (London: SCM
Press, 1965), p. 128. Also see Torrance, *Christian Doctrine*, p. 1.

[40]Thus "Christian Dogmatics from beginning to end is an empirical and personal engage-
ment of the tangible reality of Jesus Christ." Torrance is quoting H. R. Mackintosh with
approval. See Thomas F. Torrance, "Hugh Ross MacKintosh: Theologian of the Cross," *The
Scottish Bulletin of Evangelical Theology* 5, no. 2 (autumn 1987): 161. For Torrance, in genuine theology the "coherent body of informal truth embedded in the foundation of the

God-humanward activity of the incarnate Son in the hypostatic union assuming, healing and atoning for our diseased, broken, and sinful humanity in Christ's life, death and resurrection. Yet Torrance also stresses the human-Godward activity of Christ in his vicarious humanity, making the perfect human response to God in faith, conversion, worship, and obedience, though not in such a way as to undermine, but rather undergird, the integrity of *our* human response in repentance, faith, worship and obedience.[41]

This means that Torrance's theology is emphatically *evangelical*, as well as *christocentric*. The immediate focus is on Jesus Christ as divine-human mediator. Chapters two and three deal respectively with the God-humanward and human-Godward mediation of Christ.

Who is this God that we know through Jesus Christ? This is the focus of chapters four and five. Here Torrance regularly appeals to Athanasius' famous dictum that "it is more godly and accurate to signify God from the Son and call him Father, than to name him from his works and call him Unoriginate.'[42] The Creator-creature relation is vague and general because it is a relation *external* to God, whereas the Father-Son relation is internal or intrinsic to God. To know the Father through the Son in the Spirit is to share in the Son's knowledge of the Father, a knowledge incarnate in Christ within our human and creaturely conditions in space and time.

To know God in *this* way is also to know that God exceeds all we can ever think or say about God *(Deus semper maior)*. We can apprehend God, though we cannot comprehend God. Here the doxological element of Torrance's theology comes to the forefront, for to know God in this way is to know that God loves us more than God loves himself, and to know the love of God that surpasses knowledge leads to faith, obedience and worship which stand in lieu of definition and keep all of our concepts heuristically open to the inexhaustible reality of God. Genuine theology is linked to a depth of truth in God far greater than can ever be brought to formal articulation. Since through Jesus Christ and in the Holy Spirit

---

Church in Christ and his gospel" comes to "formal expression" as it presses "upon the mind of the Church in its worship of God and in the fulfillment of its mission to mankind." See Thomas F. Torrance, "The Deposit of Faith," *Scottish Journal of Theology* 36. no. 1 (1983): 12.

[41]Torrance maintains that Jesus' historical human agency is at the very center of the gospel. Torrance, *Trinitarian Faith*, p. 4.

[42]See Thomas F. Torrance, *Trinitarian Perspectives: Toward Doctrinal Agreement* (Edinburgh: T & T Clark, 1994), p. 8.

we know more of God than we ever can tell, theological statements are always incomplete and open-textured, given from faith to faith in doxology.

The God-world relationship, the relation between being and act in God, and all of God's attributes are thought out by Torrance from within the mutual knowing between the persons of the Trinity in which we may share through the grace of Jesus Christ and in the communion of the Holy Spirit. The almightiness of God the Father is the personal power of freely self-giving love and not the abstract sovereignty of a God who controls and determines everything, but can do nothing new, such as enter into the broken history of God's creation, and cannot suffer with and for lost humanity in life and in death on the cross. This is the subject matter covered in chapter four.

Since, for Torrance, Jesus Christ is "the Origin or Principle," not only of all our knowledge of God, but also of all that God has done and will continue to do in the created universe, it is in light of the relation between the incarnate Son and the almighty Father that Torrance develops his understanding of the Creator and creation (chapter five).[43] It is as Father that God is Creator, so God's Fatherhood governs what we say about God's creative activity and omnipotent sovereignty.[44]

God has always been Father, but God has not always been Creator. Here Torrance emphasizes freedom and spontaneity of God speaking the world into existence out of nothing and giving it its own creaturely integrity purely and profusely out of God's ungrudging goodness. Creation *ex nihilo* distinguishes the Christian God-world relation (which Torrance describes as *interactionist*) from many others including classical theism and the manifold panentheisms that have become so monotonous in the modern theology. This Christian perspective underscores the creaturely contingence, intelligibility and freedom of creation.

Here Torrance finds points of convergence between theological science and natural science, a perspective quite different from the kind of hostile relations between the two disciplines in much of the modern period. Modern science rests on certain ultimate beliefs (like the contingence, intelligibility and freedom of creation) that it did not (and cannot) generate on its own, Torrance contends, beliefs which really have their

---

[43]Torrance, *Trinitarian Faith*, p. 7.
[44]Torrance, *Christian Doctrine*, p. 209. Also see Torrance, *Trinitarian Faith*, pp. 78-80.

origin in Judeo-Christian tradition. He sees the scientist as the "priest of creation" who brings the astonishing patterns and subtle symmetries of the created order to joyous articulation in praise and adoration of the Creator.

Since it is within the universe of space-time and its contingent rational order that the revelation of God in Jesus Christ takes place, Torrance thinks that there must be a kind of profound consonance between the intelligibilities and rationalities of revelation and those of the created universe, though not in terms of any kind of static analogy of being. Understood in this way, theology and natural science are not adversaries, but partners working together in service to God and humanity.

Drawing on the Greek fathers, particularly Athanasius and Epiphanius, Torrance develops a pneumatology that completes and qualifies the doctrines of the Son and the Father.[45] His doctrine of the Spirit arises not simply from biblical texts but out of the inherent structure of God's self-revelation and self-communication.

The Holy Spirit is not a divine presence, energy or gift detachable from God. Rather in the sending of the Spirit, *God* acts directly again and gives *himself* anew in God's intensely personal and dynamic reality (the Giver and the Gift are identical) to the creatures God has redeemed in Christ.

Torrance's pneumatology is fully integrated with Christology. Jesus Christ and the Holy Spirit mutually mediate one another throughout the economy of salvation. The doctrine of the Spirit must fully interpenetrate all of our understanding of Christ's revealing and reconciling work. Everything Christ does in the flesh is done through the Spirit. This in turn means that when the Spirit comes on the church at Pentecost, it is no naked or isolated Spirit, but rather the Spirit charged with all the earthly encounter of the historical Jesus. The new mode of activity on the part of the Spirit at Pentecost is conditioned by the evangelical events that lie behind it.

The Holy Spirit actualizes within us what God has accomplished for us in Jesus Christ in such a way that we come to share in Christ's divine life, light and love. Here Holy Spirit is the astonishing and distinctive freedom of God to be present to the creature and bring to completion the relation of the creature to Creator without violating the creaturely freedom and real-

---

[45]Torrance, *Trinitarian Faith*, p. 8.

ity of the creature.[46] Chapter six develops Torrance's understanding of the self-effacing activity of the Holy Spirit who directs attention to the Son and to the Father in the Son. Knowledge of the Spirit, as well as the Father, through the Son completes, qualifies and deepens knowledge of God as triune.[47]

This union and communion with God in the Spirit is actualized within the concrete structures of our human, personal and social being. Here the Spirit mediates not only personal but corporate communion between Christ and us so that the church is the body of Christ.[48] This is the basis of Torrance's realist conception of the church as the body of Christ, the earthly historical form of Christ's continued existence (Barth), for through the Spirit Christ himself is present in the church mediating his life to the church. Chapter seven addresses this subject.

Chapter eight on the triunity of God draws the discussions of the Christian doctrine of God in the earlier chapters into a final synthesis, as the ultimate focus of Torrance's theology moves from its constitutive trinitarian structure to the doctrine of the Trinity. This movement from the economic to the ontological Trinity, from the evangelical to theological Trinity, is crucial, for it reveals that the doctrine of the Trinity is not simply deduced from Scripture, but is rather much more deeply embedded in the church's evangelical and doxological encounter with the reconciling and revealing self-communication of God in the gospel.

Here Torrance utilizes the concept of *perichoresis* to bring the mutual indwelling and loving of the Father, the Son and the Spirit to clear articulation. This movement generates a distinctive idea of *person* in which the relations between persons are as essential and real as the persons themselves. This, in turn, influences how Torrance conceives of the one being of God which is every bit as personal as the trinitarian persons.

The being *(ousia)* of God is essentially personal, dynamic and relational being—self-grounded being for others. The being of God that we come to know through the grace of the Lord Jesus Christ in the communion of the Holy Spirit *is* the being of God for others, for while this being of God is not constituted by that relation to God's sinful creatures in revelation and reconciliation, the free unstinting outward movement in gratuitous love for

[46]Torrance, "My Interaction," p. 54.
[47]Torrance, *Trinitarian Faith*, p. 8.
[48]Ibid., p. 9.

others (for us) reveals something of God's own inmost nature. God in him-self and God for us, divine *ousia* and *parousia*, are so linked that we need never fear that there is some dark and sinister deity behind the back of the God we know face to face in Jesus Christ. For this reason, Torrance argues that "the doctrine of the Trinity belongs to the very heart of saving faith where it constitutes the inner shape of Christian worship and the dynamic grammar of Christian theology: it expresses the essential and distinctly Christian understanding of God."[49]

The final chapter of the book brings to focal awareness the theological method inherent and implicit in all of the previous material covered in the book.[50] A significant portion of Torrance's career has been devoted to the rigorous delineation of realist epistemology and method in theology ("philosophy of theological science" is Torrance's preferred designation). This chapter delineates Torrance's understanding of the integration of form (how concepts are derived) by locating it within a narrative on mod-ern epistemology from Descartes and Newton, through Hume and Kant, to Clerk Maxwell, Albert Einstein and Michael Polanyi. It will also relate this discussion to the theological interpretation of Scripture, the role of the church and tradition in theology, the nature of doctrine and the character of truth and authority in theology.

Since Torrance grants that no one, no matter how brilliant and self-crit-ical, operates outside a tradition, language and form of life, it is important to know some of the biographical details of Torrance's life that shed light on his theology. This is the subject of chapter one.

---

[49]Torrance, *Christian Doctrine*, p. 10.

[50]Torrance argues that it is scientifically false to begin with epistemology. See Torrance, *Theological Science*, p. 10. The reason for this is that the correct epistemology and a proper theological method emerge and develop in interrelation to the actual material content of theological knowledge, rather than in abstraction from it. Thus Torrance can say, "Strictly speaking, it is only at the end of the work of dogmatics, therefore, that it will be possible to offer a proper account of an adequate epistemology." See Torrance, *Karl Barth*, p. 72.

1

TORRANCE'S LIFE & ACHIEVEMENT

We did not stop at Guanshien but skirted round it and crossed over the main
course of the Min river by a wide new bridge that was still being constructed,
and then turned left on to the road winding through the steep
awesome gorges of the Minvalley. The road leads on to Songpan County
and where the giant Panda Reserve is located about 265 kilometers from Chengdu. . . .
The road up the left bank of the Min was very broken and very rough,
for here and there the surface had been churned up by floods
and was even washed away at places. . . . Every now and then we had to negotiate
a landslide, so travel slow and up and down. Unfortunately after about ten kilometers or so, we
hit a rock which holed the sump, so that all the oil leaked out, and we were left stranded.
THOMAS F. TORRANCE, JOURNAL OF MY VISIT
TO HONG KONG, CHENGDU AND WENCHUAN

I n 1994 Thomas F. Torrance traveled to the remote Minshan mountains of Wenchuan area of China as a Christian emissary to the indigenous Qiang people. He carried with him a money belt bearing 11,200
yuan, part of a larger gift of money for rebuilding churches destroyed by
the communist takeover in 1935.[1] Needless to say, the undertaking offers
a rather unusual image of an eighty-year-old scholar and theologian. The
incident is important because it reveals part of the origin of Torrance's

---

[1]Torrance writes that he returned to the area "particularly with the hope of encouraging the
Qiang Christians in the Mountains of Wenchuan County and finding ways to help them
rebuild some of the churches destroyed by the contingents of Mao's forces in the summer
of 1935 when in the course of their 'Long March' they found Christian communities in the
valleys of the Min and To rivers. I had particularly in mind the Church at Tongmenwai at
the entrance to Longqi Township where my father has established his mission headquarters in the summer months" (unpublished *Journal of My Visit to Hong Kong, Chengdu and
Wenchuan, April 22-June 3, 1994*, p. 1).

evangelical and missionary perspective that informs his life as a Christian, a minister of the gospel and a theologian concerned with evangelizing all areas of human life and thought.[2] You see, Torrance was also on his way to the place he called home for the first fourteen years of his life.

Childhood Years

Thomas F. Torrance was born in Chengdu, in the province of Sichuan, West China, on August 30, 1913. He lived there until 1927 when he returned to Scotland with his parents (a furlough year).[3] The oldest son of missionaries (Rev. Thomas and Mrs. Annie E. Torrance), Torrance says, "My parents were my first and best teachers in theology and that still remains true."[4] He describes his father as coming from a strong evangelical Church of Scotland piety and his mother as an Anglican trained to be a missionary.[5] She left a particularly strong imprint on Torrance, for after their furlough in 1927 his father returned to the mission field for another seven years while the rest of the family remained in Scotland.

Torrance describes his mother as "a woman of the greatest spiritual depth, prayer life, and theological insight," and the real theologian of the family.[6] Being raised in a Christian and missionary home meant that "belief in God simply pervaded everything" and so belief in God "always seemed so natural" to Torrance.[7] Torrance's younger brother, David, tells that their parents gathered the family for worship, reading of Scrip-

---

[2]See I. John Hesselink, "A Pilgrimage in the School of Christ," *Reformed Review* 38, no. 1 (autumn 1984): 49, 60. As a theologian, Torrance sees himself as an intellectual evangelist helping the church evangelize the entire culture. His years of dialogue with scientists needs to be viewed in this light. See Torrance's interview with Michael Bauman in Bauman's book, *Roundtable: Conversations with European Theologians* (Grand Rapids, Mich.: Eerdmans, 1990), p. 114. Also see Thomas F. Torrance, *Reality and Scientific Theology* (Edinburgh: Scottish Academic Press, 1985), pp. ix-x for the general foreword to the first volume in the series *Theology and Science at the Frontiers of Knowledge*. Torrance was the general editor of the series.

[3]Hesselink, "A Pilgrimage," p. 49.

[4]Ibid.

[5]Ibid.

[6]Ibid., p. 50. Also see Torrance's interview with Michael Bauman, in Bauman, *Roundtable*, p. 111. He also tells of a rather amusing incident while the family was still in China in which his mother and father were having an argument about bishops and his father was getting the worst of it. As his father went out into the garden somewhat "crestfallen," Thomas went after him and slipped his hand into his father's who looked down at him "and shook his head and said, 'Your mother and her bishops!' " (Hesselink, "Pilgrimage," p. 50).

[7]Bauman, *Roundtable*, p. 111.

ture and prayer (while kneeling) every day.[8]

All of the Torrance children (Torrance has two brothers and three sisters) are in full-time Christian ministry of one form or another.[9] From his earliest memories through his years at New College under H. R. Mackintosh, Torrance intended to be a missionary.[10] Unquestionably, the life and piety of his parents had an enormous impact on Torrance which appears repeatedly in the evangelical and doxological ambiance of his life and publications.[11]

Early Education

In Scotland, Torrance attended school and worked extremely hard to catch up on his studies. The Chengdu Canadian Mission School that he attended in China (1920-1927) was very deficient by Scottish standards. However, by 1931, after several years of intense study, Torrance had become a Dux (a senior scholar in Latin and Greek), and moved on to the university a year early.[12]

During this period (1927-1931) Scotland experienced dramatic unemployment and housing shortages. The Torrance family (minus his father who had returned to China) lived in a house in Bellshill in Lanarkshire. Torrance describes it as a "very, very difficult life" which he does not "look back upon with pleasure."[13]

---

[8]See David W. Torrance, "Thomas Forsyth Torrance: Minister of the gospel, Pastor and Evangelical Theologian," in *The Promise of Trinitarian Theology: Theologians in Dialogue with T. F. Torrance*, ed. Elmer M. Colyer (Lanham, Md.: Rowman and Littlefield, forthcoming), p. 3. The Torrance family continued this practice even when the children were attending university, though still living at home. It was "a very happy home" (see p. 2).

[9]Hesselink, "Pilgrimage," p. 50. Torrance's brothers are both ministers in the Church of Scotland. His three brothers-in-law are also ministers: two went as missionaries to Nyasaland and Rhodesia and the other, Ronald Wallace, was a Calvin scholar and professor at Columbia Seminary in the United States.

[10]A missionary to Tibet, no less! Ibid., pp. 49, 52.

[11]Ibid., pp. 49-50. Torrance refers to the impact of his parents on his life even in his theological writings: "I had been brought up by my parents in the Evangelical and Reformed Faith and learned from them how to dwell in the Holy Scriptures by reading several chapters of the Bible every day and letting them soak into the depths of my being, a habit I have continued all my life. The godliness of my father and my mother begot in me a biblical and theological instinct similar to their own upon which I have implicitly relied in all my basic judgements as a minister of the gospel and a theologian" (Thomas F. Torrance, *Karl Barth: Biblical and Evangelical Theologian* [Edinburgh: T & T Clark, 1990], p. 83).

[12]Torrance's mastery of other languages is impressive. He has published scholarly articles in Greek, Latin, French and German.

[13]Hesselink, "Pilgrimage," p. 51.

At the University of Edinburgh (1931-1934) Torrance studied classics
(Latin and Greek) and philosophy. Two of his most formative teachers were
Norman Kemp Smith, an authority on Kant and Hume, and A. E. Taylor,
who was an expert in Platonic thought.[14] As a missionary family maintaining two households on a meager income, the Torrances were not well off fi-
nancially. This meant that Thomas had to complete his M.A. in three years
rather than four and then move on to New College and the divinity faculty.

Graduate Studies

Here he concentrated on systematic theology, though the first two years
(1934-1936) were largely devoted to Greek, Hebrew and biblical studies.
Torrance's proficiency in all phases of Greek—classical, septuagintal,
New Testament, patristic and modern—earned him a John Stuart Blackie
Fellowship and enabled Torrance to pursue studies in the Middle East,
three months in Palestine and the Arab countries, and in Turkey and
Greece for an additional three months.[15]

At New College, Torrance's influential mentors were H. R. Mackintosh
and Daniel Lamont.[16] Mackintosh introduced Torrance to the theology of
Karl Barth in 1935. Torrance purchased and read Karl Barth's *Church Dogmatics* I/1 as soon as it came out in English translation in 1936.[17] This was
an "immensely exhilarating" experience and Torrance found himself captivated by Barth's insight into the ontology and objectivity of the Word of
God, God himself in his revelation. What especially gripped Torrance, was
Barth's "account of the Trinitarian content, structure and dynamism of
God's self-revelation as Father, Son and Holy Spirit, expounded in terms
of the biblical roots of our Christian faith and the Nicene-Constantinopolitan Creed."[18]

At this early stage of his theological development Torrance became utterly convinced that any rigorous scientific approach to Christian theology
must begin with actual knowledge of God reached through God's self-revelation in Christ and the Holy Spirit. Theology's task is to inquire into the

---

[14]References to the work of Smith and Taylor appear regularly in the footnotes of Torrance's
books.
[15]Ibid., p. 52.
[16]Ibid. Also see D. Torrance, "T. F. Torrance," pp. 6-7. Mackintosh died while Torrance was in
Syria.
[17]Thomas F. Torrance, "My Interaction with Karl Barth," in *How Karl Barth Changed My
Mind*, ed. Donald K. McKim (Grand Rapids, Mich.: Eerdmans, 1986), p. 52.
[18]Ibid.

essential connections embodied in this knowledge of God as it arises out of God's self-revelation and self-communication to us.[19] This implied for Torrance "that the Incarnation constitutes the ontological ground of our knowledge of God and must be allowed to occupy its controlling centre. But it also meant that if the activity of the Holy Spirit is to be taken seriously both divine revelation and our understanding of it must be thought out in *dynamic* and not in static terms."[20]

Despite his intense interest in these kinds of fundamental theological questions, Torrance's intention at this point was still to enter the mission field. During his second year at New College, he had organized a large meeting (a missionary conference) with students and invited Robert Wilder, one of the founders of the Student Volunteer Movement, from the United States as a speaker in order to recruit others for missionary service.[21]

However, Torrance won a scholarship for three years of postgraduate work and decided to study in Basel with Barth. So in 1937 he went off first to the Hegelhaus in Berlin to work on his German. He stayed for only a month since Mussolini was coming to Berlin and Torrance sensed that he was already under suspicion.[22] From there he traveled to Marburg where he continued his German studies and met Rudolf Bultmann.

When Torrance finally arrived in Basel to study with Karl Barth, he "proposed as a thesis to work out a scientific account of Christian dogmatics from its Christological and soteriological center and in the light of its constitutive Trinitarian structure."[23] Barth thought this was a bit ambitious! After Torrance told Barth that he saw the inner bond giving coherence to the whole structure of Christian theology in "the unique kind of connection found in *Grace*," Barth suggested that Torrance look at the way in which grace came to be understood in the second century.[24] The result was Torrance's thesis, *The Doctrine of Grace in the Apostolic Fathers*.[25]

---

[19]Ibid., pp. 52-56.

[20]Ibid., p. 53.

[21]Hesselink, "Pilgrimage," p. 52.

[22]Ibid., pp. 52-53.

[23]Torrance, "My Interaction," p. 54. There is an irony to this, since Torrance has spent his life preparing the ground for this kind of Christian dogmatics, yet he has been unable to complete the three-volume dogmatics that has been his ambition since his early encounter with Barth. See Hesselink, "A Pilgrimage," p. 61.

[24]Torrance, "My Interaction," pp. 54-55. Also see Hesselink, "A Pilgrimage," p. 53.

[25]Thomas F. Torrance, *The Doctrine of Grace in the Apostolic Fathers* (Edinburgh: Oliver & Boyd, 1948).

The two semesters spent with Barth "made an immense impact" on Torrance.[26] He heard Barth's lectures on the doctrine of God that later became *Church Dogmatics* II/1, read I/2 and engaged in intense theological discussion with his *Doktorvater* (academic supervisor) in public and private seminars.[27] Many years later Torrance commented that Barth's "doctrine of God is simply the best thing of its kind."[28]

A Year in the States

Upon returning home to Scotland in 1938 after his first two semesters with Barth, Torrance was persuaded by John Baillie to take over his old position at Auburn Seminary in upstate New York. This provided an opportunity for Torrance to work through all that he had learned from Barth in the context of preparing lectures to seminarians.

At the same time Torrance lectured on the interrelation between Christian theology and natural science and "began to clear the ground for a rigorous Christian dogmatics expressed within the contingent rational order with which the Creator has marvelously endowed the universe."[29] It was an extremely enjoyable year and Torrance made many life-long friends, which helps account for his numerous trips to the United States over the years.

This early emphasis on the interrelations between theology and science is crucial since it reveals a theme that runs throughout Torrance's career and his publications: the need for dialogue between theology and natural science and for a scientific theology as methodologically rigorous as the hard sciences.[30]

Part of the impetus behind Torrance's concern here is the fact that he had relatives who were scientists, like Sir Bernard Lovell, a cousin of Torrance's wife. In the course of a conversation about science and theology, Lovell asked Torrance about his scientific method in theology. Torrance

---

[26]Torrance, "My Interaction," p. 54.

[27]Ibid.

[28]Bauman, *Roundtable*, p. 112. Torrance views the doctrine of God in *Church Dogmatics* II/1, 2 as the high point of Barth's *Dogmatics*. See Torrance, "My Interaction," p. 54.

[29]Torrance, "My Interaction," p. 55.

[30]Thus a significant element of Torrance's intent as a theologian has been "to clear the ground for a dogmatics in the modern era, because the kind of dogmatics that we have learned from Calvin and Barth needs to be thought out and expressed more succinctly within the rigorous scientific context in which we work and which will undoubtedly dominate the whole future" (Hesselink, "A Pilgrimage," p. 60).

found that he had a lot of work to do to even be able to talk with Lovell about the interrelations between science and theology. This led Torrance into twenty years of hard study of modern science, particularly physics and philosophy of science, and has marked him as one of the most knowledgeable theologians in this area.[31]

Toward the end of the academic year (1939) Princeton University contacted Torrance (now twenty-five years old) concerning their new Department of Religion which was to be the first such department at any university in the United States.[32] He met with the committee; Theodore Green, the professor of philosophy, told Torrance that he would have students from diverse backgrounds—unbelievers and believers, agnostics and atheists, Christians and Jews—and that he would have to teach in a disinterested and detached kind of way so as not to offend anyone. Green added, "There must be no proselytizing."[33] Torrance responded that he would rather "teach theology as a science" where you do not "think in a detached, disinterested way; you think as you are compelled to think by the evidential grounds upon which you work."[34] Torrance further explained what he meant and added that he could not guarantee that if he taught theology in this way no one would be converted!

Much to Torrance's surprise, they offered him the position. But it was well after Easter in the spring of 1939 and the situation in Europe was ominous. After breakfast one morning, as he and Emil Brunner (who had been lecturing at Princeton) walked past the Institute for Advanced Study in Princeton discussing all of this, Brunner turned to Torrance and said, "I think we should both return [to Europe] before the submarines start!"[35] Torrance immediately decided to turn down the position at Princeton and shortly thereafter left for Scotland intent on becoming an army chaplain.[36]

The War
However, there was a two-year waiting list for chaplains, so Torrance went to Oriel College, Oxford, to work on his dissertation. Within a year he completed the basic work for the thesis. Toward the end of the school

---

[31]Ibid., p. 62. Also see Torrance, "My Interaction," p. 125.
[32]Hesselink, "Pilgrimage," p. 54.
[33]Torrance, "My Interaction," p. 56.
[34]Hesselink, "Pilgrimage," pp. 54-55.
[35]Torrance, "My Interaction," p. 56.
[36]Hesselink, "Pilgrimage," p. 55.

year (1940), under some pressure from the Church of Scotland, Torrance accepted a call to serve the parish of Alyth, Perthshire, a small country town of three thousand a few miles northwest of Dundee, where he was a parish minister from 1940 to 1943. He describes this as one of the happiest times of his life in ministry.[37]

Again in 1943 Torrance went to Edinburgh with the hope of becoming an army chaplain. Once again there were no openings, though he discovered that the Church of Scotland desperately needed a minister for the Huts and Canteens project in the Middle East. Within a few days, Torrance was on his way to the Holy Land where he served not only as a chaplain for the Huts and Canteens, but acted as an army chaplain as well.[38]

Six months later Torrance joined the Tenth Indian Division and he served in Italy until the end of the war as a chaplain working primarily with an English battalion, The King's Own Royal Rifles. Torrance insisted on serving front-line troops whenever possible. This placed him in constant danger. Once while on patrol, Torrance and the English soldiers crossed the German line and came under heavy fire. Only Torrance and one soldier made it out alive. Another time, lying in a ditch while being shelled, the soldiers on either side of Torrance were killed, though Torrance escaped uninjured.[39]

Experiences like these crystallized for Torrance that Christian theology has to be able to ground one's existence amidst the most acute moments of life and death. Torrance later called theologies without this kind of existential depth "paper theology"—interesting reading, but inadequate for living and dying.[40] His service was exemplary not only as a minister of the gospel to wounded and dying soldiers, but as an entrepreneur in various causes during the Italian campaign.[41] In 1944 Torrance was awarded the M.B.E. (Member of the British Empire) for his bravery.

The Postwar Period

After the war, Torrance returned to the parish in Alyth where he com-

---

[37]Ibid. Torrance was ordained in 1940.

[38]Ibid., pp. 55-56. Also see D. Torrance, "T. F. Torrance," pp. 15-17, for an in-depth discussion of Torrance's years as an army chaplain.

[39]See D. Torrance, "T. F. Torrance," pp. 16-17.

[40]See ibid.

[41]Hesselink, "Pilgrimage," p. 56. David Torrance recounts a number of hair-raising incidents where T. F. Torrance's life was in grave danger.

pleted his thesis on *The Doctrine of Grace in the Apostolic Fathers* and had
it published (1946 and again in 1948). Torrance returned to Basel for
what he describes as a "fearful" *rigorosum* (the oral examination for his
D.Theol.).[42]

Once he had completed his degree, Torrance returned to the parish in
Alyth. That same year (1946) he married Margaret Spear, who, like his
mother, was an Anglican. Torrance regards being married and having a
family as the best thing he ever did in life.[43]

The following year (1947) they moved to the large Beechgrove Church
in Aberdeen where H. R. Mackintosh, A. J. Gossip and J. S. Stewart had all
been ministers.[44] Torrance has no regrets about having served ten years in
parish ministry. Again and again he found that "the fundamental theological questions were the very stuff of the deep anxieties of the human
heart."[45] Indeed, parish ministry enabled, rather than hindered, him to
think theologically.[46]

During his three years at Beechgrove, Torrance published a book called
Calvin's Doctrine of Man (1949) in an attempt to untangle the debate between Barth and Brunner, who both appealed to Calvin on the relation between nature and grace.[47] He also founded the *Scottish Journal of Theology*
which he co-edited with J. K. S. Reid for over thirty years (1948-1982). He
had already started the *Scottish Church Theological Society* in 1945.[48] Thus
Torrance became heavily involved in theological education and renewal in
Scotland.

Professor in Edinburgh

In 1950 the Torrance family (now with two children; the third was born in
Edinburgh) moved to Edinburgh where Tom began his teaching career as
professor of church history at New College. After two years, he switched
to the chair of Christian dogmatics, which he held until his retirement in
1979.[49]

During the early years at New College, Torrance taught most of the

---

[42]See ibid., pp. 56-57.
[43]Bauman, *Roundtable*, p. 117.
[44]Hesselink, "Pilgrimage," p. 57.
[45]Bauman, *Roundtable*, p. 113.
[46]Ibid.
[47]Torrance, "My Interaction," p. 57.
[48]Hesselink, "Pilgrimage," p. 57.
[49]Ibid., pp. 57-58.

main loci of theology, except for the doctrine of God, including the Trinity (much to Torrance's disappointment), which fell under the domain of the chair of divinity held first by John Baillie, and then his successor, John McIntyre.[50] In the postgraduate program, however, he was free to teach in other areas such as ecumenical and historical theology (including regular seminars on the Greek patristic texts) and epistemology (what Torrance calls "philosophy of the science of theology").[51]

Also in 1952 Torrance organized a team of scholars (including Geoffrey Bromiley as coeditor) and began the monumental task of preparing and overseeing the English translation of Karl Barth's *Kirchliche Dogmatik*. The project took twenty-five years (the index volume published in 1977) and kept Torrance in sustained and intense interaction with Barth's theology throughout much of his career.[52] Despite some rather significant disagreements with Barth, this extended encounter with the *Kirchliche Dogmatik* unquestionably shaped the contours of Torrance's own theological horizon.[53]

The connection between Torrance and Barth is extremely significant. In fact, Torrance says that one of his greatest regrets in life is that while Barth wanted Torrance to be his successor at Basel (the Rektor of the University, Professor Oscar Cullmann, wrote Torrance about the position), Torrance was unable to do so because he did not want to subject his children (two sons and a daughter) to the disruptive change in culture and language in a move from Edinburgh to Basel.[54]

Torrance's literary productivity from 1952 onward is phenomenal. In addition to the *Church Dogmatics*, he also edited (with an introduction and historical notes) the three-volume *Tracts and Treatises on the Reformation by John Calvin* (1958) and the twelve-volume *Calvin's New Testament Commentaries*, with D. W. Torrance (1959-1973).[55]

Two other important early works are *Karl Barth: An Introduction to His*

[50]See D. Torrance, "T. F. Torrance," p. 21.

[51]Hesselink, "Pilgrimage," p. 58.

[52]Torrance, "My Interaction," pp. 57-58.

[53]Ibid., p. 60. Torrance writes, "To interact with the *Church Dogmatics* as I had to in the process of their publication in English was an immensely enlightening and exciting experience, that opened up for me the evangelical and ontological depths of the biblical message in such a profound and moving way that again and again I found myself on my knees before God in thanksgiving and adoration."

[54]Bauman, *Roundtable*, p. 113.

[55]Ibid., p.112. During his life as a minister, Torrance found Calvin's *Institutes* and his commentaries immensely helpful.

Early Theology (1962) and *Theology in Reconstruction* (1965). The latter is a roughly trinitarian collection of Torrance's lectures, many of which were previously published in various journals in the early sixties. Between 1946 and 1965 Torrance published more than ten books and roughly 150 articles and reviews.

One of his important books, *Theological Science* (1969), received the first Collins Award in Britain for the best work in theology, ethics and sociology relevant to Christianity for 1967-1969. It is part of an early trilogy of books—along with *Space, Time and Incarnation* (1969) and *God and Rationality* (1971)—designed to prepare the way for a rigorous dogmatics expressed within the modern scientific context.[56] All three books are methodological in focus and together present theology as a distinct and dogmatic science rigorously governed by the unique nature of its object, God in his self-revelation. Torrance intends to lay bare and test the rational basis of knowledge of God, including the theological concepts used to express this knowledge along with their spatial and temporal ingredients.

Torrance has also contributed significantly to Reformation and Patristic studies. In addition to his book on *Calvin's Doctrine of Man* mentioned above, Torrance has written on the eschatology of Luther, Butzer and Calvin (*Kingdom and Church*, 1956), *The Hermeneutics of John Calvin* (1988), and *Scottish Theology From John Knox to John McLeod Campbell* (1996). His book *The Trinitarian Faith* (1988) deals with the theology embodied in the Nicene-Constantinopolitan Creed, and is one of the books with which Torrance is most pleased.[57]

Recently Torrance published a collection of essays on *Divine Meaning: Studies in Patristic Hermeneutics* (1995). This represents the first of a three-volume history of hermeneutics and epistemology designed to "collapse modern biblical interpretation from behind" since Torrance thinks it "is basically wrong."[58] Though the subsequent volumes have not appeared in print, quite a bit of the material has been published as long articles in various journals and other books.

---

[56]Hesselink, "Pilgrimage," p. 60. Torrance links the three texts in Thomas F. Torrance, *God and Rationality* (New York: Oxford University Press, 1971), p. ix.

[57]See Torrance's interview in Bauman, *Roundtable*, p. 117. Torrance has written numerous articles on the Greek fathers. He also identifies Athanasius (not Karl Barth) as his favorite theologian, all of which reveals his appreciation of the Greek fathers and helps explain his connection with the Greek Orthodox Church (p. 111).

[58]See Hesselink, "Pilgrimage," p. 61.

Academic Societies

In 1969 Torrance became a member of the International Academy of Religious Sciences (*Académie Internationale des Sciences Religieuses*) through Stanislav Dockx, a Dominican scientist and theologian, and Gerard Phillips of Leuven, a Belgian dogmatician who had written the final edition of the *Lumen Gentium* for Vatican II and who was president of the Academy at the time. Two years later when Phillips died, Torrance was elected president of the Academy and served in this position from 1972 to 1981. This further expanded Torrance's contact with continental theologians through involvement in international seminars and discussions.[59]

These connections led Torrance into the sister academy, the International Academy of the Philosophy of Sciences (*Académie Internationale de Philosphie des Sciences*), in 1976. This is an organization primarily of scientists, mathematicians and physicists. Here Torrance became even more deeply immersed in international scientific work and in cross-disciplinary dialogue between theology and the natural sciences.[60] In fact, Torrance's recognition from scientists is sometimes greater than from other theologians. He is one of the few theologians who have edited a scientific text: James Clerk Maxwell, *A Dynamical Theory of the Electromagnetic Field.*[61]

Ecumenical Endeavor

Torrance had also been deeply involved in the ecumenical movement under the auspices of the World Council of Churches.[62] He attended the Faith and Order Conference in Lund, Sweden, in 1952 and served on the Faith and Order Commission from 1952 to 1962. Between 1950 and 1958 Torrance participated in the conversations between the Church of Scotland and the Anglican Church. Torrance was also involved in the 1954 meetings of the World Council of Churches in Evanston, Illinois; the Faith and Order Commission in Chicago, Illinois; and the World Alliance of Reformed Churches in Princeton, New Jersey. The essays contained in *Conflict and Agreement in the Church, Volumes I & II* (1959 and 1960, many

---

[59]Ibid., p. 59. Though Torrance was unable to accept an invitation to the Second Vatican Council, he was involved in the summer interim with some of the theologians who did participate.

[60]Ibid. Torrance's curriculum vitae lists his involvement in eleven different societies, centers and institutes.

[61]James Clerk Maxwell, *A Dynamical Theory of the Electromagnetic Field*, ed. Thomas F. Torrance (Edinburgh: Scottish Academic Press, 1982).

[62]See Hesselink, "Pilgrimage," pp. 58-59.

published previously in various journals) all arise directly or indirectly out of Torrance's early years in ecumenical dialogue.[63]

As noted above, Torrance's family has embodied ecumenicity. There have been several generations of familial interconnections between the Church of Scotland and the Church of England, as in the case of Torrance's parents. In addition, Torrance's wife, Margaret, has been a member of both churches, and two of their children were confirmed in both as well.[64]

Torrance has been a key figure in the dialogue between the World Alliance of Reformed Churches and the Greek Orthodox Church, which began in 1977. This led to a series of consultations between 1979 and 1983. The progress during these years was so impressive that all fourteen Orthodox Churches in the Pan-Orthodox Communion were invited to participate.

Further consultations led to a "Joint Statement of the Official Dialogue between the Orthodox Church and the World Alliance of Reformed Churches" issued on March 13, 1991, in Geneva announcing that an "agreed Statement on the Holy Trinity" had been reached.[65] The results of these discussions are found in two volumes edited by Torrance: *Theological Dialogue Between Orthodox and Reformed Churches, Volumes I & II* (1985 and 1993).[66] These connections with the Orthodox Church are so significant that in 1973 Torrance was made an honorary Protopresbyter of the Greek Orthodox Church within the Patriarchate of Alexandria, and in Addis Ababa he was consecrated during a Eucharistic service as a Presbyter by Methodios, the Archbishop of Axum.

Honors and Lectureships
In 1978 Torrance was awarded the Templeton Foundation Prize for Progress in Religion for his contributions in theology and its relation to natural science. He has received at least eight honorary doctorates. Torrance is a Fellow of the British Academy (1982) and of the Royal Society of Edinburgh (1979). Always deeply involved in the church, Torrance served as Moderator of the Church of Scotland in 1976-1977.

---

[63]See Thomas F. Torrance, *Conflict and Agreement in the Church* (London: Lutterworth, 1959), 1:7.

[64]See Hesselink, "Pilgrimage," p. 50. Torrance also served on the Reformed-Roman Catholic Study Commission on the Eucharist in Woudschoten, Holland (1974).

[65]Thomas F. Torrance, *Trinitarian Perspectives: Toward Doctrinal Agreement* (Edinburgh: T & T Clark, 1994), pp. 110-11.

[66]Thomas F. Torrance, ed., *Theological Dialogue Between Orthodox and Reformed Churches*, 2 vols. (Edinburgh: Scottish Academic Press, 1985, 1993).

Among his many lectureships, several are especially noteworthy. Torrance has lectured all over the world and in the United States nearly every year since 1959 when he gave the Hewett Lectures at Union Theological Seminary (New York) and Andover Newton Theological School (Massachusetts). He gave the Taylor Lectures at Yale in 1971, the Warfield Lectures at Princeton in 1981 and the Payton Lectures at Fuller Theological Seminary that same year.[67] Many of Torrance's books are related to these lectureships.[68]

Recent Publications

Anyone intent on seriously reading Thomas F. Torrance must carefully work through a series of his mature publications. This is not to say that his earlier works are unimportant. Indeed there are significant theological topics in Torrance's previous publications not covered in his later writings. But the following books are crucial for understanding the basic topography of Torrance's thought.

Transformation and Convergence in the Frame of Knowledge: Explorations in the Interrelations of Scientific and Theological Enterprise (1984) is a collection of previous published articles primarily on epistemology.[69] These essays locate Torrance's epistemic convictions within modern philosophy and science from Descartes and Newton through Hume and Kant to Clerk Maxwell, Albert Einstein and Michael Polanyi. It also includes a chapter, "Natural Theology in the Thought of Karl Barth," indicating where Torrance differs from Barth on this subject in relation to epistemology.

Another of Torrance's most important books, *Reality and Scientific Theology* (1985), deals with many of the same themes; however, this book develops them into a more comprehensive statement of his theological method, what he prefers to call "philosophy of theology," a rigorous discipline roughly analogous to philosophy of science and aimed at clarifying

---

[67]Torrance's curriculum vitae lists nineteen lectureships from 1959 to 1995.

[68]*The Ground and Grammar of Theology* (Charlottesville: University Press of Virginia, 1980), *Reality and Evangelical Theology* (Philadelphia: Westminster Press, 1982); *The Mediation of Christ*, rev. ed. (Colorado Springs: Helmers & Howard, 1992); *Reality and Scientific Theology* (Edinburgh: Scottish Academic Press, 1985); and *The Trinitarian Faith: The Evangelical Theology of the Ancient Catholic Church* (Edinburgh: T & T Clark, 1988) are all published versions of lectures previously given.

[69]The first chapter, "The Making of the 'Modern' Mind from Descartes and Newton to Kant," was not previously published, but is extremely important for understanding Torrance's epistemic convictions.

the process and epistemological structure of theological science.[70] This book is the first volume of a series called *Theology and Science at the Frontiers of Knowledge,* written by scientists and theologians, and designed to further a reconstruction of the foundations of knowledge taking place in the post-Einsteinian, post-Barthian era. Torrance is the editor of this series of inter-disciplinary and creative works intended to carry the transformation forward.[71]

In *Reality and Evangelical Theology* (1982) Torrance deals with the nature of theological and biblical interpretation of divine revelation and should be read in relation to the two books just mentioned. Together these three books provide an overview of Torrance's mature reflections on theological method and related areas. They can also be read along with Torrance's earlier trilogy (*Theological Science*; *Space, Time and Incarnation*; and *God and Rationality*) and the introduction in *Space, Time, and Resurrection* (1976) for a more comprehensive picture of this whole area of Torrance's thought.

Four additional recent books provide an overview of the doctrinal content of Torrance's theology. The first, *The Mediation of Christ* (1984, 1992), deals with the person and work of Christ and is the most accessible entry into Torrance's theology for seminarians and pastors. Readers should use the revised edition, which contains an additional chapter on "The Atonement and the Holy Trinity."

The Trinitarian Faith (1988), mentioned above, is an exposition of *The Evangelical Theology of the Ancient Catholic Church* (the book's subtitle) as it came to expression in the Nicene-Constantinopolitan Creed formulated in A.D. 381. However, since Torrance has been so deeply influenced by the Greek fathers, the book also serves as an introduction to many of the principal themes of Torrance's own theology. It is an excellent choice for those interested in his position on the doctrines covered in the creed.

Torrance's recent book *Karl Barth: Biblical and Evangelical Theologian* (1990) is significant because it not only reveals Torrance's relationship to Barth, but because Torrance's own theological vision shines through many

---

[70]See Torrance, *Scientific Theology*, pp. xi-xvi. This book is prefigured by one of Torrance's earlier works, *The Ground and Grammar of Theology*, which should be read in light of the more recent and developed text. *The Ground and Grammar of Theology* is the most accessible book dealing with methodological issues in Torrance's theology. The other books discussed in this section are all difficult.
[71]See Torrance, *Scientific Theology*, pp. ix-x.

of the book's essays. In particular, the chapters "Karl Barth, Theologian of the Word," "My Interaction with Karl Barth," "Natural Theology in the Thought of Karl Barth," "Karl Barth and Patristic Theology" and "Karl Barth and the Latin Heresy" all provide important insights into Torrance's own theological agenda and also the way in which he has appropriated Barth's achievement.

The doctrine of the Trinity is the subject of Torrance's book *The Christian Doctrine of God* (1996). It is probably the most significant and difficult of all of his publications. It represents what might have been the first volume of a three-volume dogmatics that Torrance proposed fifteen years ago.[72] The book is of particular interest for several reasons. The first four chapters deal with methodological considerations concerning how the doctrine of the Trinity arises out of the biblical witness and within the evangelical and doxological life of the church.[73] This is an intriguing section because here one can see Torrance's epistemology and method in operation on one of the central and methodologically perplexing doctrines of the Christian faith.

The second half of the book presents Torrance's creative restatement of the Christian doctrine of God, which will undoubtedly be one of the most important treatments of the Trinity well into the new millennium. What is particularly impressive and illuminating is that Torrance's approach is *holistic* rather than *discursive*—the whole is understood out of itself with subsidiary attention to the parts, not simply by progressing through the constitutive parts.[74] As I noted in the introduction, this is also one of the features of Torrance's theology that accounts for its difficulty and for repeated misunderstanding of it even by professional theologians.

These key recent publications present the core of Torrance's theological achievement. They represent his mature Christian theological position on issues related to theological method and on the positive content of his work on the central themes of theology. Students and scholars should begin with these publications and then branch out into Torrance's various articles written over the past fifteen years and into his earlier publications.

The Man Behind the Persona

My first personal encounter with Tom Torrance was nothing like what I

---

[72]See Hesselink, "Pilgrimage," p. 61.
[73]See my review of Torrance's book in *The Scottish Journal of Theology* 50, no. 3 (1997): 389-91.
[74]Ibid.

had expected. I had heard stories about a scholar whose erudition and passion often intimidated and demolished theological opponents.[75] In the spring of 1991 I was part of a small group of pastors and doctoral students who met with him at Princeton to discuss his new book, *The Trinitarian Faith*. He was most certainly erudite, but his unassuming humility and graciousness made the two-day event all the more memorable.

I liked the man immediately. There was a certain childlike humor and joy about him that was quite winsome and reminded me of Elton Trueblood in his later years. *Life and Work* magazine carried an article about Torrance when he was elected moderator of the Church of Scotland, describing him as a "brilliant, unassuming, immensely likeable man."[76] It may be that Torrance has mellowed with age, as did his *Doktorvater*, Karl Barth.

The characteristic of Torrance's life, and Torrance the man, that intrigues me the most is his missionary sensibility. His childhood on the mission field in inland China and his return to the mountains of Wenchuan county in 1994 to deliver financial resources for the rebuilding of churches planted by his father serve somewhat like bookends for his life. I view Thomas F. Torrance as an evangelical missionary who became a theologian without ever ceasing to be an evangelist. His audience has not been the indigenous people of China, but his goals have been the theological renewal of the church and the evangelization of the foundations of modern scientific culture.

---

[75]See Hesselink, "Pilgrimage," p. 64. I also have a number of friends who have said similar things about Torrance. At a conference held in Brussels in 1970 called "The Future of the Church," Torrance "caused a mild sensation by denouncing some of the more radical Roman Catholics for introducing into the Roman communion the worst features of nineteenth-century Liberal Protestantism." See E. L. Mascall, *Theology and the Gospel of Christ* (London: SPCK, 1977), p. 46

[76]See Hesselink, "Pilgrimage," p. 64.

PART I

THE GRACE OF OUR LORD JESUS CHRIST

2

THE MEDIATION OF CHRIST

Homoousios, Hypostatic Union, Atonement

We needed an incarnate God, a God put to death, that we might live.
We were put to death together with him, that we might be cleansed; we rose again with him,
because we were put to death with him; we were glorified with him,
because we rose again with him.
GREGORY NAZIANZEN

The holism characteristic of Thomas F. Torrance's thought is rooted in his fundamental convictions concerning the dynamic interrelationality of reality (ontology—form inherent in being) and the kind of inquiry required in order to grasp and articulate this interrelatedness (epistemology—the integration of form in knowing).[1] These interrelations or "ontorelations," as Torrance calls them, are relations so basic that they are inseparable from, and characteristic of, what realities *are*.[2] If we are to

---

[1]These basic convictions or ultimate beliefs arose out of Torrance's attempt to understand and articulate the basic interrelations embedded in the gospel. Here Torrance has found the early church and the Nicene theologians involved in the formulation and defense of the Nicene-Constantinopolitan Creed as extremely helpful. Torrance has also learned from Karl Barth and modern natural science (as found in Clerk Maxwell, Albert Einstein and Michael Polanyi, among others) in their effort to grasp and express the interrelated character of the realities they investigate (God in God's self-revelation or the creaturely universe of space-time) and their struggle against the dualism embedded in the received framework of thought.

[2]An example of this kind of holism in natural science (physics) is the development of field theory. See Torrance, *The Mediation of Christ*, 2nd ed. (Colorado Springs: Helmers & Howard, 1992), pp. 47-49.

really understand realities, Torrance argues, we must investigate them in the nexus of their interconnections, rather than in isolation, for they are what they are by virtue of the relations in which they are embedded.[3]

The goal of theology, according to Torrance, is to investigate and bring to coherent articulation the essential interrelations embodied in our knowledge of God through Jesus Christ in the Holy Spirit. As we examine the central realities of the Christian faith in this way, we come to know what they really are in their inherent organization and intrinsic significance.[4]

The rest of this book is really an exploration of the essential interrelations and intrinsic structure (form in being) of our knowledge of God in the gospel, and the conceptual patterns (doctrines) that rigorous theological activity generates (integration of form in knowing) in its examination of these realities and relations. This chapter and the next discuss Torrance's view of the mediation of Christ, Christ's person and work, in light of these basic relations and in light of the conceptual patterns that rigorous theological investigation develops in order to apprehend and articulate these relations.

To really understand Jesus Christ and the gospel, Torrance thinks that we have to adopt a twofold approach in which we examine Christ, (1) in and through the actual field or matrix of his interrelations with the history and people of Israel in covenant with God and (2) in light of who Christ is (within Israel) in relation to God.[5] This is the kind of approach that Torrance finds in the early church, for the followers of Jesus sought to map his significance within the real dynamic field of God's covenantal interaction

---

[3]Ibid., pp. 2-3.   Mediations of Christ

[4]Ibid., pp. 1-5, 47-50.

[5]Ibid., pp. 3, 5, 50. Particle physics provides an example within natural science of what Torrance has in mind. Classical physics viewed nature as composed of an infinite number of particles which are connected through external relations. Now (after Clerk Maxwell and Einstein) we view particles as interconnected within dynamic fields of force where the interrelations between the particles are part of what they are. Thus particles are not separated realities, but knots of energy within dynamic, indivisible fields of force. In addition, atomic physicists succeeded in cracking open atoms and also began to investigate their internal or intrinsic relations. Here, at the micro-physical level, natural science investigates the interrelations between particles that are part of what particles are, but also the intrinsic or internal constitutive structure of atoms themselves (pp. 2-3, 47-48, 50-51).

Torrance sees physical science throwing off epistemological dualism and an obsession with observationalism that restricts knowledge of reality to appearances, and embracing a critical realism in which science seeks to understand the way things appear in light of their interrelations and intrinsic structures.

with Israel through the ages, and also in light of Christ's relation to the God he called "Father." As the early church developed its inquiry along these lines, "the startling events in the life, death, and resurrection of Jesus fell into place within a divinely ordered pattern of grace and truth [*oikonomia*], and the bewildering enigma of Jesus himself became disclosed: he was the incarnate Son of God and Saviour of the world."[6]

This chapter follows this basic twofold approach by first (section two) examining Torrance's understanding of the way in which the reality and significance of Christ and the gospel are embedded in the matrix of God's dealings with Israel, where we find the forms of life and thought in which Jesus lived and within which he must be understood.[7] Equally important for Torrance is that Jesus Christ and the gospel have to be viewed in light of Jesus' relation to God as revealed in his life, death and resurrection.[8] Sections three through five will examine three interrelated and constitutive elements (and related theological concepts) of Torrance's perspective on the person and work of Christ. Section three deals with Christ's relation to God (the *homoousion*). Section four examines Christ's incarnate person as mediator (the *hypostatic union*). The final section (five) investigates Torrance's understanding of Christ's incarnational reconciliation (the *atonement*). Before turning to the actual discussion of Torrance's Christology and soteriology, it is important to take note of his rejection of dualism.

1. Torrance's Rejection of Dualism

Torrance's holistic approach leads him into sharp conflict with ancient and modern forms of dualisms. This rejection of dualism clarifies two points crucial to Torrance's theological perspective: his understanding of the God-world relation and his critical realist epistemology.[9]

Torrance believes that the church has had to struggle repeatedly with the problem of dualism, especially in the patristic period and throughout

---

[6] Ibid., p. 5.

[7] Ibid., pp. 5, 23.

[8] Ibid., pp. 3, 5, 50.

[9] Torrance does not begin by rejecting dualism, and then develop his God-world relation and epistemology. Rather his God-world relation and epistemology arise out of his theological investigation and lead to his rejection of dualism. We will examine Torrance's God-world relation and epistemology in much more detail in chapters four and nine. Here it is important to have a basic grasp of his position on these two themes in order to understand his Christology and soteriology, and also to signal the interrelations of this discussion to themes covered later in this book.

the modern era. Dualism connotes the division of reality into two incompatible or independent domains. Torrance's repudiation of cosmological and epistemological dualism is decisive for grasping his understanding of the mediation of Christ, and the rest of his theology as well.

Cosmological dualism posits a separation between God and the world. In both Greco-Roman philosophy in the cultural milieu of the early church and in Newtonian, deistic and other dualist perspectives of the modern period, there is a deep chasm between God and the world that makes direct activity of God in the world problematic (God's involvement becomes a radical disruption of "natural law") or altogether impossible.

Within a dualist cosmology it is difficult to make sense of all that Scripture has to say about God's activity in the world and history. Those who operate within a dualist framework tend to interpret the biblical accounts of God's agency in the world as nonliteral symbolism or premodern mythology, and therefore subject to allegorical or demythological strategies of interpretation in order to extract or explain the meaning embedded in the symbol or myth.

Epistemological dualisms assert or presuppose a disjunction between the human knower and the reality that the human subject seeks to know. Dualism in this form maintains that we cannot really know reality or the thing in itself (Kant's *Ding an sich*), but only how it appears to us, since all human knowing is colored by the language, culture and the activities and structures of the human mind always operative in the process of knowing.[10]

---

[10] Torrance speaks of the "damage which dichotomous ways of thinking" have done to our knowledge of God, for their effect has been "to detach Jesus Christ from God, to detach Jesus Christ from Israel, and to detach Christianity from Christ himself" (Torrance, *Mediation*, p. 1). Within epistemic dualism it is difficult or impossible to know much of anything about Jesus in himself, for what we have in the New Testament is Jesus as he has been appreciated and interpreted by various authors/communities in light of their perspectives and agendas. Modern interpreters are thus at least two steps removed from Jesus. The Jesus of the New Testament is not necessarily the Jesus of history, and modern readers live within a modern-postmodern context quite different from first-century Christianity.

At this point epistemic and cosmological dualisms often coalesce and operate together. Modern cosmological dualisms reject an "interactionist" God-world relation and therefore interpret what the Bible says about God's activity in the world in Jesus Christ (the resurrection, for instance) in terms of the mythopoetic or apocalyptic imagery of first-century Christian faith historically distant from modern-postmodern readers and communities.

David Strauss is an example of this. In his controversial work *The Life of Jesus Critically*

Torrance rejects both forms of dualism. In contrast to a dualist separation of God from the world,[11] Torrance adopts an "interactionist" or "realist" perspective in which God is understood as personally interacting with the world of nature and history while remaining distinct from it.[12] As we will see, this allows Torrance to utilize a "realist" interpretation of God's self-revelation in Israel, in the incarnation in Jesus Christ, and in the outpouring of the Spirit at Pentecost. Revelation is not a series of symbols or myths arising out of breakthrough experiences and produced purely by the active powers of a culturally bound human imagination. Rather revelation is the living God entering history, interacting with humanity and providing real and redemptive self-communication not of purely human construction.[13]

In contrast to epistemic dualism, Torrance argues for a critical "realist" epistemology in which reality discloses itself to human knowing in such a way that the human subject is capable of real understanding, both of the created world and of God. Rather than perceiving a radical disjunction between the human subject and object, Torrance sees a *po-*

Examined, ed. and trans. Marian Evans (London: SCM Press, 1973), originally published in 1835, Strauss interpreted the miraculous events in the Gospels as myth, "the representation of an event or of an idea in a form which is historical, but, at the same time characterized by the rich pictorial and imaginative mode of thought and expression of the primitive ages" (p. 53). Indeed "the sages of antiquity . . . deficient themselves in clear abstract ideas, and in ability to give expression to their dim conceptions . . . sought to illumine what was obscure in their representations by means of sensible imagery" (p. 54). Strauss adds that the biblical writers had "a ready disposition to derive all things . . . as soon as they appear particularly important, immediately from God. He . . . gives the rain and the sunshine . . . he hardens hearts and softens them. . . . Our modern world, on the contrary, after centuries of tedious search, has attained a conviction that all things are linked together by a chain of causes and effects, which suffers no interruption" (p. 78). Also see Colin Gunton, *Enlightenment and Alienation: An Essay Towards a Trinitarian Theology* (Grand Rapids, Mich.: Eerdmans, 1985), pp. 116-17. Here in Strauss we see the cosmological dualism of a cause-and-effect universe that suffers no interruption from a God outside of it, and an epistemological dualism, at least for primitive peoples whose "mythological" modes of apprehension, thought and expression are incapable of generating enlightened knowledge of reality; however, Strauss implies that the modern Western mentality is much more epistemically competent.

[11]Torrance's interactionist God-world relation is also very different from panentheist perspectives that posit an inner identity of the world with God as the world's "Ground of Being."

[12]Thomas F. Torrance, *Karl Barth: Biblical and Evangelical Theologian* (Edinburgh: T & T Clark, 1990), pp. 136-41; Thomas F. Torrance, *Reality and Evangelical Theology* (Philadelphia: Westminster Press, 1982), pp. 97-99.

[13]See Elmer M. Colyer, "Thomas F. Torrance," in *A New Handbook of Christian Theologians*, ed. Donald W. Musser and Joseph L. Price (Nashville: Abingdon, 1996), p. 465.

tential continuity, a *possible* correlation, *presupposed* by all human beings in everyday intercourse with the world and *confirmed* by successful scientific endeavor.[14]

Yet there is no inherent or automatic isomorphism between the human mind/thought and reality (no analogy of being in knowledge of God), but only an actual correlation or transparence *if* the human knower actively responds to the self-presentation of reality in the *appropriate* manner.[15] Successful knowledge is neither inevitable nor impossible for Torrance. The human mind does play an active role in knowing and that active role requires the generation (discovery *and* creation) of suitable forms of thought, speech and even life in order to know reality in its interrelations and intrinsic intelligibility.

Chapter nine outlines the precise relation between the discovery and creation of form in Torrance's understanding of human knowing. What is important for this discussion is that there is neither a disjunction nor an *inherent* isomorphism or correlation between the human mind/thought and reality. Genuine knowledge of reality in its interrelations is possible, but it requires the generation of suitable forms of thought and speech within successful human epistemic activity.

Torrance's rejection of cosmological and epistemological dualisms is bound up with his understanding of the mediation of Christ. God has *interacted* with humanity in history, within the creaturely conditions of the created world of space and time. God has revealed himself to humanity in Israel and in Jesus Christ. Yet, "If we are to know him [God] and speak about him in a way that is appropriate to him, we need to have fitting modes of thought and speech, adequate conceptual forms and structures, and indeed reverent and worthy habits of worship and behaviour governing our approach to him."[16] This means that for human beings to know God, they require not only a self-revelation from God, but also suitable forms of thought and speech, an active and appropriate human response, a communal reciprocity where God's reconciling self-revelation is actualized and mediated within the conditions of our creaturely existence.

---

[14]Ibid., pp. 465-66.

[15]Daniel Hardy is correct on this point. See Daniel Hardy, "Thomas F. Torrance," in *The Modern Theologians: An Introduction to Christian Theology in the Twentieth Century,* ed. David Ford (Oxford: Basil Blackwell, 1989), 1:77.

[16]Torrance, *Mediation,* p. 6.

2. The Mediation of Christ Within Israel

The prehistory of mediation in Israel. It is this generation of suitable form of thought and speech, this communal reciprocity that Torrance sees taking place in God's dealings with the nation of Israel in preparation for God's final self-revelation in Jesus Christ. Out of all of the peoples of the world God selected the Israelites and subjected them "to intense interaction and dialogue with himself in such a way that he might mould and shape this people in the service of his self-revelation" (the interactionist God-world relation).[17] God establishes this intimate covenant relationship with Israel in order to provide the appropriate forms of thought and speech, worship and life, through which apprehension and knowledge of God could take root in human history and become accessible to all human beings (critical realist epistemology).[18] *Mediation P7*

Torrance sees that "a two-way movement was involved: an adaptation of divine revelation to the human mind and an adaptation of articulate forms of human understanding and language to divine revelation."[19] This is a revelation that posits and sustains humanity (first in Israel and then in Jesus Christ and the church) as "the partner" in its movement from God to humanity and humanity to God.[20] Such a "profound reciprocity" is created between God and humanity that in assuming a human form this divine revelation evokes a responsive movement from humanity toward God "which is taken up into the movement of revelation as a constitutive ingredient in God's revelation of himself to man."[21] In this way divine revelation is anchored and realized within the actual creaturely conditions of human existence and rationality.[22]

---

[17]Ibid., p. 7. God's self-revelation entered our creaturely human condition through the people of Israel in the concrete trajectory of this people's historical existence so that God's self-revelation could be actualized and made accessible for all humanity. See Torrance, *Evangelical Theology*, p. 86.

[18]Torrance, *Mediation*, p. 7.

[19]Ibid. Torrance views God's interaction with Israel as producing a reciprocity between God and humanity where our knowledge of God and God's knowledge of us are interlocked so that we come to share in part in God's knowledge of himself. God's intrinsic intelligibility and our human understanding are correlated in God's self-revelation in such a way that authentic knowledge of God is actualized in an equally authentic human response. See Thomas F. Torrance, *Reality and Scientific Theology* (Edinburgh: Scottish Academic Press, 1985), p. 139.

[20]Torrance, *Evangelical Theology*, p. 85. Also see Torrance, *Mediation*, p. 12.

[21]Torrance, *Evangelical Theology*, p. 85. This includes communities of reciprocity—Israel and the church—which serve as social coefficients in knowledge of God.

[22]Ibid.

Yet this prehistory of the mediation of Christ in Israel involves not only revelation, but also reconciliation. Indeed, in Torrance's perspective, revelation and reconciliation are inseparable.[23] This inseparability accounts for the painful experience of Israel in mediating knowledge of God, for the holy truth and love of God burned like a fire in Israel, consuming every alien preconception Israel brought to its reception of God's Word.[24] For Israel to know God, Israel's communal worship, life, thought and very being had to be cleansed, renewed and transformed. Torrance sees God at work in Israel through the ages adapting Israel into the appropriate medium for mediating revelation and reconciliation to all humanity.

The actualization of revelation and reconciliation in Israel is progressive. Torrance depicts it as an ever-deepening, spiral movement of intensifying conflict and deepening conformity with God. Israel was subjected to God's patterned interaction (oikonomia) in such a way that Israel's responses in obedience and disobedience were shaped progressively into structures of thought, speech and life that serve as an appropriate medium for the continuing communication of God to humanity[25]

---

[23]Torrance, Mediation, p. 24.

[24]Ibid., p. 25. This is a principle that Torrance finds in all genuine knowledge where we attempt to know things in accordance with their natures, for epistemic activity involves a kind of cognitive union of the human mind with its object; this requires the removal of any alienation or estrangement that distorts or obstructs human knowledge of realities in accordance with their natures. Torrance points out that in areas like mathematics, where we are dealing with impersonal or abstract truth, our personal being is relatively unaffected. This, however, is not the case with knowing other persons, where genuine knowledge entails mutual respect, trust and openness that are reciprocal and mutually modifying.

In our knowledge of God this is even more the case, for here the removal of everything that distorts or obstructs the cognitive union and reciprocity established is of the most intense and personal kind and cannot but impact every aspect of our lives (see pp. 24-25). Torrance maintains that to know God in accordance with God's nature "requires cognitive union with him in which our whole being is affected by his love and holiness. . . . To know God and to be holy, to know God and worship, to know God and to be cleansed in mind and soul from anything that may come between people and God, to know God and be committed to him in consecration, love and obedience, go inseparably together" (p. 26).

[25]Ibid., pp. 17, 26. Divine agency and human agency are involved: there are actual divine self-communication and real transformed patterns of human life and thought within the creaturely conditions of space and time.

Elsewhere Torrance speaks of this as "an orderly continuum of successive patterns of change and coherent structures within which God may reflect and fulfil his own creative and redemptive intentionality . . . not a movement that passes over these structures [of this world] or gets stuck in them, for it continues to operate livingly and creatively in space-time . . . fulfilling the divine purpose within it and pressing that fulfillment to its consum-

Furthermore, the covenant established between God and Israel for the mediation of revelation and reconciliation was a covenant between God and an unholy people. The progressive mediation of revelation and reconciliation within Israel not only disclosed something of the nature of God, it also revealed the natural offence to God embedded in the human heart, "for it was the will and way of God's grace to effect reconciliation with man at his very worst, precisely in his state of rebellion against God."[26]

This led to the incessant conflict between the worship of God and the worship of idols reflected throughout the pages of the Hebrew Scriptures, a conflict leading to intense suffering, death and renewed life in Israel as the bearer of divine revelation and reconciliation. Torrance even calls this the "pre-history of the crucifixion and resurrection of Jesus in Israel."[27]

Within the prehistory of the mediation of Christ in Israel and the intense conflict it generated, God provided a covenanted way of response for Israel in the ordinances of worship and liturgies of atoning sacrifice described in the Pentateuch.[28] Torrance indicates that this does not mean that ritual sacrifices had any intrinsic power to undo sin or guilt, but that they bear witness "to the fact that while the holy and living God could not be approached apart from atoning reconciliation, he himself promised to provide propitiation for the sin of his people."[29] Chapter three will develop the covenanted way of response in more detail.

---

mation in the new creation" (Thomas F. Torrance, *Space, Time and Incarnation* [London: Oxford University Press, 1969], p. 72). Also see Torrance, *Evangelical Theology*, pp. 86-87. Here we see significant convergence between Torrance's position and that of what might be called the "ontological" narrative theology of someone like Gabriel Fackre. See Gabriel Fackre, *The Christian Story*, 3rd ed. (Grand Rapids, Mich. : Eerdmans, 1996), pp. 77-81; Thomas F. Torrance, *Theology in Reconstruction* (London: SCM Press, 1965), pp. 37-39, 51-52; and Thomas F. Torrance, *Theology in Reconciliation: Essays Towards Evangelical and Catholic Unity in East and West* (Grand Rapids, Mich.: Eerdmans, 1975), pp. 253-66, where Torrance deals with this theme in Athanasius' theology.

[26]Torrance, *Mediation*, p. 28. "Thus, the more fully God gave himself to this people, the more he forced it to be what it actually was, what we all are, in the self-willed isolation of fallen humanity from God."

[27]Ibid., pp. 10-11. It is also here that Torrance finds one of the roots of anti-Semitism, for the conflict between sinful humanity and God mirrored in Israel mirrors the hostility of all of humanity toward God. Torrance argues that this human resentment toward God has often been sublimated and vented toward Israel (see p. 8).

[28]Ibid., pp. 28, 74.

[29]Ibid., p. 36. Torrance suggests that "the rich pattern of sacrifice and offering instituted in the liturgy [of the Day of Atonement] gave the minds of the worshippers something definite to lay hold of even though it pointed far beyond itself to what God alone could do and would do for his people [in Christ]."

The mediation of revelation and reconciliation through Israel must also be viewed not as merely through the rituals and worship of Israel, or through the prophets or the authors of the Old Testament Scriptures, but rather through Israel as a whole in the totality of Israel's existence and mission. The reciprocity between divine revelation/reconciliation and Israel takes corporate form as a community of reciprocity. It involves not simply the surface of Israel's moral and religious consciousness, but an embodied and unitary mediation of revelation and reconciliation in which the physical and the spiritual, the visible and invisible, the temporal and eternal, the natural and supernatural, interpenetrate and coinhere in each other in the actual life and existence of Israel.[30]

Here Torrance views the Old Testament Scriptures, which arose within the ongoing reciprocity with God etched out in Israel's communal life and thought, not as "free-floating divine oracles with an independent existence of their own, in spite of their written form, for they cannot properly be detached from their embodiment in the whole historical fact of Israel and its vicarious role in the reception and communication of the Word of God to the human race, not least in the incarnate form of Jesus Christ."[31]

For this reason, Torrance argues that it is not "theologically appropriate" to offer an account of the inspiration of Scripture apart from the dynamic mediation of revelation and reconciliation between God and

---

[30]Ibid., p. 17. In more technical terms Torrance describes it this way: "God's revelation was mediated to Israel in the continuous indivisible field of space-time." (p. 16). Torrance views the created universe as a continuous unitary field of space-time that is organized in terms of a series of interrelated levels. Torrance develops a nondualist anthropology in which human beings span these levels from the molecular, through the biological, to the personal and spiritual. Body and soul, for Torrance, are not distinct realities, but rather distinguishable and interrelated levels. See chapter five below, pp. 180-82, for further discussion of this. He views Israel as spanning the various levels of the indivisible field of space-time. The revelation and reconciliation mediated through Israel therefore also span all of these levels, fulfilling the divine purpose for humanity and all of creation, and pressing toward the final consummation in the new creation. To grasp what Torrance intends here requires the ability to think of the nation of Israel (and the church) as a spatial-temporal reality spanning the various levels of the created order (from the molecular to the personal and spiritual) and moving through a successive pattern of change and development involving both divine and human agency together.

[31]Torrance, *Mediation,* p. 15. Torrance can even say that we cannot detach the Old Testament from the *land* of Israel, for when Israel itself was cut off from its land, it suffered a radical detachment that tended to transpose Judaism into an "abstract ethical religion, largely bereft of its all-important priestly and redemptive tradition" (see p. 16). Torrance sees Judaism in Israel today as struggling to recover its lost concreteness.

humanity just described.[32]

Within the dynamic mediation of revelation and reconciliation through the medium of Israel, God has provided humanity with "permanent structures of thought and speech about him."[33] Torrance, of course, acknowledges that there are certainly transient and variable structures that are not of permanent significance. Even the Holy Scriptures "are characterized by features that are of a time-conditioned significance."[34]

Nevertheless, nearly all the basic concepts and patterns appropriated by Christianity for interpreting Jesus Christ and the gospel "were hammered out by the Word of God on the anvil of Israel."[35] Torrance points to examples of the permanent structures he has in mind, including the Word and name of God, revelation, mercy, truth, holiness, messiah, prophet, priest, covenant, sacrifice, forgiveness, reconciliation, redemption, atonement and those basic patterns of worship found in Israel's ancient liturgy or in the psalms, for example.[36]

Thus what we find in Torrance's theology is not a timeless and spaceless revelation and reconciliation conceived exclusively in terms of an "event," provoking the charge of "occasionalism" (a noninteractive relation between the human mind and God in revelation), but rather a pattern of continued interaction between God and the time-space structures of this world in God's historical dialogue with Israel (the interactionist God-world relation). It is a revelation and reconciliation that includes and sustains the human response in Israel and provides suitable forms of thought, speech and life through which to really know God (critical realist epistemology). It is within the dynamic field of God's covenantal interaction with Israel that we come to understand Jesus Christ and the gospel.

Christ within the matrix of Israel. If we are to understand the mediation of Christ, it must be within the matrix of relations in which he is

---

[32]Torrance, *Evangelical Theology,* pp. 85-89. Torrance argues that God's self-revelation has to be actualized in the sinful alienated existence through a revelation that is also an atoning reconciliation and recreation. This also means that the inspiration of Scripture has to be thought out in light of Christ's atoning mediation between God's Word and our human response (see p. 163).

[33]Torrance, *Mediation,* p. 17.

[34]Ibid., p. 18.

[35]Ibid. See Torrance, *Evangelical Theology,* p. 87, where Torrance argues that God adapted Israel to be a womb for the incarnation, a matrix of concepts for the reception of revelation.

[36]Torrance, *Mediation,* p. 18.

found, the actual field of interrelations that God has established within the life and history of Israel and out of which Jesus Christ and the gospel arose. Apart from Israel, the incarnation of the Word of God in Jesus Christ would have been a bewildering enigma.[37]

Mediation of revelation. In the fullness of time within the life and litera-ture of the Jewish people, the Word of God became human flesh in Jesus Christ. In God's final revelation to humanity in Jesus Christ, the personal self-communication of God gathered up the forms of life and thought in Israel's faith/worship and provided in Jesus Christ (within Israel) an ut-terly faithful human response and truthful human understanding of that self-communication.

In Jesus Christ we find that the intensely personal self-revelation of God and the fully human understanding of that revelation coincide. The Word of God made flesh once and for all is indivisibly united with the perfect hu-man response within the structures of human existence.[38] Here Torrance argues that "as both the incarnate revelation of God and the embodied knowledge of God, Jesus Christ constitutes in himself the Way, the Truth, and the Life through whom alone access to God the Father is freely open for all the peoples of mankind."[39]

Torrance points out, therefore, that "Jesus Christ, not Israel, constitutes the reality and substance of God's self-revelation, but Jesus Christ in Israel and not apart from Israel, so that Israel the servant of the Lord is neverthe-less included by God forever within his elected way of mediating knowl-edge of himself to the world."[40] This means that only as we appropriate the prehistory of the mediation of revelation in Israel, including the perma-nent concepts and patterns mentioned above, are we able to understand Jesus Christ.

Yet it also means that since Jesus Christ is God's personal self-revela-tion, Christ fills these concepts and patterns with new and fuller meaning, and in the process reshapes and transforms them.[41] In this way Israel is

---

[37]Ibid., p. 18.

[38]Ibid., pp. 22-23.

[39]Ibid., p. 9.

[40]Ibid., p. 23.

[41]Ibid., pp. 9, 18, 22-23. In the birth of Jesus, son of Mary and Son of God, "the whole prehis-tory of that mediation was gathered up and brought to its consummation in Christ in such a way that while transient, time-conditioned elements fell away, basic, permanent ingredi-ents in God's revelation to Israel were critically and creatively taken up and built into the intelligible framework of God's full and final self-revelation to mankind" (p. 22). In this

gathered up, transformed and fulfilled, and has a permanent place in the mediation of God's revelation. Thus the Old Testament, arising within its embodiment in the life and history of Israel, must be understood in light of its fulfillment in Jesus Christ. And when the Old Testament is viewed in light of the New Testament in this way, it provides the normative framework of thought within which Jesus Christ can be recognized as the Son of God and Savior of the world and his death on the cross understood as an atoning sacrifice for sin.[42]

Mediation of reconciliation. God, the Holy One of Israel, drew near to Israel and drew Israel near to himself in such a manner that the covenant, with its way of response set out in the liturgy of atoning sacrifice, was translated into Israel's very existence as the elected servant of the Lord.[43] Already in the Isaianic "servant songs" Torrance sees Israel as the suffering servant of the Lord drawn into closest proximity to God as "the Holy One of Israel" in the mediation of reconciliation. The servant songs point ahead to the incarnation where the Holy One of Israel and the suffering servant actually coincide.[44]

Within this matrix of mediation in Israel we interpret the incarnation as God and humanity so near to each other that they are perfectly one in Jesus Christ.[45] There in Jesus, son of Mary in Israel, the Son of God gathers up the prehistory of reconciliation in the interaction of God with Israel and the intensifying conflict of Israel with God.

The fearful contradiction between God and humanity vicariously embodied in Israel's conflict with God reaches its climax in Jesus Christ.[46] Throughout his earthly life Jesus embodied this fearful tension, repeating

---

[41]regard Torrance suggests that the old Testament Scriptures "proclaimed far more than they could specify at the time and so by their very nature they pointed ahead to the full disclosure of the divine reality they served" (Thomas F. Torrance, *God and Rationality* [London: Oxford University Press, 1971], p. 149).

This is a clever move on Torrance's part, for it allows him to accept many of the problems and questions regarding the Old Testament posed by modern historical-critical biblical studies and sociology of knowledge. Yet at the same time he can appropriate elements of the Old Testament in light of Jesus Christ as permanent structures in the mediation of revelation and reconciliation. It is really an extremely sophisticated form of the christological exegesis of the Old Testament that we find in the early church and in Luther, for example.

[42]Torrance, *Mediation*, pp. 18-19. Also see Torrance, *Reconciliation*, p. 28.

[43]Torrance, *Mediation*, p. 28.

[44]Ibid.

[45]Ibid., p. 29.

[46]Ibid. See Simeon's prophecy in Luke 2:25-35.

the conflict between God and humanity represented in Israel, grappling with the root of evil in the human heart in enmity toward God, uncovering and decisively overcoming it in life and in atoning sacrifice on the cross.[47]

In fact, God uses Israel's rebellion, Israel's rejection of God's Messiah, as the very means by which God accomplishes God's final purpose of reconciliation in Jesus Christ.[48] Here God deals with human sin "at the point of its ultimate denial of the saving will of God."[49] God uses Israel's rejection and the disciples' shame and horror over forsaking and denying Jesus as the very means by which to bind them to Christ. Thus the disciples come to understand the passion of Christ as God's provision for the reconciliation of sinners to God.[50]

For Torrance, the most important point that comes to light when viewing Christ's mediation of reconciliation within the matrix prepared by God in Israel is that the incarnation represents "the coming of God to save us in the heart of our *fallen* and *depraved* humanity, where humanity is at its wickedest in its enmity and violence against the reconciling love of Christ."[51] In the incarnation God assumes not a neutral humanity different

---

[47]Ibid., pp. 29-31. Torrance sees the deadly inhumanity and source of human violence in the wickedness of the human heart. Torrance argues, in contrast to certain theologies today, that Jesus was resented and crucified precisely because he would have nothing to do with the role of a political/social/national messiah (see pp. 30-31).

[48]Ibid., p. 27.

[49]Ibid., pp., 28-29, 31-34.

[50]Ibid. This is true even of Israel's rejection of God's Messiah, for "within the totality of his atoning and reconciling work, Jesus took upon himself and made his own all the disobedience and guilt of Israel, and above all the sin of rejecting him and handing him over to be crucified" (p. 34). This, of course, is why Torrance argues that there is no room for anti-Semitism, because Israel is the vicarious representative of the hostility of all humanity toward God and because Christ bore even Israel's sin rejecting him and handing him over to be crucified. If we are to appreciate Israel's place in the mediation of revelation and reconciliation at this point, Torrance argues that we must view Israel as having a vicarious role to play.

Torrance has an astonishing and suggestive discussion of Israel's vicarious role on behalf of all humanity (see pp. 32-46, especially pp. 35-39). Torrance argues that Israel's vicarious mission in the mediation of reconciliation does not cease with Christ's death and resurrection, but has significance through all of history. Torrance further maintains that the deep schism between Christianity and Judaism that developed in the early centuries of the church, and perpetuated in history since, has impaired Christianity's attempt to understand the gospel, especially the atonement (see pp. 37-46).

Torrance's discussion of the relationship between Christianity and Judaism, the continued place of Israel in God's economy, and the need for dialogue between Christians and Jews is extremely insightful. Torrance has written a number of articles on the subject in addition to his discussions in *Mediation*.

[51]Ibid., p. 39.

from our own, but rather our fallen humanity, our actual diseased human nature laden with sin and guilt.

Here Torrance sees the ancient liturgy of Israel for the Day of Atonement (Yom Kippur) pointing forward to Christ. In that liturgy one goat is sacrificed within the Holy Place, whereas a second goat is driven away alive into the wilderness carrying the iniquities of Israel confessed over it by the high priest.[52] Torrance argues that we have to keep both sacrifices in mind if we are to understand what God has done for us in Jesus Christ.

Jesus Christ was vicariously baptized at the Jordan River and consecrated as Lamb of God to bear the sin of world. He was immediately driven by the Spirit into the desert like the scapegoat under the burden of our sin and tempted by the forces of darkness to abandon his mission as the suffering servant. Throughout his ministry Jesus was oppressed and afflicted, despised and rejected, reckoned with sinners and cut off from the land of the living. Yet he was pierced for our transgressions, crushed for our iniquities, for the Lord laid on him the sin and guilt of us all (Is 53).[53] Torrance finds both sacrifices from the ancient liturgy combined and fulfilled in the passion of Christ.[54]

Thus for Torrance, it is impossible to detach Jesus Christ from Israel, and the incarnation "from its deep roots in the covenant partnership of God with Israel," without effacing the very matrix of clues within which God's activity in Jesus Christ becomes intelligible.[55] If we are to know Jesus Christ, we must understand him within the dynamic interrelations of God's interaction with Israel, for this is the matrix within which Jesus Christ is found,[56] and it is the matrix in which his significance comes into view.

Yet if we are to really understand Jesus Christ, Torrance contends that we must also examine Christ's intrinsic significance or logos: (1) Christ's inner relation to God, (2) Christ's incarnate constitution as mediator and (3) Christ's incarnational reconciliation.[57] We will discuss these themes in the sections that follow.

---

[52]Ibid., pp. 36-37.
[53]Ibid.
[54]Ibid., p. 37.
[55]Ibid., p. 23.
[56]Ibid., pp. 2-3, 5, 50.
[57]Ibid.

3. The Inner Relation of Christ to God: *Homoousios*

The homoousion. As the early Christians carried the gospel outside of its Hebraic milieu in Judea, and Christianity began to develop within Greco-Roman culture, the church had to cope with the dualist patterns of thought characteristic of that culture, patterns that drew a sharp distinction between the eternal and the temporal, between the divine realm of changeless ideas and the mutable earthly world of space and time.[58] The antithesis between God and the earthly world of space and time invariably generated conflicting attempts concerning how to understand the relation between Jesus Christ (the Son of God incarnate within the changeable material realm) and the God whom Jesus called Father.

Thus the so-called Ebionite and docetic Christologies of various types arose each starting on one side or the other of the chasm between God and the material world and then employing various strategies to bridge the divide and connect with the opposite realm.[59]

The controversial teaching of Arius (among others) forced the church to ask and answer even more precisely the question of the exact nature of the relation between Jesus Christ and God. The critical question in the great patristic debates of the fourth century surrounding the Council of Nicaea was, What do the biblical expressions "by God," "from God" and "of God" mean when applied to Jesus Christ the incarnate Son?[60] Do they signify, as Arius maintained, that the Son is of or from the Father by an act of will, created out of nothing, and therefore different in being and act from God the Father?[61] How are we to conceive and articulate the relation of the Son to the Father?[62]

---

[58] Torrance has numerous discussions of the dualistic tendencies of Greco-Roman culture and the problems it created for the intellectual integrity of Christian faith. See Torrance, *Trinitarian Faith*, pp. 110-125, for a discussion of how dualism affected the church's understanding of Christ.

[59] Yet according to Torrance, all of them in one way or another broke up the wholeness of the New Testament witness to Jesus Christ as both truly human and fully divine. See ibid., pp. 110-121 for a detailed discussion of this. Also see Torrance, *Mediation*, pp. 52-53. Torrance notes a strange dialectic between ebionite and docetic Christologies in which each tended to pass over into the opposite. The root problem is that because of the cognate dualisms each presupposed, neither approach was really capable of starting from the essential datum of the gospel that *God* has come into our midst as Jesus Christ who is completely human as well as fully divine (see Torrance, *Trinitarian Faith*, pp. 113-14). Also see Torrance, *Mediation*, pp. 52-53.

[60] Torrance, *Trinitarian Faith*, p. 119. Also see Torrance, *Evangelical Theology*, pp. 111-12.

[61] Torrance, *Trinitarian Faith*, p. 119.

[62] Torrance, *Mediation*, p. 76. Already in the Isaianic "servant songs" in the Old Testament the prophet spoke in the same breath of Israel as the servant of the Lord (*ebed Jahweh*) and

The Nicene theologians, Torrance contends, carefully examined what the New Testament in its various expressions has to say about the relation between the incarnate Son and God the Father.[63] They gathered the import and mutual modification of these various texts in their conjoint focus on this relation and summarized the essential connection between Jesus Christ and God implicit in the evangelical and apostolic message in the second article of the Nicene Creed:

> [We believe] In one Lord Jesus Christ, the only Son of God, eternally begotten of the Father, God from God, Light from Light, true God from true God, begotten not made, of one being [homoousios] with the Father, through whom all things were made.[64]

The clauses in the middle of the article, "eternally begotten of the Father, God from God, Light from Light, true God from true God," were added to the creed specifically to clarify the unique nature of the relation of the incarnate Son to God the Father.[65] Furthermore, the Nicene fathers cut away all remaining ambiguity by concentrating the intent of the clauses in the final emphatic phrase "of one being with the Father" (homoousios to Patri). The additional clause, "through whom all things were made," made indubitably clear the identification of the incarnate Son with God the Creator.[66]

Since homoousios was a nonbiblical term, it had to be interpreted with greatest care, and it was, for the same reason, subjected to severe testing and

---

the Redeemer who is the Holy One of Israel (goel). Torrance argues that it was as if "the prophet wanted to say that the real servant of the Lord is the Lord himself who as goel-Redeemer has bound himself up in such a tight bond of covenant kinship with Israel that he has taken upon himself Israel's afflicted existence and made it his own in order to redeem Israel." In the New Testament, Jesus Christ is presented as both the divine redeemer and the servant of the Lord.

[63]Torrance, Trinitarian Faith, pp. 121-22.

[64]Torrance suggests that the Nicene theologians developed their basic insight through careful examination and testing of a whole host of biblical texts that deal with the relationship between Jesus Christ and God. One of the most important distillations of the essential core of the gospel on this point is in Matthew 11:27 (and Luke 10:22): "All things have been handed over to me by my Father; and no one knows the Son except the Father, and no one knows the Father except the Son and anyone to whom the Son chooses to reveal him." These texts, combined with parallels in John's gospel (chaps. 10, 14 and 17), enabled the church to integrate the overall fabric of biblical witness to the oneness between the incarnate Son and God the Father so as to develop the basic insights the church needed in order to cut through the confusing debates and articulate the essential nerve of the gospel on this point (see Torrance, Evangelical Theology, pp. 111-13). Also see Torrance, Mediation, pp. 53-54.

[65]Torrance, Trinitarian Faith, p. 121.

[66]Ibid., p. 117.

prolonged criticism throughout the fourth century between the Councils of Nicaea and Constantinople.[67] As the debates in the fourth century wore on, the church became ever more certain that the *homoousion* was not some novel intrusion into the apostolic gospel,[68] but rather a technical theological term that distills the very essence of the New Testament gospel.[69]

Torrance maintains that the *homoousion* expressed the essential content of the New Testament witness to Jesus Christ "in which faith in Christ perfectly coincided with faith in God."[70] The New Testament does not present "Jesus Christ in contrast to God or alongside of God, or argue from one to the other," as in Arianism and its Ebionite and docetic precursors. Rather the New Testament depicts Christ in his full and undivided divine-human reality as God become a human being.[71]

Only as the church focused on this undivided divine-human reality of Jesus Christ could it formulate a Christology that did justice to the whole New Testament presentation of Jesus Christ and the gospel.[72] *Homoousios* is, therefore, not a speculative concept or a transmutation of the simple gospel into the complex categories of Hellenistic philosophy, but a precise

---

[67]Ibid., pp. 116, 124.

[68]Ibid., pp. 114-15.

[69]In Torrance's words, *homoousios* "came to be used as a theological instrument to make clear the fundamental sense of the Holy Scriptures in their many statements about the relation of Christ the incarnate Son to God the Father, and to give expression to the ontological substructure upon which the meaning of these biblical statements rested. . . . Far from being an explicit definition, *homoousios to Patri* in the context of the Nicene declaration of faith was essentially an exegetical and clarificatory expression to be understood under the control of the objective relation in God which it was forged to signify" (Thomas F. Torrance, "The Deposit of Faith," *Scottish Journal of Theology* 36 [1983]: 11). Also see Torrance, *Evangelical Theology*, p. 112. *Homoousios* asserts that the incarnate Son is identical in being with the Father, for the Son is everything the Father is, except Father (see Torrance, *Trinitarian Faith*, p. 124).

Here we see that the *homoousion* carries within it an additional point that will become important in chapter eight. *Homoousios* expresses not only the oneness between the Father and the Son, but also a distinction between them within that oneness, for nothing can be *homoousios* with itself (see Torrance, *Trinitarian Faith*, p. 124-25).

[70]Ibid., p. 117. Elsewhere Torrance says that *homoousios* is simply a concise expression of the fact that the New Testament presents Jesus Christ's unbroken oneness to God the Father (see Torrance, *Karl Barth*, p. 166).

[71]Torrance, *Trinitarian Faith*, pp. 114-15. Arius viewed God as utterly transcendent and undifferentiated. The Son, like everything else, was created out of nothing and therefore alien and radically different from the Father. This of course means that for Arius the Father is finally ineffable and incomprehensible.

The irony, however, is that Arius also held that the Son is a creature, but different from other creatures. This means, Torrance contends, that the Son or Logos was actually an intermediary between humanity and God and not really human or divine (see p. 118).

[72]Torrance, *Mediation*, p. 53.

and accurate statement of Christian faith in the face of the Arian denial of the central relation of the gospel.

Torrance sees the formulation of *homoousios* as an absolutely fundamental and irreversible event in the history of Christian faith.[73] The church made an utterly crucial step forward in understanding and articulating the gospel, for the character of the all-important relation between the incarnate Son and God the Father, and therefore the intrinsic significance or *Logos* of Jesus Christ, came to rigorous expression by Nicene theologians.[74]

Torrance does not view *homoousios* as sacrosanct or irreformable, but as amazingly generative and of immense heuristic significance.[75] In order to clarify this point, it is illuminating to draw out some of the implications of the *homoousion* for the mediation of revelation and reconciliation.

Homoousios and revelation. That the incarnate Son is *homoousios* with the Father has astonishing implications for the mediation of revelation, for it expresses the fact that what God is in our midst in and through the Son of God made flesh, God really is in himself. Thus Torrance argues that, "Jesus Christ confronts us as One who is identical with the divine self whom he reveals."[76] Revelation is not simply information, but a full and final self-revelation, a self-communication of the living God. Jesus Christ *is* God's revelation.

In the post-Nicaea period of the fourth century the Nicene theologians came to recognize that what is true of the incarnate Son of God is also true of the outpouring of the Holy Spirit at Pentecost. What God imparts to us in the Holy Spirit is not something different than himself, but his very own self. As a result of the post-Nicene debate concerning the status of the Holy Spirit in relation to God, the Nicene theologians like Athanasuis concluded that the Spirit is also *homoousios* with the Father and the Son.[77] We will deal with this theme in chapter six.

Homoousios and a dynamic, ontological, trinitarian revelation. If God is—in

---

[73] Thomas F. Torrance, *The Christian Doctrine of God: One Being Three Persons* (Edinburgh: T & T Clark, 1996), p. ix-x.

[74] Ibid., p. ix. Torrance views the gospel working itself out in the life and thought of the early church in such a way that it had the effect of transforming the thought-forms of the Hellenistic world. Ibid., p. x. Also see Torrance, *Trinitarian Faith*, p. 124.

[75] Torrance, *Christian Doctrine*, p. x. Indeed, Torrance acknowledges the Nicene-Constantinopolitan theology as providing the insights he has found most helpful in his theological reformulation (see p. xi).

[76] Torrance, *Mediation*, p. 23.

[77] See Torrance, *Trinitarian Faith*, pp. 201-5.

the internal relations of God's own being—the same Father, Son, and Holy Spirit that God is in God's revealing and reconciling activity toward us,[78] and if through Jesus Christ and in the Holy Spirit God reveals himself through himself, then God's revealing and reconciling activity is essentially triune.[79] The "Grace of our Lord Jesus Christ" who gave himself up for us all, the "Love of God the Father" who did not spare his own Son, and the "Communion of the Holy Spirit" through whom we are united to Christ as redeemed children of God, together enshrine the essentially trinitarian, Christian doctrine of God.[80] This trinitarian doctrine of God will be developed in greater detail in chapter eight.

What is important in this context is that since it is through himself in Jesus Christ (and in the Holy Spirit) that God reveals himself as he is in himself, Torrance sees the content, the nature and the event of revelation as inseparable.[81] God *is* the content of revelation, as Torrance repeatedly asserts in his various publications. Divine revelation is inherently trinitarian in nature. And the self-revelatory activity of God through Jesus Christ and in the Holy Spirit, Torrance contends, is *dynamic*. The incarnation is not a static union of static divine and human natures.[82]

Thus in light of God's self-revelation in Jesus Christ, Torrance (like Barth) thinks that revelation must be thought out in *dynamic* as well as *ontological* categories in relation to Jesus Christ, the Holy Spirit and Scripture. Here Torrance argues that "by its very nature divine revelation does not cease to be the *act* of God revealing himself, the dynamic occurrence of his self-communication to us and among us; nor does it revolve itself into some static content detached from the living reality of God's own being."[83] To think of revelation as essentially propositional, for instance, is to abstract revelation from its connection with the trinitarian persons and their relations, and to reduce revelation to the communication of information about God (a revelation that is neither dynamic nor ontological), rather than a *self*-communication of God.

Here Torrance insists that while God continues to reveal himself through

---

[78]Ibid., pp. 130-31.

[79]Torrance, *Karl Barth*, p. 172. Also see Torrance, *Christian Doctrine*, pp. 1-3.

[80]Torrance, *Christian Doctrine*, p. 2.

[81]Thomas F. Torrance, "The Legacy of Karl Barth (1886-1986)," *Scottish Journal of Theology* 39 (1986): 299. The essay is reprinted in Torrance, *Karl Barth*, pp. 160-81.

[82]Torrance, "Legacy," p. 300.

[83]Ibid.

the creaturely structures that the mediation of revelation has assumed (in the Old and New Testaments, as noted above), it is still the dynamic and ontological modality of "God-in-his-revelation," "God-in-his-Word," or God in his own "Personal Reality" who speaks to us the Word that God is.[84] The Bible is not simply a grand narrative that depicts a followable world of faith (as in some forms of narrative theology); nor is it a deposit of divinely revealed propositions (as in some forms of evangelical rationalism). Rather Scripture is a divinely prepared (the interactionist God-world relation) and suitable medium of thought and speech (critical realist epistemology) through which we hear God speaking in person (Calvin): God speaking the living Word of God through Jesus Christ in the Holy Spirit.[85]

The homoousion and a revolutionary doctrine of God. The *homoousion*, however, does not only clarify the essential oneness of the content, nature and event of revelation; Torrance argues that it signifies a self-revelation of God in the gospel which demands a *revolution* in how we think about God.[86] Athanasius and other Nicene leaders were not slow to grasp the staggering implications of this, for the *homoousion* clarifies the utterly decisive point that the Father-Son relation falls within the very being of God.[87]

If what God is in the person and activity of Jesus Christ, God is in God's own being *(ousia)*, then God's being must be conceptualized in a way that is rather *un*-Greco-Roman. "God's being is not wordless" or mute, empty-of activity and static, Torrance argues, but "divinely eloquent" being that is dynamic and personal.[88] This entails the radical redefinition of *ousia*, as is also the case with the *homoousion* itself.[89]

---

[84] Ibid., p. 301.

[85] Ibid., pp. 300-301. This is what Torrance means when he says that his early encounter with Barth's theology in relation to God's self-revelation to us in Jesus Christ and the Holy Spirit signifies a reformulation and deepening of the doctrine of Scripture (see Torrance, *Karl Barth*, p. 122).

[86] Torrance, *Christian Doctrine*, p. 3.

[87] Torrance, *Trinitarian Faith*, p. 119. Torrance argues that this implies that the Father and the Son inhere and coexist eternally, wholly and perfectly in one another. Also see Torrance, *Mediation*, p. 54.

[88] Thomas F. Torrance, "Theological Realism," in *The Philosophical Frontiers of Christian Theology: Essays Presented to D. M. MacKinnon*, ed. Brian Hebblethwaite and Stewart Sutherland (Cambridge: Cambridge University Press, 1982), p. 187. Also see Torrance, Trinitarian Faith, p. 131. Here Torrance appropriates and develops Athanasius' concepts of enousios logos and enousios energeia. God's Word, God's activity in Jesus Christ inheres in God's being.

[89] Ibid. Torrance views the *homoousion* as forged under the impact of God's self-revelation in Jesus Christ. It is an exegetical term molded within the evangelical and doxological life of

Here Torrance emphasizes the language-molding power of God's self-revelation in the gospel and cites an illuminating hermeneutical principle from Athanasius: "Terms do not detract from [God's] nature; rather does his nature draw terms to itself and transform them. For terms are not prior to beings, but beings are first and terms come second."[90] This principle holds true for biblical terms and expressions, but also for concepts utilized in the interpretation and elucidation of Scripture.

Thus from Torrance's perspective, in light of Jesus Christ, we cannot think of God and God's being as immutable and impassible, as remote and unknowable, but rather as dynamic, active and intensely personal being, speaking being. (Chapters four and eight will develop Torrance's discussion of this much more fully.) This is a God whose being is "not limited by our feeble capacities or incapacities," but a God "who is free to go outside of himself," free to "enter into fellowship with us, to communicate himself to us, in such a way as to be received and be known by us."[91] The God who we know in Jesus Christ is a God who coexists in the fullness of relationship, a God who does not in any way need other relations in order to be complete, but yet a God who freely wills not to be without us, and out of ungrudging love wills and acts to be known by us.[92]

For Torrance this means that in Jesus Christ, the Word of God incarnate in our humanity, God defines himself for us and identifies who God really is so that we may rightly apprehend and know God as he is in himself.[93] The *homoousion* discloses the intrinsic significance of who Jesus Christ is in relation to God, and therefore the essential connections embodied in the

---

the church designed to help the church grasp the significance of revelation mediated through the biblical images and expressions (see p. 128). Thus a technical term like *homoousion* is given radically new meaning under the impact of God's self-revelation than it had in previous use in Greek textbooks. This entails an intense personalization of the term *homoousios* that it does not have in classical Greek, for it refers to the personal relations in the Godhead and is the key to the development of a distinctively Christian doctrine of God. This is also true of many other Greek words appropriated by Nicene theologians in their theological activity, as we will see in chapters four and eight. Torrance passionately disagrees with those who see Nicaea and Constantinople, and their use of Greek terms like *homoousios* and *hypostatic union*, as a Hellenization and deformation of the gospel (see Torrance, *Karl Barth*, p. 198).

[90]Torrance, *Trinitarian Faith*, p. 129.
[91]Torrance, *Christian Doctrine*, p. 4.
[92]Ibid.
[93]Ibid., p. 1.

material content of our knowledge of God.[94] For Torrance, the intrinsic trinitarian relations embodied in God's self-revelation, and brought to explicit articulation through the application of the *homoousios* first to Jesus Christ and then to the Holy Spirit, provide the basis for a rigorous, scientific account of Christian theology from its Christology and soteriological center and in light of its constitutive trinitarian structure, with an immediate focus on Jesus Christ as mediator, and an ultimate focus on the Holy Trinity.[95]

The homoousion and the canon of Scripture. A final implication of the *homoousion* for the mediation of revelation is that Torrance sees it as playing a significant role in the clarification of the canon of Holy Scripture. While the Gospels and many of the Epistles were already informally accepted as canonical (along with the Old Testament) prior to Nicaea, Torrance points out that it was only after Nicaea that the exact determination of the canon was formalized, first by Athanasius, perhaps the greatest of the Nicene theologians.[96]

This is no coincidence, for the final delimitation of which Scriptures mediate divine revelation only took place as the substructure of that revelation came to expression in the *homoousion*. The decisive articulation by the Nicene theologians of the oneness of being and activity between incarnate Son and God the Father rendered conceptually explicit the crucial dynamic and ontological relation on which the evangelical message about Jesus Christ rests. But it also brought to light the implicit integration of all the truly apostolic writings on the basis of their mutual and complementary witness or connection to the inner structure of the gospel.

---

[94]Ibid.

[95]See the introduction above, pp. 21-25. Torrance maintains that if we do not have a self-revelation of God as God is in God's own being, then we are left with mythology not theology (Torrance, *Trinitarian Faith*, p. 134).

Torrance argues, as I noted in the introduction, that "it is the incarnation of the Word [in Jesus Christ] which prescribes to dogmatic theology both its proper matter and its method, so that whether in its activity as a whole or in the formulation of a doctrine in any part, it is the Christology pattern that will be made to appear" (Thomas F. Torrance, *Theology in Reconstruction* [London: SCM Press, 1965], p. 128). Also see Torrance, *Christian Doctrine*, p. 1. What Torrance intends by this will become evident in chapter five, for example, in relation to the doctrine of creation. Elsewhere, Torrance says it this way: "Now it is because we do not know the Father or the Son except through the revealing and reconciling work of Jesus Christ, that our knowledge of the Father and the Son and the Holy Spirit is, as it were, a function of our knowledge of Jesus Christ" (Torrance, *Mediation*, p. 55).

[96]Ibid.

By clarifying the ontological substructure of the gospel, the *homoousion* also aided the church's recognition of which Scriptures are of canonical authority.[97] Thus "only those Scriptures were accepted as mediating divine revelation which were in accord with the canon of truth in the Apostolic Deposit of Faith," whereas the only explication of the gospel that was authentically apostolic was one in harmony with the witness of the accepted Scriptures.[98]

Homoousios and reconciliation. By now it should be clear that Torrance sees the oneness of the incarnate Son with God the Father in being, act and word as essential to the integrity of the gospel. Torrance even calls it the "supreme evangelical truth" by which the church stands or falls *(articulus stantis aut cadentis ecclesiae)*, the crucial insight into the mystery of the gospel at the center of the Nicene Creed to which the church has returned again and again for theological and spiritual rejuvenation.[99]

When we think out reconciliation in relation to the *homoousion*, we can not think of God's grace or God's incarnate love as an impersonal substance or transferable quality dispensed by the church and possessed by us. Rather, for Torrance *homoousios* signifies that in the same way that God is the content of his self-revelation, God is also the content of his saving grace in Jesus Christ.[100] Thus, "In Jesus Christ the Giver of grace and the Gift of grace are one and the same, for in him and through him it is none other than God himself who is savingly and creatively at work for us and for our salvation."[101] Indeed God freely gives himself in Jesus Christ and thereby freely gives us all things in Christ.[102]

Throughout reconciliation, in all that Jesus Christ is and does for us, there is an unbroken homoousial relation in being and activity between the incarnate Son and God the Father. Torrance sees grace and reconciliation as the

[97]Torrance, *Trinitarian Faith*, pp. 126-27.

[98]Torrance, "Deposit," p. 13. Also see Torrance, *Trinitarian Faith*, p. 126.

[99]Ibid., p. 132. It is for this reason that the second article of the Nicene-Constantinopolitan Creed, immediately after the *homoousios to Patri,* turns to the soteriological horizon of the incarnation: "Who for us and for our salvation came down from heaven and was made flesh from the Holy Spirit and the Virgin Mary, and was made man, and was crucified for us under Pontius Pilate." The Son, who is Light from Light, true God from true God, has condescended not only to be with us and to reveal God the Father to us, but also to be one of us in our estranged, broken, and sinful condition precisely to reconcile us to God and recreate and save us (see pp. 146-48).

[100]Ibid., p. 138. Also see Torrance, *Karl Barth*, p. 174.

[101]Torrance, *Trinitarian Faith*, p. 138.

[102]Torrance, *Christian Doctrine*, p. 5.

intensely objective and personal being-in-activity and activity-in-being of the triune God, from the Father through the Son and in the Holy Spirit.[103]

Torrance argues that this is, in fact, what the Nicene theologians intended by *theosis* or *theopoiesis*, "which does not mean 'divinisation,' as is so often supposed, but refers to the utterly staggering act of God in which he gives *himself* to us and *adopts us* into the communion of his divine life and love through Jesus Christ and in his one Spirit, yet in such a way that we are not made divine but are preserved in our humanity."[104] In the unbroken oneness in being between Jesus Christ the incarnate Son and God the Father, our diseased, alienated and sinful humanity assumed by Christ is not only judged and condemned, but forgiven, reconciled and redeemed so that we come to participate in the eternal union and communion of the triune God through Christ in the Holy Spirit who unites us to Christ.

Theopoiesis in relation to the *homoousion* carries within it an additional point that there is not only oneness in being between the incarnate Son and God the Father, there is oneness in agency. This means that the reconciling and saving actions of Jesus Christ in the gospel are the absolute acts of God for us and our salvation. For Torrance this underscores the divine finality and validity of all God's saving acts for us in Jesus Christ for they are acts that *only* God can do.[105] This is true even of Christ's death on the cross, which Torrance argues must be seen as a vicarious act of God effecting atoning reconciliation in the dark depths of our fallen human existence.[106]

The atonement will be covered in more detail later in this chapter. Here it is important simply to note that the *homoousion* signifies the coming of God into the utter darkness, despair, misery, condemnation and guilt of our fallen human condition. The *homoousion* is of crucial evangelical significance for all of Jesus Christ's saving acts on our behalf.[107] In short, if the *homoousion* were not true, Torrance thinks that the gospel would be in jeopardy, for there would be no final identity between the activity of Jesus Christ and the activity of God.[108]

---

[103]Torrance, *Trinitarian Faith*, p. 139-41.

[104]Torrance, *Mediation*, p. 64.

[105]Torrance, *Trinitarian Faith*, p. 141.

[106]Ibid., p. 142.

[107]Ibid. Also see Torrance, *Karl Barth*, p. 168.

[108]Torrance, *Trinitarian Faith*, p., 134. Elsewhere, Torrance argues that if God is not love in

Yet if *homoousios to patri* is true, then not only is there divine agency and finality in all the saving acts of Jesus Christ, there is also an *identity* between the saving activity of Jesus Christ and the reality of God: God is not different in God's own being than God is in God's activity in the incarnation and crucifixion of Christ.[109] This means that in the cross of Christ in particular we come to know the astonishing character of God's love. God reveals that God loves us more than God loves himself.[110] There is no dark, inscrutable deity behind the cross of Christ, but only the God who loves us to the uttermost.[111]

In fact, Torrance argues, "In loving us in the gift of his dear Son and the mission of his Spirit he loves us with the very Love which he is."[112] The active love of God that we come to know in the activity of God in reconciliation from the Father through the Son in the Spirit is the dynamic, self-giving reciprocal love that God is within God's own eternal life.[113] We will examine this theme in more detail in chapters four and eight.

Homoousios is crucial for Torrance's theology, since it brings to articulation this central relation in being and activity between Jesus Christ incarnate Son, the Spirit Christ poured out at Pentecost, and God the Father

---

God's own reality, then the love of God in Jesus Christ and in the Holy Spirit would have no basis in God's own being (see Torrance, *Christian Doctrine*, p. 5).

[109]Torrance, *Christian Doctrine*, p. 5. This again reinforces the inseparability of revelation and reconciliation in Torrance's theology. Throughout the entire historical life, death and resurrection of Jesus Christ, the continuous incarnate movement of the Son of God is revelatory and redemptive (see Torrance, *Karl Barth*, p. 178). "Reconciliation constitutes the the inner dynamic content of revelation, and revelation becomes effective precisely as reconciliation for thereby it achieves its end" (Torrance, *Mediation*, p. 103). Elsewhere Torrance quotes Barth on this point with approval: "Revelation is reconciliation, as certainly as it is God himself: God with us, God beside us, and chiefly and decisively, God for us" (Thomas F. Torrance, "Karl Barth and the Latin Heresy," *Scottish Journal of Theology* 39 [1986], p. 473; reprinted in Torrance, *Karl Barth*, pp. 213-40).

[110]Ibid., p. 5.

[111]See Torrance, *Karl Barth*, p. 176; Torrance, *Trinitarian Faith*, p. 8; and Torrance, *Mediation*, p. 59.

[112]Torrance, *Christian Doctrine*, pp. 5, 7. Because God's activity inheres in God's being and God's being inheres in God's activity, we cannot but move from the evangelical significance of the *homoousion* to the God who engages in this activity. Torrance sees this principle as central in all pastoral care, for often people harbor in their heart of hearts the fear that there is some arbitrary deity behind the back of Jesus Christ. But if the incarnate Son of God is *homoousios* with the Father, then the love and forgiveness that we come to know in Jesus Christ is backed up by the being and agency of God.

[113]Ibid. Thus the "evangelical Trinity" (economic Trinity) and the "theological Trinity" (ontological Trinity) are inseparable in Torrance's theology (see p. 6).

who loves us more than he loves himself. Its formulation by the Nicene theologians is a fundamental event in the mind and memory of the church because it is the "ontological and epistemological linchpin of Christian theology," both for the mediation of revelation and the mediation of reconciliation.[114] The very essence of the gospel in Torrance's theology is rooted in the ontological relation of being and agency between the incarnate Son and God the Father. The *homoousion*, Torrance contends, brings the inner being-constituting relations, the "onto-relations," of Jesus Christ to God the Father to focal awareness and expression, and thereby discloses something of Christ's intrinsic significance and Logos. Jesus Christ *is* God's revelation and reconciliation.

We must now examine the internal relations of Jesus Christ within the constitution of his incarnate person as mediator.

4. The Person of Christ as Mediator: The Hypostatic Union

Divine and human. The *homoousion* is vital, for if the homoousial bond between Jesus Christ and God is cut, the bottom falls out of the gospel, because only God can atone for sin and save. Yet it is also critical that Jesus Christ is of one and the same being and nature with humanity, for if the incarnate Son is not fully human, the gospel is also emptied of soteriological substance. All that Christ has done would have no connection with our side of the chasm between humanity and God created by human sin, guilt and alienation. To be mediator, Jesus Christ has to be as fully human as he is *homoousios* with God the Father.[115]

It was out of soteriological concern that the Nicene fathers developed the famous principle given epigrammatic expression by Gregory Nazianzen: "The unassumed is the unhealed." It is for us and our salvation that the Son of God became a human being, identifying himself with us fully in every aspect of our humanity, taking our place, reconciling and redeeming us.[116]

Torrance follows this Nicene principle that if the humanity of our Lord Jesus Christ was in any way deficient, then at precisely that point the salvation of *our* humanity is called into question. The incarnate assumption of our humanity by Christ must include a fully human soul and mind or

---

[114]See Torrance, *The Ground and Grammar of Theology* (Charlottesville: University Press of Virginia, 1980), pp. 160-61; and Torrance, *Trinitarian Faith*, p. 144.
[115]See Torrance, *Trinitarian Faith*, pp. 4, 8, 146, 149.
[116]Ibid., p. 8.

we remain unredeemed in our mental reality.[117]

Yet the Son of God became not simply a human being, for in Jesus Christ the incarnate Son took the form of a servant and assumed our actual sinful servile status in an act of humiliation and self-abasement.[118] Only by identifying with us completely in our estranged and sinful humanity, acting on our behalf, for our sake, in our place, could the incarnate Son save us in our alienated existence as those who have become separated from the life of God.[119]

Here Torrance applies the *homoousion* to the *incarnate* Son thereby stressing both the full humanity and the complete deity of Jesus Christ as Mediator: "Jesus Christ is Mediator in such a way that in his incarnate Person he embraces both sides of the mediating relationship. . . . In Jesus Christ we have to do with One who is wholly God and yet with one who is wholly man."[120] This means that there is not only an internal relation between Jesus Christ the incarnate Son and God the Father, there is also an internal relation between Jesus Christ the incarnate Son and our humanity assumed by the Son in the incarnation.

Hypostatic union. In light of the fact that the relation of the Father to the Son falls within the communion and union between the *persons* of the Trinity in the being of God, the incarnation of the Son of God in our human creaturely existence takes the form of *hypostatic* union in which the unique divine nature is fully united with a truly human nature in Christ's *one person*.[121] Jesus Christ is not two realities joined together, but rather "one Reality who confronts us as he who is both God and man."[122]

Here Torrance rejects any sort of dualism that would break up the unified integrity of the hypostatic union in the one person of Jesus Christ. All of the divine and human activity of Christ flows from his one person. This

---

[117]Torrance finds support for his position in Athanasius. See ibid., p. 152.

[118]Ibid. Torrance sees this *kenosis* not in metaphysical terms of a self-limitation of God, but as "self-abnegating love" assuming our sinful human nature in order to redeem us. The hypostatic union is a healing and saving union with our actual diseased, alienated and sinful humanity, humanity in conflict with God (see p. 153).

[119]Ibid., pp. 4, 8, 152.

[120]Torrance, *Mediation*, p. 56. This union of the divine and the human in Jesus Christ entails not the slightest impairing or diminishing of either nature. Neither are the two natures confused or separated in the one person of Christ (see pp. 64-65).

[121]This hypostatic union is rooted in and sustained by the communion and mutual indwelling of the trinitarian persons in the one being of God.

[122]Ibid., p. 65.

mediation of Jesus Christ involves a twofold movement, from God to humanity and also from humanity to God, but this movement is always the activity issuing from Christ's person.[123] In all of his earthly historical human actuality, Christ embodies the activity and presence of God. Yet, this act of God includes the fully *human* activity of Jesus Christ, who is one with us in human being and nature. For Torrance, Jesus Christ himself is God's act, for it is God who acts personally and immediately as a human being and therefore in a simultaneously divine and human manner.[124]

Torrance sees this as involving real *becoming* on the part of God. The incarnation expressed in terms of a hypostatic union "is an act of *God himself* in which he really became man . . . and acts *as man,* all for our sake—from the beginning to the end God the Son acts among us in a human way . . . within the measures of our humanity."[125] In Jesus Christ, God becomes what we are and acts in our place in order to save us.[126]

The incarnate assumption of that humanity in Jesus Christ takes an earthly historical form of a whole human life from birth to death and beyond death in Christ's resurrection to the restoration of human life into union and communion with God in Christ's ascension. For Torrance the incarnation, and the hypostatic union it entails, is not a transient historical episode forever past. In the resurrection and ascension Jesus Christ remains forever the Son of God incarnate, God with us, God beside us and decisively God for us.

Thus the hypostatic union entails dynamic and ontological interrelations with God and with humanity within the personal constitution of Jesus Christ the Mediator throughout the life of Christ from birth through life, death and resurrection. According to Torrance these internal relations define the intrinsic significance, or logos, of Jesus Christ. Jesus Christ is *homoousios* with God and with diseased, sinful humanity, ministering the

---

[123]Torrance, *Trinitarian Faith*, p. 149.

[124]Ibid., p. 149. Rather than starting with abstract concepts of God and humanity and then asking how the incarnation is possible, Torrance starts with the incarnation and then attempts to understand what kind of God and what kind of humanity we come to know in and through Jesus Christ.

[125]Ibid., p. 150.

[126]Christ is not just the Word of God coming upon a human being as is the case of the prophets in the Old Testament. Nor is Christ some created intermediary halfway between God and humanity. Torrance sees Jesus Christ the incarnate Son as *God* coming to us not *in* but *as* a particular human being without ever ceasing to be the eternal God who called all of creation into existence. See Torrance, *Mediation*, p. 56, and Torrance, *Trinitarian Faith*, p. 147.

things of God to humanity, reconciling, healing and restoring humanity to proper relation to God, and therein ministering the things of humanity to God. All of this is worked out dynamically and soteriologically for our sake within the life history in space-time of Jesus, son of Mary within Israel and yet Son of God, of one being with the Father.

The evangelical and doxological perspective. The "for our sake" character of Christ's person and work underscores the evangelical and doxological perspective within which the event of our redemption in Jesus Christ is properly understood and articulated. Only in the context of worship as redeemed sinners loved to the uttermost by God in Christ do we begin to understand, Torrance argues, the intrinsic significance of Jesus Christ and simultaneously the God who has so loved us in Jesus Christ.[127] Knowledge of God is participatory in Torrance's theology in an *evangelical* movement from the Father through the Son and in the Spirit, and a *doxological* movement in the Spirit through the Son to the Father. It is a movement to take place first in Christ and his vicarious humanity, and then in us in the Spirit who unites us with Christ's vicarious humanity. We come to know and experience the love of God through the grace of Jesus Christ in the communion of the Holy Spirit in such a way that we share evangelically and doxologically in the trinitarian life and love that God is.

This assuming of our actual human nature and being by God for us is the pivotal premise behind Torrance's understanding of Christ's saving work. Torrance develops his doctrine of the atonement within the intrinsic interrelations of the hypostatic union, the incarnational constitution of the Christ as mediator.

5. Incarnational Redemption: Christ's Atoning Reconciliation

The unity of Christ's person and work. Torrance sees the incarnation and the atonement intimately interconnected throughout the earthly life, death and resurrection of Jesus Christ.[128] In light of the fact that Jesus Christ is fully God and wholly human in one person, and since all of Christ's divine and human activity flow from his one person, Torrance sees the atoning reconciliation Christ accomplishes for us as occurring *within* the being and life of Jesus Christ, not *outside* of Christ as something

---

[127]Torrance, *Karl Barth*, p. 230.
[128]See Torrance, *Trinitarian Faith*, pp. 155-90; Torrance, *Mediation*, pp. 62-72; and Torrance, *Karl Barth*, pp. 177-79, 201-5, 229-36.

external to the incarnate constitution of Christ's person as mediator (Heb 1:3; 2:14-18; 4:14—5:10; 9:11—10:10).[129]

In the hypostatic union the Son of God assumes our sinful and corrupt humanity in conflict with God. This does not mean that Jesus Christ the incarnate Son sinned himself or became contaminated by our corrupt and fallen condition. Rather it signifies that the hypostatic union is a reconciling union in which the Son of God condemned sin in our sinful humanity and overcame the estrangement, sin, guilt and death entrenched in our humanity via a transforming relation between the divine and the human natures within the incarnate reality of Jesus Christ.[130] The incarnation is inherently redemptive, and redemption is intrinsically incarnational (2 Cor 5:21; Heb 2:14; 4:14-16).

As noted in the section on the mediation of Christ within Israel, Torrance views the incarnate Jesus Christ as embodying the tensions and contradictions of our sinful and rebellious humanity in such a way that atoning reconciliation takes dynamic form and is worked out within actual historical relations and structures of our human existence all through Jesus' life from birth to death, resurrection and ascension.[131] Throughout his earthly life the incarnate Savior shared all our experience, endured fearful temptations and the onslaught of the forces of darkness, yet overcame them in a life of purity and faithfulness, withstanding the strain of human sin and God's judgment on it, sanctifying every phase of human life within the hypostatic union of the divine and human natures in the oneness of his person as mediator.[132]

This atoning reconciliation between God and humanity from Christ's birth to its consummation in his death and resurrection must be understood in terms of a continuous vicarious sacrifice in which "his incarnate life and

---

[129]Torrance, *Trinitarian Faith*, p. 155.

[130]Torrance, *Mediation*, p. 65. By making our sin and guilt, our condemnation and death, his own, the Son of God through the hypostatic union brought God's perfect holiness and power to bear upon our fallen nature, reconciling and redeeming it and converting our disobedient humanity back to communion with God (see Torrance, *Karl Barth*, pp. 178-9, 202-4, 230-31).

[131]Torrance, *Mediation*, p. 65.

[132]See Torrance, *Trinitarian Faith*, p. 166-67. "Thus there took place in Christ as Mediator," Torrance argues, "an agonizing union between God the Judge and man under judgement in a continuous movement of atoning reconciliation running throughout his obedient and sinless life and passion into the resurrection and ascension when he presented himself to the Father on our behalf and presented us in him as those he had redeemed and consecrated to be his brethren" (Torrance, "Latin Heresy," p. 475).

his redeeming activity . . . [are] completely interwoven" in such a way that
"his Person, his Word, and his Act are one and undivided."[133] For Torrance
the incarnation and the atonement, the hypostatic union and atoning reconciliation, interpenetrate and imply one another within the mediation of
Christ.[134] Given the conditions of our corrupt and sinful humanity, the hypostatic union could not be actualized without overcoming human sin and
guilt through the atonement and through the sanctification our human nature assumed by Christ into union with Christ's divine nature.[135] Yet atoning
reconciliation could not take place within the depths of our corrupt and sinful humanity unless Christ penetrated into those depths in the hypostatic
union between Christ's divine and human natures.[136]

The hypostatic union of the divine and human natures in the incarnate
Son, Torrance argues, is the source for all of Christ's mediatorial activity
on our behalf.[137] The atonement, or atoning reconciliation, falls within the
one person of Jesus Christ as mediator, and therefore Christ's person and
work are one.

The Latin heresy: A "gospel" of external relations. Torrance sees a
growing tendency in Latin theology from the fifth century on to reject the
idea that Christ assumed our sinful, alienated and fallen humanity, and to
embrace the notion that Christ assumed a neutral or an original and perfect human nature from the Virgin Mary.[138] This understanding of the incarnation, however, conflicts with the soteriological principle of the
Nicene theologians that the unassumed is the unhealed, for in the Latin
view the Son of God has not assumed our *actual* fallen humanity, but a per-

---

[133]Thomas F. Torrance, "The Atonement, the Singularity of Christ and the Finality of the
Cross: The Atonement and the Moral Order," in *Universalism and the Doctrine of Hell*, ed.
Nigel M. de S. Cameron (Grand Rapids, Mich.: Baker, 1993), pp. 236, 232. Torrance sees
God's saving act in Jesus Christ as continuous and indivisible (see Torrance, *Karl Barth*, p.
200).

[134]Torrance can say that "the hypostatic union between the divine and human natures in
Jesus Christ is the ontological aspect of atoning reconciliation and the atoning reconcilia-
tion is the dynamic aspect of hypostatic union." (Torrance is describing Barth's position,
though it is clear that Torrance is sympathetic with Barth on this point.) See Thomas F.
Torrance, "Karl Barth and Patristic Theology," *Theology Beyond Christendom: Essays on the
Centenary of the Birth of Karl Barth, May 10, 1886*, ed. John Thompson (Allison Park, Penn.:
Pickwick, 1986), p. 229.

[135]Torrance, *Mediation*, p. 66.

[136]Ibid.

[137]Ibid., p. 64-65.

[138]See ibid., p. 40, and Torrance, *Karl Barth*, pp. 203, 231-32. Torrance sees Leo's *Tome* as one
of the chief sources.

fect and sinless humanity different from our own.[139]

Yet if in incarnation the Son of God did not assume our fallen and sinful human nature, Torrance argues that Christ's atoning sacrifice can only be understood in terms of *external* (*forensic*, for example) relations between Christ and humanity's sins.[140] The incarnation thus becomes *instrumental* in relation to the atonement. It is the means of providing the sinless human being capable of living a life in perfect obedience to God's law, and of taking our place on the cross and enduring the judgment and wrath of God which we deserve because of our sin. In Christ's suffering and death there is an external judicial transaction in the transference of the penalty for sin and of the judgement and wrath of God from us to Jesus Christ who dies an agonizing death fulfilling the just and inexorable penalty against those who transgress God's laws.[141]

In this theory of the atonement we are freed from the *penalty* for sin, Torrance contends, but the actual *root* of our alienation and sin in the ontological depths of our corrupt and fallen humanity is left untouched by Christ's atoning sacrifice. Christ's death on the cross deals only with our *actual* sins, but not original sin.[142] In conservative Protestant circles this can lead to a reductionist soteriology of forgiveness now and heaven in the hereafter.

Torrance finds a similar tendency in Roman Catholic theology, which has also often understood the atonement in external juridical categories. Original sin is cured through the "healing medicine" of transferable grace merited by Christ and dispensed by the church through the sacraments.[143]

In modern Protestant theology, Torrance finds further evidence of theories of the atonement conceived in terms of external relations. Here Jesus is viewed as a kind of moral/religious leader/teacher whose principles or

---

[139] According to Torrance this also forced the Roman Catholic tradition into the notion of the immaculate conception of Mary to ensure the sinless humanity of Christ (see Torrance, *Mediation*, p. 40).

[140] Torrance, *Mediation*, p. 40, and Torrance, *Karl Barth*, p. 178.

[141] Torrance, *Mediation*, p. 40.

[142] Torrance, *Karl Barth*, p. 203.

[143] Ibid., p. 232. Protestantism has its own ways of dealing with the problem of original sin within the framework of the atonement conceived in forensic categories. It often handles the problem of original sin by an appeal to an additional and subsequent soteriological source for regeneration and sanctification (or for power and gifts for ministry in the charismatic tradition) in the person and work of the Holy Spirit. Even John Wesley occasionally succumbed to this kind of characterization of the *ordo salutis* (order of salvation): "The

example of love/justice/consciousness of God exert a powerful and transforming influence on humanity.[144] Christ's death on the cross is the model
of suffering love or solidarity in the struggle for justice (rather than forensic transference of the penalty of sin). But Torrance argues that the cross is
still interpreted in extrinsic categories, the socio-moral or spiritual influence of Jesus' example for others.[145]

In each of these theories, and their many variations, Torrance sees a
"gospel" of external relations in which the sacrifice of Christ on the cross
is interpreted in terms of moral influence or a juridical transaction between
Jesus Christ and the rest of humanity. Torrance refers collectively to these
various forms of the "gospel" of external relations as the "Latin heresy."[146]
He even asserts that, "almost all Protestant theology, not the least in its
evangelical forms, has followed Latin theology down this road—although
here too there have been notable exceptions such as Martin Luther and
H. R. Mackintosh" and, of course, Karl Barth.[147]

Personal and ontological redemption. In contrast to the various forms
of the gospel of external relations, Torrance argues for an incarnational redemption in which atoning reconciliation takes place within the one person of Jesus Christ, the mediator between God and humanity.[148] In the
incarnation God has penetrated the dark depths of human sin and alienation from God, taking our fallen and diseased humanity on himself in order to get at the very ontological roots of the sin and guilt entrenched in
the recesses of human existence (2 Cor 5:21; Heb 2:14; 4:14-16). Throughout
his vicarious life, death and resurrection, atoning reconciliation was accomplished by Jesus Christ within the hypostatic union, his incarnate di-

---

one [justification] implies what God *does for* us through his Son; the other [sanctification],
what he *works in* us by his Spirit" (see John Wesley's standard sermon, "Justification by
Faith" II.1, in *John Wesley,* ed. Albert C. Outler [New York: Oxford University Press, 1964],
p. 201). Here, it seems the atonement deals with our standing before God, providing par-
don for actual sin. The overcoming of original sin appears to be the provence of the third
person of the Trinity. Wesley's theology, of course, is far better than this quotation indicates, but this transition from the atonement of Christ interpreted in external juridical
terms to the work of Spirit understood as the inner transformation of the sinful human
nature (or empowerment to live an authentic human existence in liberal Protestant theology) has had a significant impact on Protestantism, especially in North America.
[144]See Torrance, *Mediation,* p. 61-62.
[145]Ibid., pp. 61-62.
[146]See Torrance, "Latin Heresy," pp. 461-82.
[147]Ibid., p. 477.
[148]See Torrance, *Trinitarian Faith,* pp. 154-55.

vine and human reality as mediator.[149]

Torrance acknowledges that this way of linking redemption and the incarnation has been characterized and criticized as the "physical theory" of redemption.[150] This criticism implies that the human salvation is accomplished through a physical union between fallen humanity and the divine Logos. Torrance argues, however, that this is a serious misinterpretation since the incarnate Son of God acts *personally* from within our entire unitary (body-soul) humanity which he assumed for our sake.[151]

This entails an intense personalization of salvation and is related to Torrance's understanding of the *homoousion* in which person, being and activity are all inseparable, a point to which we will return in chapters four and eight. Here what is crucial is that Torrance's understanding of incarnational redemption unites the *personal* and the *ontological* within the incarnate reality of Jesus Christ as mediator. Atoning reconciliation takes place within the personal life and being of Jesus Christ.

While there are forensic and exemplar elements within this incarnational reconciliation, Jesus Christ embodies the reality of salvation in his divine-human reality.[152] Christ does not mediate an atoning reconciliation other than what he is. He is in his own incarnate person the reality and content of the atoning redemption that he mediates.

The precise nature of vicarious atonement. Torrance contends that when Christ's atoning reconciliation on the cross is not understood in close relation to the incarnational assumption of our fallen humanity, the atonement is inevitably interpreted in terms of external forensic relations, as noted above. In addition, without a unifying center in the incarnation, the various aspects of the atonement in the biblical witness break up into various theories of the atonement, each stressing one element or another found within Scripture.[153]

Torrance, however, finds a realist and holistic understanding of the atonement in the New Testament based on a "Christological reinterpre-

---

[149]Torrance asserts that the hypostatic union "is the immediate ground of all Christ's mediatorial and reconciling activity in our human existence" (Torrance, *Mediation*, pp. 64-65).
[150]Torrance, *Trinitarian Faith*, p. 156.
[151]Ibid.
[152]Ibid., p. 156.
[153]See ibid., pp. 159-60, and Torrance, "Atonement," p. 239.

tation" of God's redemptive acts in the Passover and exodus—delivering
Israel out of bondage in Egypt—that unifies the various aspects of the
atonement in the New Testament.[154] Here again, Torrance develops his
formulation of the mediation of Christ within the matrix of forms of life
and thought arising out of Israel's covenant with God.

It was Jesus Christ's own interpretation of his passion, revealed in his
words to his followers about his mission, and in the institution of the Holy
Supper on the night he was betrayed and perpetuated in the eucharistic liturgy, Torrance contends, that provided the church with its point of reference for interpreting the atonement.[155] Jesus told his disciples that the Son
of Man came to serve and give his life a ransom for lost humanity, and the
cup Jesus offered them represented the new covenant in his blood poured
out for the forgiveness of sins.[156] In this way Christ interpreted his life and
his passion in light of the suffering servant and cultic atonement in the Hebrew Scriptures.[157]

Torrance sees the New Testament understanding of redemption developed in light of Jesus' own self-interpretation through an appropriation of the three Hebrew terms associated with redemption in the Old
Testament—*pdh*, *kpr* and *g'l*—as well as their cognates.[158] These concepts
and images had already been taken up by the great prophets and applied to God's anointed servant who would mediate a new covenant,
bearing the sins of God's people and providing God's ultimate redemption.[159]

Under the impact of the life, death and resurrection of Jesus Christ,
these three basic themes are transformed and utilized by the church "in expressing something of the indescribable mystery of Christ's Passion and
the ineffable truth of atonement in its various but profoundly interrelated
aspects."[160] Torrance develops his realist and holistic doctrine of the atonement by drawing together these three aspects (the dramatic or dynamic,
the priestly or cultic, and the ontological), with the ontological (incarnational) providing the overall pattern.[161]

---

[154]Torrance, *Trinitarian Faith*, p. 171, and Torrance, "Atonement," p. 239.

[155]Torrance, *Trinitarian Faith*, pp. 168-70.

[156]See Mark 10:45 and Matthew 20:28; and Mark 14:24, Matthew 26:28 and Luke 22:20.

[157]Torrance, *Trinitarian Faith*, p. 169.

[158]See Torrance, "Atonement," pp. 239-40, and Torrance, *Trinitarian Faith*, p. 170-72, for discussions of these three Hebrew terms.

[159]Torrance, "Atonement," p. 240, and Torrance, *Trinitarian Faith*, p. 171.

[160]Torrance, "Atonement," p. 239. Also see Torrance, *Trinitarian Faith*, p. 158.

The dramatic aspect or theme *(pdh)* refers to redemption as a mighty act of God delivering God's people from bondage or oppression and God's judgment on it, as in the case of the deliverance of Israel out of Egypt. In its christological fulfillment Torrance sees the dramatic aspect of the atonement as Christ delivering us from the threat of the law, the power of death, the forces of evil and the judgment of God.[162]

Closely related to the dramatic is the priestly *(kpr)* aspect of redemption "through atoning sacrifice for the expiation of sin and guilt whereby God incarnate in Christ draws near to us and draws us near to himself, cleansing us through his blood, sanctifying and healing us . . . ransoming us from servitude to the world, delivering us from slavery into liberty . . . thereby constituting us as a . . . special people belonging to himself."[163] This aspect of Christ's atonement, of course, draws on the ritual acts of sacrifice in the Old Testament.

It also reveals that Torrance incorporates forensic elements within his understanding of the atonement.[164] He can even speak of this aspect as an "expiatory sacrifice offered in atonement for sin and in propitiatory reconciliation with God,"[165] though Torrance is adamant that God is always the subject of this act of reconciliation of atonement and never the object of it.[166] Torrance repeatedly emphasizes that Christ is always priest and sacrifice, offerer and offering.[167]

The ontological *(g'l)* aspect of the atonement refers to redemption out of bondage, destitution or forfeited rights through the advocacy of someone with a kinship, affinity or bond to the person in need. The emphasis is on the nature of this redeemer (called the *go'el* in the Old Testament) who claims the cause of the person in need and stands in for that person. This

---

[161]Ibid., p. 173, and Torrance, "Atonement," p. 240. Torrance develops these three themes in the Old Testament and in the early church up through the Nicene theologians in significant detail in Torrance, *Trinitarian Faith*, pp. 170-79.

[162]Ibid., p. 175.

[163]Torrance, "Atonement," pp. 240-41.

[164]See Torrance, *Trinitarian Faith*, pp. 161, 170, 173, and Torrance, "Atonement," pp. 239-42.

[165]Torrance, "Atonement," p. 239.

[166]Torrance, *Trinitarian Faith*, p. 170.

[167]See ibid., pp. 154, 170, 173, 177. The servant form of this act underscores the fact that Jesus Christ in his incarnate constitution as mediator is both priest and sacrifice, both the one who offers and the one who is offered for us throughout the course of his life from conception and birth through his sinless life to the triumphant fulfillment of this dynamic vicarious reconciliation in the resurrection of Jesus Christ from the grave and the rebirth of humanity in him.

concept of redeemer is even applied to God who takes up the cause of
God's people, as in Deutero-Isaiah where there is the promise of a new exodus when the divine *Go'el* will redeem Israel through an anointed suffering servant who bears the iniquities of God's people.[168]

While the Old Testament never identifies this suffering servant with the
divine *Go'el*, this identification is precisely what Torrance sees taking place
in Jesus Christ in the New Testament as noted above in section two. The
emphasis in the christological reinterpretation of this theme is on the incarnate person of Jesus Christ the Redeemer who is *homoousios* with God,
but who has also established an ontological covenant bond with us in our
lost condition through Christ's incarnational assumption of our sinful humanity. The incarnate Son identifies with us in our diseased, destitute,
damned and dying condition, and makes our cause his own by taking our
fallen and sinful humanity on himself.[169]

This incarnational aspect provides the overall framework for Torrance's
doctrine of the atonement, for the incarnate person of Jesus Christ, in his
oneness with us, "sums up and is intensively in himself all that he under-
takes in atoning activity on our behalf."[170] By virtue of this ontological
identification with us in the incarnation, Christ claims us for the redemption he has accomplished in his overcoming of sin, judgment and death,
and the offering of himself in propitiatory sacrifice to God on our behalf
and in our place.[171] All the elements of the Christ's atoning work interpenetrate one another in a dynamic whole within this overall ontological or incarnational pattern.[172]

Torrance is clear, however, that the reality of the atonement, like the incarnation, cannot be fully grasped by human theological activity. It is a
mystery more to be adored than expressed: "The saving act of God in the
blood of Christ is an unfathomable mystery before which the angels veil
their faces and into which we dare not and cannot intrude, but before
which our minds bow in wonder, worship and praise."[173]

Atoning exchange. There is one final theological concept related to the
incarnation and atonement of significance for understanding Torrance's

---

[168]Ibid., p. 171.
[169]Torrance, "Atonement," p. 241.
[170]Ibid., p. 241.
[171]See ibid. and Torrance, *Trinitarian Faith*, p. 176.
[172]Torrance, "Atonement," pp. 241-42, and Torrance, *Trinitarian Faith*, p. 175.
[173]Torrance, *Karl Barth*, p. 239.

perspective on the mediation of Christ. This is the blessed exchange or atoning exchange which involves the "redemptive translation of man *from* one state *into* another brought about by Christ who in his self-abnegating love took our place that we might have his place, becoming what we are that we might become what he is."[174]

Atoning exchange is at the center of Torrance's understanding of incarnational redemption, for Christ's union with us in our actual broken and sinful nature entails the humiliation and self-sacrifice of the incarnate Son, but also the transformation and the exaltation of our humanity that is lifted up in and through Christ to share in the communion that God is in God's own trinitarian life. All of this is worked out within the incarnate person of the Mediator. Thus the descent and ascent, the humiliation and exaltation, the death and resurrection of the Son of God are inseparable in the oneness of Jesus Christ's person and involve from beginning to end this blessed exchange between Christ and ourselves (Rom 5:15-21; 2 Cor 5:21; Heb 4:14—5:10; 9:26-28).

This point brings out the decisive significance of Jesus Christ's resurrection and ascension in Torrance's theology, for they are more than simply the verdict of the Father's complete approval of the self-offering of Son on the cross. Torrance argues that redemption takes place through Jesus Christ's resurrection and ascension and not just Christ's death on the cross. Incarnational redemption involves not only forgiveness and freedom from bondage, but also new life in union with God.[175] The end and goal of the atonement is more than the restoration of relations between God and humanity, for it includes "union with God in and through Jesus Christ in whom our human nature is not only saved, healed and renewed but lifted up to participate in the very light, life and love of the Holy Trinity."[176]

It is also important to note that for Torrance this is *bodily* resurrection and ascension in which Jesus Christ in his risen *humanity* is exalted into the immediate presence of God the Father where Christ "presented himself to the Father on our behalf and presented us in himself as those he had redeemed

---

[174]Torrance, *Trinitarian Faith*, p. 179. Torrance finds support for this in the early church through the Nicene fathers and in Calvin and Karl Barth, as well as in the New Testament (2 Cor 8:9, for example). See ibid., pp. 179-81, and Torrance, *Karl Barth*, pp. 204, 223. Torrance, however, is critical of Reformed theology on this point since he thinks that on the whole Reformed theology tends to formulate the blessed exchange within a rather Latin conception of the incarnation (see p. 231).

[175]Torrance, *Trinitarian Faith*, p. 180.

[176]Torrance, *Mediation*, p. 66.

and consecrated to be his brethren."[177] This is another way of expressing what is conveyed in the concept *theosis* or *theopoiesis*—not the divinization of humanity, but the recreation of our lost humanity in the dynamic, atoning interaction between the divine and human natures within the one person of Jesus Christ, through whom we enter into the communion God is in God's trinitarian life.[178] We are brought into union and communion with the divine life and love of God, yet preserved in our humanity (2 Pet 1:3-8).

For Torrance, this blessed exchange involves the entire relationship between Jesus Christ and ourselves, "between his obedience and our disobedience, his holiness and our sin, his life and our death, his strength and our weakness . . . his wisdom and our ignorance, his joy and our misery . . . and so on."[179] The atoning exchange *is* incarnational redemption, and incarnational redemption *is* atoning exchange, all worked out in the one person of the incarnate Son of God within the twisted depths of our fallen humanity.

The range of Christ's atoning redemption. The range and significance of the atoning exchange that took place in Jesus Christ, according to Torrance, is as comprehensive and boundless as the eternal nature, being and love of the Triune God incarnate in Jesus Christ.[180] If God did not spare his own Son and gives us with him all things (Rom 8:32), then the benefits of God's gift of Christ to humanity are inexhaustible.[181] Torrance sees the redemptive exchange as opening the door to all of God's creative and sanctifying purposes for humanity.

Following Athanasius, Torrance also emphasizes the universal range of

---

[177]Torrance, "Latin Heresy," p. 477; cf. Heb 4:14—5:10; 8:1-6; 9:11-28; 10:5-14. Torrance is critical of Barth's account of the humanity of Jesus Christ in *Church Dogmatics* IV/3 where "Christ seemed to be swallowed up in the transcendent Light and Spirit of God, so that the humanity of the risen Jesus appeared to be displaced by what he called 'the humanity of God' in his turning toward us" (Torrance, "My Interaction," p. 134). Torrance provides a fascinating narrative of his final conversation with Karl Barth on the importance of the *bodily* resurrection and ascension of Jesus Christ (see pp. 133-34).

[178]Torrance, *Trinitarian Faith*, p. 189. Indeed, Torrance argues that as Christ's vicarious death on the cross had its beginning in the virgin birth where the Son of God assumes our estranged humanity and takes our place, so also Jesus' resurrection had its genesis in Christ's birth when the incarnate Son began the redemptive translation of alienated humanity into filial communion and final union of humanity with the triune God in Jesus Christ's bodily resurrection, ascension and exaltation of us with Christ in the presence of God the Father (see Torrance, *Karl Barth*, pp. 207-8, and Torrance, *Trinitarian Faith*, pp. 180-81).

[179]Torrance, *Trinitarian Faith*, p. 181.

[180]Ibid., pp. 181-82, and Torrance, "Atonement," pp. 244-47.

[181]Torrance, *Trinitarian Faith*, p. 181.

Christ's redemptive activity, for Christ's life, death and resurrection on our behalf and in our stead: "Christ as Man represents all mankind . . . all who belong to human nature are involved and represented—all human beings without exception."[182] Torrance rejects any and every idea of limited atonement, for if in the incarnation the Son of God assumed the actual fallen nature of humanity, then all human beings without exception are involved and represented.[183] Only if Christ's humanity (and atoning reconciliation) has no "inner ontological connection with those for whom he died, but is regarded as an external instrument used by God as he wills, in effecting salvation for all those whom God chooses," can the atonement be limited to only some people.[184]

The universal range of Christ's effective incarnational redemption, Torrance contends, includes not only all people, but the entire universe: "The universal range of the redemptive work of Christ takes in not only all humanity, but the whole created universe of space and time, including all things (ta panta) visible and invisible, earthly and heavenly alike."[185] This includes the fulfillment of salvation for all time until the final consummation when Christ returns, for Christ's incarnation, death and resurrection are not a momentary episode, but rather a perfected event within the divine-human reality and person of Jesus Christ who is even now in the presence of God the Father and remains unceasingly present and active as God incarnate.[186]

In light of statements like these some might think that Torrance embraces universal salvation. This, however, would be a grave misunderstanding of his position. Torrance sees universalism and limited atonement as "twin heresies which rest on a deeper heresy, the recourse to a logico-causal explanation of why the atoning death of the Lord Jesus Christ avails or does not avail for all people."[187] Torrance has a radically different understanding of God's grace in relation to divine agency and human agency in salvation, which the next chapter will address.

Here it is important to note that Torrance rejects universalism because we cannot explain why some people believe and others do not, "any more

---

[182]Torrance, "Atonement," p. 245.

[183]Ibid.

[184]Torrance, "Latin Heresy," p. 481. Torrance has a detailed and sophisticated analysis of limited atonement and universal salvation, which he sees as both bound up with the "Latin Heresy." See pp. 481-82, and Torrance, "Atonement," pp. 244-50.

[185]Torrance, "Atonement," p. 249; cf. Eph 1:9-10; Col 1:19-20.

[186]Torrance, "Atonement," p. 249. Ibid. Also see p. 232.

[187]Ibid., p. 248.

than we can explain why evil came into the world."[188] The gospel, Torrance argues, does not even tell us precisely how evil is vanquished by Christ and the cross. It *is* a mystery before which the angels veil their faces. But the gospel does tell us that God has loved us to the uttermost and has entered the dark depths of our sinful humanity within this fallen creation in order to make our misery, shame, sin, guilt, alienation and godlessness his own, substituting himself for us, thwarting evil, redeeming and restoring us to union and communion with the triune God who loves us more than he loves himself.

[188]Torrance, *Karl Barth*, p. 239.

3

THE MEDIATION OF CHRIST

Christ's Vicarious Humanity

I am crucified with Christ: nevertheless I live, yet not I but Christ lives in me;
and the life which I now live in the flesh I live by faith,
the faithfulness of the Son of God who loved me and gave himself for me.
GALATIANS 2:20
AS TRANSLATED BY T. F. TORRANCE

I n chapter two we examined Torrance's holistic approach to the mediation of Christ. Torrance argues that to really understand realities we cannot investigate them in isolation from one another. Rather we must examine them in their nexus of interrelations, for only then will their dynamic reality and intrinsic significance come into view.

For the mediation of revelation and reconciliation in Jesus Christ, this means that Christ has to be understood in the dynamic field (form in being) of God's covenantal interaction with Israel (the interactionist God-world relation), for it is within the actual matrix of divinely prepared forms of thought, speech and life in Israel and the Old Testament (critical realist epistemology or integration of form in knowing) that Jesus Christ is recognized as the incarnate Son of God and Savior of the world and his death on the cross is understood as an atoning sacrifice for sin.

Within this matrix in Israel we also examined Torrance's interpretation of the mediation of Christ (1) in relation to God (the *homoousion*), (2) within the incarnate divine-human reality of Christ's person as mediator (the *hypostatic union*) and (3) as that mediation is accomplished in Christ's atoning reconciliation (the *atonement*). In Christ, *God* has taken up the cause, and taken on the condition, of our *sinful alienated* humanity. Jesus Christ, fully God and completely human, embraces both sides of the mediating relationship in the hypostatic union and acts at once in a divine and human manner. This divine and human activity issues from Christ's one person, condemning human sin, overcoming guilt and death, and transforming and restoring our broken humanity back to union and communion with God.

Jesus Christ is *homoousios* with God and with humanity, ministering the things of God to humanity and ministering the things of humanity to God. Torrance sees the God-humanward and human-Godward ministry "as an inseparable whole in the oneness of our Lord's Person as God and Man, and as continuous throughout all the reconciling movement of his life to its culmination in his vicarious death and resurrection, but also extending after his ascension into his heavenly intercession as our High Priest and Advocate before the Face of the Father."[1]

The last chapter emphasized the ministry of Jesus Christ, the incarnate Son of God, toward humanity overcoming sin and guilt, reconciling and redeeming humanity. This chapter focuses on the ministry of the incarnate Son as a man toward God, or Christ's *vicarious humanity*. The chapter will develop this theme first within the matrix of Israel and then in relation to revelation and reconciliation. The final sections discuss the vicarious humanity of Christ in connection with *our* human response to God (faith, conversion, worship, evangelism), including Torrance's understanding of *the logic of grace*, his alternative to monergism and synergism with reference to the relation between divine agency and human agency in soteriology.

1. Israel and the Covenanted Way of Response
The covenantal relation between God and Israel is normally viewed as involving two parties, God and Israel. Torrance finds this kind of covenant relation within the biblical witness in declarations such as, "I will be your God, and you will be my people," and "I am holy, be ye holy."[2]

Yet within this covenantal reciprocity between God and Israel, Torrance sees an all-important third factor or middle term between the two

[1] Thomas F. Torrance, *The Mediation of Christ*, 2nd ed. (Colorado Springs: Helmers & Howard, 1992), p. 73.
[2] Ibid., pp. 73, 77.

covenant polarities or partners: "*a covenanted way of response,* such as a divinely provided sacrifice replacing the best that the human partner may think he can offer, as in the paradigmatic case of the offering God provided instead of Isaac, Abraham's beloved son" (Gen 22).[3]

This covenanted way of response, Torrance argues, is also central in the covenant relation between God and Israel established at Mt Sinai because God knew that Israel would not fulfill the covenantal obligations in Israel's life or worship of God. It is a covenant between God and an unholy people (Israel as representative of all humanity), as noted in chapter two.

Thus while the covenant involved God and Israel, it is a covenant of pure grace established by God in which God effects reconciliation with humanity at its worst in rebellion against God. Within the conflict between God and Israel, God provides Israel with a covenanted way of response in the ordinances of worship and liturgies of atoning sacrifice so that the Israelites could come before God, receive forgiveness and restoration to covenant partnership with God, and fulfill Israel's vicarious priestly mission in history.[4]

In the sacrificial scheme and the details of the liturgies described in the Pentateuch, Torrance finds a pattern "designed to bring home to the people of Israel that they are not to appear before the Face of God with offerings embodying their own self-expression or representing their own naturalistic desires, or with kinds of sacrifice thought up by themselves as means of expiating guilt or propitiating God, for that was how the heathen engaged in worship, as ways of acting upon God and inducing his favour."[5] The holy and living God cannot be approached by sinful human beings without atoning reconciliation, and God alone can provide propitiation for the sin of God's people and expiate their guilt.

All of the detailed regulations about the temple and everything done within it prohibited unprescribed oblation, uncovenanted offering and all other ritual of people's own invention. Even the priesthood itself and all of the liturgical ordinances associated with it, Torrance maintains, "were regarded as constituting the vicarious way of covenant response in faith, obedience and worship which God had freely provided for Israel out of his steadfast love."[6]

---

[3] Ibid., p. 74.
[4] Ibid.
[5] Ibid.
[6] Ibid., p. 75.

Likewise, as noted in chapter two, in the prehistory of the mediation of revelation and reconciliation in Israel, God's purpose set forth in the Torah and reinterpreted by the prophets had to be etched into the minds, inscribed on the hearts, translated into the very being and life of God's people. If Israel was to be a light to the nations, the vicarious way of response had to be embodied in Israel as a whole in the totality of Israel's existence as a community with a priestly and vicarious life and mission in history.[7]

This kind of vicarious embodiment within the covenant comes to expression in the Isaianic prophecies where the priest/mediator and the guilt-bearer/sacrifice are conflated in the vicarious role of the "servant of the Lord" in relation to the redemption of Israel.[8] Torrance sees this Isaianic "servant of the Lord" as an "hypostatised actualisation within the flesh and blood existence of Israel of the divinely provided way of covenant response. . . . A messianic role was evidently envisioned for the servant in which mediator and sacrifice, priest and victim were combined in a form that was at once representative and substitutionary, corporate and individual."[9]

Here Torrance sees the Isaianic prophet struggling to articulate a vision in which, (1) the servant of the Lord is identified with Israel, (2) the divine *Go'el* or redeemer is identified with the Holy One of Israel and (3) the two (the servant and the redeemer) are united and repeatedly spoken of together. Torrance argues, "It is as though the prophet wanted to say that the real servant of the Lord is the Lord himself who as *goel*-Redeemer has bound himself up in such a tight bond of covenant kinship with Israel that he has taken on himself Israel's afflicted existence and made it his own in order to redeem Israel."[10] This, of course, would imply an actual state of incarnation, and as noted in sections two and four of chapter two, this is precisely what Torrance finds taking place in Jesus Christ within the matrix of Israel as reflected in the New Testament.

2. The Vicarious Humanity of Christ

It is in Christ that the divine redeemer, the incarnate Son of God *homoou-*

---

[7]Ibid.
[8]Ibid., p. 74.
[9]Ibid., pp. 75-76.
[10]Ibid., p. 76.

sios with God the Father, has identified himself with not only Israel but all people. As noted in sections two, four and five in chapter two, Torrance argues that this divine redeemer has come in the form of a suffering servant of the Lord sent to unilaterally fulfill a new covenant of universal range, bearing (and bearing away) the sins and guilt of the whole world as both priest and self-sacrifice, offerer and self-offering. Thus the New Testament recognition and presentation of Jesus Christ within the matrix of Israel as both divine redeemer and suffering servant of the Lord, Torrance argues, must be regarded as the very essence of the gospel.[11]

In Torrance's perspective this incarnational identification of the Son of God with us in our sin and alienation from God includes the assuming of our transgressions and estranged humanity, and the reconciling and restoring of humanity to proper relation to God. Yet the incarnation also entails the sanctification, perfection and bending of our wayward human nature back in perfect obedience to God at every point in Jesus Christ's life, ministry, death and resurrection. Incarnational redemption includes the entire earthly historical and *fully human vicarious activity* of the man, Jesus, who acts in his humanity on our behalf and in our place.

What Torrance finds in the New Testament witness is not simply a new covenant between two partners, God and humanity. He discerns in Jesus from the human side of the covenant toward God, "the divinely provided counterpart" to God's self-revelation and self-communication to humanity, the divinely provided and utterly faithful human response of the servant/son that replaces the best we (all human beings) think we can offer God. The all-important middle factor within the covenant polarity between God and humanity, in Torrance's theology, is *the vicarious humanity of Jesus.*[12]

Here Torrance argues that "Jesus Christ constitutes in his own self-consecrated humanity the fulfillment of the vicarious way of human response to God promised under the old covenant, but now on the ground of his atoning self-sacrifice once for all offered as a vicarious way of response which is available for all mankind."[13] Christ's incarnational redemption involves mediation not only from God to humanity but also

---

[11]See sections two, four and five of chapter two. Also see Torrance, *Mediation*, p. 76.
[12]Ibid., p. 77.
[13]Ibid., pp. 76-77.

from *humanity* to God in which Jesus Christ fulfills the covenant from both sides.

This is one of the distinctive features of Torrance's Christology and soteriology, for it discloses what he calls the *logic of grace*, in reference to which "we may give careful formulation to all the ways and works of God in his interaction with us in space and time."[14] The nature of grace is one of the basic theological concepts and relations crucial for Torrance's *scientific* account of theology, for it provides a pivotal insight into God's relation to the world in redemption and creation.[15] God acts in such a way as to sustain the integrity of the creature and realize the creature's relation to God. God is free in the freedom of grace to be present to the creature in such a way as to sustain the creature in a free relation to God.

We will examine Torrance's understanding of the vicarious humanity of Christ first in relation to revelation and reconciliation and then in relation to our human response. The final section of this chapter deals with the logic of grace and its significance.

Christ's vicarious humanity and revelation. Section two of chapter two outlined Torrance's understanding of the mediation of revelation in Israel in which God subjected the Israelites to intense and often painful interaction with himself so as to adapt Israel's thought, speech, worship and life into the appropriate human response or creaturely vessel progressively purified and assimilated to God's Word for the communication of that word to all people. This historical covenantal ordeal provided the matrix of life and literature in Israel, the basic concepts and patterns of life, within which the mediation of God's final self-revelation and self-communication in Jesus Christ is understood, even though Christ fills, fulfills and transforms that matrix with new and fuller meaning.

The Word of God assimilates the creaturely human word. In Jesus Christ the movement of God's self-revelation begun in Israel reaches its climax, for here the eternal Word of God graciously condescends and participates in our finite, creaturely existence in a particular human being "who embodies in himself the personal address of God's Word and the

[14]See Thomas F. Torrance, "My Interaction with Karl Barth" in *How Karl Barth Changed My Mind*, ed. Donald K. McKim (Grand Rapids, Mich.: Eerdmans, 1986), p. 55.
[15]See the introduction above, p. 24. As such, this "unique kind of connection found in *Grace*" provides "the inner connection giving coherence to the whole structure of Christian theology" (Torrance, "My Interaction," p. 54).

personal response of man to God's Word."[16] In Jesus Christ, Torrance sees the Word of God as assimilating creaturely and human hearing and speaking as a constitutive ingredient in divine revelation so that "a correlation and correspondence" is established "between God's self-giving and man's receiving within which alone God's revelation could be actualized in man and a true and faithful response could be yielded by man to God."[17]

This, of course, is extremely important for Torrance, since there is no *inherent* or *automatic* transparence or isomorphism (similarity or correlation in structure) between the human mind (and its forms of thought and speech) and the reality the mind seeks to know, as discussed in section one of chapter two. This is even more the case with knowledge of God in Torrance's perspective because (1) creaturely rationality and human word are radically different from God's eternal Word and rationality and (2) the human mind is alienated from God due to sin.[18] There can be genuine knowledge of God only when, in addition to the self-revealing of God (form in being), (1) there is a true and faithful human response, a transparency or isomorphism between God's eternal Word and rationality and creaturely rationality and human word, a transparency or isomorphism that must be generated or created (an integration of form in knowing) since it is not *inherent* in creaturely rationality and human word, and (2) the human mind, which is alienated from God due to sin, is reconciled and redeemed. The vicarious humanity of Christ answers both of these issues.

Torrance points out that the Word of God incarnate in Jesus Christ is the same Word of God through whom all of creation has been called into

---

[16]Torrance, *Mediation*, p. 78.

[17]Thomas F. Torrance, *God and Rationality* (London: Oxford University Press, 1971), pp. 144-45. Also see Thomas F. Torrance, *Reality and Evangelical Theology* (Philadelphia: Westminster Press, 1982), p. 88.

[18]Torrance discusses both points in parallel essays found in Torrance, *Evangelical Theology*, pp. 84-97, and in Torrance, *Rationality*, pp. 139-53, though the discussion in *Evangelical Theology* contains significant development of the second point beyond what is found in *Rationality*.

Also, Torrance does not first develop his anthropological and epistemic convictions and then apply them to his Christology and soteriology. Like Calvin, Torrance sees knowledge of humanity and knowledge of God as arising together. Therefore, knowledge of the problems associated with human knowledge of God and knowledge of the possibility of real knowledge of God arise together within real or actual knowledge of God mediated through Jesus Christ.

existence out of nothing and given a contingent reality and order of its own, a contingent reality and order which the Word of God respects and preserves. In creating the universe, Torrance maintains, God "confers upon it a created rationality different from, yet dependent on, His own transcendent Rationality."[19] Chapter five develops this theme more fully.

What is important in this context is that it is this created rationality and human word (logos) that the Word (Logos) of God assimilated to himself in the incarnation.[20] Even though the contingent human modes of thought and speech in themselves are "utterly inadequate to speak of God or convey divine Truth," yet they have nevertheless been assumed by God in Jesus Christ and "transformed and used in God's self-revelation" in such a way that "they are made to indicate more than they can express and to convey divine Truth beyond their natural capacity."[21] Thus in the hypostatic union between the divine and human natures in Jesus Christ, Torrance sees a complete union between God's uncreated rationality and Word and contingent creaturely rationality and human word so that it is in and through Christ's creaturely human word that the Word of God is mediated to all humanity.[22]

Yet in the incarnation, Torrance argues, the Son of God assumed not only a fully human, but an alienated and sinful, mind "in order to redeem it and effect reconciliation deep within the rational center of human being."[23] Here in the vicarious humanity of Christ, the human mind is redeemed and real knowledge of God is actualized within our humanity

---

[19]Torrance, Rationality, p. 139. Also see Torrance, Evangelical Theology, p. 90.

[20]It is a bodily incarnation that involves all of the interrelated levels of our created human existence and rationality from molecular through the biological to the personal. See footnote 30 of chapter two, p. 64, and chapter five, pp. 180-82.

[21]Torrance, Evangelical Theology, p. 108. Torrance asserts, "For the eternal Word of God to become understandable and communicable in the mode and character of word to man He had to share to the full in the space-time distinctions, and connexions of human existence in this world and operate within the finite conditions of created rationality" (Torrance, Rationality, p. 142). Also see Torrance, Evangelical Theology, p. 91.

[22]Ibid.

[23]Torrance, Mediation, p. 49. Also see Torrance, "The Reconciliation of Mind," TSF Bulletin 10, no. 3 (1987): 4-7. This emphasis on the Son of God assuming our fallen and sinful humanity, Torrance contends, is found throughout the first five centuries of the early church, especially among the Greek fathers (see Torrance, Mediation, p. 39). Athanasius and Gregory of Nazianzen especially emphasized that sin is entrenched in the human mind. See Thomas F. Torrance, The Trinitarian Faith: The Evangelical Theology of the Ancient Catholic Church (Edinburgh: T & T Clark, 1988), p. 165.

which the Son of God assumed in the incarnation.[24]

Thus Torrance concludes that through his atoning self-consecration on our behalf, Jesus Christ "is Himself the hearing [and speaking] man included in the Word of God, and He is that in a final and definitive way."[25] Here we have neither a Word of God and a response of humanity only loosely related in a Nestorian dualism,[26] nor an Apollinarianism in which the human word is displaced by the eternal Word of God,[27] but rather "the all-significant middle term, the divinely provided response in the vicarious humanity of Jesus Christ."[28] Jesus Christ is God's exclusive language to humanity, Torrance argues, and Jesus Christ *is* humanity's exclusive language to God as well.[29]

The apostolic word, the communicable form of God's Word in history. In order for the actualization of God's self-revelation in the vicarious humanity of Christ to achieve its end and avail for all people throughout history, the created word assimilated to the eternal Word of God in the mind of Jesus Christ had to enter the interpersonal medium of thought and speech embodied in a community of human persons. Here Torrance sees Jesus as forming a "nucleus within the speaker-hearer relations" among his disciples so that Christ could continue his speaking and acting through history.[30]

---

[24]Torrance, *Trinitarian Faith*, p. 166. Torrance argues that the prophetic office of Christ cannot be separated from Christ's priestly office and that Jesus' teachings passed on through the Gospels are integral to Christ's saving work.

[25]Torrance, *Rationality*, p. 145.

[26]Torrance, *Evangelical Theology*, p. 88.

[27]Torrance, *Rationality*, p. 142.

[28]Torrance, *Evangelical Theology*, p. 88.

[29]Ibid. Here Torrance affirms the *exclusive* character of God's self-revelation in Jesus Christ. Also see Thomas F. Torrance, *Karl Barth: Biblical and Evangelical Theologian* (Edinburgh: T & T Clark, 1990), pp. 93-95.

[30]Torrance, *Evangelical Theology*, p. 91. Torrance's understanding and account of the mediation of the vicarious creaturely human word (assimilated and adapted to the Word of God) in Jesus Christ through Christ's first disciples and the apostolic church to the writing, redacting and final formation of the New Testament canon is rather complex. It includes the disciples' knowledge of Jesus before his death and resurrection, but also the transformation of that knowledge by the resurrection and Pentecost.

While Torrance understands it as a fully historical mediation involving all of the complexity uncovered by critical-historical investigation of this history by modern biblical scholars and historians, it is not purely historical. That is to say, Torrance adamantly refuses to exclude from his account of this history the activity of a living God who interacts with the created order and human history. Readers interested in the subtlety of Torrance's development of this should consult the sources indicated in the footnotes for this

In so doing, Christ established "the controlling basis among believers for the extended communication of the Word of God and the translation of the self-witness of Christ into witness to Christ,"[31] "informed, empowered, and used by Christ's self-witness so that it could take the field as the communicable form of his self-witness in history, i.e. , as the specific form intended by Christ for the proclamation of God's Word to all men."[32] This is what Torrance sees taking place in the apostolic formulation of the *kergyma* and apostolic foundation of the church.

Of course, it was only after the resurrection of Jesus Christ from the dead and the outpouring of the Holy Spirit at Pentecost, Torrance contends, that all that Jesus had said and done "broke forth in its self-evidencing power and seized hold of the church as the very Word or *Logos* of God" incarnate in the very human life and words of Jesus the Jew from Nazareth.[33] The resurrection is crucial in Torrance's theology on a number of levels. Here the resurrection casts entirely new light on all that Jesus had said and done, which like pieces of a jigsaw puzzle suddenly come together in a depth of meaning and consistency impossible for Jesus' followers to conceive before the resurrection.[34] Here finally "is the key to the . . . enigma of Jesus, for it [the resurrection] provides it with a structure consistent with the whole sequence of events leading up to and beyond the crucifixion."[35] Thus the significance embedded in God's whole *oikonomia* (the pattern of God's revealing and reconciling activity) back through Jesus to God's dealings with Israel and forward through the ascension and Pentecost is disclosed through Jesus Christ's resurrection from the dead.

Under the continuing influence of the risen Christ through the outpouring of the Spirit at Pentecost, the apostolic church was so reconciled and joined to the *mind* of Christ that it came to reflect that *mind* in its own witness

---

section and particularly the following material: Thomas F. Torrance, *Space, Time and Resurrection* (Grand Rapids, Mich.: Eerdmans, 1976), pp. 1-26, 159-93, especially pp. 1-7, 159-79; Torrance, *Evangelical Theology* pp. 91-120, especially 94-100; Thomas F. Torrance, "'The Historical Jesus': From the Perspective of a Theologian," *The New Testament Age: Essays in Honor of Bo Reicke*, ed. William C. Weinrich, 2 vol. (Macon, Ga.: Mercer University Press, 1984), 2:511-26; and Thomas F. Torrance, *Theological Science* (London: Oxford University Press, 1969), pp. 312-37.

[31]Torrance, *Rationality*, p. 151-52.

[32]Torrance, *Evangelical Theology*, pp. 91-92.

[33]Torrance, *Mediation*, p. 4.

[34]See Torrance, *Resurrection*, p. 164.

[35]Ibid.

to Christ.[36] This involves both the fully historical mediation from the vicarious humanity of Jesus through the eye and ear witness of his first disciples, but also the ongoing activity of the risen Christ through the Holy Spirit.[37]

Here Torrance explains that just as Christ's vicarious humanity is integral to the mediation of the Word of God to humanity, "so the response of the apostles was assumed by Christ into oneness with His own [response] to form the means by which the Word of Christ reached out into history."[38] The risen Christ himself was at work through the apostles and the early church bearing witness to all that he had accomplished in his life, death and resurrection, thereby communicating himself as Savior and Lord through their witness.[39]

Christ's vicarious humanity and the New Testament Scriptures. It is here that Torrance finds the genesis of the New Testament Scriptures which gives them their ontological grounding and distinctive quality.[40] He

---

[36]See Thomas F. Torrance, *Theology in Reconstruction* (Grand Rapids, Mich.: Eerdmans, 1965), pp. 136-40. Torrance asserts that "the apostolic proclamation of Christ was so geared into his self-proclamation that it was used by him as the shared and corporate medium of understanding and communication through which he brought his Word in human and historical form to bear upon mankind throughout the ages" (Torrance, *Rationality*, p. 152).

[37]This can be viewed as another example of Torrance's critical realist epistemology and interactionist God-world relation.

[38]Ibid. Also see Torrance, *Evangelical Theology*, p. 92.

[39]Torrance, *Evangelical Theology*, p. 92.

[40]For Torrance, the character of Scripture is not simply determined by the inspiration of the Spirit so that one ends up with an essentially oracular conception of revelation embodied in the Bible. Nor is Scripture merely a human witness to a divine Word, a divine Word understood as exclusively an event. Rather Torrance's perspective must be understood in light of his *realist* view of the ontology and objectivity of the Word and the dynamic activity of the Spirit. This, I believe, clarifies what Torrance meant when he spoke of an exciting rethinking and deepening of the doctrine of Scripture. See Torrance, *Karl Barth*, p. 122.

Here we see another point of difference between Torrance and fundamentalism (and some strands of evangelicalism) and also some forms of narrative theology, for they both view the character of Scripture in primarily literary terms. Fundamentalism construes the character of the Bible on the basis of its verbal inspiration and identifies the words of the Bible with the Word of God. Certain strands of narrative theology speak of the Bible projecting a "followable world" that is rendered through the literary devices of narrative depiction, but the ontological reference of the narrative remains obscure or eschatological, as in the case of Ronald Thiemann who thinks that theology should dispense with the category of revelation altogether. See Ronald Thiemann, *Revelation and Theology: The Gospel as Narrated Promise* (Notre Dame, Ind.: University of Notre Dame Press, 1985), pp. 47-71, 141-55. Both are attempts to overcome the problems posed for Christian faith and Scripture by modern natural science and historiography, though the attempts are very different from one another in detail. In a sense, they both represent a retreat from science and history into the literary character of the Bible. Torrance's view has a theological and historical depth that I find missing in these other perspectives.

maintains, "It was out of this corporate reciprocity centered in and creatively controlled by Christ through the outpouring of his Spirit of Truth on it that the New Testament Scriptures were born and took shape within the church. They constitute, therefore, the divinely provided and inspired linguistic medium which remains of authoritative and critical significance for the whole history of the church of Jesus Christ."[41]

The New Testament writers maintained that their proclamation about Christ had its genesis in Jesus himself, for in the light of his resurrection from the dead and the sending his Spirit, the apostolic church understood Christ as the Word of God who had proclaimed himself to them in a life of self-disclosure in word and deed.[42] Torrance argues that the New Testament writers do not obtrude themselves and foist their spirituality on us, but rather direct us to Jesus Christ and his vicarious humanity, a vicarious humanity that provides the life-giving basis as well as the normative expression for all of our human response to God.[43]

The purpose of their inspired witness in its written form, according to Torrance, is that it enables us to "stand with the original witnesses under the impact of the Word . . . and to be drawn into the sphere of its effective operation . . . where we, like them, may learn to repent and believe the gospel, give thanks to God and live in communion with Him."[44] God continues to make himself know to us through Scripture, this articulate form of human word, first spoken and then written, initially unfolded in the nucleus of disciples around Jesus, but ultimately grounded in the assimilation of the human word to the divine Word in the vicarious humanity of Jesus Christ.

Yet Torrance contends that "*the real text* of New Testament revelation is *the humanity of Jesus.*"[45] Jesus Christ is the "real text of God's Word ad-

---

[41]Torrance, *Evangelical Theology,* pp. 92-93.

[42]Torrance, *Theological Science,* p. 333. Torrance also notes that the ascension of Christ sends us back to the incarnation, the historical Jesus, and of course, the apostolic witness to Christ locked into Christ's self-witness which we have been discussing. See Torrance, *Resurrection,* pp. 133-34.

[43]Torrance, *Evangelical Theology,* p. 93.

[44]Torrance, *Rationality,* p. 153.

[45]Torrance, *Mediation,* p. 88. The emphasis appears in Torrance's text. Elsewhere Torrance writes, "The real text of the New Testament Scriptures is the humanity of Christ. He is God's exclusive language to us and He alone must be our language to God. . . . Jesus Christ is God's self-address to man" (Torrance, *Rationality,* p. 151). Torrance argues that Jesus

dressed to us" and he is also "the real text of our address to God."[46] In Christ our human forms of thought and speech are assumed, sanctified and addressed to God on our behalf, in our place, as our very own. It is a word from humanity to God with which God is well pleased. And it is human response to God, Torrance asserts, "in which we all may share through the Spirit of Jesus Christ which he freely gives us."[47]

Christ's vicarious humanity and reconciliation. As noted in the last chapter, Torrance thinks that all genuine knowledge involves an element of participation or cognitive union of the mind with its object, a participation that requires the removal of any alienation or estrangement that obstructs or distorts genuine knowledge.[48] While Torrance sees this principle as applying to all knowledge, the element of participation is heightened in our knowledge of other persons where we are not really able to know them without "a rapprochement or communion of minds characterized by mutual respect, trust and love."[49]

This is even more the case with knowledge of God, for we cannot know God without being "adapted in our knowing and personal relations to him . . . without being reconciled to him."[50] Yet this is also precisely the human dilemma, for we have, in fact, broken our relationship with God, forfeited our privilege as children of God and, in Torrance's words, twisted "our personal and interpersonal being-constituting relations as sons and daughters . . . of God . . . into the opposite so that instead of expressing genuine filial relation to our heavenly Father they express what we are in our self-centered alienation from him and from one another."[51] In so doing we turn the "truth of the very image of God in which we have been created into a lie."[52]

Thus we cannot actualize a Word of God addressed to us or respond to God without a reconciliation effected within the depths of our alienated being and existence. Once again, Torrance argues that what we find in

---

Christ "does not mediate a revelation or a reconciliation that is other than what he is. . . . He embodies what he mediates in himself, for what he mediates and what he is are one and the same" (Torrance, *Mediation*, p. 67). Also see Torrance, *Evangelical Theology*, p. 14-16.
[46]Torrance, *Mediation*, p. 78.
[47]Ibid.
[48]Ibid., pp. 24-25.
[49]Ibid., p. 25.
[50]Ibid., pp. 25-26.
[51]Ibid., p. 79.
[52]Ibid.

Jesus Christ is not just a covenantal parity between God and humanity, but the all-important middle factor, the divinely provided, but fully human and fully reconciled, vicarious humanity of Christ.

It is in Jesus Christ that the eternal Son, who is ever *homoousios* with God the Father, has penetrated the perverted personal and interpersonal reality of our fallen and estranged humanity and made it his own. In assuming our disobedient humanity in rebellion against God, Christ converted it back to a true and faithful filial relation to God in love, obedience, holiness, trust and praise throughout his vicarious human being and life for us. Torrance maintains that the Word of God incarnate in Jesus Christ not only delivered humanity from subjugation to sin and alienation, but also recreates humanity's relation to God by realizing perfect humanity on the earth, offering God the *true human response* to God on our behalf and in our place, which we cannot make for ourselves.[53]

As we saw in sections four and five of chapter two, this is a reconciliation worked out throughout the entire course of Jesus Christ's vicarious obedient life as Servant-Son, including his atoning sacrifice on the cross.[54] Torrance sees this vicarious restoration of our alienated and fearful humanity to filial relation to God taking place especially in the passion and death of Jesus Christ.

In Gethsemane and at Calvary, Jesus "penetrates the utmost extremity of our self-alienating flight from God where we are trapped in death, and turned everything round so that out of the fearful depths of our darkness and dereliction we may cry with him, 'Our Father.'"[55] Torrance sees Jesus' prayer to God in Gethsemane, "Not my will, but your will be done," as *vicarious*; it is *our* selfish human will that Christ Jesus assumed and turns back to God in Gethsemane in an agonizing obedience to the Father worked out on our behalf and in our place.[56] Here the resurrection, according to Torrance, does signify the "verdict" or answer of God the Father who is "well pleased" with the obedient vicarious humanity of Jesus Christ.

---

[53]Torrance, *Rationality*, p. 143.

[54]Torrance, "Atonement," p. 233. Torrance views the vicarious humanity of Christ as Word and Act of God become human word and human act, "moving and operating creatively and redemptively within the space and time of our world in the acutely personalised form of the Lord Jesus Christ."

[55]Torrance, *Mediation*, p. 79.

[56]Ibid., pp. 79-80.

It is also significant that Torrance understands the atoning exchange operative here in the depths of Jesus Christ's vicarious penetration of human suffering as taking place within the incarnate divine-human reality of one person of the mediator. In Gethsemane and on Golgotha, it is God who has entered our passion in Jesus Christ and assumed our fear and hurt, our condition under judgement, even our deepest dereliction and godlessness that we overhear in Christ's cry, "My God, my God, why have you forsaken me?"[57] And yet in his vicarious *humanity*, Jesus Christ turns *our* fearful, derelict, godless humanity back to God in faith and surrender: "Father, into your hands I commit my Spirit." It is in light of God's involvement in the passion of Christ that Torrance deals with the question of both the suffering and impassibility of God, a subject developed in the next chapter.

For this discussion, what is significant is that Torrance understands the entire life and activity of Jesus from birth to death "as constituting the vicarious human response to himself which God has freely and unconditionally provided for us."[58] It is a response that Christ has made within *our* humanity taken up in the incarnation. It is not only a vicarious human response that God has made for us in our place in Jesus Christ, but a response that Christ made as *one with us and one of us*. It is a single continuous and indivisible saving and sanctifying act of atoning reconciliation by God, reaching from Jesus' birth and earthly life and ministry, to its consummation in Christ's death, resurrection and ascension.[59] In other words, Jesus Christ, in his vicarious humanity, *is* God's act of incarnational atonement and therefore the very heart of the gospel.[60]

For this reason Torrance repeatedly asserts that Jesus Christ *is* our propitiation, justification, sanctification, redemption, salvation, and so

---

[57]Mark 15:34. Also see Torrance, *Trinitarian Faith*, p. 185.

[58]Torrance, *Mediation*, p. 80.

[59]Thomas F. Torrance, "Karl Barth and Patristic Theology," in *Theology Beyond Christendom: Essays on the Centenary of the Birth of Karl Barth May 10, 1886*, ed. John Thompson (Allison Park, Penn.: Pickwick, 1986), p. 229. Torrance is describing Barth's position, but it is clear that it represents Torrance's position as well.

[60]Torrance, *Trinitarian Faith*, p. 4, 8, 145-54. Torrance draws out the astonishing character of Christ's vicarious humanity in a fascinating quotation from Gregory of Nyssa concerning why God descended to such humiliation: "Our faith staggers at the thought that God, the infinite, inconceivable and ineffable reality, who transcends all glory and majesty, should be clothed with the defiled nature of man, so that his sublime activities are debased through being united with what is so degraded" (see p. 153).

on (1 Cor 1:30).[61] Christ's vicarious humanity thus becomes a concept more fundamental than the various themes discussed under the rubric of the *ordo salutis* (order of salvation), for Christ *is* our response to God in whom we come before God and are accepted by God "as those who are inseparably united to Jesus Christ our great High Priest in his eternal self-presentation to the Father."[62] Jesus Christ himself, in his vicarious life, death and resurrection, *is* our salvation in all of its manifold, though indivisible, facets. Thus the vicarious humanity of Christ becomes one of the few crucial concepts which simplify and unify theology's grasp of God's self-revelation and provide Torrance with his coherent and rigorous scientific account of theology from its christological and soteriological center.

The radical character of the vicarious humanity of Jesus Christ at this point comes into view through the way Torrance combines the themes of substitution and representation in a concept of *total substitution*.[63]

An account of what Christ has done for humanity purely under the concept of representation is inadequate, Torrance contends, because on this model Jesus is the leader of humanity. His response *represents* our response to God, but it is not a *substitute* for our response.[64] In an exclusively substitutionary theory Christ's mediation is restricted to his death on the cross, where there is a transference of the penalty for sin from sinful humanity to the sinless Jesus who suffers and dies the death we deserve as those who have transgressed God's law. The problem with this doctrine of substitution is that Christ, in his perfect or neutral humanity, acts only in an external or forensic manner that has no ontological connection with our actual sinful humanity. Our *actual* sinful humanity remains untouched by this kind of substitution transacted by Christ's *neutral* humanity on the cross.

In Torrance's view representation and substitution must interpenetrate one another in such a way that within Christ's incarnational union with our sinful humanity, Jesus Christ acts on our behalf, in our stead, and in

---

[61]See Torrance, "Atonement," p. 233, and Torrance, "Latin Heresy," p. 230.

[62]Torrance, *Mediation*, p. 80. I also believe that this is why Torrance seldom deals with the *ordo salutis* (order of salvation) or the various elements within it (justification, sanctification, etc.) in his various discussions of Christology and soteriology.

[63]Torrance discusses this in a number of places. See Torrance, *Karl Barth*, pp. 234-36; Torrance, *Trinitarian Faith*, pp. 168-78; and Torrance, *Mediation*, pp. 80-81.

[64]See Torrance, *Mediation*, p. 80.

our place in *all* of *our* basic responses to God from *within* our *actual* humanity from birth, through life, death and resurrection: "The vicarious humanity of Jesus Christ . . . fulfills a representative and substitutionary role in all our relations with God . . . such as trusting and obeying, understanding and knowing, loving and worshipping. . . . Jesus Christ . . . in and through His humanity took our place, acting in our name and on our behalf before God, freely offering in Himself what we could not offer and offering it in our stead, the perfect response of man to God in a holy life of faith and prayer and praise, the self-offering of the Beloved Son with whom the Father is well pleased."[65]

Furthermore, Torrance argues that since God's grace has taken this particular form and is now *the* provision for all of humanity's response, the true and faithful response in the vicarious humanity of Christ thereby invalidates every other way of response.[66] In order to clarify precisely what Torrance intends by these last points, the next section of this chapter develops some of what the vicarious humanity of Christ means for the mediation of *our* human response to God.

3. Christ's Vicarious Humanity and Our Human Response

The relation between the vicarious humanity of Jesus Christ in revelation and reconciliation and our human response to Christ is a controversial area of Torrance's theology and a distinctive facet of his work. This section examines four representative aspects of *our* human re-sponse to Jesus Christ and the gospel in relation to *Christ's* vicarious humanity.

Faith. Torrance points out that often people view faith as something we do, or something we have, an activity we embody in our response to Christ and the gospel. There are places in the New Testament, Torrance acknowledges, where people are called to repent, have faith and be saved. Yet Torrance argues that this does not mean that faith is "an autonomous, independent act" grounded solely in our human agency.[67] Torrance sees faith in the New Testament as intensely personalized, for Jesus Christ himself in his personal being turns our wayward, unfaithful personal being back to God.[68]

---

[65]Torrance, *Rationality*, p. 145.
[66]Ibid.
[67]Torrance, *Mediation*, p. 82. Those interested in the development of Torrance's thought in this area should compare ibid., pp. 81-98, with Torrance, *Rationality*, pp. 153-64.
[68]Torrance, *Mediation*, p. 82.

The radical character of what Torrance intends is revealed in the following statement: "Jesus steps into the actual situation where we are summoned to have faith in God, to believe and trust in him, and he acts in our place and in our stead from within the depths of our unfaithfulness and provides us freely with a faithfulness in which we may share. . . . That is to say, if we think of belief, trust or faith as forms of human activity before God, we then must think of Jesus Christ as believing, trusting and having faith in God the Father on our behalf and in our place."[69] Torrance grants that this is difficult for many to accept, especially those from Western culture with its emphasis on the competent and autonomous individual.

Faith does entail a polar relation between God and people, but in the gospel the human pole is, in fact, actualized in Jesus' vicarious faith and faithfulness on our behalf where "through his incarnational and atoning union with us our faith is implicated in his."[70] Yet our faith is in no way depersonalized or dehumanized by Christ's vicarious human faith. Rather through union with Christ's vicarious humanity, our faith arises "freely and spontaneously out of our own human life before God."[71] Torrance maintains that the faith we confess is in the faith *of* the historical Jesus Christ who lived in utter trust in God the Father in life and death (Gal 2:20; Heb 12:2). Precisely how *our* faith is implicated in *Christ's* faith is the subject of the next section in this chapter, "The Logic of Grace."

Conversion. Jesus Christ calls us to repent and believe the gospel, to convert and make a personal decision to follow Christ as Savior and Lord. Torrance says that this "is something that each of us must do, for no other human being can substitute for us in that ultimate act of man in answer to God—no other, that is except Jesus."[72]

Here again, Torrance argues that Jesus Christ's incarnational reconciliation is representative *and* substitutionary. Our sinful rebellious humanity runs further and further from God into the far off country (the parable of the prodigal son). Christ united himself to our wayward humanity there in the far-off country and "reversed its direction and converted it back in obedience and faith and love to God the Father."[73] Christ effected a full

---

[69]Ibid., pp. 82-83. See Gal 2:20; Jn 15:1-8.
[70]Ibid., p. 84.
[71]Ibid.
[72]Ibid.
[73]Ibid.

and complete repentant restructuring *(metanoia)* of the human mind and soul from within where we are all unrepentant, unconverted and at enmity with God (Heb 2:14-18; 4:14-16).

The New Testament, Torrance notes, uses the term for regeneration *(paliggenesia)* not for what takes places in our human hearts, but rather for the regeneration that took place in the incarnation (Tit 3:4-7) and for the final eschatological transformation when Christ returns (Mt 19:28; Acts 3:21). In this connection, Torrance recounts an incident when he was Moderator of the Church of Scotland and was once asked whether he had been "born again." Torrance responded affirmatively but shocked his questioner when he added that he had been born again when Jesus Christ was born of the Virgin Mary and when Christ rose again on the third day out of the virgin tomb![74]   *Mediation*

Torrance sees our conversion or new birth as first having taken place in Jesus Christ. We, of course, share in Christ's regeneration or conversion, but only as we first "think of him as taking our place even in our acts of repentance and personal decision, for without him all so-called repentance and conversion are empty."[75]

Worship. Once one grasps the basic structure of the relation between the vicarious humanity of Jesus Christ and our human response, one can anticipate how Torrance works this theme out in relation to other aspects of the human response. He sees the same kind of pattern in the Bible regarding worship as we find in faith and conversion. Earlier in this chapter we saw how Torrance interprets the Old Testament sacrificial scheme and the pattern of liturgy as fundamentally vicarious in character, for it was God who provided both the priesthood and the form of worship whereby the Israelites could come into God's presence and find forgiveness.

Jesus Christ, of course, fulfilled the messianic trajectory of the Old Testament found for example in the Isaianic servant songs, as noted above. In so doing, Torrance contends, Jesus Christ himself embodies the new covenant in worship in his vicarious humanity, so that all human beings now find their worship and prayer grounded in Christ himself. Indeed, "Jesus Christ in his own self-oblation to the Father *is* our worship and prayer in an acutely personalised form, so that it is only through him and with him

---

[74]Ibid., pp. 85-86.
[75]Ibid., p. 86.

and in him that we may draw near to God with the hands of our faith filled with no other offering but that which he has made on our behalf and in our place once and for all."[76]

Prayer and worship, Torrance maintains, are therefore not what we do in ways that fill worship and prayer with our own self-expression. Rather worship and prayer become acts in which Christ acts on our behalf and in our place, yet in such a way that what Christ does in our stead becomes our very own offered freely out of ourselves, but interpenetrated and assimilated by Christ in his one self-oblation to God the Father.[77]

Evangelism. Torrance contends that there is an *un*evangelical as well as an evangelical way to preach the gospel. The gospel has to be proclaimed in a way that does not make Christ's redeeming activity on our behalf dependent on *our* activity of repentance, decision and faith. When the gospel is preached in such a way that we cannot be saved unless *we* make a decision for Christ or give *our* lives to Christ, Torrance sees that kind of evangelism as decidedly *un*evangelical, for at whatever point the gospel becomes something *we* do only out of ourselves, there is a "weak link" that jeopardizes the whole chain of salvation.[78] At precisely that point the human self ends up relying on its own resources rather than on Christ.

How does Torrance envision an *evangelical* proclamation of the gospel? It has to be done in a way that gives full place to the vicarious humanity of Jesus:

> God loves you so utterly and completely that he has given himself for you in Jesus Christ his beloved Son, and has thereby pledged his very Being as God for your salvation. . . . He has bound you to himself by his love in a way that he will never let you go, for even if you refuse him and damn yourself in hell his love will never cease. . . . He has acted in your place in the whole range of your human life and activity, including your personal decisions, and your responses to God's love, and even your acts of faith. He has believed for you. . . . Therefore, renounce yourself, take up your cross and follow Jesus as your Lord and Saviour. Repent and believe in Jesus Christ your Lord and Saviour.[79]

Torrance thinks that the unevangelical way to preach the gospel all too

[76]Ibid., p. 87.
[77]Ibid., p. 88. Also see Thomas F. Torrance, "The Mind of Christ in Worship: The Problem of Apollinarianism in the Liturgy," in *Theology in Reconciliation: Essays Towards Evangelical and Catholic Unity in East and West* (Grand Rapids, Mich.: Eerdmans, 1975), pp. 139-214.
[78]Torrance, *Mediation*, p. 93.
[79]Ibid., p. 94.

often creates a dynamic in which believers are always overly concerned over whether they have *really* given themselves to Christ, whether they *really* have faith, whether they are *really* converted. Anyone who has been an observant pastor for even a short time will recognize the problem Torrance identifies.

The vicarious humanity of Jesus liberates us from all this, Torrance argues, because it is, in fact, the real good news of the gospel: throughout the whole Christian life, in every aspect of our human response, we rely on Jesus Christ who *is* the good news in his personal and incarnate reality, *the* one human response efficacious for everyone in every situation in relation to God the Father.

It is *this* gospel, Torrance contends, that really sets us free for *full* and *authentic* human and personal spontaneity and freedom in all of our human responses to the love of God. Thus despite the fact that this emphasis on the *total substitutionary* character of Jesus Christ's vicarious humanity might seem to undermine or displace *our* humanity and *our* human response, Torrance argues that really the opposite is true. *All* of grace does not, in fact, mean *nothing* of humanity. Torrance sees this paradox expressed in Galatians 2:20, the epigram at the beginning of this chapter (in Torrance's translation). This text underscores that we have been crucified with Christ, nevertheless *we* live, yet not we, but Christ lives in us; and the life that we live in the flesh we live by faith, the *faithfulness* of the Son of God who loved us and gave himself for us.[80]

In light of the total substitutionary character of Christ's vicarious humanity and our human response, how does Torrance conceive of the relation of divine and human agency in the *ordo salutis* (order of salvation)?

4. The Logic of Grace
Given Torrance's radical emphasis on *total substitution* in what Jesus Christ does for us in his vicarious humanity, it comes as no surprise that some have questioned whether this is not, in fact, an overemphasis that in the end undermines the importance of *our* personal response of faith or the role of *our* human agency at every point of the *ordo salutis*.[81] This is a

---

[80]Ibid., p. 98.

[81]Thomas Smail criticizes Torrance on this point. See Thomas Smail, *The Giving Gift: The Holy Spirit in Person* (London: Hodder and Stoughton, 1988), pp. 109-112. Also see Christian D. Kettler, *The Vicarious Humanity of Christ and the Reality of Salvation* (Lanham, Md.: University of America Press, 1986), pp. 139-42. Kettler notes that Smail also critiques Torrance

point where evangelicals, among others, may also feel rather uncomfortable with Torrance's theology.

I intend to show that Torrance does stress the place of our human agency or our human response in the *ordo salutis*, but understanding him on this point may require a transformation in one's basic conceptual framework for thinking about the relation between divine and human agency. The best way to enter Torrance's thinking in this area is by considering what he means by "the logic of God's grace" as disclosed in the theological couplet of *anhypostasis/enhypostasis*.[82]

Anhypostasis/enhypostasis. The negative term *anhypostasis* asserts that in the incarnation there is *no independent* personal reality or human *hypostasis* assumed by the Son of God. *Anhypostasis* signifies that the man, Jesus, would not have come into being apart from the incarnation, and it therefore undercuts all forms of adoptionism.

Enhypostasis declares that in the incarnation there is nevertheless a real and complete human Jesus *in* the *hypostatic union*. There is no independent human *hypostasis*, but there is "a complete human *hypostasis* in and in perfect oneness with the divine *hypostasis* of the Son."[83] The term *enhypostasis* asserts that there is, in fact, an absolutely real human Jesus in the incarnation and it therefore cuts off all forms of monophysitism. Together the two terms also undermine any kind of Nestorian dualism between the two natures of Jesus Christ.[84] Page 227 - 229

The significance of the *anhypostasis/enhypostasis* couplet for Torrance is that it affirms in the strongest and fullest way that in the incarnation all

---

for not differentiating between the work of Christ and the work of the Spirit, which appears to be where Smail thinks the real problem in Torrance's theology finally rests. Kettler provides a telling analysis of Smail's criticism of Torrance and an able discussion of the points where Smail misreads Torrance, including a pointed counter-criticism of cleavage in Smail's account between the work of the second and third persons of the Trinity. Kettler's chapter "Vicarious Humanity as Theological Reality (T. F. Torrance)" is an excellent introduction to this theme in Torrance's theology.

[82]See Torrance, *Karl Barth*, p. 125. It appears that Torrance got the *anhypostasis-enhypostasis* couplet from Barth when studying Barth's *Church Dogmatics* I/2, though Torrance finds it expressed in the history of theology from Cyril of Alexandria onward. Torrance discusses the couplet in many places in his theology. See ibid., pp. 125, 198-201; Torrance, *Reconstruction*, p. 131-32; Torrance, "Atonement," p. 230; and Thomas F. Torrance, *Scottish Theology: From John Knox to John McLeod Campbell* (Edinburgh: T & T Clark, 1996), pp. 70-74.

[83]Torrance, "Patristic Theology," p. 227. The term *enhypostasis* "refers to the fact that . . . in the incarnation the human nature of Christ was given a real hypostasis *in* the hypostasis of the eternal Son of God" (Torrance, "Atonement," p. 230).

[84]See Torrance's discussion in Torrance, "Patristic Theology," pp. 227-29.

of grace involves all of humanity. The incarnation is "wholly an act of God" but it is "no less true human life truly lived in our actual humanity."[85] Instead of discounting or displacing or in any way degrading humanity, the act of God's grace incarnate in Jesus Christ creates, upholds and fulfills the humanity assumed by the Son of God. In Torrance's words, "It is by grace alone that man comes into being and by grace alone he is saved and made a child of God, which he cannot achieve for himself. However, by grace alone does not in any way mean the diminishing, far less the excluding, of the human but on the contrary its full and complete establishment."[86]

The archetypal or paradigmatic instance of this logic of grace for Torrance is the virgin birth, though he also mentions Jesus Christ's resurrection from the grave.[87] But it also has much wider implications, for Torrance maintains that by reference to this logic of grace embodied in the incarnation we may give careful formulation to "all the ways and works of God in his interaction with us in space and time."[88]

The relation between divine and human agency. Just as there is not simply grudging space, but a full and glorious place, for the *human* being and *human* response of Jesus in the incarnation (no one is as fully human and personal in response to God as Jesus was), so also there is an analogous full and complete place for our human response within Christ's vicarious human response for us. "All through the incarnate life and activity of the Lord Jesus we are shown that 'all of grace' does not mean 'nothing of man,' but precisely the opposite: *all of grace means all of man,* for the fullness of grace creatively includes the fullness and completeness of our human response in the equation."[89] If all of grace includes all of humanity in the incarnation in Jesus Christ, how could it be otherwise with us in *our* human response? Just as there is full divine agency and human agency in Jesus Christ, so also there is an analogous full divine agency and human agency in the realization of redemption in our lives throughout the *ordo salutis.*

---

[85] Torrance, *Reconstruction*, p. 131.
[86] Torrance, "Patristic Theology," pp. 227-28.
[87] Ibid. Also see Torrance, *Mediation*, p. xiii.
[88] See Torrance, "My Interaction," p. 55. I think that Torrance means this quite literally, and its importance in his theology should not be underestimated.
[89] Torrance, *Mediation*, p. xii. This, I believe, is an analogy in the strict sense in Torrance's theology (see Torrance, *Reconstruction*, pp. 111-16).

Part of the problem, Torrance argues, is that the relation between grace and the human response, between divine agency and human agency, "is not something that can be understood logically, for logically 'all of grace' would mean 'nothing of man.' "[90] Thinking of this in logical, causal or necessary relations/categories has generated classical competing explanations for the relation between divine agency and human agency in the *ordo salutis*: (1) monergism in which God *alone* brings about (is the agent of) salvation (in the entire *ordo salutis* or in part), or (2) various forms of synergism in which agency is apportioned to God and the human person in salvation (God does part and we do part).[91]

When Torrance says that this is not something that can be understood logically, he does not mean that it is illogical. Rather he thinks that the reality of divine agency and human agency, and their relation, are of such a complex, ineffable, and *sui generis* character that they are not amenable to simplistic causalist categories, necessary relations or static formal logic in explicating what they entail. The *reality* of this relation between divine agency and human agency in this case is incommensurate with these kinds of categories, and more adequate ones need to be developed, though God's agency, of course, cannot be fully depicted in human categories.

A similar sort of problem arises even in natural science where, at times, the reality under investigation is so complex that it is not amenable to a simple definition within the framework of scientific knowledge at a particular point in history. The characteristics of light as both wave

---

[90]Ibid. *Marginalia*

[91]Construing grace (and human will) in terms of force, necessity or cause at any point in the *ordo salutis* is theologically pernicious and an example of categorical inadequacy, for this kind of thinking easily misrepresents the personal and ineffable presence of the Holy Spirit whose activity in mediating Christ's vicarious humanity to us is also as *sui generis* as the divine-human agency of Christ's mediation. Thinking of grace in logico-causal categories in particular is the root of much mischievous error in theology. If grace is *God himself* in his activity through Jesus Christ and in the Holy Spirit, how can we not but think of grace in radically *sui generis* trinitarian, personal modes, rather than logic-causal categories? Torrance is adamant that we cannot read logico-causal categories back into God or interpret God's agency in grace in terms of logico-causal terms or necessary relations. See Thomas F. Torrance, *Christian Theology and Scientific Culture* (New York: Oxford University Press, 1981), pp. 134-37.

Torrance's position is a viable alternative to monergism and synergism. Here I disagree with Clark Pinnock who thinks that we have to choose between monergism and synergism. See endnote 43 of his essay "The Holy Spirit in the Theology of Donald G. Bloesch," in *Evangelical Theology in Transition: Theologians in Dialogue with Donald Bloesch*, ed. Elmer M. Colyer (Downers Grove, Ill.: InterVarsity Press, 1999), p. 229.

and particulate is a classic example. We simply lack a completely adequate conceptuality to schematize the actual reality of light as it has come
into view in scientific investigation. To reduce light to one line of explanation over the other for the sake of logical consistency would thus be
more irrational than to employ multiple, though seemingly paradoxical,
lines of explanation.

What Torrance means when he says that the relation between grace and
the human response "is not something that can be understood logically"
is that, while it is logically simpler to affirm either monergism (all of God/
grace, nothing of humanity) or synergism (partly God/grace and partly
humanity), both are more irrational (or more precisely, categorically inadequate) than the *anhypostasis/enhypostasis* couplet expressing the inner logic of grace in which all of grace (full divine agency) includes all of
humanity (full human agency), first in Jesus Christ, and then in us. Indeed
the relations of divine agency and human agency in Jesus Christ and in us
throughout the *ordo salutis* are *sui generis* and must be understood out of
themselves and with categories that are adequate to their actual reality.
Torrance's understanding of the relationship between language and being
or reality, and the other epistemological convictions presupposed here are
developed in more detail in chapter nine.

What is significant at this juncture is that throughout Torrance's discussion of Christology and soteriology, he emphasizes that in all of Christ's
soteriological activity in relation with us, "Jesus Christ is engaged in personalising and humanising (never depersonalising and dehumanising) activity, so that in all our relations with him we are made more truly and
fully human in our personal response of faith than ever before.["]92 Torrance
argues that in the incarnation and the *ordo salutis*, the human person is never emptied of agency or overpowered by the divine agency. Rather the human person is upheld and intensified, personalized and humanized, in
relation to God. Jesus Christ was and is only all too different from the impersonal, insincere, uncentered, duplicitous and inhumane humanity that
we so often see in ourselves and others in the way we relate to God and to
each other.

What Torrance is driving at in his development of the vicarious humanity of Christ and the inner logic of grace, is that it is precisely this impersonal and dehumanized humanity that the Son of God assumed in the

---

92Torrance, *Mediation*, p. xiii.

incarnation in order to reconcile and redeem, to repersonalize and rehumanize.[93] Our telos in Torrance's theology is *personal* sharing in union and communion with God the Father through Jesus Christ and in the Holy Spirit in which we become ever more fully human and free, and respond in thanksgiving, faith and joyous freedom, as children of God, in the Spirit through the Son to the Father. It is a personal sharing of our humanity in union and communion with God, first in Jesus Christ through *his* vicarious humanity, and then in *our* humanity as we are incorporated by the Spirit into Christ and his union with our humanity in the incarnation.

When you think of the times in your life when you are most fully aware of the love of God, the grace of the Lord Jesus Christ and the communion of the Holy Spirit, are you not the mostly fully personal and fully human being God has created and redeemed you to be, though this is only a foretaste of what is to come? Is it not the case that all of Christ and all of you are fully compatible? And does this not propel you out of self-centered selfishness into love for and relations with God and others?[94]

Torrance's understanding of the vicarious humanity of Christ clarifies the fact that Jesus Christ, in his humanity (our humanity), has already faced every decisive struggle against the sinful, faithless, fallen, impersonal, dehumanized and rebellious human condition and has already reconciled and redeemed, personalized and humanized this condition. Thus even though the struggle still rages within our lives as Christians, all of the utterly crucial battles have been won within *our* actual human condition as it has been and still is assumed and transformed in Christ's vicarious humanity even now in the presence of God. What we have then is not just a forensic forgiveness and an ever-present Spirit who enables us to join Christ in the fray; we have a forgiveness and a full and final transformation of our very humanity in Jesus Christ in which we may participate in

---

[93]See ibid., pp. 67-72.

[94]I am not in any way implying that our "experience" of the gospel is the ultimate criterion for understanding this "inner logic of grace." Nor am I suggesting that we have to be conscious of the presence of God in order to live in the reality of the gospel. I have just discovered after years as a pastor and a seminary professor that most Christian lay people and seminarians can grasp the basic point that Torrance intends in this "inner logic of grace" when they think of it in light of their most vivid encounters with God in the gospel; however, theologically we should think of it the other way around, as Torrance formulates it, first in Jesus Christ, and then by analogy in our relationship with God through Christ in the Spirit.

the Spirit, the Spirit who is sent to us from the risen and ascended divine-human person of our Lord and Savior, Jesus Christ—the Spirit imbued with all of the earthly, historical struggle and victory of Jesus Christ on our behalf. We walk by faith and not by sight, but it is the faith and faithfulness of Jesus Christ, the incarnate Son of God who loved us and gave himself for us (Gal 2:20).

PART II

THE LOVE OF GOD
THE FATHER

4

THE LOVE OF GOD
THE FATHER ALMIGHTY

*It is more godly and accurate to signify God from the Son and call him Father,
than to name him from his works and call him unoriginate.*
ATHANASIUS

T hroughout his career, Thomas F. Torrance has pursued the vision
of a rigorous scientific theology governed from beginning to end by the
nature of theology's object or subject-matter (God in God's self-revelation). The intent of Torrance's version of scientific theology is to bring to
careful and concise expression the essential relations (onto-relations), that
define or better constitute the reality and nature of theology's "Object."[1]
The clarity of Torrance's scientific intent is nowhere more important than
in this chapter dealing with knowledge of God the Father Almighty.

Here Torrance appeals to Athanasius' famous dictum, quoted above.
Torrance sees the eternal Father-Son relation revealed in and through the
incarnation to be the supreme truth on which everything in the gospel depends, and also the key that unlocks knowledge of God.[2] The reason for
this is that to know God the Father through Jesus Christ, the incarnate Son
of God who is *homoousios* with the Father, is to know God strictly in accordance with God's nature and therefore in a most accurate manner.[3] It is the
ontological and epistemological relation of *being* and *agency* between the

---

[1]See the introduction above, pp. 21-25. Torrance's interpreters need to be clear as to what he
means by "science" lest they miss his vision on this point.

[2]Thomas F. Torrance, *The Trinitarian Faith: The Evangelical Theology of the Ancient Catholic
Church* (Edinburgh: T & T Clark, 1988), p. 3.

[3]Ibid., pp. 3, 49-52.

Trinitarian Faith

incarnate Son and God the Father brought to precise expression in the *homoousion* that opens up the possibility of a rigorous scientific theology.

The Father-Son relation not only affords accurate knowledge of God, it reveals that Jesus Christ is the *"arche*, the Origin or Principle of all God's ways and works."[4] This means that *everything* to be known of God, God's creation and the relation between the two must be meticulously thought out in light of this *arche*, Jesus Christ himself. Thus Torrance develops his understanding of God as Creator and of God's creation in light of the relation of Jesus Christ the incarnate Son to God the Father.

This also means that Torrance first unfolds knowledge of God the Father Almighty in relation to Christ, and then deals with God as Creator and God's creation, all on the basis of the Father-Son relation. We follow Torrance's pattern here in part two, "The Love of God the Father Almighty," first treating Torrance's understanding of the God the Father Almighty in this chapter and then developing his perspective on the Creator and creation in the next.

The initial section of this chapter deals with the question of access to the Father and presupposes the material covered in chapters two and three, especially the discussion in chapter two concerning the *homoousion*. The section exegetes Athanasius' epigram that the godly and accurate way to know God is through the Son, and not through creation.[5] To know God the Father through Jesus Christ the Son is to know God in an accurate way. Yet this accurate way of knowing God through the Son is via evangelical and doxological participation, not on the basis of an objectivist, impersonal and uncommitted approach.

The second section of this chapter develops the material content of Torrance's doctrine of the person, love and being of God the Father Almighty. To know the Father through the Son and in the Spirit is to know that Fatherhood belongs to the being of God. The Father-Son relation provides a window into the very heart of God, where we come to know that God the Father loves us more than God loves himself, for God spared not his Son, but gave him up for us all.[6] This section also discusses Torrance's

---

[4]Ibid., pp. 3, 7.

[5]Thomas F. Torrance, *Trinitarian Perspectives: Toward Doctrinal Agreement* (Edinburgh: T & T Clark, 1994), p. 8.

[6]Thomas F. Torrance, *The Christian Doctrine of God: One Being Three Persons* (Edinburgh: T & T Clark, 1998), p. 55. Also see Thomas F. Torrance, *The Mediation of Christ*, 2nd ed. (Colorado Springs: Helmers & Howard, 1992), p. 109.

perspective on language for God, especially in relation to the trinitarian name.

The final section of this chapter takes up the question of the almightiness of God the Father. Here, as in the case of all of the attributes of God, God's omnipotence (that is, God's power over all creation visible and invisible) is not to be defined in some abstract metaphysical manner, but rather concretely and decisively by reference to God as "Father."[7] Torrance understands the nature of God's divine being and *power* precisely in light of the Fatherhood of God revealed in Jesus Christ.[8] This section also serves as a bridge to the next chapter on the Creator and the creation.

1. Access to the Father

Torrance's questioning of natural theology. Athanasius' statement that it is "more godly and accurate to signify God from the Son and call him Father, than to name him from his works alone and call him unoriginate,"[9] underscores the centrality and the primacy of the Father-Son relation over the Creator-creature relation. The reason for this, according to Torrance, is the radically different character of the two relations.

The Father-Son relation is a oneness in being *(homoousios)* between the incarnate Son and the Father, what Torrance calls an onto-relation or being constituting relation which is basic, characteristic or defining of what the realities implicated in the relation really are.[10] This inner relation between the incarnate Son and the Father allows us, sinful and finite though we are, to approach God the Father through the mediation of the Son and know God in a way that is godly (that is, as forgiven sinners reconciled to God through Christ)[11] and accurate (that is, according to God's nature or the onto-relations constitutive of God's reality).

The Creator-creature relation is radically different in Torrance's perspective. There is no oneness in being between God and the creation. This means that creation is of such a character that it is external to God and

---

[7] Torrance, *Christian Doctrine*, p. 138.

[8] Ibid., p. 118.

[9] See Torrance, *Trinitarian Perspectives*, p. 8. Also see Torrance, *Trinitarian Faith*, p. 49.

[10] Torrance, *Trinitarian Faith*, p. 49. See chapter two above, pp. 55-56, 70-81, for a discussion of onto-relations and the *homoousion*.

[11] Our knowledge of God requires a cognitive union with God in which our entire being is affected by God's love and holiness. See chapter two, endnote 24, p. 62.

utterly different from God and therefore cannot really tell us who God is or what God is like.[12]

The irreversibility of the Creator-creature in Torrance's theology is linked to his understanding of creation *ex nihilo*, for creation is called into existence by God's creative Word and will, and not by any kind of eternal generation from the being of God. Thus on the basis of the unoriginate-originate relation it is only possible to speak of God in vague and negative terms indicative of the distance and utter difference between God and creation.[13]

Precisely at this point we find the motive and the principle that have consistently constrained Torrance to question any independent natural theology. Within the horizon of Torrance's scientific predilection and rigor, and his God-world relation, an independent natural theology is really a form of mythology, for it has no realist basis in any kind of intrinsic ontological and epistemological relation to God in light of which knowledge of God can be developed: "If we try to reach knowledge of God from some point outside of God, we cannot operate with a point *in God* by reference to which we can test or control our conceptions of him, but are inevitably flung back upon ourselves."[14]

Torrance's questioning of traditional natural theology arises on the "two-fold ground of theological content and scientific method."[15] Natural theology is radically undermined and relativized by the *actual* knowledge of God mediated through Jesus Christ. If one examines Thomas Aquinas' *Summa Theologiae* for example, one discovers, Torrance contends (follow-

---

[12]Torrance, *Trinitarian Faith*, p. 50. Also see Thomas F. Torrance, *Reality and Evangelical Theology* (Philadelphia: Westminster Press, 1982), p. 24.

[13]Torrance, *Trinitarian Faith*, p. 50. This, of course, does not imply an ontological dualism that prohibits God from interacting with the world God has created. Rather it simply underscores the irreversibility of relation between God and creation. It is the *contingent* character of creation that is at the root of this irreversibility. The following chapter will deal with Torrance's understanding of the created universe characterized by contingence, intelligibility and (limited) freedom.

[14]Torrance, *Trinitarian Faith*, p. 51. It thus becomes difficult to say anything at all about God that is not a form of autobiographical mythology. Torrance notes the additional danger identified by the Nicene theologians, that if we allow the contrast between Creator and creature to provide the initial approach and terms, we may very well reduce the Son to one of God's created works, as the Arians did (see p. 50).

[15]Thomas F. Torrance, "The Problem of Natural Theology in the Thought of Karl Barth," *Religious Studies* 6, no. 2 (June 1970): 128. Torrance is describing Barth's position, but it is clear that it is Torrance's as well. This is an extremely important article for understanding Torrance's perspective on natural theology and his relation to Karl Barth.

ing Barth), a split concept of God, in which "the doctrine of the Trinity be-comes attached to an independently reached doctrine of the one God."[16] Only after Aquinas develops arguments or proofs for the existence of God and establishes something of the nature or essence of the one God (*First Part, Questions 2-26*) does he offer an account of the three persons in God (*Questions 27-43*), an account that bears little relation to the investigation of God's existence and essence that precedes it.

It is not all that different, Torrance argues, with the Westminster Confession of Faith, where in chapter two—"Of God, and of the Holy Trinity"—once again "the main paragraphs are devoted to an account of the infinite being of God and his attributes expressed in rather abstract and negative terms, to which two brief sentences are appended on the Trini-ty."[17] The question addressed in the main paragraphs is *what* is the essence of God, rather than the personal question of *who* is this God who has actu-ally revealed himself to us through Jesus Christ and in the Holy Spirit.[18]

The result, Torrance contends, is that natural theology generates a doctrine of God that terminates on some being or essence of God in general, rather than on the triune God who really is Father, Son and Holy Spirit in God's undivided being, as God has actually revealed himself through Jesus Christ and in the Holy Spirit.[19] Torrance challenges the understand-ing of God that natural theology generates in this manner because it is an *abstraction* that falls hopelessly short of the trinitarian God revealed in Jesus Christ, an abstraction that is relativized and set aside because it miss-es the mark of God's triune reality as revealed on the ground of our actual knowledge of God through Jesus Christ.[20]

Furthermore, in this kind of approach, the doctrine of the Trinity comes as an addendum to an independently developed doctrine of the One God in which the two are not integrally related. The result is that the doctrine of the Trinity is isolated in the dogmatic structure of theol-ogy and therefore has little bearing on other theological themes such as the nature and content of the gospel or the Christian life (Torrance is re-

---

[16] Torrance, *Mediation*, p. 100. Torrance points to Bernard Lonergan, in our own day, as a theologian who draws a clear distinction in doctrinal formulation between "The One God" and "The Triune God."
[17] Ibid.
[18] Ibid.
[19] Torrance, "Natural Theology," pp. 131-32.
[20] Ibid., pp. 126-27.

ferring to the Westminster Confession and the Catechism, though it is not all that different with Aquinas's *Summa*).[21] Thus natural theology, which arises on an independent ground outside God's self-revelation, proves to be a source of confusion for theology, since the concept of God it generates adversely affects other aspects of Christian faith, life and thought.[22]

In his recent magnum opus, *The Christian Doctrine of God*, Torrance forcefully declares, "The one trinitarian way of thinking of God forced upon us through the incarnation calls into question . . . any alternative way of thinking of him, apart from the incarnation. . . . To admit any other than a trinitarian way of thinking about God is in fact not only to relativise and question the truth of the Trinity but to contradict the Trinity and to set aside the gospel."[23] Torrance's questioning of natural theology arises out of the actual trinitarian theological content of God's self-revelation.[24]

The other reason for Torrance's rejection of an independent natural theology is his concern for scientific methodology. Theology is not subject to some preconceived notion of science that is universally applicable *(scientia universalis)* or to a methodology developed outside of theological inquiry.[25] Theology, like any proper science, clarifies its epistemological structure and develops its rigorous methodology, not independent of or antecedent to its subject matter, but rather within the process of investigation and in conformity to the actual progress in understanding the character of the reality disclosed in the course of the inquiry.

---

[21]Torrance, *Mediation*, p. 100.

[22]Torrance, "Natural Theology," p. 127. I suspect that double predestination is an example of what Torrance has in mind here. See Thomas F. Torrance, *Scottish Theology: From John Knox to John McLeod Campbell* (Edinburgh: T & T Clark, 1996), pp. 16-17, 136-37, 265.

[23]Torrance, *Christian Doctrine*, p. 24. Indeed, Torrance argues that even theism must be rejected in light of the one trinitarian way of thinking about God.

[24]Ibid. This, however, does not mean that Torrance denies that God made himself known to people in history from creation on, but this did not include the kind of revealing of God's "own self" in the intensely personal way that we find in Jesus Christ and the outpouring of the Holy Spirit at Pentecost. Torrance also grants that there are "lights of creation" (Barth), but the sinful and alienated human mind twists apprehension of these little lights, thereby generating refracted concepts and distorted understanding of God (see p. 25). Thus, in the end, the doctrine of the Trinity "sets aside all other religious approaches and abolishes any entertainment of alternative devotions and conceptions of God as invalid."

[25]See the introduction, pp. 21-22.

Like any *a posteriori* science, theology must be free to engage in rigorous methodological questioning of all previous assumptions, antecedent conceptualities and independent epistemologies that conflict with the actual way knowledge of God arises within God's self-revelation and comes to articulation in the theological investigation.[26] Thus on the ground of scientific methodology Torrance questions any natural theology that operates as a *praeambula fidei* (preamble to faith) or as an independent movement of thought.

The next chapter will discuss how Torrance radically reconceives natural theology and incorporates it into his positive theology. What is of significance at this point is that we cannot know God in a godly or accurate way through an independent natural theology on the basis of the Creator-creature relation. In rigorous scientific knowledge of God, Torrance contends, we have to develop what we think and say about God in light of God's nature as it comes into view in God's actual self-revelation.[27]

---

[26]See the introduction, pp. 21-25. Also see Torrance, "Natural Theology," pp. 127-28. Here Torrance points to Albert Einstein's lecture on "Geometry and Experience," republished in English in *Ideas and Opinions* (New York: Wing Books, 1954), pp. 232-49, and the relation of geometry to physics as illustrative of Torrance's (and Barth's) questioning of an independent natural theology. Einstein pointed to Euclidean geometry as an example of an axiomatic deductive science developed independently of natural science as an abstract conceptual system.

What Einstein discovered in actual natural scientific inquiry is that Euclidean geometry does not completely conform to the character of nature as disclosed in the advance of physics. To force nature into the rigid Euclidean conceptuality developed independent of and antecedent to physics would be to falsify our understanding of the universe as it is actually disclosed within the process of scientific inquiry. Einstein argued that what had happened (and had to happen) is that geometry is transformed by our actual knowledge of physical reality, thus becoming four-dimensional in indissoluble unity with physics and thereby bringing to expression the nature of the universe as disclosed within the course of scientific investigation.

In other words, Torrance argues that Einstein "questioned the validity of schematising physics to the rigid framework of Euclidean geometry, that is of an independent and antecedent conceptual system detached from actual experience, and set about dismantling the rational superstructure of mathematical time and space which the Newtonian system clamped down upon the universe of bodies in motion and thereby distorted knowledge of it" (Thomas F. Torrance, *Transformation and Convergence in the Frame of Knowledge* [Grand Rapids, Mich.: Eerdmans, 1984], p. ix). Similarly, rigorous scientific method in theology cannot allow itself to be controlled by an antecedent conceptuality or independent epistemology, but must be developed in light of the nature of actual knowledge of God mediated through Jesus Christ disclosed within the process of theological inquiry. See Torrance, "Natural Theology," pp. 129-30, and Thomas F. Torrance, *Space, Time & Resurrection* (Grand Rapids, Mich.: Eerdmans, 1976), pp. ix-x.

[27]Torrance, *Trinitarian Faith*, p. 52.

This is what takes place when we approach God the Father in and through Jesus Christ the incarnate Son.

Access to the Father. Torrance finds support for his scientific approach to theology among the Nicene theologians. In Alexandria in particular, Torrance detects significant attention to scientific inquiry (leading to the work of John Philoponos, a sixth-century Christian physicist), which influenced Christian theologians like Athanasius.[28] In this Alexandrian tradition the only way to reach exact scientific knowledge is by a form of inquiry that is in strict accordance with the nature *(kata physin)* of the reality under investigation, rather than through an arbitrary approach.[29]

Since in the case of knowledge of God, there is no inherent isomorphism between the eternal being of God and the created being of creaturely reality as noted above, Torrance argues that God can only be known out of himself.[30] Here he draws on Irenaeus who argued that only God can know God, since God alone is adequate to know God strictly in accordance with God's nature. If this is the case, Torrance asserts, then the only way we can really know God is by somehow sharing in the knowledge which God has of himself.[31]

This means that if *we* are to know God in a precise and scientific way in accordance with God's nature, we must somehow share in God's knowledge of himself yet within the creaturely conditions of our earthly historical existence. There has to be a way to access knowledge of God from within God's knowledge of himself, but at the same time within our creaturely existence.[32]

The utterly astonishing thing for Torrance is that this is precisely what he finds happening in the incarnation, where the mutual being and knowing of God the Father and the Son is lived out within our humanity assumed by the Son of God for the mediation of revelation and reconciliation, as outlined in chapter two and especially chapter three.[33] In Jesus Christ "the closed circle of knowing between the Father and the Son"

---

[28]Ibid., p. 51. Also see Thomas F. Torrance, *Theology in Reconciliation* (Grand Rapids, Mich.: Eerdmans, 1975), pp. 215-31, 23-62; Thomas F. Torrance, "John Philoponos of Alexandria, Sixth Century Christian Physicist" in *Texts and Studies* (London: Thyateira House, 1983), 2:253-59.

[29]Torrance, *Trinitarian Faith*, p. 51.

[30]Ibid., p. 52. Also See Torrance, *Christian Doctrine*, pp. 6, 11, 13, 16, 21, 28, 74, 77.

[31]Torrance, *Trinitarian Faith*, p. 54.

[32]Ibid., p. 52.

[33]See chapter two above, pp. 78-84, and chapter three, pp. 102-13.

has been realized with our creaturely and contingent human reality and existence in space and time "in such a way that in Jesus Christ we may share in the very knowledge which God has of himself."[34]

Of course, the incarnate Son reveals God the Father not by being the Father, but precisely by being the Son.[35] Jesus Christ, the incarnate Son, reveals God the Father not simply by teaching us who God is and what God is like, but through being who he is as the Son of the Father, the Son of God incarnate in our human reality.[36] Torrance repeatedly emphasizes that knowledge of God the Father and knowledge of Christ, the incarnate Son of God, arise together and regulate the meaning of each other.[37] Only by sharing in the Son's knowledge of the Father are we ever able to know God according to God's nature, and when we do, Torrance contends, all of our previous "knowledge" of God is inevitably and radically reconstructed, as we will see in section two of this chapter.

Torrance notes, however, that it is only through the communion of the Spirit, who is the Spirit of the Father and the Son, that we may come to share in the sonship of Jesus Christ and his knowledge of, and access to, God the Father.[38] We will examine Torrance's pneumatology in detail in chapter six. Here, however, it is important to note that the Holy Spirit, poured out on the church at Pentecost, is the Spirit of the Father and the Son, sent *from* the Father *through* the Son to unite us with the Son, and through the Son with the Father.

Jesus received the Holy Spirit without measure into our human nature, which the Son assumed in his incarnation, and through the same Spirit, Jesus offered himself in atoning self-sacrifice on our behalf.[39] It is this Holy Spirit, the Spirit already integrally involved in the mediation of Christ, that the incarnate Son mediates to us. In Torrance's theology the Holy Spirit unites us with Christ, so that through Christ and in the communion of the

---

[34]Torrance, *Trinitarian Faith*, p. 60. Elsewhere Torrance states that we "have access to the Father through the blood of Christ and in one Spirit, and on that ground of divine propitiation and reconciliation which God himself has freely provided for us to be allowed really to draw near to God in personal response of faith and to know him as he is in himself, what is more, to be certain that what he is toward us in the gospel of Christ as Father, Son and Holy Spirit, he really is and always will be in himself" (Torrance, *Mediation*, p. 115). Also see Torrance, *Christian Doctrine*, pp. 1, 16-18.

[35]Torrance, *Trinitarian Faith*, p. 59.

[36]Ibid., p. 55.

[37]Ibid., pp. 55, 60. Also see Torrance, *Christian Doctrine*, pp. 11, 17-18, 54, 56, 58-59, 138-39.

[38]Torrance, *Trinitarian Faith*, pp. 55-56. Also see Torrance, *Christian Doctrine*, pp. 2, 16.

[39]Torrance, *Trinitarian Faith*, p. 61.

Holy Spirit we may have access to God the Father and we come to participate in the communion between the Father, the Son and the Holy Spirit.[40]

When we approach God through the Son in the Holy Spirit and call God "Father," Torrance contends, our knowledge of God the Father through the Son and in the Holy Spirit is in strict accordance with God's nature *(kata physin)* and therefore precise and true. Indeed, the Spirit and the Son are not external to God, but in fact belong to the eternal and essential reality of God and are the onto-relational persons constituting the one triune God who, Torrance says, really is fully Father, fully Son and fully Spirit, in the unity of the one being of God.[41]

Here again we see Torrance's holism, for the Trinity is a differentiated whole, which we apprehend holistically out of itself with subsidiary awareness of the trinitarian persons.[42] In other words, in hearing the gospel and coming to know God the Father through the Son in the Holy Spirit, we encounter the Trinity as a whole simultaneously, even if at the time we are unable to articulate in an explicit manner the trinitarian persons and relations we encounter. Christian *faith* is aboriginally *trinitarian*, for the Father-Son relation in which we participate through the communion of the Holy Spirit is the actual ontological and epistemological connection embedded in the gospel message on which knowledge of God arises.[43]

In this triune self-revelation of God as Father, Son and Holy Spirit in the gospel, God tells us something absolutely new that we could never tell ourselves.[44] Indeed, Torrance notes that it is only because God has actually made himself known to us in this trinitarian manner that we can even begin to speak of God in this way.[45] This knowledge provides the basis for an accurate scientific theology in accordance with God's nature.

Thus, for Torrance, accurate knowledge of God is not via a narrow biblicist approach to thinking about God.[46] Rather than piecing together various biblical statements about God, Torrance maintains that we have to *look through* Scriptures to the truth of God out of which they arose (form in being) and to which they bear witness. We indwell the biblical witness

---

[40]Torrance, *Christian Doctrine*, p. 148, cf. p. 16.
[41]Torrance, *Trinitarian Faith*, p. 64.
[42]See the introduction, pp. 16-17, 21-25; and Torrance, *Christian Doctrine*, p. xi.
[43]Torrance, *Christian Doctrine*, p. 138.
[44]Ibid., p. 18.
[45]Ibid.
[46]Torrance, *Trinitarian Faith*, p. 57.

within the evangelical and doxological life of the church and allow the Scriptures to direct us to the divine realities to which they bear witness and then to articulate accurately and precisely what we come to know of God (integration of form in knowing).[47] This does not mean that we leave Scripture behind. Indeed it is through the Holy Scriptures alone, Torrance contends, that God's self-revelation and self-communication reaches us. Yet we cannot be satisfied with simply quoting and summarizing Scripture, for we should try to ground "our thinking and speaking upon the truth of God himself who addresses us through those biblical statements."[48]

The evangelical and doxological perspective. When we know God the Father through Jesus Christ and in the Holy Spirit in this way, however, Torrance contends that we also come to know that God infinitely exceeds everything we can ever conceptualize and articulate of God.[49] When we *apprehend* God, we come to the acute realization that we can not *comprehend* God, as Torrance points out repeatedly throughout his publications.[50] The ineffable, unlimited, inexhaustible reality of God cannot be captured within the confines of human knowing and explicit concepts and definitions.[51] For this reason theology needs to operate with concepts that are always open to further modulation in light of our deepening awareness and understanding of God, who is always greater *(Deus semper maior).*

→ Yet in Torrance's theology, this sense of the ineffable and inexhaustible reality of God is not because God is an inscrutable deity of undifferentiated oneness whom we can only speak of in vague and general negative modes of thought and speech *(via negativa).* Rather it is due to the fact that when we know the love of God through the grace of Jesus Christ in the communion of the Holy Spirit, "we know much more than we can grasp or express; we feel or experience far more than we can put into thought or word."[52] Torrance can even speak of theology as "a kind of ecstatic passion" in which we are lifted up by God's Spirit "to share in

---

[47]Ibid. See chapter two above, pp. 65-67, 73-78, and chapter three, pp. 102-13, for Torrance's understanding of revelation, Scripture and the relation between the two.

[48]Torrance, *Trinitarian Faith*, p. 57. In chapter nine we will deal with Torrance's theological method and his understanding of the relation between language and reality.

[49]Ibid., p. 53.

[50]See ibid., also pp. 24-27. Also see Torrance, *Christian Doctrine*, pp. 10-11, 19, 26, 73-74.

[51]Torrance, *Christian Doctrine*, p. 4. The more we know God, Torrance contends, the more wonderful we know God to be.

[52]Torrance, *Trinitarian Faith*, p. 53.

God's own self-knowing and self-loving.[53]

At this evangelical and doxological level, human reason is molded and adapted to real knowledge of God according to God's trinitarian nature so that we are initiated into an accurate knowledge of God in which we "are enabled to apprehend" God "in some real measure" of conformity to what God is in himself.[54] In light of God's self-revelation and self-communication through Jesus Christ and in the creative operation of the Holy Spirit, the human mind is renewed, transformed and spiritually reorganized, and it begins to reflect to a degree the triune God that we know in this way.[55]

All rigorous scientific inquiry, Torrance points out, is grounded in "an informal undefined knowledge, from which it cannot be cut off without becoming empty of significance and useless."[56] This also applies to theological inquiry, Torrance contends, for theology arises (or should arise) out of our implicit knowledge of God through Christ in the Spirit as we indwell the Scriptures within the evangelical and doxological life of the church.[57]

In fact, Torrance argues that theology can never be more than a clarification of the actual knowledge of God that takes place at this evangelical and doxological level within this evangelical and doxological perspective. This is what it means to know God in a way that is in some sense commensurate with God's nature, "for knowledge of God arises and takes shape in our mind under the determination of his revealed nature, and is maintained in the experience of prayer, holiness and godliness."[58]

When theology clarifies *this* knowledge of God, which is knowledge of God according to God's nature *(kata physin)*, theology is *scientific*. In chapters eight and nine we will examine Torrance's understanding of the stratified structure that develops in our knowledge of God from the

---

[53]Thomas F. Torrance, *The Ground and Grammar of Theology* (Charlottesville: University of Virginia Press, 1979), p. 155.

[54]Torrance, *Ground and Grammar*, p. 155. Also see Torrance, *Trinitarian Faith*, pp. 56-57. Here Torrance points to a fascinating statement from fourth-century church father Hilary of Poitiers: "The perfect knowledge of God is so to know him that we are sure that we must not be ignorant of him, yet cannot describe him. We must believe, must apprehend, must worship; and such acts of devotion must stand in lieu of definition" (see p. 53).

[55]Torrance, *Trinitarian Faith*, p. 56.

[56]Torrance, *Christian Doctrine*, p. 73.

[57]Ibid.

[58]Torrance, *Trinitarian Faith*, p. 54.

evangelical level through the economic Trinity to the ontological Trinity, and Torrance's theological method implicit throughout this section. Within this evangelical and doxological perspective theology develops a knowledge of God that is "godly and true" to God's nature, for an objectivist, impersonal and uncommitted theology is incommensurate with the living and loving personal being of God the Father whom we come to know through the incarnate Son and in the outpouring of the Spirit.[59]

2. The Person, Love and Being of God the Father

Torrance grants that God did reveal something of himself to Israel in the course of the historical ordeal through which God molded and shaped Israel into a special medium for the communication of God's saving revelation to all people, as we saw in chapter two above.[60] Yet it is only in the incarnation of God's beloved Son in Jesus Christ that God reveals not just something of himself, but an intensely personal and familiar revelation of God's very self in accordance with God's own divine nature as Father.[61] In the incarnation, true knowledge of God is realized within our human and creaturely condition in Jesus Christ and we can share in the incarnate Son's knowledge of (and communion with) God the Father through the power and presence of the Holy Spirit sent to us from the Father and through the Son.

In and through this trinitarian self-revelation, God reveals and proclaims himself to all humanity, Torrance contends, as God the Father Almighty, the Creator of heaven and earth.[62] We formulate our doctrine of God not in an abstract manner, but in terms of the personal being and love of God the Father whom we know through the grace of Christ and in the communion of the Spirit. We apprehend God, Torrance contends, simultaneously in God's differentiation as Father, Son and Holy Spirit, but also in God's oneness as the one Lord God.[63]

The Person of the Father. This oneness of God, as well as trinitarian differentiation, is already implied in the *homoousion*, as we noted in chapter two, for the oneness in being between the Father and the Son also expresses the distinction between them, because nothing can be *homoou-*

---

[59]Torrance, *Christian Doctrine*, p. 88.
[60]See chapter two, pp. 61-69; and Torrance, *Christian Doctrine*, p. 14.
[61]Torrance, *Christian Doctrine*, pp. 13-15, and Torrance, *Trinitarian Faith*, p. 54.
[62]Torrance, *Christian Doctrine*, p. 15.
[63]Ibid.

sios with itself, but only with another.[64] This same oneness of being, and yet distinction between persons, of course, applies to the Holy Spirit in relation to the Father and the Son as well, as we will see in chapter six.

We will not recapitulate the discussion of Torrance's understanding of the *homoousion* and its application to Jesus Christ the incarnate Son here, except to say that the *homoousion* is soteriologically and evangelically evoked, especially in light of the resurrection of Jesus Christ from the dead, for the resurrection invested Jesus Christ and his death on the cross with a redemptive and divine significance that led the disciples to confess him as Savior and Lord, and thereby bracket together their faith in Christ with their faith in God, something Torrance finds evident throughout the New Testament.[65] This is true even for us today, for on the basis of indwelling the biblical witness, absorbing it in a way that we come to know Jesus Christ who lived and died for us, we confess that *Jesus is Lord*, for he is raised from the dead and ascended to the right hand of God; and we pray to him and worship him, and thereby acknowledge his deity along with the Father and the Holy Spirit.[66]

At the same time it is especially the cross and the resurrection, Torrance contends, that also lead us to distinguish between Jesus Christ the incarnate Son, and God the Father.[67] Here Torrance finds especially significant Jesus' agonizing "Abba, Father" in the garden on the night that he was betrayed, Jesus' fearful "My God, my God, why have you forsaken me?" which Jesus cried in our place on the cross, but also Jesus' triumph over our doubt and dereliction in the face of death saying, "Father, into your hands I commit my spirit." These events together compel us to differentiate between the incarnate Son and God the Father, even while we confess Jesus as Lord and God.[68]

Of course, it was after the resurrection and glorification of Christ that the Spirit of holiness and power was poured out on the church at Pentecost from the Father through the Son, so that the church then and the church today confess this same Spirit as Lord again.[69] In light of these relations and distinctions revealed in God's *oikonomia* (economy), the or-

---

[64]See Torrance, *Trinitarian Faith*, p. 125 and Torrance, *Christian Doctrine*, p. 129.
[65]See chapter two above, pp. 70-81, and Torrance, *Christian Doctrine*, pp. 51-53.
[66]Torrance, *Christian Doctrine*, pp. 52-53.
[67]Ibid., p. 54.
[68]Ibid.
[69]Ibid.

dered pattern of God's revealing and reconciling activity in our world of space and time (form in being), we are constrained to think (integration of form in knowing) of a differentiation, as well as a oneness, in the inner life of God between the Father and the Son and the Holy Spirit.[70]

Thus for Torrance, knowledge of and belief in God the Father and Jesus Christ the incarnate Son arise together. Here the *homoousion*, the unique oneness in being and act between God the Father and Jesus Christ the incarnate Son, underscores that the Son reveals not just something about God the Father, but reveals the Father's very self. Torrance sees Jesus Christ as the one form or *Eidos* of the Godhead through whom the Father grants knowledge of himself as he actually *is*.[71]

Indeed the mission of the Son is to reveal the Father and to redeem us so that we too may call on God as *our* Father. Through God's beloved Son incarnate for us in Jesus Christ, God reveals that God is Father as God, and that God loves us with the love that God is as Father of the Son.[72] The incarnate Son's filial relation to the Father reveals that God is eternally Father in himself as God irrespective of God's relation to creation.[73]

The threefold manifestation of God as Father, Son and Holy Spirit, Torrance argues, compelled the early church to develop a theological concept of "person" in order to express the implicitly trinitarian self-revelation of

---

[70]Ibid., p. 54.

[71]Torrance, *Trinitarian Faith*, p. 63.

[72]Torrance, *Christian Doctrine*, p. 55. This knowledge of the Father is actualized redemptively within the vicarious humanity of Jesus Christ in whom our alienated humanity is reconciled to God the Father.

Jesus Christ, of course, as we saw in chapter two, was a Jew, and therefore knowledge of God as Father is not cut off from what was revealed of God under the Old Covenant. Torrance points out that Father is used to designate God very infrequently in the Old Testament, and almost exclusively in contexts indicating God's redemptive relation to Israel. Torrance acknowledges that the general sense of God as Father, the Creator of humanity, is found in a few places in the Old Testament. But in the Old Testament, "Father" is not a proper name for God, but rather a title or epithet. Torrance says that *Yahweh* is the one ineffable substantive name of God found in the Old Testament (see pp. 55-56).

In the New Testament, however, there is a radical change in how God is conceived, for Jesus Christ vicariously embodies the filial relation of Israel (indeed all humanity) to God within his own incarnate life and mediation as true servant-Son. See chapter two above, pp. 61-69. Torrance argues that in so doing the concepts of sonship and fatherhood are taken up to express the unique relation of Jesus Christ and God the Father. As noted above, the primary purpose for the coming of the Son is to reveal God the Father and to reconcile and redeem us so that we can be God's daughters and sons by the grace of our Lord Jesus Christ (see Torrance, *Christian Doctrine*, pp. 138-39).

[73]Torrance, *Christian Doctrine*, p. 138.

God.[74] As the early church thought out the relations between the Father, the Son and the Holy Spirit, it became evident that the relations between the divine persons belong to what the persons are as persons, and are therefore *constitutive* relations, or *onto-relations*, ontic and holistic relations between the Father, the Son and the Holy Spirit that define who God is.[75]

The three divine persons coexist inseparably and eternally together in the one being of God. It is, of course, this threeness and oneness of God's personal activity and personal being that generates the *Christian* doctrine of the Trinity. We will deal with Torrance's concept of person in more detail in chapter eight on the doctrine of the Trinity. The crucial issue here is that the *homoousion* expresses the relation in being, but also distinction between the Son and the Father. It therefore enables us to grasp and articulate knowledge of God rooted in constitutive relations in God so that we come to know that God is "eternally Father in himself, as Father of the Son, before the foundation of the world and apart from creation, and so is Father in a sense that is absolutely unique and transcendent."[76]

Torrance points out that in the New Testament and the theology of the early church, "Father" designates God in a twofold though indivisible manner, for the two senses always overlap and we do not know the one without the other.[77] On the one hand, "Father" refers to God the heavenly or almighty Father as the Creator and Lord of all that is, as in the Lord's prayer, "Our Father who art in heaven," or as given definitive expression in the Nicene Creed, "We believe in God the Father Almighty, Creator of heaven and earth."[78] In this sense "Father" signifies the one being *(mia ousia)* of the Godhead, the "one supreme almighty being, uncreated, self-sufficient, all-perfect, who is the transcendent Fount, Source, and Author of all other being."[79]

On the other hand, "Father" in a specific sense refers to the Father of our Lord and Savior Jesus Christ whose person is distinct from the person of the Son, and of course the person of the Holy Spirit.[80] Torrance is adamant that God is God the Father Almighty, Creator of heaven and

---

[74]Ibid., p. 156.

[75]Ibid., p. 157.

[76]Ibid., p. 57.

[77]Ibid., pp. 136, 141, and Torrance, *Trinitarian Faith*, pp. 78-79.

[78]See Torrance, *Christian Doctrine*, pp. 56-57, 137-38, and Torrance, *Trinitarian Faith*, pp. 78-79.

[79]Torrance, *Trinitarian Faith*, pp. 78-79.

[80]Torrance, *Christian Doctrine*, pp. 56-57, 137-38. It is important to note that for Torrance, the Son proceeds from the *being* of the Father in unique coinherent relation to the *person* of the Father (see p. 141).

earth, only because God is eternally Father of the Son, a point to which we will return at the beginning of the third section of this chapter.[81] Jesus Christ the incarnate Son first makes God known as precisely and peculiarly *his* Father and therefore reveals the Father through *his* own divine sonship lived out in and as Jesus the man from Nazareth.[82]

It is also as eternally Father of the Son that God in unstinting love freely chose to become *our* Father, by reclaiming and reconciling us in and through his Son, our Lord and Savior, Jesus Christ. Christ identified with us in our sinful and alienated humanity where we are anything but children of God, so that through his incarnational redemption we might become daughters and sons of God by grace and come to know God as *Father*.

It is by reference to this Father-Son relation revealed in the gospel and made efficacious by the Holy Spirit that all knowledge of God as Father is defined and all prior conceptions God and fatherhood are critically evaluated and replaced.[83] Thus the God and Father that we know through Jesus Christ may not be identified, Torrance contends, with any concept of God whom we claim to know apart from Jesus Christ, for there is no other way to the Father than through Jesus Christ, and there is no other God the Father Almighty except the God who is eternally Father of our Lord Jesus Christ.[84]

Language for God. In the New Testament, in light of the revelation of God the Father through the incarnate Son, Torrance maintains that "Father" becomes the personal name for God, and not just a title or epithet, as in the Old Testament. Here Torrance points to Jesus' high-priestly prayer in John 17: "Father . . . I have finished the work which you gave me to do. . . . I have manifested your Name unto men."[85]

In the Old Testament, God proclaims God's name to be "I am who I am" ("I will be who I will be"), a name, Torrance contends, that only God can speak.[86] However, in Jesus Christ, Torrance contends, God's historical redemptive and revealing dialogue with the nation of Israel is brought to

---

[81]Torrance, *Trinitarian Faith*, p. 79, and Torrance, *Christian Doctrine*, pp. 57, 138.

[82]Torrance, *Christian Doctrine*, p. 57. Here Torrance points, as he does so often, to Matthew 11:25-27 (also in Lk 10:21-22), which was also so pivotal for the Nicene theologians (see pp. 57, 139). Also see chapter two above, p. 71 n. 64.

[83]Ibid., p. 138.

[84]Ibid., p. 57.

[85]Ibid., p. 139. This appears to be Torrance's own translation.

[86]Ibid., p. 14.

its culmination, disclosing not simply something further about God, but God's very self as the God and Father of our Lord Jesus Christ. In so doing, God provides the specific personal content of God's name, "I am who I am/I will be Who I will be," for "God identifies and defines Himself for us as Father, Son, and Holy Spirit."[87] We are set free in the Spirit to speak the resulting name in thanksgiving and praise.

In this incarnational self-revelation of the Father through the Son and in the Holy Spirit, Torrance thinks that form and content are inseparable.[88] We can no more bypass the trinitarian name and name God ourselves than we can bypass the Hebraic character of the Old Testament or the particularity of the man, Jesus of Nazareth, *enhypostatic* in the Word or Son of God incarnate.

The trinitarian name is, therefore, bound up with the radically new understanding of God inherent in God's self-revelation as Father through the Son and in the Holy Spirit. As the church carefully thought out the implicit content of that self-revelation, it became increasingly clear, Torrance maintains, that Father, Son and Holy Spirit are in fact proper names signifying three distinct persons or *hypostases* who are unique, while at the same time of the one being of God.[89] This led to a distinctively Christian (trinitarian) doctrine of God. It is also the reason why baptisms and ordinations must be, Torrance argues, in the name of the Father and of the Son and of the Holy Spirit, for the trinitarian name is inextricably embedded in the very reality and content of the gospel.

However, it is this same radically new understanding of God that arises out of God's self-revelation through Jesus Christ and in the Spirit and comes to expression in the trinitarian name that also transforms the content of "Father," "Son" and "Spirit" when used to designate God.[90] To call God "Father" is *not* to say that God is like a human father. Torrance sees the biblical use of "Father" for God as an example par excellence of how divine revelation radically transforms ordinary forms of human thought and speech. When applied to God, Torrance maintains that "Father" means something "utterly different from its ordinary use when applied to a human being.[91] Here we see again the language-molding

[87]Ibid., p. 15.
[88]Ibid., p. 56.
[89]Ibid., p. 155.
[90]Ibid., p. 138.
[91]Ibid., p. 57. ← Christian Doctrine

power of the gospel.[92] God as Father, as defined by God's own self-revelation, stands in judgment on, not analogical relation to, human fatherhood.[93]

Torrance sees the Hebraic prohibition, especially in the second com-
mandment of the Decalogue, against all sensual imagery for God as important here. He is adamant that we may not think of God as having
gender, whether masculine or feminine. The Hebraic perspective is further reinforced by the doctrines of the incarnation and Holy Spirit.

Torrance points out that the incarnation signifies not an analogical or
mythological movement from the human to the divine.[94] Rather, the incarnation signifies God assuming the human and radically transforming
it in the process. Analogies of being and mythological symbolism constructed on the basis of human experience are overturned and ruled out
by the content of God's actual self-revelation as Father, Son and Holy
Spirit.[95]

The application of the *homoousion* to the Holy Spirit is also crucial
for Torrance at this point because it signifies that what God is toward us
in the Holy *Spirit*, God is antecedently and eternally in himself. Since
God *is* Spirit, Torrance argues that we cannot read back into God the
creaturely content of our human notions (fatherhood and sonship, for example) back into God.[96] Here Torrance appeals to Athanasius who said
that while the Son is the one form *(Eidos)* of the Godhead, the Spirit is
the image *(Eidos or Eikon)* of the Son.

This might appear puzzling until one realizes that the Spirit is, in
fact, *imageless*. Torrance argues, that because the Father, Son and Holy
Spirit are *homoousios*, of one *spiritual* being and nature, it is "in an ineffable, imageless and wholly spiritual way that we are to think of them
in their relations with one another in the Holy Trinity."[97] Father and Son
refer to imageless relations when they are used to designate God. All of the

---

[92]See chapter two, pp. 75-77.

[93]Torrance says that we should "set aside all analogies drawn from the visible world in
speaking of God," for when we use "Father," "Son" and "Holy Spirit," we must think of
imageless relations (Torrance, *Christian Doctrine*, p. 157).

[94]See ibid., pp. 157-59, and Torrance, *Trinitarian Faith*, p. 71.

[95]Torrance, *Christian Doctrine*, p. 105. Torrance argues that God's triune self-revelation rules
out any mythological projection by us into God of the creaturely relations and images
latent in the pre-theological use of "father," "son" and "spirit."

[96]Ibid., p. 158, and Torrance, *Trinitarian Faith*, p. 71.

[97]Torrance, *Christian Doctrine*, pp. 158; also, 99.

trinitarian interrelations are essentially spiritual.[98] Thus in Torrance's perspective, the trinitarian name and all other language used for God undergoes a radical alteration under the impact of God's self-revelation. Whether it be "Father," "Son," "Spirit," "Word," "being," "communion," "persons," etc., the terms and concepts borrowed or created are transformed in their use in reference to God.[99]

The same language-molding power of the gospel is evident in relation to the *love (agape)* of God the Father. The New Testament meaning of the term *agape* is not drawn from any fatherly or motherly human love toward a child, but rather from the self-revelation of God's utter self-giving love, especially in the cross.

The love of God the Father. It is because God the Father actually and actively loves us so much, Torrance contends, that God sent his only Son into the world to save us and in so doing reveals himself as the "Loving One."[100] God, in ungrudging love for us, freely and passionately wills and acts to be with us, to graciously reconcile and redeem us.[101] God does not need us to be the ever living and loving God that God is, nor is God constituted by the relations God establishes with us in God's saving activity for us, but God seeks us and reconciles us so that God may share God's own eternal life and love with us.[102]

Only because of God's self-revelation in Jesus Christ the beloved Son, Torrance argues, do we come to know and understand something of this love of God that surpasses knowledge.[103] It is not a kind of love that we think up on our own and analogically attribute to God.[104] Rather it is love defined, according to 1 John, in the concrete terms of the life and especially the death and resurrection of Jesus Christ.[105] In Jesus Christ the love of God comes to us and is lived out among us in the form of a servant, touching and healing lepers, associating with people of ill-repute and washing his disciples' feet, finally dying that we might experience new life.

Torrance points out that it is in the giving of God's beloved Son over to atoning sacrifice on the cross for our sin that we see the full extent of God's

---

[98]Torrance, *Trinitarian Faith*, p. 72.
[99]Torrance, *Christian Doctrine*, pp. 20-22.
[100]Ibid., p. 5.
[101]Ibid., p. 4.
[102]Ibid., pp. 4, 166.
[103]Torrance, *Mediation*, p. 109.
[104]Torrance, *Christian Doctrine*, p. 139.
[105]Ibid., p. 8. This is another example of Torrance's interactionist God-world relation.

love.[106] Torrance speaks of the cross as a window into the heart of God.[107] The fact that the incarnate Son is *homoousios* with the Father means that God the Father was also personally present and active in the crucifixion of Jesus Christ such that the atoning sacrifice of the Son for our sin reveals the inner nature of God the Father as compassionate love.[108]

The cross of Jesus Christ is a trinitarian event because God's being inheres in the *activity* of the Son of God incarnate as Jesus of Nazareth even in death, and the Father, the Son and the Holy Spirit coinhere inseparably in the one being of God. Of course, this does not mean that the Father was crucified, since it was the incarnate Son in differentiation from the Father who died on the cross. Yet Torrance is adamant that the cross of Christ entailed not just human, but divine suffering, the suffering of God, the very being of God in God's redemptive and passionate act on our behalf.[109] "Thus we cannot but think of the atonement," Torrance argues, "as a threefold act grounded in and issuing from the triune being of God," for the activity of trinitarian persons interpenetrate one another in the one and indivisible Godhead (Eph 2:13-18; Heb 9:14).[110]

In and behind the crucifixion of the incarnate Son is God the Father who also along with the Son "paid the cost of our salvation."[111] For this reason Torrance repeatedly emphasizes that in Jesus Christ, who has been delivered up for us all, God has revealed that God loves us to the uttermost, without reserve, even more than God loves himself.[112] We come to see that God wills not to exist for himself alone, for God has made us for himself and will not be without us.[113]. Mediation P.140

Indeed through our union with our Lord Jesus Christ and in com-

---

[106]Torrance, *Mediation*, p. 109.

[107]Ibid., pp. 11, 112, 133, and Torrance, *Christian Doctrine*, pp. 58, 69.

[108]Torrance, *Mediation*, p. 109.

[109]Ibid., p. 113.

[110]Ibid., p. 117. Torrance asserts that "the oneness in being and activity between the incarnate Son and God the Father means that we cannot but speak in a significant way of the sacrifice of the Father in and with the sacrifice of the Son, whom he did not spare but gave up for our sake." Also see Torrance, *Christian Doctrine*, pp. 249, 246-54 (especially 252). It is important to note that Torrance does not here embrace patripassionism. It is the incarnate Son who is crucified in differentiation from the Father and the Spirit, though still in unbroken oneness with the Father and the Spirit. The whole Trinity is involved in the sacrifice of Christ, but the Father does not suffer in the same way as the Son. Patripassionism was really a form of modalism and therefore rightly condemned as heretical.

[111]Torrance, *Mediation*, p. 109.

[112]Torrance, *Christian Doctrine*, pp. 5, 162, 166, 244.

[113]Ibid., p. 140.

munion of the Holy Spirit, because of the love of God the Father, God gathers us up into union and communion with the eternal life and love of God.[114] In the incarnation and the cross, God in the freedom of God's boundless love has irreversibly committed himself to us, for God's activity in loving us is an activity backed up by God's very being.[115] God does not love us because God has reconciled us, rather Christ's atoning and reconciling blood flows toward us from the love of God, the love that God is.[116]

This means that love is not simply something God does, for God's loving is not different from God's own living being and reality. Here Torrance points to 1 John, which tells us that God is love.[117] When combined with the account in John's gospel of the mutual loving between the Father and the Son, it becomes clear that God is himself the love with and through which God loves us.[118] The loving relations between the triune persons reveal that God *is* the ever-loving, self-sacrificing and living God, only and always in this dynamic communion of loving and being loved in relation within God's own life as God.[119]

This giving and receiving love that God is eternally as Father, Son and Holy Spirit constitutes in Torrance's mind the "Communion of Love," a reciprocal loving, which God is in God's one being.[120] This means that God's love is as inexhaustible as God's being, for God's love is God's being in a ceaseless trinitarian movement, a movement of love that freely overflows toward others.[121] It also signifies that love is, in

---

[114]Ibid., pp. 8, 164.

[115]Ibid., p. 244. If God were not the absolutely "Loving One" in God's own being, Torrance maintains, God's love toward us in Christ's death on the cross and outpouring of the Spirit at Pentecost would be groundless (see p. 5).

[116]Ibid., p. 245, and Torrance, *Mediation*, p. 110. This is the very center of the gospel, for God so loved the world that he gave his only begotten Son (Jn 3:16), but this is a love that we know only through Christ who died for us and in the Holy Spirit who pours this love into our hearts (Rom 5:5) so that rooted and established in that love, we may know something of the love of Christ that surpasses knowledge and be filled with the fullness of God who is love (Eph 3:17-19, 1 Jn 4:7-18).

[117]Torrance, *Christian Doctrine*, pp. 245; also, 5, 6, 59, 139, 163.

[118]Ibid., pp. 139, 165, 245. From Torrance's perspective, all of this should also be understood in light of the Synoptic Gospels of the mutual knowing and being between the Father and the Son (Mt 11:25-27 and Lk 10:21-22), discussed above in this chapter's first section, "Access to the Father."

[119]Ibid.

[120]Ibid., p. 165.

[121]Ibid., p. 5.

fact, the primary act of God's being.[122]

Therefore, God could no more cease loving, and loving us, than God could cease being the triune God whose being is a ceaseless reciprocity of personal love.[123] This is the ultimate ontological ground, Torrance thinks, of why nothing can ever separate us from the love of God the Father in Jesus Christ our Lord.[124]

The being of God. Thus God's being is not being that also *loves*, but rather being that *is* love.[125] Following Athanasuis, Torrance contends that to call God "Father" is, in fact, to express God's very being, for the being of God is *personal being* who loves.[126] Indeed the personal being and loving activity of God mutually qualify and define each other.[127] Here Torrance argues that the reason this is so, and the reason that we know this is so, is that the *being* of God and the *activity* of God in loving are inseparable, as noted at several points above.[128]

When we think of God's being *(ousia)*, we are not to think of *ousia* in terms of some preconceived abstract static essence, but rather in the concrete, dynamic and intensely personal sense injected into *ousia* by God's *parousia* with us in Jesus Christ.[129] Here Torrance appropriates Athanasius's twin concepts of *enousios logos* (word that inheres in God's being) and *enousios energia* (activity that inheres in God's being).[130]

The Word of God, incarnate in Jesus Christ, and God's being are essentially one, for they coinhere in one another. Thus God's being is not silent and impersonal, but rather inherently being that is eloquent, self-communicative being, being that speaks.[131] In a parallel manner, God's activity or

---

[122]Ibid., p. 244.

[123]Ibid., pp. 59; also, 5-6.

[124]Ibid., p. 59. Torrance understands God's love as a dynamic constancy that is always new in its free outpouring for others. It is a dynamic kind of love characteristically free from rigidity with "an infinite range of variability and mobility in which its dynamic constancy as love is brought to bear consistently and differentially upon every and any state of affairs beyond itself" (p. 245). It is because God's love is always the same, unconditioned by anything beyond it, that God's love acts differentially with different people and events. Torrance argues that this is true in God's judgement of the sinner (see p. 246). This is why Scripture can speak, Torrance contends, of the wrath of God as the wrath of the Lamb.

[125]Ibid., p. 139.

[126]Ibid., pp. 118, 137-40.

[127]Ibid., p. 106.

[128]Ibid., p. 4.

[129]See ibid., pp. 4, 104, 116, 129, 132.

[130]Torrance, *Trinitarian Faith*, p. 72.

[131]Ibid., p. 73.

active presence in Jesus Christ and God's being are not separate, for they are essentially and eternally coinherent.[132] Together the *enousios logos* and *enousios energia* lead to a dynamic and active concept of God and God's being that is rather different, Torrance contends, from the Greek philosophical understanding of being and of God, as in the case of Aristotle's unmoved mover who timelessly affects and moves the world as the object of the world's desire.[133]

So Torrance's understanding of the *ousia* (being) of God is governed by what we know of the ever-living God the Father who speaks to us through his Word and reveals who God is in God's own being through God's saving activity in the Son.[134] "What God is toward us," Torrance asserts, "in the Word and Activity of Christ and the Spirit, he is in his ultimate being or *ousia* from which, or rather from whom, they issue and to whom they direct us."[135] The Fatherhood of God revealed through Jesus Christ and in the Holy Spirit determines how we understand God's being.[136]

This also means that the one being of God must be thought of as *personal*, indeed as intrinsically and fully personal as God is in God's trinitarian self-manifestation in the gospel.[137] Here Torrance argues that the personal character of God's being is reinforced by the "I am who I am" of *Yahweh*, particularly when related to the "I am" statements of Christ, as we will see in chapter eight.[138] Together they emphasize the essentially personal understanding of *ousia* in reference to the God of Christian faith.

It is also significant, in Torrance's mind, that the "I am" statements of *Yahweh* and of Jesus Christ are all related to God's *redeeming* personal presence *to*, *for* and *with* God's people, whether it be Israel in the Old Testament or the church in the New Testament. Torrance argues that this signifies

---

[132]Ibid.

[133]See ibid., pp. 73-74. Torrance's dynamic understanding of the *ousia* of God also radically differs from the many forms of panentheism so popular in theology these days, for God's relation to the world is one of freedom characterized by personal interaction, not an inner necessity and continuity of being that God and the world share.

[134]Torrance, *Christian Doctrine*, p. 116.

[135]Ibid., p. 129.

[136]Ibid., pp. 118, 137; also, 18, 140. Remember that Torrance argues that "Father" is used in a twofold way in reference to God: "Father" can refer to the one being *(ousia)* of God or to the *hypostasis* or person of the Father, though the two senses always overlap one another and may not be separated (see pp. 137-41, especially p. 141, for a discussion of this).

[137]Ibid., p. 129.

[138]Ibid., p. 119.

that God's personal being is *being for others*.[139] This, of course, does not mean that God's being is constituted by the relations that God establishes with others, but rather that the free movement of God's being toward and for others reveals something of God's personal *ousia*.[140]

Thus Torrance understands the being of God as "personal, living, dynamic, relational Being," "communion-constituting Being," because God is "Being-in-Communion" in himself.[141] In fact, Torrance argues that God's fullness of personal being, this communion of the trinitarian persons, *is* the one being God.[142] We will return to this subject in chapter eight, "The Tri-unity of God."

For now, it is important to reiterate that for Torrance it is only because God has revealed himself to us through Christ and in the Spirit that we can speak about God in this manner. Here the *homoousion* is utterly decisive and revolutionary in Torrance's mind, for it expresses the supreme evangelical truth of the gospel that *God* is the content of what God is toward us in God's love and grace, what God has done and continues to do for us in Jesus Christ and the Holy Spirit, God really *is* in himself.[143] Through the grace of our Lord Jesus Christ and in the communion of the Holy Spirit our minds and our lives are adapted so that we may know the love of God the Father in a godly and accurate manner, at least in some sense in accordance with God's own personal being.[144] Indeed, Torrance argues, because God loves humanity to the uttermost, God wants all people to participate in the love of God the Father through Christ and in the Spirit, and therefore in the living communion that God is as Father, Son and Holy Spirit, who together are the one "Being of God in Communion" (*Ousia* as *Koinonia*).[145]

3. God the Father Almighty

As noted above, Torrance argues that knowledge of and belief in God as Father must be formulated within the evangelical interrelations of the grace of our Lord Jesus Christ and the communion of the Holy Spirit. The

---

[139]Ibid., p. 123.
[140]Ibid.
[141]Ibid., p. 124. Torrance appropriates the phrase "Being-in-Communion" from James B. Torrance.
[142]Ibid., pp. 104, 161.
[143]Ibid., p. 130.
[144]Ibid., pp. 127, 129, 136.
[145]Ibid., p. 133.

reason for this is that the Father-Son and Son-Father relation in which we participate in the Holy Spirit is a relation of oneness in being (*homoousios*) or an onto-relation which enables us to know God in an accurate way according to God's nature. It is on the ground of what God has actually revealed of God's nature through God's self-revelation and self-communication in Jesus Christ that everything else to be known of God and God's relation to the world is understood.[146]

This principle also applies to how we conceive of *almightiness* of God the Father and conceive of *God* the Almighty Creator, for it is through Jesus Christ "that the distinctive nature of the sovereign power of God is made known."[147] The almightiness of God the Father that we know through the Son and in the Spirit transcends everything that we could ever think or say about God's almightiness apart from Jesus Christ and the Holy Spirit.[148]

Not abstract omnipotence. In fact, Torrance contends that God's omnipotence, as revealed in Jesus Christ, actually conflicts with concepts of unlimited arbitrary power that humanity often constructs on the basis of worldly experience, absolutizes, and then attributes to God.[149] "We must reject," Torrance declares, "all abstract notions of divine omnipotence, for omnipotence is not to be understood in terms of what we think God can do, defining it as potence raised to the nth power, i.e., as omni-potence, but in terms of what God actually *is* and actually *has done*."[150] For this reason Torrance argues that every abstract question about what God can and cannot do and any discussion of God's power apart from who God is as Father revealed in Jesus Christ the Son is an empty movement of thought.[151]

This also means that God is not defined in terms of omnipotence, but rather omnipotence is delimited by the nature and being of God the Father revealed through the incarnate Son. Here Torrance points out that God's power is in no way separate from or different than God's being and nature, for God's being inheres in all God's activity (as we have noted at various points in this chapter), so that the exercise of God's power *is* God's

---

[146]Torrance, *Trinitarian Faith*, pp. 3, 7.
[147]Torrance, *Christian Doctrine*, p. 204.
[148]Torrance, *Trinitarian Faith*, p. 82.
[149]Ibid., p. 82.
[150]Torrance, *Christian Doctrine*, p. 204.
[151]Ibid., p. 205.

"Being in Action" in accordance with the nature of God as Father.[152] In Torrance's mind only God has real power, and only on the basis of God's self-revelation as God the Father Almighty are we able to properly conceive and express what God's omnipotence is like.

Christological qualification of God as almighty. So for Torrance, it is never in terms of what *"we* think God *can do*, but in terms of what God *has done and continues to do* in Jesus Christ that we may understand something of what divine almightiness really is."[153] How does Torrance understand this power of God in Jesus Christ? It is the transforming personal energy of God to enter the disordered and fallen creation that borders on non-being in death and decay in order to recreate what is in danger of crumbling into chaos. It is in the *new creation* that God inaugurates in Jesus' birth and consummates in Christ's resurrection that we learn that the almighty power of God is *omnipotent grace*.[154]

The omnipotence of God in the incarnation is the indescribable and astonishing power of God for self-humiliation in the cradle and on the cross, the power of God to become weak, poor and helpless for our sake. Torrance notes that this kind of condescension or kenosis of God is not a curtailing of God's power, but the astonishing exercise of that power within our contingent, material, creaturely existence in space and time for the *new creation*.[155]

Of course it is the death of Christ that reveals the full unqualified depths to which God descends in sacrificial love, and also the unfathomable power of God in weakness, for God enters into our sin and guilt, our inability to change our past and ourselves, our shame and death, and, in an expiatory act of sheer omnipotent grace, undoes the past and our sin and guilt.[156] It is an act in which God gives *himself*, dies our death, sets us free and reveals that God's power is utterly different than what we would ever think or imagine.[157] Torrance sees the cross as the preeminent example of God's almightiness, for God does not prevent the crucifixion, but does something greater: God personally enters and uses human wicked-

---

[152]Ibid.

[153]Torrance, *Trinitarian Faith*, p. 82. Elsewhere Torrance argues that the *homoousion* leads us to view the sovereignty of God and Father as identical with the sovereignty of Jesus Christ, the incarnate Son, and vice versa (see Torrance, *Christian Doctrine*, p. 205).

[154]Ibid., p. 214.

[155]Ibid., pp. 214-15. Also see Torrance, *Trinitarian Faith*, p. 82.

[156]Torrance, *Christian Doctrine*, p. 215.

[157]Ibid.

ness "as the unintended means" through which God accomplishes God's plan to reach and to redeem sinners.[158]

Yet the power of God in the cross must be viewed in light of the resurrection of Jesus Christ from the dead, and us with him, for the presence of God in the midst of death annuls death's power and manifests the lordship of God over life and death, and thereby discloses God's sovereign power over all of the destructive powers of disorder, disease, darkness and decay that so threaten our world and our lives, but cannot and will not overwhelm the omnipotent grace of God.[159]

The almightiness of God the Father is not some impersonal brute force that God exerts at a distance. Rather Torrance thinks it is intensely personal, for it is God himself in the midst of our world in its disorder and despair, God present in such a way as to preserve, heal, save, reconcile and redeem. The power of God is the power of the cross, the power of the resurrection, the power to bring good out of evil, for God in the midst of the crucifixion of Jesus, the most heinous act of unfathomable evil, in love atoned for sin, redeemed lost humanity and raised Christ to life, thereby conquering destruction and death.[160]

The sovereign freedom of God's almighty power. One of the astonishing things about God's almighty power revealed in Jesus Christ is that God's power is capable of bringing about absolutely new events, *new even for God*, since God *became* incarnate.[161] Of course, God was always able to become incarnate, but Torrance maintains that God actually became incarnate in what the Scripture defines as the fullness of time.[162] Torrance argues that Pentecost also represents a radically new form of divine presence initiated in the world, new even for God.[163]

While God was and is always Father and always almighty, the new acts of God in creation, in the incarnation and in the outpouring of the Spirit at Pentecost reveal the sovereign *freedom* of God's almighty power. God's omnipotence is not that of a static, inertial deity who determines every-

---

[158]Ibid., p. 215. This phrase is actually from H. R. Mackintosh, though Torrance quotes it with approval.

[159]Ibid. In the death and resurrection of Christ, Torrance contends, God demonstrated that God's power, or omnipotence, is so utterly distinct that it cannot be described by analogy to any kind of power we can know outside of Jesus Christ.

[160]Ibid., pp. 222, 228

[161]Ibid., p. 208.

[162]Ibid.

[163]Ibid.

thing that happens while remaining unmoved and apathetic to it all. Rather, Torrance contends, it is the omnipotence of the living and personal God who "is absolutely free to do what he had never done before, and free to be other than he was eternally . . . and even to become incarnate as a creature within his creation, while nevertheless remaining eternally the God that he always was."[164] It is this incredible freedom of God's almighty power that reveals the astonishing character of God's activity that always seems to take us by surprise, Torrance thinks, for God's activity is always new while ever true to what it was and is and ever will be in Jesus Christ our Lord.[165]

This almighty power and freedom of God creatively calls forth creaturely freedom in God's creatures. The personal power of God does not override the creature, but rather lovingly sustains the freedom of the creature before God within a relation of the creature to God.[166] The omnipotence of God's grace toward us is always a unique kind of humanizing and personalizing power that sets us free for free response in praise and thanksgiving, in faith and obedience, as we noted in chapter three.[167]

God the Father's astonishing almightiness, Torrance concludes, "is the sovereignty of his Holy Love revealed to us in the gospel."[168] Nothing in all of creation will ever be able to separate us from the love and the power of God the Father Almighty revealed in Jesus Christ and in the outpouring of the Holy Spirit, any more than anything can separate the Father, the Son and the Holy Spirit from one another.[169] This is knowledge of God's omnipotence strictly in accordance with God's nature.

For Torrance, it *is* more godly and accurate to signify God from the Son and call God "Father" than it is to name God from his works and call God "unoriginate." And it is in terms of the love of God the Father Almighty that Torrance develops his understanding of God as sovereign Creator.

---

[164]Ibid.

[165]Ibid.

[166]Ibid., p. 206.

[167]Ibid., p. 211. It is in light of this kind of power that we are to understand the kingdom of God that has no end. And it is in light of this sovereign freedom of God's almighty power, Torrance argues, that we are to understand Jesus' words to his disciples (and us) after the resurrection: "All authority has been given unto me in heaven and on earth. Go therefore and make disciples of all nations. . . . And remember, I am with you always, to the end of the age" (Mt 28:18-20).

[168]Ibid., p. 211.

[169]Ibid., p. 140.

5

SOVEREIGN CREATOR, CONTINGENT CREATION

Only when we keep before us what the Triune God has done for us men in Jesus Christ
can we realise what is involved in God the Creator and his work.
Creation is the temporal analogue taking place outside of God, of that event in God himself
by which God is Father of the Son. The world is not God's Son,
is not 'begotten' of God, but is created. But what God does as the Creator
can in the Christian sense only be seen and understood as a reflection,
as a shadowing forth of the inner divine relationship between God the Father and the Son.
And that is why the work of creation is ascribed in the Confession to the Father.

KARL BARTH

T hroughout chapter four on Thomas F. Torrance's doctrine of the love of God the Father Almighty, the emphasis fell on the primacy of the Father-Son relation over the Creator-creature relation in all of our knowledge of God. This was summarized in Athanasius' memorable epigram quoted at the beginning of chapter four that it is more godly and accurate to signify God from the Son and call God "Father." The reason for this is the radically different character of the two relations. The Creator-creature relation is vague and general because it is a relation external to God, whereas the Father-Son relation is one internal to the being of God.

An accurate and redemptive knowledge of God must come from the Father-Son relation, which is a oneness of being (the *homoousion*). To know the love of God the Father through the grace of Jesus Christ, the Son of God incarnate, is to know God in accordance with God's nature and in the most accurate way. Torrance argues that theology must be developed in strict conformity to God's self-revelation and self-communication in Jesus Christ and when it does so it is scientific.

Since *everything* to be known about God must be thought out on the basis of this Father-Son relation, Torrance defines his doctrine of the *almightiness* of God the Father in light of what God has done and continues to do in Jesus Christ (who is God's self-revelation), not by absolutizing our earthly experiences of power and developing a concept of infinite power which is then applied to God.[1] Thus, knowledge of the almightiness of God the Father is taken from Jesus Christ, God's incarnate Son and our Lord and Savior.

This is also true of our knowledge of the sovereign Creator. It is as *Father* that God is Creator. Therefore, Torrance contends that our knowledge of God as Creator is also derived from our knowledge of God in Jesus Christ, who is *homoousios* with the Father. This chapter examines Torrance's christocentric and trinitarian doctrine of the sovereign Creator and the contingent creation.

The first section of the chapter develops Torrance's understanding of the sovereign Creator, (1) in light of the inherently generative being of God the Father Almighty who is eternally Father of the Son and (2) in light of the love of God revealed particularly in the cross, the superabundant love that God is in God's trinitarian life; this love overflows and calls a universe into existence on which God showers God's goodness, not because of any necessity, but simply out of sheer grace. Since God's intrinsic relations are trinitarian, the activity of God the Father in creation is never without the activity of the Son and the Spirit.

Torrance sees the freedom and spontaneity of God in calling the universe into existence out of nothing reflected in the creaturely contingence, intelligibility and freedom of creation. The second section of this chapter develops Torrance's understanding of the contingent creation. The third section also deals with the contingent creation, but focuses on the human creature.

It is the contingent and subtle intelligibility and freedom of creation that invites, even in a sense demands, a certain kind of human inquiry and exploration, for creation can only be known out of itself. Torrance thinks that modern science rests on certain specific ultimate beliefs about

---

[1]Thomas F. Torrance, *The Trinitarian Faith: The Evangelical Theology of the Ancient Catholic Church* (Edinburgh: T & T Clark, 1988), p. 82.

the universe (like those just mentioned) that science did not generate on its own and that actually have their origin in the Judeo-Christian tradition. Here Torrance finds significant points of convergence between natural science and theological science. The relation between theology and natural science is the subject matter of the fourth section of this chapter. I have included much more explanatory material in the footnotes of this section for those without significant background in the natural sciences.

The final section takes up the question of natural theology, one of the most difficult themes in Torrance's theology. While he rules out an *independent* natural theology, Torrance allows a place of a reconceived natural theology, one that is "natural" to the kind of scientific theology he advocates, as discussed throughout the chapters of this book.

1. The Sovereign Creator

The concept of God as the Creator of the universe is found in the Old Testament, of course, and had been developed within Judaism. Even creation *ex nihilo* occurs in explicit form in inter-Testament Jewish literature.[2] But in the New Testament the concept of God as Creator is radicalized, Torrance argues, in connection with what it has to say about God in light of God's self-revelation in Jesus Christ.[3]

As noted above, it is as Father that God is sovereign Creator. However, our knowledge of the fatherhood of God is mediated through the person and work of Jesus Christ, for it is only through Jesus Christ, the Word made flesh, that we have access to God the Father (Mt 11:25-27; Lk 10:21-22; Jn 6:43-47; 14:6-12; 17:1-26), as the first section of chapter four discussed at length.[4] Thus Torrance contends that we cannot think about the creatorship of God in terms of abstract generalities of what we imagine God is or is not, or from creation itself in its utter difference from God, any more than we can think of the Father's almighty power in this way. Rather our thought about God as sovereign Creator must be grounded in our knowledge of God the Father Almighty, which arises out of God's self-revelation in Jesus Christ who is *homoousios* with the Father.

The Father and the Son are of one being, nature and activity, as noted

---

[2] Torrance, *Trinitarian Faith*, p. 96.
[3] Thomas F. Torrance, *The Christian Doctrine of God: One Being Three Persons* (Edinburgh: T & T Clark, 1998), pp. 203-4.
[4] Torrance, *Trinitarian Faith*, p. 77.

in chapter four. This means that all that God the Father Almighty does is done through the Son or Word of God, for the Father is never without the Son, and what the Son does is identical with what the Father does.[5]

This is also true of creation. According to the New Testament Scriptures in the opening sections of John's Gospel, Colossians and Hebrews, Torrance finds that it is through the Word, by the Word and in the Word of God incarnate in Jesus Christ that all things have been created.[6] It is from the Word of God that all creation derives its creaturely intelligibility and order, and it is in Jesus Christ that creaturely reality holds together.[7]

This christocentric understanding of creation is further radicalized for Torrance by the actual *way* in which God has chosen to come into our midst in the Word or Son of God, the *way* of a servant, the *way* of condescension becoming incarnate, the *way* of suffering and death. Torrance views the creaturely humanity and suffering love of Jesus Christ as God's actual way of self-revelation and self-communication, and therefore the *archetype* of all of God's activity toward us in redemption and creation.

Here once again, Torrance follows Athanasius who linked together the uncreated *arche* which God is in himself with this created *arche*, the servant form in which God reveals his almightiness, thereby identifying Christ's condescension in the incarnation as both "the Beginning of a new beginning within the creation and as the . . . archetypal pattern of God's gracious provision for his creation."[8] It is in Jesus Christ, Torrance maintains, that we meet God the Father, the sovereign Creator, face to face and come to understand the nature and work of the Creator in an intimate manner impossible apart from Christ.[9] In the remainder of this chapter we will examine some of the implications of Torrance's christocentric approach to the sovereign Creator and the contingent creation.

God was not always Creator. While God is always Father, God was not always Creator. The crucial distinction here is between the generation of the Son from the *nature* of God and the creation of the world by the *will* of God.[10] There is an ontological identity or oneness of being be-

---

[5]Ibid., pp. 77, 78, and Torrance, *Christian Doctrine*, p. 205.
[6]Torrance, *Trinitarian Faith*, p. 77.
[7]Torrance, *Christian Doctrine*, pp. 203-4, and Torrance, *Trinitarian Faith*, pp. 77, 83.
[8]Ibid., p. 83; also, pp. 7, 84.
[9]Torrance, *Christian Doctrine*, p. 204.
[10]Torrance, *Trinitarian Faith*, p. 84.

tween the Father and the Son. There is utter disparity of nature between the Creator and the creature, for it is a contingent relation that exists only because God freely and graciously called creation forth from non-being, giving it an absolute beginning and a reality external to God.[11]

Thus while God has always been Father, and Father independent of all that God created, Torrance notes that as Creator, God acted in an altogether new way, bringing into being entirely new events, for the creation of the world *ex nihilo* is something new *even for God*.[12]

Of course, God always had the power to create, and creation was in the mind of God before God called it into being.[13] But it does mean that in some sense God *became* Creator of all things. When combined with God's *becoming* human in the incarnation, Torrance finds breathtaking implications for our understanding of God. It underscores the astonishing freedom and sovereignty of God's dynamic being, for God is utterly free to do what God had never done before, free to become what God had never been before, the sovereign Creator, who called creation into existence, while remaining eternally God the Father Almighty.[14]

Indeed, Torrance contends that God is the ultimate source of all other being precisely because God is intrinsically and eternally productive as Father of the Son.[15] This, of course, does not mean that God is fount of creation in the same way that God eternally generated the Son, but it does mean that God is inherently generative in God's own being as God the Father Almighty.[16] Torrance sees the universe called into being by the creative activity of God as "the temporal analogue taking place outside of God, of that event in God himself by which God is Father of the Son."[17]

---

[11]God's fatherhood is in no way constituted by a relation to what God created, whereas the created order is completely dependent upon God's will and grace for its existence.

[12]Torrance, *Christian Doctrine*, p. 208.

[13]Ibid. Also see Torrance, *Trinitarian Faith*, pp. 88-89.

[14]See Torrance, *Christian Doctrine*, p. 208. Torrance always points out that terms like "was," "beginning" and "before" are not used of God in the same sense as they are in relation to our creaturely reality (see Torrance, *Trinitarian Faith*, pp. 87-88).

God's almighty power and sovereign freedom, Torrance argues, are not exhausted by all that God has done, does do, and ever will do (see p. 89). Torrance sees God's *becoming* Creator and *becoming* incarnate as conflicting sharply with the philosophical categories such as necessity, immobility and impassivity so often associated with God in Hellenistic philosophy.

[15]Torrance, *Christian Doctrine*, p. 209.

[16]See chapter four, pp. 142-43, for the discussion of the twofold sense in which God is Father.

[17]Karl Barth, *Dogmatics in Outline*, trans. G. T. Thomson (New York: Philosophical Library, 1949), p. 52. Torrance cites Barth with approval (see Torrance, *Christian Doctrine*, p. 140).

While the world is created, not begotten, it is the product of the love of God, the ever living communion of loving and being loved that God is.[18]

God wills not to exist for himself alone. While the creation of the universe in its astonishing array of creaturely realities and order is an act of staggering omnipotent power, Torrance contends that we should not think of the Creator's sovereignty in the abstract manner of pure unlimited power as noted in the final section of chapter four. Rather, the Creator's sovereignty is the living power of God the Father that flows from God's inmost nature and life as the movement of love that God is as Father, Son and Holy Spirit.[19]

God is not solitary, but an inner fellowship, an eternal communion of personal being in himself as Father, Son and Holy Spirit. God does not need a creaturely world, Torrance argues, in order to be the fullness of personal being in relation and fellowship that God is within the one being of the triune God.[20]

It is as this self-sufficient fullness of personal being and fellowship of love in himself that God is sovereign Creator who creates not of necessity, but purely in this freedom of love that God is. Torrance asserts that it is out of this intrinsic fellowship of personal being and love that God wills not to exist for himself alone and brings a world into existence, forms human beings out of the dust of the earth, and gives them an integrity of their own out of sheer grace so that God may share God's communion of love and personal being with them.[21]

Here Torrance finds "the ultimate rational ground" of the universe "in the beneficent nature and love of God."[22] Its *raison d'être* lies in the truth revealed in Jesus Christ that God wills not to be alone without us.[23] The *why* of the world is the ungrudging goodness of the triune God. This is a truth we could never know apart from the incarnation of God's love in Jesus Christ.[24]

---

[18]Torrance, *Trinitarian Faith*, p. 6.

[19]Ibid.

[20]Ibid., p. 90. God is in no way conditioned by any kind of necessary relation to any reality other than himself and is therefore independent of, and exalted above, the contingent creation as the free Lord, sovereign Creator and source of all being beyond himself (see pp. 89-90).

[21]Ibid., pp. 90-91, and Torrance, *Christian Doctrine*, p. 140.

[22]Torrance, *Trinitarian Faith*, p. 93.

[23]Ibid. Also see Torrance, *Christian Doctrine*, pp. 211-12.

[24]Torrance, *Trinitarian Faith*, p. 92; also pp. 7, 83-84, 90-94, and Torrance, *Christian Doctrine*, pp. 5-6, 59, 139-40, 209-12. Only in the light of Christ's death and resurrection from the dead do we learn that God is Lord over life and death, over the being of creation and its non-being, and over creation's past and future as well.

It is from the standpoint of the incarnation of God's love in Christ, the Word of God through whom all things were created, that Torrance thinks out the baffling origin of the universe and the character of its objective reality and rationality external to God, yet dependent on God.[25] Creation, like redemption, is an astonishing act of the free grace of God revealed in Jesus Christ, for the sovereign Creator could never act in a way incompatible with what has been revealed of God in Jesus Christ.

Thus God's relation to the created universe is neither necessary nor arbitrary. In Torrance's perspective, the universe did not come into being by itself, but is the free and intelligible handiwork of the free and eternal Word or wisdom of God. This means, Torrance argues, that the universe is neither self-sufficient nor is its existence self-explanatory.[26] Rather it is a product of God's will and the free activity of God's love.

God the triune Creator. Torrance maintains that it is ultimately in a trinitarian manner that we must think of God as sovereign Creator, for the only God, and therefore only sovereign Creator, there is, is God the Father Almighty whom we know through the Lord Jesus Christ in the communion of the Holy Spirit. Indeed, the *homoousion* asserts that there is a oneness of being, nature and activity between the Father, Son and Holy Spirit. Yet it is a differentiated oneness in which each person engages in the activity of the one God in a distinctive manner, though always together in the coactivity of the persons in their relations. Since creation is the work of the one triune God, Torrance argues that there are distinctions within God's threefold activity of creation, for creation takes place within the homoousial and perichoretic interrelations of the trinitarian persons, from the Father through the Son and in the Spirit.[27]

The creative activity of the Father. Torrance traces the reason for creation and its distinctive characteristics to the activity of God's love peculiarly appropriate to the Father, for the Son and the Spirit both proceed in their own unique ways from the Father.[28] Creation *is*, and is *what it is*, rather than something else, because it is grounded in the ultimate love that God is as Father, as noted in the previous subsection.[29]

---

[25]Torrance, *Trinitarian Faith*, p. 91.
[26]Ibid., pp. 92-93.
[27]Ibid., pp. 206, 212.
[28]Ibid., p. 212.
[29]Ibid.

The holy love of God, which cannot be other than it is, Torrance argues, is also the ultimate ground of all intelligibility and moral order in creation, for all physical and moral laws operating in the universe function under the constraint of that love and are recognized and formulated in light of it.[30] Here Torrance views all of created heaven and earth as called into existence and ordered by the love of God the Father to bear witness to the wonder of God's holy love, in praise of God's transcendent beauty, goodness and glory (Calvin's *theatrum gloriae Dei*—theater of God's glory).[31]

The creative activity of the Son. While the existence and order of creation are ultimately traced to the love of God the Father, it is through the Son or Word of God who is with the Father that all things have been made. Torrance thinks that all things are not only created *through* Christ, but *for* him, and it is *in* him that all things are held together, for all things on earth and in heaven are reconciled in Christ (Col 1:15-20).

In Jesus Christ the Word or wisdom of God, through whom all things were created, entered the sinful and lawless creation subject to futility in order to reconcile, redeem, and overcome the disordered state into which creation has fallen, and in order to restore it to the law of God's divine love.[32] Here the gospel reveals a sovereign Creator who does not remain aloof from the world of space and time, but who is actively and personally involved preserving, and redemptively interacting with, and intervening in the world and the historical affairs of humanity.

Torrance is adamant that this interaction ought not to be conceived as interference with, or suspension of, the natural order of things. Rather, since the Word of God is the ultimate source of the natural order, God's redemptive interaction in the incarnation ought to be viewed as the reordering activity of the Creator Word with the natural order, the creaturely world, deepening its relation to God so that the world can find its fulfillment in the eternal purpose of God's love.[33] In the incarnation, Torrance sees redemption as intersecting and overlapping creation so that all of history and the en-

---

[30]Ibid., p. 213. For a fascinating discussion of how Torrance conceives of the objective and ontological, yet subtle and nondeterminist, character of natural and moral law see Thomas F. Torrance, *Juridical Law and Physical Law: Toward a Realist Foundation for Human Law* (Edinburgh: Scottish Academic Press, 1982).

[31]Torrance, *Christian Doctrine*, p. 213.

[32]Ibid.

[33]Ibid., p. 214.

tire universe is encompassed by Christ and his kingdom.[34]

The creative activity of the Spirit. The Holy Spirit is also Creator, Torrance contends, but Creator in accordance with God's distinctive reality and character as Spirit.[35] As Creator *Spirit*, Torrance emphasizes the distinctive quality of God's transcendent and unlimited *freedom*, freedom from any sort of necessary relation to the creation that God called into existence out of nothing and in differentiation from God. Creation is given a relative independence and freedom that is nevertheless dependent on God's free creative activity, as will become evident later in this chapter.[36]

Torrance finds this aspect of God's activity as sovereign Creator associated with the *Spiritus Creator* (Creator Spirit) in the third article of the Nicene Creed which speaks of the Spirit as "the Lord and Giver of Life." This is the liberating, life-giving and quickening activity of the Creator Spirit who is able to sustain the creature in *open-ended relation* toward God without over-

---

[34]Ibid. Torrance can speak of this as a "Christological and soteriological interrelation between eschatology and cosmology," which he finds in the New Testament book of Revelation. In fact, Torrance sees creation as *proleptically conditioned* by redemption (see pp. 204, 210). What Torrance has in mind here becomes clear in a quotation he cites from H. R. Mackintosh, *The Doctrine of the Person of Jesus Christ* (New York: Charles Scribner's Sons, 1928), p. 70: "Christ is conceived as Creator of the world *qua* the Person in whom the universe was in due time to find its organic centre in virtue of his work of reconciliation; he was the initial cause of all things, as being destined to be their final end. His function as Creator is proleptically conditioned by his achievement as Saviour." Also see Torrance, *Christian Doctrine*, p. 204.

Torrance does not intend a kind of predestination in which God, by some form of causality or necessity, predetermines everything that will happen, so that even the fall of humanity becomes part of God's proleptic preparation for the coming of Christ. This kind of predeterminism is absolutely antithetical to Torrance's understanding of the contingent freedom of the creation, and especially the character of the gospel, as noted in chapters two and three above. What Torrance intends, I believe, is that God's ultimate telos for creation from the beginning is revealed and actualized in the incarnation, death and resurrection of Christ, a telos in which all creation comes to share in the eternal communion of love that God is. This is the ultimate goal of both redemption and creation. It is actually realized in redemption after the Fall, and it is a telos that proleptically conditions the creation. Torrance even indicates that in light of the eternal purpose of God's love revealed in Jesus Christ to unite all things to God through Christ (the origin and goal of creation), "we may feel urged to say that even if our world did not need redeeming grace, Christ still would have become incarnate within the creation" (see pp. 210, 214).

[35]Ibid. Chapter six will deal with Torrance's doctrine of the Holy Spirit in detail. Here the focus will be on those themes in Torrance's pneumatology germane to creation, though Torrance's full pneumatology is presupposed.

[36]Torrance, *Christian Doctrine*, p. 216. When Torrance thinks of the unlimited and unrestricted freedom of God the Creator Spirit, it is in light of God's actual activity in the incarnation where we see that God is utterly free to do what God has never done before without ceasing to be who God eternally is and ever will be.

whelming or negating the reality and freedom of the creature.[37] Torrance thinks of this life-giving power of the Spirit as God's freedom to be present to the creature, to sustain the creature and to bring the creature to its true end in relation to God.

God does not "deistically abandon" (Barth) creation, but is present to and within creation and upholds it within God's embrace so that through the Spirit we and all creation live and move and have our being in God (see Acts 18:28). In so doing, the Spirit comes to creation in and from the inner communion, life and love of the triune God; and from within, the creature realizes the purpose of God the Father embodied in the grace of the incarnate Son, which is to share God's communion of love with others.[38] It is also from within a trinitarian perspective that Torrance thinks out his doctrine of divine providence.

God's providence. By now it will come as no surprise that Torrance develops his doctrine of God's providence in light of Jesus Christ, for God is not different in God's being or in any of God's activity than God is in the being and activity in Jesus Christ, the incarnate Son of God.[39] Here in Jesus Christ we discover what the sovereign Creator's activity in providence is like. We see the sovereignty of God personally and patiently clothed with and at work "in creaturely littleness and human weakness,"[40] not as some impersonal and deterministic brute force.

It is above all in the cross that we come to know the power of God as love overflowing in free and total self-sacrifice supreme over sin and guilt, evil and death, over anything and everything that might separate us from God. Christian faith in God's providence, Torrance argues, is the converse of Christian faith in the redemption.[41] Indeed, in the words of H. R. Mackintosh (which Torrance cites with approval), "The same Father who saves the world at the cost of Jesus is he who omnipotently guides the world, and the single lives within the world to a blessed end. Providence is correlative to the Cross."[42]

Torrance sees providence not as the perpetuation of the original act of

---

[37]Ibid., p. 217.

[38]Ibid., pp. 218-19.

[39]See chapter four, pp. 153-55.

[40]Torrance, *Christian Doctrine*, pp. 221-22.

[41]See ibid., p. 222.

[42]H. R. Mackintosh, *The Originality of the Christian Message* (New York: Charles Scribner's Sons, 1920), p. 70. Also see Torrance, *Christian Doctrine*, p. 222.

creation, but as God conserving the creation in a *covenanted coexistence* with himself, preserving creation by interacting positively toward and within it, and caring for creation out of limitless grace by the Word and through the Spirit.[43] The purpose of providence has to do with what Torrance calls the "redemptive overruling of history," which constrains history so that it serves God's love. God continues and preserves the creation in space and time toward the fulfillment of creation in the order of redemption, thereby disposing creation for God's eternal purpose of love.[44]

God's providential activity is not exercised from afar, as if God were deistically or dualistically separated from the world. In light of Jesus Christ, Torrance sees the nature of God's providential activity and power as God personally and directly present and active to creation, even in its fallenness, without surrendering God's transcendence and holiness.[45] God does not abandon the world to chance or necessity, let alone to the forces of evil.[46] Divine providence must be conceived in terms of the free and personal activity of the Creator and Redeemer who "rules over all things in the world without detracting from their reality or impairing their contingent nature, freedom or order, yet in such a way that in his absolute freedom he makes everything to serve his ultimate purpose of love and of fellowship with himself."[47]

On this point Torrance is adamant that this providential power and activity cannot be construed in logical-causal or deterministic categories, but only in terms of the inexplicable power and activity of the immediate personal presence and operation of God.[48] When we take our cue from the kind of power and activity of God that we see in the virgin birth and bodily resurrection of Jesus, we see that all of God's activity manifests an astonishing subtle flexibility entirely different from what we find in the intramundane world around us.[49] The ultimate "how" of providence is

---

[43]Torrance, *Christian Doctrine*, pp. 222-43.
[44]Ibid., especially pp. 221-22.
[45]Ibid.
[46]Ibid., p. 224.
[47]Ibid.
[48]Ibid., p. 231. Torrance understands the nature of divine providence strictly in light of the kind of relation between divine agency and human agency that we saw in chapter three in the discussion of the logic of grace (see chapter three, pp. 117-23).
[49]Torrance, *Christian Doctrine*, p. 231. This tells us, Torrance argues, that God is free to interact with the world "in innumerable multivariable ways while being consistently true to his own nature as Holy Love and consistently true to his creation of the world with a contingent rational order of its own" (see p. 222).

the same as that of creation *ex nihilo*; it is an incomprehensible mystery that we may understand only as far as we are able in light of the activity of the triune God revealed in Jesus Christ.[50]

Also, only in light of God's self-revelation in Jesus Christ do we understand the scope of divine providence which extends, like Christ's atoning reconciliation, to all things. In Torrance's perspective God rules over the entire universe and everything that goes on within it in the subtle, personal, graceful manner described above.[51]

This includes even those things that defy God's will.[52] God is sovereignly free to take hold of that which resists God's will (including evil and death) and make it bow down and serve God's love. Yet it is a paradoxical power over evil and death as revealed in the cross, for it is the love and grace of God in Christ that plumbs the fearful depths of sin, evil and death, overruling them in order to undo and vanquish the evil entrenched in creation from within it through the power of suffering incarnational love.[53]

Through the kind of power revealed in Christ's death and resurrection, Torrance contends, God exercises an overruling sovereign and providential care for all of creation so that all things work together for good and serve God's ultimate purpose.[54] Though we cannot fully grasp *how* God does this, Torrance thinks that just as God made the wicked crucifixion of Jesus serve God's supreme purpose of love, so by the same cross God makes the worst things that happen to us serve God's design and the purpose of God's grace in our lives.[55]

---

[50]Ibid., p. 233.

[51]Ibid., p. 224.

[52]Ibid.

[53]Ibid., pp. 224-26. Torrance offers an illuminating treatment of the mystery of evil in connection with his discussion of divine providence. Torrance views evil not as merely privative but actively negative. Its fearful depth is revealed by the cross, where only the passion of God himself can overcome it. The cross also reveals that God does not condone or permit evil, but rather opposes, judges and overcomes it. While God does not condone or permit evil, it has a strange, impossible, yet "deadly, real existence." Torrance sees evil as infiltrating all creation, including the material and the spiritual. While evil is essentially anarchic and irrational, Torrance also contends that it is strangely personal, "a malevolent will," and an organized kingdom of evil with "a kind of headquarters . . . or powerhouse of utterly rebellious evil will or spirit," which Scripture calls Satan or the devil (see pp. 224-28).

[54]Ibid., p. 228.

[55]Ibid. Torrance also provides a fascinating discussion of the role of angels in God's redemptive and providential activity. See ibid., pp. 229-33, and Thomas F. Torrance, "The Spiritual Relevance of Angels," in *Alive to God: Studies in Spirituality Presented to James Houston*, ed. James Packer and Loren Wilkins (Downers Grove, Ill.: InterVarsity Press, 1992).

2. The Contingent Creation

Thus far this chapter has focused primarily on Torrance's understanding of God as sovereign Creator. The next two sections deal with the creation itself, first in terms of creation in its totality, and then the human creature in particular.

Creation ex nihilo. Torrance maintains that the concept of creation *ex nihilo*, that God created the entire universe and everything in it out of absolutely nothing as an entirely new event, is an essentially Judeo-Christian idea.[56] This understanding of creation has roots in the Old Testament in the opening chapters of Genesis where the Hebrew word which designates God's creative act *(bara)* means bringing something utterly new to pass. The term was never used for God's activity with previously existing matter.[57]

Already by the New Testament period, Torrance finds belief in creation *ex nihilo* established and taken for granted in Judaism. However, it is an idea that was repeatedly rejected within the history of Greek thought as irrational and impossible. The early church appropriated the idea of creation *ex nihilo* and viewed God as creating the universe both in matter and intelligible order out of nothing. Torrance argues that it was the resurrection of Jesus Christ from the dead that reinforced in the mind of the church the idea of God's absolute power over death and life, and therefore over the genesis of creation and its preservation.[58]

The debates surrounding Nicaea solidified both creation *ex nihilo* and the christocentric approach (which Torrance adopts and develops) by showing that the Creator-creature relation is radically different in character than the homoousial relation that exists between God the Father and Son of God incarnate as Jesus Christ, as noted above.[59] It is the fact that the *Creator* became a *creature* in the incarnation, in order to redeem a creation gone awry, Torrance contends, that especially forces theology to reflect more deeply on creation *ex nihilo* and the nature of created reality.[60]

As theology correlates creation *ex nihilo* and the incarnation of the eternal *Logos* within creation, Torrance see three crucial and christologically qualified ideas developing concerning creation: the contingence,

---

[56]Torrance, *Trinitarian Faith*, p. 95.
[57]Ibid.
[58]Ibid., pp. 96-97.
[59]Ibid., p. 97.
[60]Ibid.

the intelligibility and the freedom of God's creation.[61]

The contingence of creation. Contingence is not an easy concept, but it is pivotal to Torrance's theology. Torrance defines the contingence of creation in this way: "By contingence is meant, then, that created out of nothing the universe has no self-subsistence and no ultimate stability of its own, but that it is nevertheless endowed with an authentic reality and integrity of its own which must be respected."[62] The universe is created freely by an act of God's will, with an absolute beginning and an existence utterly distinct from God. Creation is neither necessary nor accidental. It could have been different, and it might not have been at all. It has a reality all its own different from God and a measure of independence.[63]

Torrance finds this way of thinking of creation reinforced by the incarnation, since the incarnation of the Creator within creation presupposes a fundamental distinction between God and creation, and also the full reality of material universe and events within it even for God.[64] It is this *independent* existence and reality that is given to creation *by God* that makes contingence such a difficult concept, for it means that the independence of creation is itself dependent, or contingent, on God.[65] This is true not simply of the origin of creation, but also its continuing spatio-temporal existence.[66]

This means, Torrance contends, that the created universe is neither self-supporting nor self-explaining; but it is not merely an appearance, for its existence, its reality and its lawfulness are grounded and sustained by God's creative Word and Spirit[67] (as we saw in the previous section on providence). Thus the meaning of this kind of universe lies not in itself, but beyond itself in God who created it and sustains it as an object of God's love (a point to which we will return in the section on natural theology below).

The incarnation discloses a further point about the contingent creation

---

[61]Ibid., pp. 97-98. Also see Thomas F. Torrance, *The Ground and Grammar of Theology* (Charlottesville, Va.: The University Press of Virginia, 1980), pp. 54-74, where Torrance argues that these three ideas were generated by classical Christian theology (especially the key Nicene theologians) and played a significant role in the reconstruction of ancient philosophy, science and culture. He sees these ideas as crucial to the genesis and development of modern natural science.

[62]Thomas F. Torrance, *Divine and Contingent Order* (London: Oxford University Press, 1981), p. vii.

[63]See ibid., pp. vii-viii, and Torrance, *Trinitarian Faith*, pp. 98-100.

[64]Torrance, *Trinitarian Faith*, p. 100.

[65]Ibid.

[66]Torrance, *Christian Doctrine*, p. 217.

[67]Torrance, *Trinitarian Faith*, p. 101.

in Torrance's theology. Creation is in a precarious state. So threatened is creation that God has to step in and save it by uniting creation with himself in atoning reconciliation.[68] Human beings are infected with a corruption that only the redemptive activity of *God* can overcome. In the incarnation, God transfers our creaturely contingent existence even more fully into himself, so that Jesus Christ secures the origin and end of creation in his own eternal being.[69] Thus the incarnation redeems and completes creation in its contingent relation to God.[70]

The intelligibility of creation. In classical Greek philosophy and science "contingence" meant that which is merely accidental, the antithesis of what is logical or necessary, and therefore excluded from rational discourse or scientific explanation.[71] Thus in Greek philosophy "contingent intelligibility" was almost an oxymoron.[72] Yet, Torrance contends that this is precisely what the Christian doctrine of creation *ex nihilo* implies. God created not only the materiality of the universe out of nothing, but its very rationality and order as well, including the human mind or soul.[73]

Torrance sees a clear-cut distinction not only between the uncreated being of God and all created being, but also between the uncreated rationality (Logos) of God and the created rationality of the universe, including human rationality, as we saw in chapter three in the relation between God's Word and rationality and human word and rationality in the mediation of revelation.[74] This bracketing of human rationality as part of the created rationality of the creaturely universe of space-time is also the basis of Torrance's rejection of cosmological and anthropological dualisms between the intelligible and the sensible or material, between soul and body, or mind and matter. God created the materiality and rationality of creation and of the human creature out of nothing and utterly contingent.

---

[68]Ibid.

[69]Ibid., p. 102.

[70]Ibid.

[71]Ibid., p. 100.

[72]See Torrance, *Ground and Grammar*, pp. 53-54. Torrance notes that this was one reason for the accusation of impiety (even atheism) against Christian faith, for creation *ex nihilo* called into question the "eternal forms" which linked the rational order of cosmos to the divine and provided the stability of the cosmos over against chaos. Contingence is Torrance's alternative to the old couplet of necessity-chance for describing the relation of creation to God. This is absolutely crucial for understanding many aspects of Torrance's theology, including his God-world relation and its implications for natural theology.

[73]Torrance, *Trinitarian Faith*, pp. 102-3.

[74]Ibid., p. 103. See chapter three above, pp. 100-113.

At the same time, the fact that God created the world (including its creaturely order and intelligibility) through the Son or Word (Logos) and regrounded the fallen creation in that Word (through the incarnation) led classical theology to affirm a *single* rational order pervading all created existence, for all creation has its beginning and its new beginning in a *single* rational source, the one Word of God.[75] Torrance views this as a pervasive, multi-variable, unitary order or intelligibility in the universe, because it has a single and inherently intelligible origin in the Word (Logos) of God, in both creation and recreation.[76]

Three further implications of this contingent intelligible order of the universe are important for understanding Torrance's doctrine of creation and for the discussion of natural science later in this chapter. The first is that God not only created a single rational order that pervades the entire creation, God also created within the universe "an intelligent counterpart" to the intelligibility immanent in the creation: human beings with minds able to understand and bring to articulation the rational order immanent in the creation.[77]

Yet, because the immanent intelligibility of the created universe is *contingent* (non-necessary—it could have been different), it cannot be known *a priori*. "Only by going to the natural process itself," Torrance contends, "and probing into its natural or intrinsic order" are we able to understand the *contingent* intelligibility inherent in creation.[78] Torrance argues that this Christian doctrine of the contingent intelligibility or rationality of the created universe injected into the thought stream of Western culture by classical (Nicene) Christian theology is in fact an ultimate belief or assumption crucial to the development of modern empirical science.[79]

The third implication of the contingent intelligibility of creation is that Torrance understands the orderly universe as an *open system*, rather than a closed one.[80] Torrance sees the Nicene theologians working this out

---

[75]Torrance, *Trinitarian Faith*, p. 103.
[76]Ibid. Also see Torrance, *Ground and Grammar*, pp. 52-54. This basic point has been something of a fundamental presupposition within the rise of modern science and modern Western culture so deeply influenced by science. Certain streams of postmodernism are less inclined in this direction, preferring a kind of radical pluralism and polymorphism to unitary order.
[77]Torrance, *Ground and Grammar*, pp. 4-6, 55.
[78]Ibid., p. 56.
[79]Ibid.
[80]Torrance, *Christian Doctrine*, p. 217.

in light of the incarnation, for the incarnation (and the resurrection) implies that the created order of the universe with its spatio-temporal structures is *open* to God's recreative and reordering activities in Jesus Christ in space and time.[81] This shatters necessitarian and deterministic notions of the universe and human life, Torrance contends, whether it be the tyranny of fate, inexorable cyclical processes, or the modern determinism of the materialist cause-and-effect universe.[82]

The universe has its origin and end in the freedom and love of the triune God revealed in Jesus Christ. In place of necessitarian and determinist perspectives, Torrance sees the Nicene theologians coming up with open-textured conceptions of natural law viewed as orderly patterns, subtle sequences, enduring structures called into being and sustained by God the Creator through God's Word.[83] Torrance finds this kind of understanding of natural law as astonishingly compatible with the findings of Einsteinian and post-Einsteinian natural science.

The freedom of creation. The notion of the contingence of creation, Torrance argues, carries with it the idea of the contingent freedom of creation as well. Contingence signifies that God's relation to the universe is neither necessary nor arbitrary, since God created and sustains it freely out of his love. Creation is not enslaved to chance or fate, Torrance argues, but rather shares God's own freedom in an appropriate creaturely way.[84]

Once again Torrance finds the root of this new conception of the freedom of the universe in Jesus Christ, for in Christ the sovereign Creator has come to redeem and recreate the fallen universe.[85] Christ is the head of the new creation in which the whole creation is reconciled and reestablished in relation to God, liberated, and therefore given a new freedom grounded in the freedom of God, the kind of freedom especially evident in the resurrection.[86]

---

[81]Torrance, *Trinitarian Faith*, p. 104. This means that while the incarnation is a new event in space and time and in the life of God, Torrance does not view it as a breach of natural law. The universe is not a closed cause-and-effect system "contained" within absolute space and time.

[82]See ibid., and Torrance, *Ground and Grammar*, pp. 57-58.

[83]Torrance, *Trinitarian Faith*, p. 105.

[84]Ibid., p. 105. Also see Torrance, *Ground and Grammar*, pp. 57-60.

[85]Torrance, *Trinitarian Faith*, p. 106.

[86]Ibid., pp. 106-7. Torrance argues that this idea of the redemption of the whole creation was stronger in Greek than Latin patristic thought because of the way Greek patristic thought linked the incarnation, atonement and creation, and because of the way the dualisms between the intelligible and sensible realms influenced Augustinian theology.

This freedom of creation is contingent and therefore limited freedom (the unlimited freedom of something that is contingent is a contradiction in terms). But Torrance argues that it is no less free simply because it is limited. Here again we see the elusive character of the independence of creation, which is nevertheless dependent on God in and for its liberty.[87] Torrance thinks that because the universe is sustained by the unlimited and inexhaustible freedom of God, the created freedom of the creation reflects God's freedom, and is inexhaustible and limitless in its own creaturely way within its relation to the Creator.[88] Torrance views the created universe as having unlimited and inexhaustible possibilities because of its relation to the sovereign Creator.[89]

Thus Torrance understands the universe as endowed with an astonishing reliability and constancy, but also a kind of spontaneity and freedom that takes us by surprise and repeatedly defies what we anticipate or can articulate.[90] Of course, Torrance contends, this is what we should expect of a creation called into being and sustained by the sovereign Creator revealed in Jesus Christ, for in Jesus Christ we discern this same astonishing combination of freedom and constancy, of spontaneity and reliability, of unpredictability and order.[91] And because Jesus Christ is *homoousios* with God the Father Almighty, the sovereign Creator of all things, Torrance sees Jesus Christ as the divine pledge not only of God's freedom, integrity and reliability, but also of the freedom, integrity and reliability of creation and its order.[92]

3. The Human Creature
While Torrance has written several articles on theological anthropology, he has not given the same kind of sustained attention to this subject (at least in his published work) that he has to the broader contours of the doctrine of creation. Of course, since humanity is a facet of the created universe, what we have discussed thus far of Torrance's understanding of the contingent creation applies to the human creature as well.

In line with his overall christocentric treatment of the doctrine of creation, Torrance argues that a Christian anthropology is properly

---

[87]Ibid., p. 107.
[88]Ibid.
[89]Ibid.
[90]Ibid., p. 108.
[91]Ibid.
[92]Ibid., pp. 108-9.

"formed in light of the humanity of Christ and in accordance with his redemptive purpose in the regeneration of mankind."[93] The incarnation entails the Son of God assuming our actual human being and nature in order to heal, restore and fulfill it in accordance with the divine telos for humanity of union and communion with God.[94] Thus Torrance views the humanity that the Son of God assumed from us in the incarnation, healed in body and soul and restored to proper relation with God and others, as of *archetypal* significance for all human beings.[95] In Jesus Christ we "discern what the basic structure of humanity is and ought to be."[96]

Since Jesus Christ himself, as well as the Christian account of creation, is rooted in and presupposes the Hebraic tradition and the Old Testament Scriptures, Torrance's christocentric anthropology develops out of the Hebraic view of humanity.

A unitary concept of humanity: body and soul. Torrance points out that of the three great traditions that have contributed significantly to the image of humanity in Western thought (Greek, Roman and Hebrew), only the Hebraic view was nondualist. Both Greek and Roman perspectives understood humanity in terms of "a radical dualism of body and soul (or mind)" and viewed the soul as in a sense "temporally imprisoned" in the body.[97]

The Hebraic tradition held a unitary view of human being in which soul (including mind) and body are essentially integrated and indivisible, body of soul and soul of body.[98] In addition, Hebrew creation emphasized that the soul as well as the body is created *ex nihilo* and therefore corruptible like the rest of creation, with no inherent immortality, and subject to disintegration. Yet the gracious and creative presence of God

---

[93]Thomas F. Torrance, "The Goodness and Dignity of Man in the Christian Tradition," *Modern Theology* 4, no. 4 (1988): 309.

[94]Ibid., p. 315.

[95]Thomas F. Torrance, "The Soul and Person in Theological Perspective," in *Religion, Reason and the Self: Essays in Honour of Hywel D. Lewis*, ed. Stewart R. Sutherland and T. A. Roberts (Cardiff: University of Wales Press, 1989), p. 115.

[96]Ibid.

[97]Thomas F. Torrance, *The Christian Frame of Mind: Reason, Order, and Openness in Theology and Natural Science*, 2nd ed. (Colorado Springs: Helmers & Howard, 1989), pp. 35-36. Characteristic of Greek religion and philosophy was the view that the human soul (or mind) is essentially divine or a spark of the divine, therefore immortal, and oriented toward the eternal ideas or divine forms of truth, goodness, and beauty. Also see Torrance, "Soul and Person," p. 105.

[98]Torrance, *Christian Frame*, pp. 35-36, and Torrance, "Goodness and Dignity," p. 310.

continuously sustains the whole human creature in life and affirms the whole human being, body and soul, as good.[99]

The incarnation, death and resurrection of Jesus Christ constitute the decisive factor in the deepening and radicalizing of the Christian understanding of humanity. Christian faith asserts that in the incarnation the very Word, or *Logos*, of God has become a creaturely human being within the materiality of the universe. This conviction is devastating to anthropological dualism, Torrance argues, for it destroys the notion of the unreality or irrationality of the material world, as well as the divine character of rational forms present in the world.[100]

The incarnation of the Word or Son of God within the structures of the material world also conflicted sharply with the Greek notion of the Logos as an immanent cosmological principle, while the incarnation reinforced the Hebraic understanding that the bodiliness of humanity is real to God, and loved and reaffirmed by God. By assuming the human mind in order to heal it, the incarnation strengthened the Jewish distinction between the contingent creaturely rationality of the universe created *ex nihilo* and God's uncreated Logos or Rationality,[101] and also reinforced the Hebraic concept that all the rational forms immanent in nature, including the human mind, are created out of nothing, are transitory and are fallen, and therefore need to be secured and redeemed by the divine Logos.[102]

The enigma of the human creature: dignity and depravity. Christ's death on the cross is significant for developing a Christian anthropology, for it reveals the precarious condition into which humanity has fallen, but also the worth of humanity loved to the uttermost by God.[103]

Gethsemane and the horror of Golgotha expose the fearful depth to which humanity has fallen, for there we see that only the passion of God, at *"infinite cost* to himself," can overturn the desperate plight of

---

[99]Torrance, "Soul and Person," p. 105, and Torrance, "Goodness and Dignity," p. 310. Torrance points to all of the Old Testament teaching regarding religious cleanness in physical life and behavior as evidence of the importance of the physical and also of the unity of body and soul. Also see Torrance, *Christian Frame*, p. 36.

[100]Ibid., p. 38.

[101]Torrance, "Soul and Person," p. 103.

[102]Torrance, *Christian Frame*, p. 39, and Torrance, "Soul and Person," p. 107.

[103]Torrance, "Goodness and Dignity," pp. 315-16. Of course, the enigma of humanity as fallen was significant in the Hebraic tradition, as is evident in the vivid and profound account of the fall of humanity in the early chapters of Genesis.

depraved humanity and restore humanity to a relation with God in which alone human beings are able to be fully human.[104] Yet the cross also reveals the dignity and worth of the human creature, for the passion of God in the passion of Christ discloses "the immeasurable worth, the infinite value, that God puts upon man in the price he has chosen to pay in order to share with him his own divine Life and Love."[105]

The resurrection of Jesus Christ, body and soul, brings to fruition God's full purpose for humanity.[106] In Torrance's mind "the resurrection recapitulates and transcends the original creation of man, making good the deficiency in the unstable, fleeting nature of his contingent being, and finalizing his reality and integrity as body of his soul and soul of his body through giving him participation in the eternal life of God embodied in his Incarnate Son."[107] Our resurrection in body and soul comes through union with Christ, since his resurrection is the generating source of ours.[108]

Together the incarnation, cross and resurrection of Jesus Christ secure, affirm and finalize humanity's contingent creaturely existence as embodied soul; they expose and heal fallen and depraved humanity; and they establish a distinctively Christian anthropology.[109] In Jesus Christ's life, death and resurrection, we learn that for humanity to live without a relation with God is to be less than human and to often fall into the monstrous inhumanity so recurrent in history. Torrance contends that for humanity to live in union with God, as we see in the life of Jesus, is for humanity to become fully human and personal.[110]

The human creature as person in relation: the image of God. The archetypal significance of Jesus Christ is nowhere more important for Torrance than in connection with the concept of person. Torrance contends that God's eternal Word or Son *personally* becoming a human being in Jesus Christ generated an intense personalization of the Christian understanding of God and of humanity, and led to the development of personal and relational concepts of both God and humanity quite different from Greco-

---

[104]Ibid.
[105]Torrance, "Goodness and Dignity," p. 316.
[106]Torrance, "Soul and Person," p. 106.
[107]Ibid.
[108]Ibid., p. 107.
[109]Ibid.
[110]Torrance, "Goodness and Dignity," p. 315.

Roman perspectives which lacked a concept of person.[111]

Torrance thinks that Jesus' teaching and his mutual relationship of astonishing intimacy with God (whom Jesus called, "Abba," his Father) helped generate the concept of the personal. But of even greater significance was the developing conviction on the part of the church that in Jesus Christ, *God* has come among us in unlimited love, and that in the outpouring of the Holy Spirit at Pentecost, *God* has come again to dwell in us and unite us through Christ in communion with God the Father.[112] This compelled the early church to develop the onto-relational concept of person, mentioned at several points in previous chapters, in which the relations between the persons are as real as (and constitutive of) the persons.

In the formulation of the doctrines of Christ and the Trinity, Torrance argues, the church developed the technical theological concept of *person*, "applied in a unique way to God who is the source of all created personal being, and in another way to human beings who are personal in virtue of their relation to God and to one another within the interpersonal structure of humanity."[113]

This brings us to Torrance's understanding of humanity created in the image of God. In the Old Testament, human beings are created in God's image not as solitary individuals, but in human relations, particularly as male and female.[114]

Yet humanity's relational *imago Dei* (image of God) in the Old Testament is grounded in the even more basic relation of humanity to God, for the image of God has to do with the fact that the human being is "constituted a relational being basically through a . . . relation with the Creator."[115] In other words, this relational image of God is not something that human beings possess statically and innately, but rather is dynamic and contingent, for it is called into existence by a free relation to God and

---

[111]Torrance, "Soul and Person," pp. 103-4, and Torrance, *Christian Frame*, p. 37. While there is no specific concept of "person" in pre-Christian Hebraic thought, Torrance does find the basic framework for its development in the Old Testament teaching about God and in the commandments to love God and one's neighbor (see Torrance, *Christian Frame*, p. 37).

[112]Torrance, "Soul and Person," p. 114, and Torrance, *Christian Frame*, p. 38.

[113]Torrance, *Christian Frame*, p. 38, and Torrance, "Soul and Person," p. 114.

[114]Torrance, "Goodness and Dignity," p. 311. Torrance can even say that owing to the ontological inseparability of soul and body, "difference in sex is not simply a feature of the body . . . but is intrinsic to the human soul which . . . *is* either male or female," and that therefore man and woman "need each other to be human." Also see Torrance, "Soul and Person," pp. 108-9.

[115]Torrance, "Goodness and Dignity," p. 311.

reflects the uncreated relations within God.[116] Of course human sin, guilt and alienation disrupt this relational *imago Dei*, so that it is restored only in Jesus Christ.

Torrance argues that the Old Testament view of humanity created "in the image of God was considerably deepened and reinforced through the acute personalisation of human relations with God in Jesus Christ."[117] In fact, in light of his understanding of the vicarious humanity of Christ, it should come as no surprise that Torrance views *Jesus Christ himself* as "the image of God in a unique and supreme sense, for he is both the image and reality of God in his incarnate Person."[118] This of course means that "we human beings are held to be the image of God . . . not in virtue of our rational nature or of anything we are inherently in our own beings, but solely through a relation to God in grace into which he has brought us in the wholeness and integrity of our human being."[119]

Thus as we saw in chapter three, in Jesus Christ all of our relations with God and with one another are intensely personalized, for Jesus Christ is "the one *personalising Person*, while we are *personalised persons* who draw from him the true substance of our personal being both in relation to God and in relation to one another."[120]

This also means that the image of God restored through the vicarious humanity of Jesus Christ, and mediated to us in the Spirit who unites us in Christ, is closely related to Torrance's understanding of *theosis*. *Theosis* or *theopoiesis* is not the divinizing or deification of the human soul or creaturely being, Torrance contends, but rather is the Spirit of God humanizing and personalizing us by uniting us with Christ's vicarious humanity in a way that both confirms us in our creaturely reality utterly different from God, and yet also adapts us in our contingent nature for knowledge of God, for communion with God and for fellowship with

---

[116]Ibid., pp. 310-12, and Torrance, "Soul and Person," pp. 110-12.

[117]Torrance, *Christian Frame*, p. 39.

[118]Ibid.

[119]Ibid., and Torrance, "Goodness and Dignity," p. 317.

[120]Torrance, *Christian Frame*, p. 39. Elsewhere Torrance says that if Jesus Christ "is both the Image and Reality of God, then he is the unique image-constituting Image of God, and it is by reference to what he is that we must now think of human beings as created in the image of God" (see Torrance, "Goodness and Dignity," p. 317). Thus he maintains that "we are not human in virtue of some essence of humanity that we have in ourselves but only in virtue of what we receive from his Humanity which embodies the Life that is the Light of humanity. For us really to be human, therefore is to be in Christ" (see Torrance, "Goodness and Dignity," p. 318).

one another.[121] Thus *theosis/theopoiesis* is closely related to this relational *imago Dei*, for in Torrance's trinitarian perspective, the Spirit unites us to Christ and through Christ with the Father, and therefore brings our creaturely relations to their true end and fulfillment in union and communion with the triune God.[122]

This means that for Torrance the image of God in humanity has "to do with the way in which the basic inter-human relation called into existence by the Word and Spirit of God, is made to reflect in its creaturely difference a transcendent relations within God."[123] These creaturely relations represent a *created correspondence* (*not* an inherent analogy of being) to the uncreated trinitarian relation within God.[124]

God is a fullness of personal being, according to Torrance, or an ineffa-

---

[121]Torrance, "Soul and Person," p. 113. This is what Torrance means by "a distinctive transcendental determination" of human being for God.

[122]Ibid., p. 112.

[123]Torrance, "Goodness and Dignity," p. 311.

[124]Ibid., p. 312. There are many issues at stake here, including the fundamental character of creaturely being and the question of an inherent point of contact *(Anknüpfungspunkt)* between humanity and God that can ground an independent natural theology. Torrance argues that there is no inherent point of contact between God and humanity because of the contingent character of the created order, including the human soul and rationality, which are also created out of nothing. Torrance can say that a human being does not "possess" a "spirit" as "an ingredient or potency in his make-up, or as a 'spark of the divine.'" Rather the human "spirit" is "the ontological qualification of his soul, and indeed of his whole creaturely being, brought about and maintained by the Holy Spirit, in virtue of which he lives and moves and has his being in God, as man made in his image and likeness" (see Torrance, "Soul and Person," p. 110). He also speaks of it as a "transcendental determination" of the person's being as an embodied soul.

What Torrance is trying to say is that because of his interactionist God-world relation and his dynamic concept of God's being and activity, which inhere in each other, Torrance is able to conceptualize a dynamic and personal *relation* of the human being to God in which God is actively and personally present to the human being and maintains the human being in a personal relation to God and to other human persons. When Torrance speaks of "transcendental determination," he does not understand this in a deterministic manner, but rather in terms of the personalizing and humanizing activity of God, which respects and grounds the human creature in freedom. "All of grace" means "all of humanity," as developed in chapter three in the section on the logic of grace, pp. 117-23.

What this really signifies is Torrance's fundamental conviction of the free, dynamic, relational and personal character of God and the contingent, free, dynamic and relational character of creaturely reality, including human beings, where creaturely reality becomes *personal* in relation to God.

Because of human sin and guilt, the onto-relational being of humanity is radically disrupted and human beings "cannot overcome the disruption in their constitutive relations with God and others" (see Torrance, "Goodness and Dignity," p. 313). This, of course, affects

ble communion of persons in perichoretic relations with one another in the one divine being.[125] Human persons are not of one and the same being. Yet, Torrance says, they "are not without an inherent relatedness or 'community-ness' among themselves in which they bear a created reflection of the transcendent relatedness or 'community-ness,' inherent in God."[126] It is this onto-personal, onto-relational structure of humanity called into being *by grace* in relation to God that is the *imago Dei* in Torrance's theology.

In light of the christological and trinitarian reconstitution and personalization of the human being in the image of God, Torrance argues that while we do not understand all that this means for the person "who is 'without Christ,' it certainly means for a man 'in Christ' that his human nature as body of his mind and mind of his body is affirmed with a spiritual wholeness and a new ontological interrelation with others that transcends his original creation, for now he exists not just alongside of the Creator, but in such a way that his human being is anchored in the very Being of God."[127] Here Torrance sees humanity as having a unique place within the universe, called and appointed to serve Christ "as covenant-partner" in the on-going actualization of Christ's redemption and renewal within the universe, and also as *priest of creation* on the boundary between earthly and heavenly reality.[128]

Humanity, priest of creation. This idea that humanity lives on the boundary between two "worlds," the earthly and the heavenly or the physical and the spiritual, provides both a significant rationale for the pursuit of natural science, Torrance argues, and an important theological basis for positive dialogue between theology and natural science.[129] As unitary beings who are indivisibly integrated soul of body and body of soul, and uniquely related to God through Christ in the presence of God's Spirit, humanity spans both worlds.[130] Humanity is thus the one place in

---

the character of the Spirit's presence to the sinful, alienated human creature, for the Spirit is holy and our sinful human being cannot endure the fearful judgment of God's holiness brought to bear upon us by the Holy Spirit. This means that only through the mediation of Christ can the Holy Spirit be poured out upon human beings so that they can again come to more fully reflect the image of God that God intended them to be (see pp. 320-21).

[125]Torrance, "Soul and Person," p. 115.

[126]Ibid.

[127]Torrance, "Goodness and Dignity," p. 321.

[128]Ibid., p. 322.

[129]Torrance, *Christian Frame*, p. 41, and Torrance, "Goodness and Dignity," p. 311.

[130]Torrance, "Goodness and Dignity," p. 311.

space and time where knowledge of sovereign Creator and also knowledge of the contingent creation come to articulation.

Even modern natural science, Torrance notes, has had (and is still having) to come to terms with the emergence of conscious mind as an essential feature of the expanding universe.[131] This means that human scientific knowledge of the universe is itself part of that expanding universe as scientists continue to uncover the hidden patterns of order and symmetry of the universe. This has been called the "anthropic principle," the highly improbable development of such a finely balanced expanding universe in which humanity and science could emerge.[132]

The new science has been moving steadily away from what Torrance calls the "old-fashioned science" that tried to explain higher levels of order (conscious human mind, for example) in terms of a lower level (the chemical and physical properties of the brain).[133] Rather than reducing the order of the universe downward to the level of mechanistic, physico-chemical relations, Torrance argues, the new science discloses a universe characterized by a hierarchy of levels with an ascending gradient of richer and more complex order.[134]

Within this multilevel structure of the universe, Torrance sees that "each level is coordinated with other levels 'above' or 'below' it in such a way that its own organisation is open at its boundary conditions to the one above it, that it is finally explicable only through reference to the organization of that higher level, and that it plays the same role in relation to the level below it."[135] Human beings span all these levels as ordered open systems. The new natural science sees humanity as occupying the uppermost level of the created universe, the product of the contingent freedom and spontaneous, self-organizing order characteristic of this universe with its highly improbable anthropic principle.[136]

---

[131]See Torrance, *Ground and Grammar*, p. 4, and Torrance, *Christian Mind*, p. 59.

[132]See Torrance, *Christian Mind*, p. 59.

[133]See Torrance, *Ground and Grammar*, pp. 13, 142; Thomas F. Torrance, *Transformation and Convergence in the Frame of Knowledge: Explorations in the Interrelations of Scientific and Theological Enterprise* (Grand Rapids, Mich.: Eerdmans, 1984), p. 62; and Torrance, *Divine and Contingent Order*, pp. 18-21.

[134]Torrance, *Ground and Grammar*, pp. 13, 142, and Thomas F. Torrance, *Reality and Scientific Theology* (Edinburgh: Scottish Academic Press, 1985), p. ix.

[135]Torrance, *Christian Frame*, p. 60. This idea that each level is finally explicable only through reference to a higher level is a central and crucial point in Torrance's reconceived natural theology, as we will see later in this chapter.

[136]See Torrance, *Christian Frame*, pp. 59-62, and Torrance, *Ground and Grammar*, p. 142.

However, from Torrance's perspective as a theologian, *God* has created the universe with this astonishing and subtle order and anthropic principle. God endowed humanity with mind and the dynamic ability to investigate and interpret this astonishing order for this very purpose. In and through humanity, the universe God has created discovers and articulates knowledge of itself. Thus Torrance sees the human scientist "as the priest of creation, whose office it is to interpret the books of nature written by the finger of God, to unravel the universe in its marvelous patterns and symmetries, and to bring it all into orderly articulation in such a way that it fulfills its proper end as the vast theater of glory in which the Creator is worshipped and hymned and praised by his creatures."[137]

Without humanity, nature is mute, unable to voice the creaturely wonder and praise for the glory and majesty of the Creator. In this light, Torrance contends, proper natural science becomes a religious activity and duty done out of gratitude and obedience to God.[138] Viewed this way, natural science and theological science present complementary accounts of the created universe of space and time and ought to be regarded not as opponents, but as partners before God in service to God.[139]

4. Natural Science and Theological Science

While it is clear, in light of the previous section, that Torrance sees theology and natural science not as adversaries, but as partners in service to God, the details of the relations between them are complex, both in terms of his understanding of the history of those relations and in light of Torrance's vision for future dialogue between these special sciences. Indeed, Torrance has devoted considerable attention and publication to this subject over many years. Here we will deal with the salient features and provide the reader with a bibliographic trail for further research.

While Torrance is well aware of the difficult and hostile relations between theology and science in the modern era, as in the case of the religion and science controversies, he opposes the adversary mode of relation be-

---

[137]Torrance, *Ground and Grammar*, pp. 5-6.

[138]Ibid., pp. 1, 111-12. Elsewhere, Torrance states that humanity is "called to be a kind of midwife to creation, assisting nature out of its divinely given abundance constantly to give birth to new forms of life and richer patterns of order" (see Torrance, "Goodness and Dignity," p. 322).

[139]Torrance, *Ground and Grammar*, pp. 6-7.

tween the two disciplines.[140] Torrance also rejects the old idea that natural science is concerned with *how* nature operates in its various processes and relations, whereas theology is interested in *why* questions about the beginning of creation and its ends.[141]

Torrance's own research and experience concerning the interface between theology and science point to radically different scenario, one in which, in spite of critical questioning, there has been substantive beneficial influence and hidden commonality between the two disciplines. This has led Torrance into serious reflection on why this is so, and also to his reconceptualization of the relation between theology and natural science as one of positive dialogue, convergence and transformation.[142]

Beneficial influence, hidden commonality. As noted above, when Torrance speaks of theological *science*, he does not mean that theology is built on natural science or that theology must conform to the methods or requirements of natural science or any other special science.[143] In fact, Torrance argues that the opposite is more nearly the case: modern empirical/theoretical science actually owes its existence to several crucial concepts that really had their genesis not in natural science, but in classical (Nicene) Christian theology from the fourth through the sixth century.[144]

The rational unity of the universe. The first of these three ideas is the rational unity of the universe rooted in Judeo-Christian monotheism and the conviction that, since *one* God created the entire universe (matter and rational form) out of nothing, the universe is therefore *one* har-

---

[140]See Torrance, *Theological Science*, p. xvii, and Palma, "Thomas F. Torrance," p. 26. One could write an interesting history of theology over the past two centuries as a massive attempt to come to terms with modern science. There is a repeated tendency of modern theology to ground religion and Christian faith in a *transcendental* realm beyond the Newtonian cause-and-effect material universe and the acids of critical historiography in order to protect the essence of Christian faith.

[141]Torrance, *Christian Frame*, p. 24-25.

[142]One of the interesting facets of reading Torrance's work is the radically different perspective he so often brings to a particular area of theological conversation, as in the case here of the relations between theology and science or his idea that Nicaea represents the Christianizing of Greco-Roman culture rather than the Hellenization of Christian faith.

[143]See the introduction, pp. 21-25.

[144]Torrance argues that natural science did not, and could not, generate or demonstrate these "masterful ideas." See Torrance, *Transformation*, p. vii; Torrance, *Christian Frame*, pp. 29-30, 66; Torrance, *Ground and Grammar*, pp. 44-74; and Torrance, *Divine and Contingent*, pp. viii-ix, 1-25.

monious system characterized by a unitary, multi-variable order throughout. Thus wherever science directs inquiry into the universe, science anticipates a consistent rational order accessible to human knowing due to the single Source of the universe's being and intelligibility.[145]

The contingent rationality of the universe. A second idea important to the emergence of modern science is the contingent rationality of the universe, a rationality (including the human mind) created by God out of nothing and utterly different from God, a rationality that is neither necessary, nor arbitrary, and might have been different than it is. Torrance argues that contingent rationality means that we cannot deduce the order or intelligibility of the universe from what we know about God, nor can we regard that order as an embodiment of eternal, *a priori* or antecedent forms, ideas or formal causes that can be known and developed apart from actually investigating nature (Euclidean geometry, for example).[146] *Contingent* order or rationality has to be investigated by empirical contact with nature and by experiments in order to be discovered

---

[145]See Torrance, *Ground and Grammar*, pp. 44-74, especially pp. 52-60; and Torrance, *Divine and Contingent*, pp. 1-25, especially pp. 2-5. Torrance traces the genesis of these three ideas and also their history in Western culture up to and through the rise of modern science and the full and explicit reemergence especially of the concept of contingence in Maxwellian, Einsteinian and post-Einsteinian science.

[146]See chapter four, p. 133 n. 26, for a discussion of the way Einstein's work transformed the way geometry is integrated into scientific endeavor. Torrance sees Newton as applying or imposing Euclidean geometry on the universe of bodies in motion and thereby distorting knowledge of the universe (see Torrance, *Transformation*, p. ix). Clerk Maxwell's work already revealed the failure of Newtonian science to explain the actual reality and behavior of the electromagnetic field, which cannot be understood as discrete particles extrinsically related, but rather as a continuous field of force in which particles are intrinsically related in a unity of field and particles. But it was Einstein's work, especially in his theory of general relativity, that revealed that geometry as an independent system of ideas developed as a deductive mathematical discipline apart from actual spatial relations among physical objects, cannot be imposed upon the physical universe. This forced Einstein to reject Newton's dualism between bodies in motion and absolute mathematical space and time. See ibid., pp. viii-xii; Thomas F. Torrance, *Space, Time and Resurrection* (Grand Rapids, Mich.: Eerdmans, 1976), p. ix; and Torrance, *Ground and Grammar*, p. 11.

This was a crucial event in the development of natural science, for it undermined the Newtonian understanding of the universe as a vast mechanistic and deterministic cause-and-effect system and replaced it with a much more dynamic and open-structured order, far more congenial to classical Christian theology, but also reinforced the masterful idea of the contingent freedom of the universe. Here Torrance sees the work of Katsir and Prigogine on open or nonequilibrium systems as indicating an even more open, spontaneous, subtle and free kind of order that cannot be understood and articulated within the

and known.[147] Thus Torrance sees the idea of contingent order as absolutely essential to the genesis of modern empirical/theoretical science.

The contingent freedom of the universe. The contingent freedom of the
universe means that the universe is not enslaved to any alien power,
fate, determinism or chance, but has finite freedom, potentiality and inexhaustible possibilities deriving from God's own unlimited freedom.
Torrance sees this as part of the reason why the universe keeps surprising
science, disclosing patterns and order in an astonishing range and depth
of intelligibility that keeps science pressing forward in its inquiries.[148]

Torrance argues that "modern empirical science owes its existence to
the injection of these notions of contingence and contingent order into the
basic stock of ideas in our understanding of nature."[149] In fact, despite their

---

old couplet of chance and necessity, as noted at several points above. This does not mean
that Einsteinian and post-Einsteinian natural science simply discard Newtonian science.
Rather Newton's work has a limited range of applicability (see Torrance, *Transformation*,
pp. viii-xii). Also see Torrance, *Christian Frame*, pp. 29-31, and Torrance, *Ground and Grammar*, pp. 10-14.

Einstein's criticism of Newton's way of relating geometry and experience and the development of general relativity also raised serious epistemological questions, for Einstein's
work demonstrated a very different way of relating the empirical and theoretical elements
in epistemic activity in natural science. Analytic methods and atomistic thinking tend to
break up the actual unitary, relational, dynamic connections where being and event, geo-
metrical and dynamic aspects actually exist together (form in being) in the natural universe. Thus Einstein's combining these elements reveals that he operated with an
integrative epistemology (way of integrating form in human knowing) that transcends the
limits of analytical and deductive methodologies. We will return to this extremely significant point in chapter nine below on theological method. Here we see the deep interconnections between Torrance's God-world relation, his theological account of the character
of the created universe, and how they are generally compatible with the new science. All
of this is deeply interconnected with Torrance's epistemology and his reconceived natural
theology (see Torrance, *Transformation*, pp. viii-xii). Also see Torrance, *Christian Frame*, pp.
29-31, and Torrance, *Ground and Grammar*, pp. 10-14.

[147]Scientific inquiry involves asking appropriate questions of nature and allowing nature to
disclose its coherent patterns of behavior, order and intelligibility. Scientists develop ideas,
theories and methods of inquiry in light of what they learn from nature and refine them
through further investigation and experiment in actual contact with nature, not simply on
the basis of external authorities or preconceived systems of thought. See Torrance, *Ground
and Grammar*, pp. 44-74, especially pp. 52-60; Torrance, *Divine and Contingent*, pp. 1-25,
especially pp. 2-5; and Torrance, *Christian Frame*, pp. 29-30, 65-66.

[148]See Torrance, *Ground and Grammar*, pp. 44-74, especially pp. 52-60; and Torrance, *Divine
and Contingent*, pp. 1-25, especially pp. 2-5.

[149]Torrance, *Divine and Contingent*, p. viii. Torrance's main purpose in writing *Divine and
Contingent Order* was to clarify and carry forward the notions of contingence, and contingent order and freedom. The history of these ideas is complex, for contingence and contingent order encountered resistance when they were first generated by early Christian the-

importance for natural science, Torrance maintains that rational unity and contingent intelligibility cannot be proved by natural science, since they have to be assumed in all scientific operations.[150] All of this reveals that modern empirical/theoretical science has learned far more from theological science than is generally realized.[151]

Other examples of cross-fertilization. There are other incidents of what Torrance calls "cross-fertilization" or "hidden-traffic" in which ideas taken from theological science have positively and decisively influenced natural science.[152] Torrance contends that James Clerk Maxwell utilized an onto-relational concept of "person" drawn from theology in developing his dynamical field theory, a theory that Torrance regards as the most significant breakthrough in modern physical science between Newton and Einstein.[153]

This relation of positive influence and hidden commonality between

---

ology (as noted earlier in this chapter) and in subsequent history (see pp. viii, 5-25). Also see Torrance, *Ground and Grammar*, pp. 60-74. The first idea was damaged, whereas the other two, contingent order and freedom, were submerged and lost for a time. We cannot trace Torrance's detailed account of the history of these three masterful ideas here. What is important is that Torrance sees the kind of classical theology he embraces as having a profound influence on the genesis and development of modern natural science.

[150] Torrance, *Divine and Contingent*, p. ix.

[151] Torrance, *Ground and Grammar*, p. 7. Torrance also finds all three of these masterful concepts forced out into the open again by the progress of science through the work of Maxwell, Einstein, Polanyi and others, a point to which we will return later in this section (see pp. 110-11). This has taken place through the discovery that the universe is in a state of continuous expansion, and thus is finite, temporal, with an absolute beginning and therefore singular and contingent (see Torrance, *Christian Frame*, p. 48).

[152] Torrance, *Ground and Grammar*, p. 7.

[153] Ibid. This onto-relational concept of person, as noted above, is one in which the relations between persons are ontological and person-constituting, or part of what persons are as persons. Also see Torrance, *Christian Frame*, pp. xxvi-xxxi, for W. Jim Neidhart's account of this, and Torrance, *Transformation*, pp. 229-33. Torrance sees this onto-relation concept of person mediated from Nicene trinitarian theology through Richard of St. Victor, Duns Scotus, John Major to John Calvin and Amandus Polanus, and then to Scotland. He contrasts this concept of person with the analytic, individualist notion of person in Boethius and Thomas Aquinas, and later in John Locke and Auguste Comte, who thought of persons as separate individuals connected with one another through external relations (see Torrance, *Transformation*, p. 230).

Maxwell developed an onto-relational field theory, Torrance argues, in which particles are never isolated and only externally related, but rather are so interconnected in fields of force that they have to be conceived as converging points of force or nodules of energy within continuous fields in which particles are inseparable from their relations and interactions. See again Torrance, *Christian Frame*, pp. xxvi-xxxi; Torrance, *Transformation*, pp. 229-33; and Torrance's introduction to James Clerk Maxwell, *A Dynamical Theory of the Electromagnetic Field*, ed. Thomas F. Torrance (Edinburgh: Scottish Academic Press, 1982), pp. ix-27.

theology and natural science also flows in the other direction. Natural science has actually played an important role in Torrance's own theological work. Early on, Torrance found that the rigor of physical science's research and method forces theology to clarify its own scientific status and method, and therefore helps theological science be true to its own subject matter, God in God's self-revelation.[154]

Another area where theological science and natural science have a lot in common, Torrance argues, is in their struggle in the modern period with "epistemological problems that are basically similar owing to the framework of thought within which both have had to function and owing to their common conflict with dualist, phenomenalist and mechanistic habits of thought."[155] Torrance thinks that theological science can learn a great deal from the new science in overcoming certain persistent difficulties.[156] We will return to this point in chapter nine on theological method.

In addition, Torrance sees the new Einsteinian science playing a crucial role in "liberating theology from the tyranny of false ideas" such as a closed mechanistic and deterministic universe or a receptacle notion of space, both of which have created many serious difficulties for theology.[157] It is difficult

---

[154]Torrance, *Ground and Grammar*, p. 7, and Thomas F. Torrance, *Reality and Evangelical Theology* (Philadelphia: Westminster Press, 1982), pp. 11-12. Torrance's own dialogues with scientists such as Sir Bernard Lovell (a relative), pressed Torrance to develop the rigor of his scientific method in theology (see Torrance, "A Pilgrimage," p. 62).
  Simply examining a bibliography of Torrance's publications, or noting his numerous references to Maxwell, Einstein, Polanyi, Ilya Prigogine, John Wheeler, etc., reveals the level of resonance between Torrance's theological reflection and the new physical science. Torrance forthrightly states, "I have found the thought of great scientists like James Clerk Maxwell, Albert Einstein, and Michael Polanyi to be helpful in my theological activity" (Thomas F. Torrance, *Preaching Christ Today* [Grand Rapids, Mich.: Eerdmans, 1994], p. 62).
[155]Torrance, *Transformation*, p. xii. By framework of thought, Torrance means the overarching set of unquestioned presuppositions, concepts, attitudes and habits of mind that we acquire often tacitly and share with others in our particular culture and place in history, and which exercise a regulative influence over how we think, formulate theories and weigh evidence. Such frameworks of knowledge are, Torrance argues, resistant to new ideas and to the reconstruction or transformation of those frameworks (see pp. x-xi).
[156]Ibid. Also see Torrance, *Evangelical Theology*, p. 11-12.
[157]Torrance, *Ground and Grammar*, p. 111. Also see pp. 184-85 n. 146. Torrance treats the problem of a receptacle notion of space at great length in his important book, *Space, Time and Incarnation* (London: Oxford University Press, 1969). Also see Thomas F. Torrance, "The Relation of the Incarnation to Space in Nicene Theology," in *The Ecumenical World of Orthodox Civilization*, ed. A. Blane (The Hague: Mouton, 1973), pp. 43-70; Thomas F. Torrance, *God and Rationality* (London: Oxford University Press, 1971), pp. 123-34; and Elmer M. Colyer, *The Nature of Doctrine in T. F. Torrance's Theology* (Eugene, Ore.: Wipf & Stock, 2001). Torrance points out that relativity theory has dealt a crushing blow to the receptacle con-

to make sense of the incarnation, miracles or the resurrection within the
Newtonian cosmology other than as a breach or suspension of natural law.[158]

Torrance, however, sees Einstein's work as transcending and qualify-
ing Newtonian physics and its deterministic and mechanical conceptualization of the universe.[159] The universe revealed by the new science is not
understood "as a closed deterministic system, but as a continuous and
open system of contingent realities and events with an inherent unifying
order . . . a finite but unbounded universe with open, dynamic structures."[160] It is a finite, unbounded universe open to the activity of God and
compatible with the interactionist God-world relation that Torrance embraces and finds arising out of classic Nicene theology.[161]

In fact, Torrance finds that "the universe of space and time as understood by the new science is far more congenial to Christian theology than
that developed by ancient science or by Enlightenment science."[162] This is

---

ception of space and time as independent of what goes on within them. Yet, Torrance
unequivocally asserts—and this is an important point for those who think that he is building theology on post-Einsteinian science—that "this does not mean that Christian theology must give up the old scientific notions of space in order to adopt a more modern one,
but that dialogue with natural science in its struggle to understand space and time in the
natural processes of this world, theology on its part must strive to develop a strictly *theological* understanding of space and time in the light of God's interaction with this world as
revealed in the incarnation of His Son in space-time" (Torrance, *Rationality*, p. 131). Torrance also asserts, "This does not mean that Christian theology can or should ever be
grounded on natural science, but it does mean that as we allow ourselves to be questioned
by rigorous scientific analysis we are helped to discriminate what is truly theological, arising on the ground of God's self-revelation, from distorting foreign structures that have so
often been grafted on to it but which turn out to be no more that obsolete deposits in the
Christian consciousness from some passing phase of human culture" (Thomas F. Torrance,
Theology in Reconciliation: Essays Towards Evangelical and Catholic Unity in East and West
(Grand Rapids, Mich.: Eerdmans, 1975), p. 275.

[158]Torrance points out that Newton's understanding of a closed mechanistic universe of
determinist cause-and-effect relations leads to a deism in which any interaction of God
with the universe or human life and history is ruled out or conceptualized as a breach of
natural law (see Torrance, *Divine and Contingent*, p. 10). Torrance also notes that Newton's
vehement rejection of Athanasius' understanding of the incarnation and Newton's acceptance of Arius's position reveals Newton's tendency toward deism. God cannot become
incarnate in a universe that is inertially contained by absolute space and time that Newton
identified with the divine "sensorium" or mind of God.

[159]Of course, Newtonian physics, with its cause-and-effect relations, is not simply rejected,
but has only a limited range of applicability, as noted above.

[160]Torrance, *Divine and Contingent*, p. 11.

[161]In this way, the Einsteinian perspective frees theology from the tyranny of a closed, mechanistic, determinist universe.

[162]Torrance, *Preaching Christ*, p. 61. Also see Torrance, *Ground and Grammar*, pp. 11, 83. God's

not to say that theological science must be grounded on the new science, but that there is positive influence and commonality between theology and the new science.[163]

Reasons for the influence and commonality. The significant areas of hidden commonality and mutual positive influence between theological science and natural science have led Torrance to give substantial reflection as to why this is so.

Fundamental to Torrance's reflection on the relation between theology and natural science is his conviction that it is *within* the universe of space-time and its contingent order that God makes himself known to humanity through Israel and above all in the incarnation of the Son or Word of God in Jesus Christ. The human, historical and bodily character of the incarnation underscores the fact that God's self-revelation and self-communication come to us in and through the empirical creaturely objectivities and intelligibilities of this universe of space and time.[164]

This means that theology cannot be limited simply to the relation between God and humanity, Torrance contends, as if humanity were alien to the world of space and time. Rather theology is concerned with God-human-world relations, for God has placed humanity within the world of space-time, and humanity embodies all of the interrelated levels of creation from the sub-atomic through the bio-chemical to the mental, personal and social. By implication, God's self-revelation in the incarnation spans all of these levels as well.[165]

---

interaction with the open universe of space-time and human history in revelation, incarnation, atonement and resurrection is no longer to be regarded as a breach of natural law, but rather God's re-creative activity in a universe destined for human life, and for union and communion with the triune God who created it. Even the uniqueness of God's self-revelation in Jesus Christ is not foreign to the new science, since science itself has had to come to terms with singularities such as the invariant speed of light, the absolute beginning of the universe from an original dense state of all matter and energy (black hole), and the narrow margin in the rate expansion needed for the universe ever to sustain human life. See Torrance, *Preaching Christ*, pp. 63-65, and Torrance, *Ground and Grammar*, p. 3.

Torrance has found among natural scientists many who are more open to understanding and appreciating the singularity, uniqueness and finality of the incarnation and resurrection of Jesus Christ, than among professors in religious studies departments (see Torrance, *Preaching Christ*, pp. 64-65). Torrance notes that the concept of singularity was repugnant to classical modern science arising within the Enlightenment with its passion for universality and timeless and necessary truth, which in philosophy and science had the effect of resolving or discounting singularity and uniqueness (see pp. 63-65).

[163]Torrance, *Preaching Christ*, p. 73.

[164]Torrance, *Evangelical Theology*, pp. 10-11.

[165]Ibid., pp. 11, 24-30.

Thus it is the full incarnational reality of Jesus Christ that leads Torrance to think together the order of redemption and the order of creation, and therefore to take into account the creaturely world of space and time in all theological reflection on God's self-revelation in Jesus Christ.[166] It is in the world under investigation by natural science that God reveals himself to humanity and human knowledge of God is actualized. So there must be, Torrance contends, "an inescapable relation" between natural science and theological science.[167]

Theology and natural science overlap, for both operate in the same world and in the same medium of space and time.[168] Whereas "natural science is concerned to explore the stratified structures of contingent existence," Torrance argues, "theological science inquires of God their Creator who reveals himself through them."[169] Each science develops its own methods, conceptualities and mode of verification in accordance with the nature of the realities it investigates. Yet both are *human* inquiries. Both are forms of faith seeking understanding, since both operate on the basis of ultimate beliefs, and even share certain basic concepts like those noted above (rational unity, contingent order and freedom).

Thus, in this situation there cannot but be deep interconnections between theology and science, which Torrance contends "increasingly cry

---

[166]Ibid., p. 11.

[167]Ibid., p. 27. Torrance adds that there is an inescapable relation between "theological concepts and physical concepts, or between spiritual and natural concepts; between positive theology and natural theology, or rather between theology and natural science." This is a revealing statement, one that we will return to in the final section of this chapter on Torrance's reconceived natural theology. The theological and natural concepts Torrance is referring to are those discussed above: the unitary and contingent order and contingent freedom of the universe. I also believe that Torrance has in mind Maxwell's beneficial appropriation of an onto-relational of concept of person in the development of his field theory, as noted above.

Indeed, Torrance says that we are not really doing theology if we only focus on the God-humanity or humanity-God relationship. When theology is restricted to a God-human relation, it regularly leads to a form of symbolic objectification of inward human experience. The symbols of the faith are mytho-poetic and are constructed by human consciousness to express the inner spiritual or religious human subjectivity (see p. 29). Torrance finds this kind of approach in existentialist theologies that detach the significance of Jesus from all empirical correlates in space and time (like the bodily resurrection) and ground Christ's significance in the existential or transcendental realm of human subjectivity, safely removed from critical attack by an objectivist natural science or critical historiography. Torrance sees Bultmann as an example of this par excellence.

[168]Ibid., p. 30

[169]Ibid.

out for each other."[170] In light of all of this, Torrance thinks the understanding of the universe that is the goal of natural science cannot but be of great interest to theology.[171]

Dialogue, convergence and transformation. More and more, Torrance contends, natural science is reaching boundaries that generate questions which science cannot answer: "Scientists today frequently find themselves at the frontiers and limits of their science compelled to ask open questions directed toward an intelligible ground beyond the determinations of science."[172] Subatomic particle research is reaching the most basic structures of nature. Here science seems to be close to the very edge between being and nonbeing, and thereby encounters not only intelligibility, Torrance argues, but a boundary that raises ultimate questions concerning what is the sufficient reason for this state of affairs.[173]

The singularity of the expanding universe with its absolute beginning raises similar questions, as does the narrow window in the rate of expansion of the universe in order for it ever to develop conditions that would sustain human life. Thus "again and again today, the scientist is baffled and tempted to speculate when the intelligible connections in the universe . . . just break off owing to their contingent nature and point mutely beyond themselves."[174]

Here Torrance sees theological science as presenting a *complementary account*. God created the universe *ex nihilo* so that the universe *does* have boundaries. The contingent order and freedom of the universe *are* the product of the love of God who calls a creation into existence so that it may share in the communion of love that God is in God's own trinitarian life. Humanity is the priest of creation articulating the contingent intelligibility of the universe, including its boundary conditions, in praise of the Creator.

Torrance finds this convergence of natural science and theological science hopeful, especially in light of the fact that both have had to struggle with a dualist general frame of thought in Western culture, which has inhibited their progress.[175] Indeed, Torrance thinks that through pro-

---

[170]Ibid., p. x.
[171]Torrance, *Ground and Grammar*, p. 1.
[172]Ibid., p. 19.
[173]Torrance, *Christian Frame*, pp. 27-28.
[174]Ibid., p. 77.
[175]See Torrance, *Transformation*, pp. vii-xiv.

found dialogue, theology and science can significantly further the transformation of the frame of knowledge that has been initiated in natural science by Maxwell, Einstein and Polanyi, among others, and in theology by Barth and others.[176]

In light of all of this, Torrance thinks that the great day for dialogue, convergence and transformation in the relation between theology and natural science lies in the future.[177] To this end Torrance has devoted much of his career out of his concern "to evangelize the foundations" of modern scientific culture.[178]

5. A Reformulated Natural Theology

Within this dialogue and deepening coordination between natural science and theological science, Torrance sees a place for a radically reformulated *natural theology*.[179] We will examine Torrance's problem with traditional

---

[176]This, of course, explains the meaning of the striking title of one of Torrance's important books: *Transformation and Convergence in the Frame of Knowledge: Explorations in the Interrelations of Scientific and Theological Enterprise*.

This is also the rationale for the series of books Torrance has edited, *Theology and Science at the Frontiers of Knowledge*. In the general foreword Torrance asserts, "The universe that is steadily being disclosed to our various sciences is found to be characterized throughout time and space by an ascending gradient of meaning in richer and higher forms of order. Instead of levels of existence and reality being explained reductionistically from below in materialistic and mechanistic terms, the lower levels are found to be explained in terms of higher, invisible, intangible levels." See Carver T. Yu, *Being and Relation: A Theological Critique of Western Dualism and Individualism* (Edinburgh: Scottish Academic Press, 1987), p. viii. We will return to this point in the next section on Torrance's understanding of natural theology. Torrance states that the various volumes of the series are intended to further the transformation in the frame of knowledge now taking place. What Torrance ultimately envisages is "a reconstruction of the very foundations of modern thought and culture, similar to that which took place in the early centuries of the Christian era" when Nicene theology (and natural science) transformed the thought world of ancient culture and first injected those three masterful ideas discussed earlier in this section into the fabric of history leading in due time to the rise of the kind of new science represented in the volumes of the series (see Yu, *Being and Relation*, p. viii).

[177]Torrance, *Ground and Grammar*, pp. 7-8.

[178]I. John Hesselink, "A Pilgrimage in the School of Christ," *Reformed Review* 38, no. 1 (1984): 60.

[179]Torrance's reconstruction of natural theology is one of the most difficult aspects of his theology. See Torrance, *Ground and Grammar*, pp. 75-109; Torrance, *Evangelical Theology*, pp. 30-34; Thomas F. Torrance, *Karl Barth: Biblical and Evangelical Theologian* (Edinburgh: T & T Clark, 1990), pp. 136-59; and Torrance, *Scientific Theology*, pp. 32-63. The chapter in *Scientific Theology* is the most developed form of Torrance's discussion and adds additional lines of exposition and argumentation. It is also probably the most difficult discussion because it compresses previous material from several different publications.

natural theology and the matrix within which he develops his version of natural theology, and then summarize some of the main themes in his reformulation of this subject.

The matrix of a reformulated natural theology. Anyone who wants to understand Torrance's reformulation of natural theology must view it from within his encounter with natural science.[180] Torrance repeatedly asserts that "natural theology has its proper place and status within the area of overlap between natural science and theological science, within the overlapping of created and uncreated intelligibility where natural science presses its inquiries in one direction and theological science presses its inquiries in another direction."[181]

The previous section noted the mutual beneficial influence, the sharing of basic concepts, the common struggle with modern dualism and the complementarity that Torrance discovered between his own actual theological reflection developed on the basis of special revelation (in dialogue with Karl Barth and Athanasuis, among others) and his encounters with the discoveries of the new science (Maxwell, Einstein, Polanyi and others).[182]

Of special importance is the fact that scientists are now finding themselves at the frontiers and limits of scientific inquiry, whether it be quantum theory and the most basic constituents of the universe or cosmological theory pressing back through time to the original black hole or finite beginning of the universe.[183] Here Torrance finds science at the boundaries of existence where scientific inquiry itself raises fundamental and profound questions that science can neither suppress nor answer, sometimes even

---

Those reading the chapter in *Karl Barth* on "Natural Theology in the Thought of Karl Barth" should also compare the final pages with the earlier version of the article "The Problem of Natural Theology in the Thought of Karl Barth," *Religious Studies* 6 (1970): 121-35. Torrance makes some important and revealing additions in the later version.

[180]Remember that Torrance has been involved in intense dialogue with natural science and actual scientists over many years. See chapter one, pp. 38, 40-41, 46.

[181]Torrance, *Evangelical Theology*, p. 31. Also see Torrance, *Ground and Grammar*, pp. 75-76. Torrance points out that it is in and through the world of space and time (Israel and the historical Jesus) that God not only reveals himself to us, but does so in the modes of rationality of the created order and of us as creatures (see Torrance, *Ground and Grammar*, p. 1). At times Torrance nearly identifies natural theology with natural science: "This implies . . . that there is a necessary and inescapable relation between theological concepts and physical concepts . . . between positive theology and natural theology, or rather between theology and natural science" (Torrance, *Evangelical Theology*, p. 27).

[182]Torrance, *Ground and Grammar*, pp. x, 5, 7, 44-74.

[183]Torrance, *Christian Frame*, p. 62, and Torrance, *Ground and Grammar*, pp. 17-18.

leading scientists to ask theologians for assistance.[184]

Torrance's reformulated natural theology can be viewed partly as his attempt to make conceptual and theological sense of these profound and surprising interrelations between natural science and theological science, especially in light of his theological conviction that God's self-revelation in Jesus Christ in space and time calls for a careful rethinking of the relation between Christology and creation.

Rejection of traditional natural theology. What we find in Torrance's work is *not* a traditional natural theology as a *praeambula fidei* (preamble to faith) in which we attempt to "prove" God's existence or develop an understanding of God's essential attributes on the basis of an independent or autonomous movement of thought from the created order to God the Creator apart from special revelation.[185] Torrance rejects any notion of an *independent* natural theology as a movement of thought and an autonomous rational structure developed on the basis of nature alone, abstracted from God's actual self-revelation in Jesus Christ.[186]

We will not recapitulate the discussion in chapter four of traditional natural theology and its problems. Yet there are several additional points in Torrance's analysis and critique of traditional natural theology that are important for understanding his reformulated version.[187]

---

[184]See Torrance, *Christian Frame*, pp. 30-33, 61-63, 77-79, 89-90, 117-18. Also see Torrance, *Divine and Contingent*, p. 58.

[185]See Torrance, *Karl Barth*, pp. 141-50; Torrance, *Ground and Grammar*, p. 87-91; and Torrance, *Scientific Theology*, pp. 37-43. Torrance is clear about the subtlety of traditional natural theology, as in Thomas Aquinas for example, where Aquinas admits that his natural theology is developed by reason already infused by grace. Despite this concession, however, Torrance still points to the damaging split between knowledge of the one God and knowledge of the triune God that remains in many theologies (including Aquinas) that appeal to natural as well as special theology, as noted in chapter four, pp. 129-33.

[186]See Torrance, *Karl Barth*, p. 147.

[187]Also see chapter four, section one, "Access to the Father." In an introductory text like this one, it is not possible to trace Torrance's lengthy and insightful analysis and criticism of natural theology. Nearly all of the essay "Natural Theology in the Thought of Karl Barth" deals with this (see Torrance, *Karl Barth*, pp. 136-59). There are long sections on traditional natural theology in the other essays as well. Also see Torrance, *Ground and Grammar*, pp. 78-94, and Torrance, *Scientific Theology*, pp. 37-43.

There is reason to believe that Torrance may regret calling this reformulated version "natural theology." In several essays from the mid-eighties, published in *Christian Frame* in 1989, Torrance covers many of the same issues and themes as in his discussions of natural theology, but never mentions "natural theology" at all. Rather he speaks of *theology of nature*, "sustained only with a recovery of the full Christian framework of knowledge, for it is through the incarnation of the Word of God among us in Jesus Christ that the secret of

Torrance notes that traditional natural theology has come to the fore-front and flourished in periods of cosmological and epistemological dual-ism in science, philosophy and theology (especially the Middle Ages) and in the Age of Reason, particularly after Newton and Locke and the rise of English deism.[188] Despite the real differences between the forms of natural theology within these periods, Torrance argues that in both eras natural theology developed as a movement of thought and conceptual system in-dependent of special revelation and positive or revealed theology. Natural theology was valued precisely because of its independence for apologetic and mediating purposes.[189]

This kind of natural theology, Torrance contends, "attempts to reach and teach knowledge of God, apart altogether from any interaction between God and the world, and proceeds by way of abstraction from sense experi-ence and inferential and deductive trains of reasoning from observed or em-pirical facts."[190] Despite the differences between the medievals and mod-erns, Torrance thinks that they all wanted to develop a movement of thought from rationally demonstrable knowledge of the empirical world of space and time to rationally demonstrable knowledge of God.

The goal was to close the dualist gap between God and the world through a "logical bridge" from the world to God and thereby provide ra-tional support for faith.[191] The bridge from the world to God supposedly operated on the basis of a *logical* connection between concepts and experi-

---

the whole created order is disclosed. . . . This implies that . . . all patterns of order in the universe are finally and satisfyingly intelligible only as they are ontologically linked to the love of God, the supreme power of order" (see Torrance, *Christian Frame*, p. 83). Yet this underscores the central point of Torrance's reconceptualization of the cosmological argu-ment, as we will see later in this section. See chapters four, five and six of *Christian Frame* and compare them with Torrance's discussions of natural theology in texts mentioned in the previous note.

We see the same pattern in Torrance's essay "Creation, Contingent World-Order, and Time: A Theologico-Scientific Approach," in *Time, Creation and World-Order*, ed. Mogens Wegner (Oakville, Conn.: Aarhus University Press, 1999). See page 218, where Torrance states, "By its open-structured contingent nature the orderly universe points to God as the transcendent ground of all order. In the nature of the case there can be no logical argument from a contingent universe to its Creator, for as contingent the universe is not self-existent and does not contain a sufficient reason for itself—otherwise it would not be contingent, but would be self-existent and necessary."

[188]Torrance, *Scientific Theology*, p. 37. See chapter two above, pp. 57-60, for a discussion of dualism.

[189]Torrance, *Scientific Theology*, p. 38.

[190]Ibid.

[191]See Torrance, *Ground and Grammar*, pp. 80-81, and Torrance, *Evangelical Theology*, p. 32.

ence. This kind of epistemology, Torrance argues, assumes that ideas are
derived from sense experience or observation by abstraction or logical deduction, as, for example, in the case of Newton's account of how he derived his fundamental scientific concepts from observations and
experiments, as we will see in chapter nine.[192] It was this idea of a logical
bridge between concepts and experience or observed facts that provided
the necessary epistemological foundation for the attempt to develop logically demonstrable knowledge of God in the form of inferential and deductive reasoning from the world to God.

The problem, however, is that there is no logical bridge between concepts and experience, Torrance contends, either in the discovery of ideas
or in their verification, as will become clear in chapter nine.[193] Thus he
maintains that when these "constructions collapsed there opened up in
late medieval and modern times an unbridgeable chasm between thought
and being or between ideas and events," which in turn undermined the
possibility of any logical bridge from the world to God, and so it too "had
to collapse along with the notion that science proceeds by way of abstraction from observational data."[194]

This means that when Torrance develops his reformulated natural theology, he does *not* attempt to build a logical bridge from the world to God
on the basis of a logical bridge between experience and concepts. The epistemological relation between concepts and experience is quite different
and much more interactive and integrative, and the relation between God
and the world is neither *necessary* (it is not a relation on which we can construct a *logical* reference or argument from the world to God), nor *arbitrary*,
but contingent and free, as noted at several points above.

Thus when Torrance reformulates natural theology, he operates with a
different kind of epistemology, a different God-world relation, and therefore a different kind of argumentation. This is what makes Torrance's reformulation of natural theology confusing even for theologians who are

[192]See chapter nine, pp. 325-44, for an account of Newton's epistemology and its collapse
due to the criticism of Hume and Kant, but even more because of the kind of integrative
epistemology that arises in the work of Maxwell, Einstein and Polanyi in natural science,
and in Torrance's reflections on theological epistemology.
[193]Torrance, *Ground and Grammar*, p. 81, and Torrance, *Scientific Theology*, p. 38.
[194]Torrance, *Scientific Theology*, p. 38. In point of fact, the reason for the collapse of this logical
bridge between the world and God, Torrance contends, is the *contingent* relation between
God and the world in which God freely creates the universe and its created rationality *ex
nihilo* (see Torrance, *Divine and Contingent*, p. 21).

unaware of or do not understand Torrance's epistemology (the integration of form) and God-world relation (the subtle relation of created form in created being that points beyond itself to its contingent source in creation *ex nihilo* by the Creator).[195]

Torrance finds traditional natural theology further undermined by Karl Barth's pointed criticism of it on the basis of the actual content of our knowledge of God as it arises out of God's self-revelation and self-communication in Jesus Christ, together with the rigorous scientific methodology that Barth and Torrance develop in relation to that knowledge, as noted in the opening section of chapter four.[196] If the God we know in Jesus Christ is really *trinitarian*, how can there be an independent natural theology that terminates, not on the being of the triune God, but on some being of God in general?[197] This splits knowledge of God into two parts: a natural knowledge of the one God and a revealed knowledge of the triune God.[198]

Thus natural theology's independent movement of thought can and does become an actual source of confusion for theology as it attempts to integrate this split in our knowledge of God.[199] Barth was painfully aware of this in the German Christian movement and in certain theologians (for example, the Roman theologian Karl Adam of Tübingen) who invoked the famous dictum that grace does not destroy nature (German blood and soil!), but perfects and fulfills it, all of which provided dangerous inroads for conciliation with the Nazi regime and its natural-based ideology.[200]

In terms of methodology, Torrance follows Barth in rejecting the notion that we can develop an account of *how* we know apart from our actual knowledge and its material content. Here Torrance argues that

---

[195]Ibid. There is no *necessary* relation between God and the universe, for God remains utterly free in relation to the universe, Torrance argues, and therefore "is not at the disposal of the conceptions and necessities of any deductive argumentation or logical compulsion on our part." Even a theologian as careful and astute as Donald Bloesch has misunderstood Torrance on this point. See Donald G. Bloesch, *A Theology of Word and Spirit: Authority & Method in Theology* (Downers Grove, Ill.: InterVarsity Press, 1992), pp. 178-83, which misinterprets Torrance's position on several themes in the area of theological method. Torrance's theology is actually very similar to Bloesch's.

[196]See pp. 129-33 of chapter four above.

[197]See Torrance, *Ground and Grammar*, p. 89. Also see Torrance, *Karl Barth*, pp. 150-52.

[198]Torrance, *Ground and Grammar*, p. 91. Also see Torrance, *Karl Barth*, pp. 152-53.

[199]Once an independent ground in nature is granted, there is always the danger and tendency of a synthesis in which knowledge of God in Jesus Christ is adapted and domesticated in relation to natural theology.

[200]Torrance, *Karl Barth*, pp. 142-43.

theology, like any *a posteriori* science, must be free to develop appropriate methods and to elaborate epistemological structures in light of the nature of the object or subject matter as it comes into view in the course of actual inquiry.[201]

In all of his discussions of natural theology, Torrance utilizes an analogy drawn from geometry and physics, mentioned in footnotes earlier in this chapter and in the previous one, to clarify this point.[202] While Newtonian science with its use of Euclidian geometry was extremely successful in advancing our knowledge of the universe of bodies in motion, it was an *idealized* geometry developed as a conceptual system separate from experience and utilized as the framework in which scientific knowledge of the universe was pursued and organized.[203] This idealized framework, however, generated a radically mechanistic (cause-and-effect) understanding of the material universe that created all kinds of problems not only for science, but for Western culture generally, because higher levels of human experience such as morality, freedom and meaning were threatened by a reductionism that viewed them as epiphenomena of the brain.[204]

However, the progress of science revealed that this kind of rigid Euclidian geometric epistemological structure could not satisfactorily explain fundamental properties of the universe like electromagnetic fields, radiation or the behavior of light, all of which have an essential place in the dynamic fabric of the universe at the macro- and micro-cosmic levels.[205] It was Einstein who traced the problem to Newton's independent, idealized geometry artificially imposed on scientific inquiry. Einstein argued that

---

[201]Torrance, *Ground and Grammar*, p. 90.

[202]Also see p. 133 n. 26 and pp. 184-85 n. 146. Also see Torrance, *Ground and Grammar*, pp. 91-93; Torrance, *Scientific Theology*, pp. 39-40; Torrance, *Karl Barth*, pp. 148-49; and Torrance, *Evangelical Theology*, pp. 32-34.

Frederick W. Norris has criticized Torrance's use of this analogy of the relation of Euclidean geometry to physics. Norris implies that Torrance allows this analogy to play too much of formative role in Torrance's reformulated natural theology (see Frederick W. Norris, "Mathematics, Physics and Religion: A Need for Candor and Rigor," *Scottish Journal of Theology* 37, no. 4 [1984]: 457-70). Also see Alister McGrath's cogent response that Torrance's use is "illustrative," rather than "determinative or constitutive" (Alister McGrath, *T. F. Torrance: An Intellectual Biography* [Edinburgh: T & T Clark, 1999], 186-87).

[203]Torrance, *Evangelical Theology*, pp. 32-33.

[204]Ibid. This rigid determinist conceptualization of the material universe often led to various forms of idealism that posit a transcendental realm of human freedom, morality, meaning and religion, but in the process create *dualist* anthropologies that split the human being into a physical body and transcendental soul or *geist* (spirit).

[205]Ibid.

geometry has to be developed within the material content of physics where it suffers a transmutation and becomes four-dimensional in its integration with physics, and therefore what he called "a natural science," that is *natural* to the actual subject matter or reality of the universe disclosed by the advance of science.[206]

In a similar way, Torrance argues, theological science cannot be conceptually or methodologically constricted by an epistemology and an epistemological structure developed independent of God's actual self-revelation and self-communication. Rather than operate with two conceptual systems and their respective epistemologies (general revelation/natural theology and special revelation/positive theology), Torrance believes that theological science has to operate with one coherent and integrated framework of theological understanding.[207] Therefore, a reformulated natural theology has to give up its *independent* status and find its place *within* revealed theology where it is "developed as a complex of rational structures arising in our actual knowledge of God." There natural theology "becomes 'natural' in a new way, natural to its proper object, God in self-revealing interaction with us in space and time."[208] Precisely what Torrance means by this will become evident as we examine his reformulated vision of natural theology.

A reformulated natural theology. Torrance's reformulated natural theology has its proper place and status within the area of overlap between theological science and natural science, between created intelligibility and God's uncreated intelligibility.[209] Natural theology is *not* a movement of thought independent of revealed theology. It can be pursued as "a distinct discipline or set of disciplines" only "through being *artificially* bracketed off from the material content of actual knowledge of God, and . . . only as a *temporary* methodological device for purposes of clarifications."[210] And even then, natural theology will bear the imprint of its connection with revealed theology.[211]

As we turn to the actual development of Torrance's reformulated natural theology (we will examine his reformulation of the main point of the

---

[206]See ibid., p. 33; Torrance, *Transformation*, pp. ix-x; and Torrance, *Scientific Theology*, p. 39.

[207]Torrance, *Ground and Grammar*, pp. 76-78, and Torrance, *Karl Barth*, p. 149.

[208]Torrance, *Scientific Theology*, p. 39.

[209]Torrance, *Evangelical Theology*, p. 31.

[210]Torrance, *Scientific Theology*, p. 42.

[211]Ibid., pp. 42-43, and Torrance, *Ground and Grammar*, p. 107.

traditional "cosmological argument"),[212] it is crucial to remember that Torrance rejects (1) any notion of a *logical* bridge or connection between ideas and experience in the development of our concepts or their verification and (2) any notion of a *necessary* or logical relation between God and the world. Yet there can be an actual correlation or transparence between thought and reality, *if* the human knower actively responds to the self-presentation of reality (form in being) with the generation of suitable forms of thought (integration of form in knowing).[213]

What this means for the particular intellectual exercise in natural theology that follows is that Torrance finds a *real*, and therefore *rational*, relation between (1) the design of the universe (and its silent cry for a sufficient reason) as disclosed by natural science and (2) God the Creator as revealed in Jesus Christ and brought to articulation by revealed theology. But this relation is *not* a logical bridge from the universe to God (because the relation of the universe to God is contingent—neither necessary, nor arbitrary) built on a logical bridge or connection between concepts and experience (the integration of form in knowing is far more subtle and complex); and it is natural science *already deeply influenced* by Christian presuppositions.

What Torrance tries to do in reformulating the main point of the cosmological "argument" is provide his readers with a *reflection* or *discourse* that enables them to think of the universe as a whole, as it has come into view in the new science, in a *referential* way that *points* beyond itself toward its sufficient ground.[214] Torrance is trying to develop converging lines of discourse that will enable his readers to *apprehend* (integration of form in knowing) the *real*, though contingent (not necessary), relation (subtle form in being) of the universe to God from the creaturely side of the relation in light of the astonishing intelligibility and singularity of the universe that comes into view in natural science, and in light of the questions that science cannot help but ask

---

[212]Torrance, *Ground and Grammar*, pp. 94, 106-7. It is interesting that in his later and more developed version of this "argument" in *Scientific Theology*, pp. 32-63, he never mentions "cosmological argument" at all (or the "ontological argument" which also appears in *Ground and Grammar*, pp. 94-100). It may be that upon further reflection, Torrance wanted to downplay any connection between his reformulated natural theology and the traditional forms of the ontological and cosmological arguments.

[213]See chapter two, pp. 57-60. Chapter nine treats Torrance's understanding of the proper integration of form in detail (see chapter nine, pp. 325-44).

[214]Torrance asserts that "we now need a . . . conceptual reform in our outlook on the universe as a whole" in "its signitive or referential relations beyond itself" (Torrance, *Scientific Theology*, p. 44).

concerning the sufficient reason for this state of affairs.

Revealed theology, of course, already knows the answer: the free and sovereign Creator, revealed in Jesus Christ, called the contingent, free and intelligible creation into existence *ex nihilo* out of pure unbounded love. Revealed theology generated the ideas that are part of the ultimate beliefs on which natural science is based (unitary rationality, contingent intelligibility and contingent freedom). Thus natural theology, which attempts to articulate the way in which the astonishing and intelligible universe points beyond itself (silently cries) for a sufficient reason for this state of affairs, cannot be an *independent* discipline, but must be developed in indissoluble relation to revealed theology.

In the following summary of Torrance's "transformed" natural theology, I have cut out everything but the central points of the exceedingly detailed and complex development of Torrance's reflection. Readers interested in the comprehensive version should consult Torrance's work directly.[215] I also believe that Torrance's purpose in his several essays on natural theology is illustrative of the kind of development of this area that he intends, and not an exhaustive treatment of the subject. He is inviting others to follow up his initial work.[216]

A reformulation of the main point of the cosmological "argument." As science presses its inquiries to the very boundaries of the universe, Torrance finds that a concept of contingent intelligibility or order forces itself on scientific inquiry in light of the fact that this order of the universe is neither necessary, nor self-sufficient, nor self-explanatory.[217] This kind of universe compels us to ask questions about the reason for this state of affairs. Thus from the "pole . . . where our attention is directed in natural theology . . . *contingent* creaturely *being* and *intelligibility* require a sufficient ground or reason beyond themselves in order to be what they actually are . . . they constitute a rational question requiring a rational answer."[218]

In other words, in scientific inquiry we are faced not only with an astonishing intelligibility, but also with the question of *why* there is a contingent

---

[215]See Torrance, *Scientific Theology,* pp. 43-61.

[216]An example of someone who has developed natural theology along these lines is Ray S. Anderson, "Barth and a New Direction for Natural Theology," in *Theology Beyond Christendom: Essays on the Centenary of the Birth of Karl Barth,* ed. John Tompson (Allison Park, Penn.: Pickwick, 1986), pp. 241-66.

[217]Torrance, *Christian Frame,* pp. 30-31.

[218]Torrance, *Scientific Theology,* p. 44. But this answer is not in the form of a *logical bridge* between this intelligibility and its ground in God.

intelligible universe. But it is a question that science cannot answer. And so, Torrance contends, this contingent and intelligible universe cries out mutely for a sufficient reason, and in so doing points beyond itself. The universe as a whole, as it has come into view in modern science, has a kind of subtle referential character beyond itself in the form of a question.[219]

Science is baffled not only by the existence of an intelligible universe, but also by the fact that the forms of thought that arise within the minds of scientists enable science to grasp the reality and intelligibility of the universe. Einstein spoke of this as religious awe in the face of the openness between human knowing and the structure of the universe.[220] So it is not only the *intelligibility* of the universe but also *intelligent* human scientists and their knowledge of the universe (the anthropic principle) that cry out for a sufficient reason.

The fact that the inherent intelligibility of the universe is open to human inquiry and the fact that human beings as *active personal agents* have the capacity for this kind of unbounded inquiry into the universe, and unbounded inquiry into the sufficient reason for the universe, all suggest (are capable of) an explanation in relation to a transcendent ground or source of both the *rationality* of the universe and the *active human agency* in knowing and articulating that rationality.[221] *Active human agency* suggests or points to a *transcendent active agency* (God) as the ultimate source of the universe, its intelligibility, and the active human agents who bring this intelligibility to articulation.

Thus Torrance argues that even on "this merely 'natural' level of human inquiry, then, the fact that the intelligibility of the universe is not self-explanatory and the fact that its astonishing unity and self-identity persist through all its changing processes would seem to *suggest* that there is an *active agent* other than the inherent intelligibility and harmony of the universe, unifying and structuring it, and providing it with its ground of being."[222]

This is the core of Torrance's reformulation of the main point of *cosmological "argument."*[223] It does not prove God's existence or define God's attributes. But Torrance thinks that it does identify the kind of

---

[219]Ibid., p. 52.
[220]Ibid., p. 53.
[221]Ibid., p. 56.
[222]Ibid.
[223]Torrance, *Ground and Grammar*, p. 94.

subtle, yet intelligible, way the universe coming to articulation by the new science seems to point (in the form of a question) in the direction of the Christian God as the sufficient reason for this universe. However, Torrance argues that it is only intelligible within a specific non-dualist frame of reference.

Dualism effaces the universe's subtle reference to God. Torrance grants that some people (maybe even many) will not be able to follow this kind of reflection. Nevertheless he contends that this may not be due to the difficulty of relating the universe to an active agent, but rather because Western culture has been conditioned for so long to operate with impersonal, abstractive and deductive Cartesian models of thought that view the human subject as a "thinking thing" over against the world out there (*res cogitans* against *res extensa*—classic epistemological dualism, as we will see in chapter nine).[224]

In other words, those who operate out of epistemological dualism have curtailed their own *capacity* for the kind of holistic, integrative epistemic activity required to grasp the subtle suggestive way in which the intelligible universe points to an active agency (God) as sufficient reason for this state of affairs that Torrance wants his audience to apprehend. This also means that those who view the human subject as a thinking thing lack an adequate understanding of personal, interactive *human* agency that models or suggests in this subtle manner a *transcendent* active agency as the sufficient reason for this intelligible universe and for these intelligent human agents who discover and articulate this intelligibility.

Or to state it in reverse, those who operate with an epistemological dualism of the human knower over against the world out there, rather than with an interactive and personal human epistemic agency, will be predisposed to cosmological dualism (with its radical separation or yawning chasm between the universe and God) which is inhospitable to an interactive God-world relation, and therefore to the active agency of God as the sufficient reason for the astonishing and subtle intelligibility of the universe and its openness to active human epistemic agency at the center of Torrance's reformulation of the main point of the cosmological "argument." Epistemological and cosmological dualisms efface the context and the clues within which the universe's cry of a sufficient reason suggests the triune God as the answer.

---

[224]Torrance, *Scientific Theology,* p. 57.

The new science undermines epistemological and cosmological dualism. The new science, however, operates with an unbounded dynamic understanding of the universe (a universe open to the activity of God), and with an understanding of the human being as a personal agent actively interacting with nature and other people. The new science therefore undermines cosmological dualism between the universe as a closed determinist system over against God, and epistemological dualism between the detached "objective" observer and the external world. Torrance thinks that by undermining both dualisms, the new science generates an alternative frame of mind that does not exclude the idea of God as an active agent who interacts with the world of space and time and with human beings.[225] Thus the new science, with its rejection of cosmological and epistemological dualism, and affirmation of active human agency, Torrance argues, "will surely *suggest* even more strongly that the universe is what it is under the agency of a transcendent Being."[226]

While the contingent intelligibility of the dynamic unbounded universe (which does not exclude God) cannot give an answer to the question concerning the sufficient reason or ground of that intelligibility beyond itself, Torrance concludes that "it does more than raise a question for it seems to *cry silently* for a transcendent agency in its explanation and understanding."[227] Torrance reiterates that the kind of discourse he envisages in this reformulated natural theology is not intended as a chain of "inferential reasoning" or a "logical bridge" from a contingent creation to a "necessary" Creator (a necessary contingent creation is impossible), but this does not rule out that it *is* a deeply rational movement of thought (an integration of form in knowing discussed in chapter nine).[228] It is not *logical* necessity but rather the "obligatoriness of being," the contingent and intelligible

---

[225]Ibid.
[226]Ibid., p. 58.
[227]Ibid.
[228]Ibid. Elsewhere Torrance says,

> There is no reason, however, why the argument should be logicalized, any more than we are obliged to operate with a logical relation between the empirical reality of the universe and our scientific understanding of it. . . . Within the framework of the scientific enterprise the intelligibility of the universe . . . lays hold of our minds in a way that we cannot rationally resist, calling for a sufficient reason beyond it . . . Thus we are finally brought back to the constitutive relation between God the Creator and the contingent universe, the realization of which made the enterprise of empirical science possible in the first place, and actually set it on the course of its great achievement. (Torrance, *Divine and Contingent Order*, p. 59)

being of the universe that "suggests" or "cries silently" for a transcendent agent as its sufficient reason.[229]

In the end, Torrance grants that this kind of natural theology can

---

[229]Torrance, *Scientific Theology*, p. 54. Torrance uses phrases like "cries out," "cries silently" or "suggests" because he is searching for a way to conceptualize a subtle kind of reference or intimation of the universe beyond itself, since this subtle reference cannot be schematized within the old couplet of necessity and chance. The relation between the universe and God is neither necessary nor accidental. Therefore the kind of reference of the universe beyond itself is not explicable within the antinomies these kinds of categories.

Torrance wants to frame the subtle reference of the universe (including its intelligibility and humanity's capacity and active agency in knowing it) beyond itself in such a way that his readers will understand and perceive this reference, but without transmuting that subtle reference (which "cries silently" for a sufficient reason) into a logical or necessary relation, reference or bridge, as is the case of the traditional natural theology.

I think Torrance senses that he has not found the right conceptuality within which to formulate what he intends. This is why in the final version of his crucial essay, "Natural Theology in the Thought of Karl Barth," he adds the following (and I believe extremely illuminating statement not found in either of the earlier versions of the essay): "On the other hand, is it not rather the case that for Barth the kind of relation in question here is one that must be conceived statically or logically, but in *dynamic* and *ontological* terms? Yet our problem is that we do not really have conceptual or linguistic tools that are sufficiently adequate for this purpose" (Torrance, *Karl Barth*, p. 156).

For Torrance both of *the crucial relations* involved throughout his reformulation of natural theology (the epistemological relation between the human mind and what it seeks to know and the referential relation of the universe that "cries silently" for a sufficient reason) are *dynamic* and *ontological* relations, though we do not have the adequate categories with which to express "the truth of human [rationality] and creaturely rationality [of the universe that] . . . must be brought to light and be fulfilled within the context of grace" [new natural theology developed within revealed theology], for we cannot leave the truth of human rationality and the universe's rationality "hanging in the air" (see Torrance, *Karl Barth*, pp. 155-56).

Alister McGrath's excellent and very careful chapter on Torrance's understanding of natural theology is extremely helpful for placing Torrance's rejection of traditional natural theology and reformulation of natural theology in the appropriate context of (1) the Reformed theological tradition, (2) the legacy of Karl Barth's criticism of natural theology, (3) Torrance's rejection of cosmological and epistemological dualisms and (4) the contingent intelligibility of the universe as it has come into view in the new natural science. McGrath clearly and correctly identifies the main contours of Torrance's position on the place and purpose of natural theology (see "The Place and Purpose of Natural Theology," in McGrath, *T. F. Torrance*, pp. 175-94).

McGrath's discussion, however, is so careful (or so introductory) that he never gets to the actual examples of Torrance's reformulated natural theology found in Torrance, *Ground and Grammar*, pp. 94-109. McGrath does not mention or discuss the second half of the essay where Torrance develops the "main point" of both the traditional ontological and cosmological arguments (which are related respectively to Torrance's rejection of epistemological and cosmology dualism). See Torrance, *Ground and Grammar*, pp. 94-109. McGrath does not deal with Torrance's most fully and carefully developed essay on natural theology, chapter two, "The Status of Natural Theology," in Torrance, *Scientific Theology*, pp. 32-63.

have no "more than a quasi-validity within the artificial limits imposed."[230] A proper natural theology can only be artificially and temporarily bracketed from the content of our actual knowledge of God. Therefore Torrance's reformulated natural theology is always incomplete in itself and can only be developed within a relation to revealed theology.[231]

Readers interested in Torrance's reformulated natural theology should carefully work through the three essays or chapters mentioned in this note. Throughout Torrance's discussion, he wants to show that grace does not negate but fulfills nature (*gratia non tollit naturam sed perficit et complet*), while at the same time rejecting any and every independent natural theology in light of the reasons given in this chapter and the previous one.

When Torrance reformulates "the main point in the traditional ontological argument," what he really wants to show is the way in which human rationality (the integration of form in knowing) is *fulfilled* in revelation, not negated. Torrance thinks that Barth was in danger of negating the truth of human rationality when Barth restricted the relation between God and humanity to an *event* of grace/revelation without working out the ontology of the creaturely structures that revelation assumes (the truth of human rationality— the human integration of form in knowing and the creaturely structures [doctrines for example] that arise in human knowledge of revelation). Contra epistemological dualism, revelation includes a subtle integration of form in our human knowing (but not by a logical bridge between experience and concepts), and includes cognitive structures (doctrines, for example) that arise out of this integration. Thus grace/revelation does not negate but fulfills nature, in this case the creaturely rationality of the intelligent human active agent. See Torrance, *Karl Barth*, pp. 155-56, and Torrance, *Ground and Grammar*, pp. 95-100.

When Torrance reformulates "the bearing of the singularity of the universe" on "the main point of the cosmological argument," what Torrance really wants to show is the way in which the contingent intelligibility of the universe and its cry for a sufficient reason that is once again fulfilled, not negated by grace/revelation. Contra cosmological dualism, the cry of the intelligible universe for a sufficient reason finds its answer in the active agency and love of God the Father Almighty, the sovereign Creator, revealed in Jesus Christ, as developed in section one of this chapter. Once again grace/revelation does not negate the truth of creaturely rationality (in this case the intelligibility of the universe that "cries mutely" for a sufficient reason), but fulfills it by explaining its origin in the love and active agency of the triune God, and affirming its contingent intelligibility. See Torrance, *Karl Barth*, pp. 155-56; Torrance, *Ground and Grammar*, pp. 94, 100-109; and Torrance, *Scientific Theology*, pp. 32-63.

In other words, natural theology operating within revealed theology identifies and articulates the complementarity that exists between (1) the new science and its discovery of the intelligibility and singularity of the universe which does not and cannot provide its sufficient reason, and (2) the kind of positive theology that Torrance articulates which reveals that the free and gracious love of God the Father Almighty is the source of just this kind of contingent, intelligible and free universe, and just this kind of human science through which scientists serve as priests of creation bringing the wonder of the universe to expression in praise of the creator. In this way grace/revelation does not negate but fulfills nature.

[230]Torrance, *Scientific Theology*, p. 60.
[231]Ibid., p. 66.

This kind of natural theology is, of course, quite different from traditional natural theology which arose in periods of dualism (epistemological and cosmological), for Torrance's version provides neither proof of God's existence, nor an account of God's nature apart from special revelation. Rather, it shows the way in which the kind of theology Torrance advocates is compatible with and illuminating of (theology can successfully answer questions that natural science cannot help but raise, yet cannot answer) the findings of the *new* natural science (already grounded in ultimate beliefs of Christian origin), and therefore encourages dialogue, mutual cross-fertilization and convergence between natural science and theological science. In this way revelation/grace does not destroy natural theology, but rather brings the truth of creation to light and fulfills it, though *always and only* in the context of revelation/grace and within the orbit of revealed theology.[232]

---

[232]See Torrance, *Karl Barth*, pp. 155-56.

PART III

THE COMMUNION OF THE HOLY SPIRIT

6

THE HOLY SPIRIT

The Spirit of God is God in his freedom to be present to the creature,
and therefore to be the life of the creature. And God's Spirit, the Holy Spirit, especially in revelation,
is God himself in that he can not only come to man, but also to be in man,
open up man and make him capable and ready for himself,
and thus achieve his revelation in him.
KARL BARTH

The universal witness of the New Testament affirms both the personal and divine nature of the Spirit, Torrance notes, for the Holy Spirit, along with the Father and Son, is the subject and object of Christian faith, since it is through the Spirit and in the Spirit that we believe in Jesus Christ and are saved.[1] In Torrance's theology, the Holy Spirit is not just a divine presence or energy separable from God, but rather God himself acting directly and giving himself anew in God's own personal and dynamic reality to the creatures God has redeemed through Jesus Christ. As such, Torrance's doctrine of the Holy Spirit completes, qualifies and deepens his perspective on the Father and the Son, and thereby leads to his fully trinitarian theological orientation.[2]

This chapter examines Torrance's pneumatology first in relation to his biblical, evangelical/doxological and trinitarian approach, which grounds his doctrine of the Spirit much more deeply than simply on the various texts and triadic formulae in the New Testament that bear witness to the

---

[1]Thomas F. Torrance, *The Trinitarian Faith: The Evangelical Theology of the Ancient Catholic Church* (Edinburgh: T & T Clark, 1988), p. 191. Also see Thomas F. Torrance, *Theology in Reconstruction* (Grand Rapids, Mich.: Eerdmans, 1965), p. 209.
[2]Torrance, *Trinitarian Faith*, pp. 8-9.

coequality of Spirit with the Father and the Son (Mt 28:19, for example).[3]

The second section of this chapter focuses on the utter deity, majesty, and holiness of the Holy Spirit brought to articulation in the application of the *homoousion* to the Spirit. Torrance emphasizes the irreducible objectivity and transcendence of the Holy Spirit poured out on the church in sharp contrast with any and every confusion of the Spirit with the inward morality, spirituality or religiosity of humanity or the church.[4] As *Holy Spirit*, the Spirit of God guards the ineffable mystery of God which cannot be mastered by humanity or the church even when the Spirit is immediately, personally and experientially present to us in revelation and reconciliation.[5]

One of the characteristics of Torrance's pneumatology is the careful way he works out the relations between the persons and missions of the incarnate Son of God and the Holy Spirit. Jesus Christ and the Holy Spirit mutually mediate one another and interpenetrate one another in all of God's activity in revelation and reconciliation. This is the subject of the third part of the chapter.

The final section deals with the procession of Holy Spirit. Torrance's intensely personal understanding of the Holy Spirit, his integrated account of the mutual mediation of the Son and the Spirit, and Torrance's fully perichoretic conceptualization of the trinitarian persons and their interrelations, all enable Torrance to reconceive the divine *monarchia* in a way that the *monarchia* cannot be restricted to any one of the divine persons. This, in turn, leads Torrance to reformulate procession of the Spirit on a deeper basis which cuts behind the division between the East and West over the *filioque* clause inserted into the Nicene-Constantinopolitan Creed by the Western church.

1. A Biblical, Evangelical/Doxological and Trinitarian Approach

As in other areas of his theology, Torrance finds the Nicene-Constantinopolitan Creed and the work of the theologians associated with it extremely helpful in thinking through basic questions regarding the doctrine of Spirit. The Nicene theologians understood the church's faith in the Holy Spirit within a *trinitarian frame* as is evident in the structure of the creed:

---

[3]Ibid., p. 8-9. 191-92, 202, and Torrance, *Reconstruction*, p. 242.
[4]Torrance, *Reconstruction*, pp. 242-44, and Torrance, *Trinitarian Faith*, pp. 205-15.
[5]Torrance, *Trinitarian Faith*, p. 211.

We believe in one God, the Father Almighty . . . and in one Lord Jesus Christ, the only begotten Son . . . and in the Holy Spirit, the Lord and Giver of life.

The third clause in the creed—on the Holy Spirit—brings to articulation and completion the church's trinitarian understanding of the Godhead. The Holy Spirit was always intimately related to the Father and the Son in the evangelical and doxological faith and life of the early church. The explicit triadic formulae and overall witness of the New Testament together point to the fact, Torrance concludes, that "the message of the gospel as handed on by the apostolic tradition, is one in which the Father, the Son and the Holy Spirit together belong to the essential faith and experience of the church as it is rooted and grounded in Jesus Christ."[6]

This trinitarian frame within which Torrance develops his pneumatology does not arise simply out of faithful exegesis of the New Testament, but in light of God's *oikonomia*, the actual way in which God's revealing and reconciling activity through Jesus Christ and in the Holy Spirit has taken place in history as reflected in the biblical witness.[7] Torrance argues that the meaning of the outpouring of the Holy Spirit at Pentecost "belongs to a series of God's mighty acts which brought salvation" to humanity.[8]

In Torrance's theology, Pentecost signifies the coming of God the Holy Spirit, in response to what God the Father has done through the coming of God the Son in the incarnation, atonement and resurrection. The Son of God, without ceasing to be God, became what we are, taking our sinful humanity on himself, healing, redeeming, restoring our humanity to relation

---

[6]Ibid. Of particular significance in the early Church's faith in the Holy Spirit is the command of the risen Christ in Matthew's gospel that his followers go into the world, make disciples, and baptize them in the name of the Father, Son and Holy Spirit (see p. 196). Torrance sees this command as linked to Jesus' own vicarious baptism on our behalf in Matthew 3:13-17 where Jesus is affirmed by the voice of the Father as God's beloved Son and anointed by the descent of the Holy Spirit as the promised Messiah. Other similar triadic patterns in the New Testament such as the familiar benedictions in 2 Corinthians 13:14 and 1 Corinthians 12:3-4 also entered the central stream of the faith, worship and witness of the early Church and played a crucial role in the development of pre-Nicene and post-Nicene theology in relation to the Holy Spirit (see p. 197). The benediction in 2 Corinthians 13:14 reads: "The grace of the Lord Jesus Christ, the love of God, and the communion of the Holy Spirit be with all of you." Torrance thinks that the fact that the pattern in 1 Corinthians 12:4-6 begins with the Spirit indicates that the order in no way detracts from the equality of the trinitarian persons. Also see Acts 2:32-33; 1 Pet 1:2; 2 Thess 2:13-14; Eph 2:18; 4:4-6 for other trinitarian formulae. Torrance also points to this pervasive trinitarian pattern in many of the earliest hymns after the apostolic era (see pp. 198-99).
[7]Torrance, *Reconstruction*, p. 241.
[8]Ibid., p. 240.

with God in faith and obedience.[9]

In light of the saving presence of God in Jesus Christ and the church's evangelical and doxological encounter with God through Christ, Torrance maintains (as we saw in chapter two) that the church could not but confess that Jesus Christ is the self-revelation and self-communication of God. It belongs to the very essence of the gospel that it is God who has come into our midst in Jesus Christ to demolish our sin and alienation and to reconcile us to himself.[10] The *homoousion* brings this essential relation between the Son and the Father in the gospel to explicit articulation.[11]

Torrance argues that it was only after the church clarified the ontological relation between the Father and the Son in God's self-revelation in Jesus Christ, that the doctrine of the Holy Spirit came to full dogmatic articulation within the trinitarian frame of the early church.[12] This development takes place because the Son and the Spirit are so integrally interrelated in the gospel that the affirmation of the *homoousion* of the Son leads to a parallel formulation in the doctrine of the Holy Spirit.

In the coming of the Holy Spirit from the Father through the Son, after the ascension of Christ, Torrance sees the Spirit as the very life and breath of God renewing the life of God's people, lifting them up with Christ in a doxological life of worship and witness in response to the gospel.[13] Once again the truth and effectiveness of the gospel rests on a oneness of being and agency, this time between the Holy Spirit and God the Father, as well as the incarnate Son.

If the Holy Spirit were not as fully divine as the Father and the Son, Torrance argues, how could the Spirit unite us to Christ, and pour the love of God into our hearts and lives?[14] The church's belief in the Holy Spirit, the Lord and giver of life, belongs to the very essence of the gospel, for it is God the Holy Spirit who comes forth from the Father, receives from the Son, sheds the love of God abroad in our hearts and lives, and lifts us and

[9]Ibid., pp. 241-42.

[10]Thomas F. Torrance, *The Christian Doctrine of God: One Being Three Persons* (Edinburgh: T & T Clark, 1998), p. 16.

[11]Torrance, *Trinitarian Faith*, p. 200.

[12]Ibid., p. 195.

[13]Torrance, *Reconstruction*, pp. 241-42. Also see Torrance, *Christian Doctrine*, p. 150. Torrance views the coming of the Holy Spirit at Pentecost as something new and distinct in addition to the Spirit's original and continuing presence and operation in the world from the beginning of creation. Torrance, *Reconstruction*, p. 240.

[14]Torrance, *Christian Doctrine*, p. 18.

all creation up through the Son to the Father in a life of worship and wit-ness.[15] So from the beginning the church could not but worship and praise the Holy Spirit along with the Father and the Son.

Thus the doctrine of the Holy Spirit, Torrance maintains, is not some "extraneous intrusion" into the gospel. It is simply the natural unfolding of the inner structure of our actual knowledge of God in God's self-revelation and self-communication from the Father through Jesus Christ and in the Holy Spirit which *is* the saving content of the gospel.[16] The doctrine of the Spirit renders explicit what is already and always implicit in the gospel.

Thus Torrance derives his doctrine of the Holy Spirit not simply from the biblical witness and its triadic testimony to the Spirit along with the Father and the Son, "but from the supreme truth that God reveals himself through himself, and therefore that *God himself* is the content of his revelation [and reconciliation] through the Son and in the Spirit."[17] As in the case with the Son of God, the Holy Spirit is the self-giving of God in which the Giver and the gift are identical.[18]

Following the Nicene theologians like Athanasius, Gregory Nazianzen and Epiphanius, Torrance applies the *homoousion* to the Holy Spirit and brings the theological structure of the trinitarian understanding of the Godhead to careful articulation.[19] The application of the *homoousion* to the Son and then the Spirit enables us to trace the evangelical self-revelation and self-communication of God as Father, Son and Holy Spirit back to

---

[15]Torrance, *Reconstruction*, p. 242. The Holy Spirit *is* the Spirit of the Father and the Son, who together *are* the divine life of love that God is in God's own eternal being, and which is the source of the creation of the universe and its redemption, as noted in chapter five.

[16]Torrance, *Trinitarian Faith*, p. 202.

[17]Ibid., p. 202. Torrance will have nothing to do with an approach to the Spirit that begins with some kind of general manifestation of the Spirit within creaturely world or humanity. In the same way that the *Logos* is not a cosmological principle immanent within the universe, so the *Holy* Spirit is not a panentheist power, an organismic principle, a will to life immanent in nature or a *zeitgeist* (spirit of the time). (See p. 201.) The Holy Spirit in Torrance's theology belongs to the divine side of the distinction between creation and the Creator.

[18]Ibid., p. 201. Also see Torrance, *Christian Doctrine*, p. 147. The doctrine of the Spirit arises out of faithful exegesis of Scripture within the evangelical and doxological life of the church where the grace of our Lord Jesus Christ, the love of God the Father and the communion of the Holy Spirit embrace our lives and actualize in our midst the love that God is in God's own trinitarian life. This evangelical/doxological focus is essential, as noted in chapters two and four, since there is no knowledge *of* God without reconciliation and union *with* God.

[19]Torrance, *Christian Doctrine*, pp. 199, 201, 202-3.

what God is in himself in God's own eternal being, life and love as Father, Son and Holy Spirit.[20] In this way the doctrine of the Holy Spirit deepens our understanding of God as triune. Within this biblical and trinitarian approach—with its essential evangelical and doxological focus—Torrance develops his doctrine of the Holy Spirit.

2. God Is Spirit and the Holy Spirit Is God[21]

Spirit is used of God in two senses. Both in Scripture and in the Nicene theologians, Torrance finds a distinction in the use of "Spirit" in reference to God.[22] The term affirms that God *is* Spirit in God's very nature as God. Yet "Spirit" also designates *the* Holy Spirit who with the Father and the Son together are God, "One Being Three Persons."[23]

In the first or absolute sense, Torrance sees "Spirit" as referring to the being *(ousia)* of God without distinction to the three persons and is applicable to Father and Son, as well as to the Holy Spirit.[24] In this sense "Spirit" underscores God's invisible, immutable, immaterial, eternal and transcendent nature in absolute contrast to the material, creaturely, finite, contingent and mutable character of humanity and the rest of the created order.[25] Here Torrance argues that "Spirit" signifies the sheer perfection and holiness of God, as well as God's inexhaustible freedom and transcendence in relation to all of creation.[26]

In the specific or relative sense "Spirit" refers to the person *(hypostasis)* of the Holy Spirit in distinction to, but not in separation in being or activity from, the Father and the Son.[27] Torrance points out that when Scripture refers to the Spirit in this sense it is always with some particularized qualification such as *Holy* Spirit, *the* Spirit, Spirit *of God*, Spirit *of the Father*, etc.[28]

The Spirit clarifies the doctrine of the Father and Son. Whether the focus is on the fact that God is *Spirit* or on the Holy Spirit who *is* God, this article in the church's confession of faith stresses that God can be known by us and expressed appropriately only in a reverent and spiritual man-

---

[20]Ibid., p. 199.

[21]Ibid., p. 205.

[22]Ibid. and Torrance, *Christian Doctrine*, pp. 147-48.

[23]*One Being Three Persons* is the subtitle of Torrance's book *The Christian Doctrine of God*.

[24]Torrance, *Christian Doctrine*, p. 148.

[25]Torrance, *Trinitarian Faith*, p. 205.

[26]Ibid.

[27]Ibid., p. 206, and Torrance, *Christian Doctrine*, p. 148.

[28]Torrance, *Trinitarian Faith*, p. 206.

ner.[29] According to Torrance, the very designation of God's spiritual nature as *holy* and the third person as *Holy* Spirit emphasizes the otherness, the utterly transcendent glory and majesty of God before whom the "cherubim spread the covering of their wings," an Athanasian image that appears regularly in Torrance's publications.[30]

Here the doctrine of the Spirit clarifies the doctrines of the Father and the Son. Since the Father and the Son and the Holy Spirit are of one and the same nature, and that nature is ineffable and spiritual (God is Spirit), Torrance maintains that we must think of the "Father" and "Son" in reference to God in a wholly spiritual manner; we must avoid projecting material and creaturely images of "father" and "son" into our understanding of God, as we saw in the subsection "Language for God" in chapter four.[31]

Following Athanasius, Torrance sees Christ as the "image" (*eidos*) of the Godhead, and the Spirit as the "Image" of the Son. Yet the Spirit himself is *imageless*. By linking together the Son's imaging of the Father and the Spirit's imaging of the Son in a wholly spiritual, imageless manner, Torrance argues that we are able to think of God as Father, Son and Holy Spirit in a spiritual manner without projecting the creaturely content of "father" and "son" into our understanding of God.[32] Thus the *homoousion* of the Spirit enables the church to understand more adequately the spiritual character of the *homoousion* of the Son and the Father, and therefore of all the relations within the trinitarian being of God.[33]

This raises again from a pneumatological perspective a crucial epistemological issue discussed at the beginning of chapter four, for the fact that God is Spirit and the Holy Spirit is God, in utter differentiation from all creaturely reality means that we cannot begin with human questions and creaturely reality, and reason our way to God at all.[34] Torrance thinks that every attempt to compel God to be the content of our thought and our concepts, through a rational demonstration that we convoke, can only shatter itself on the radical transcendence and freedom of the Holy Spirit. It also

---

[29]Ibid.

[30]See ibid., p. 213.

[31]Ibid., p. 194.

[32]Ibid., pp. 194-95. In light of the spiritual and transcendent nature of God, Torrance thinks that the transfer of gender to God is silly.

[33]Ibid., p. 195.

[34]See chapter four above, pp. 127-39, for Torrance's critique of traditional natural theology and his alternative in which we come to know God according to God's nature (*kata physin*) when we know the Father *through* the Son and *in* the Holy Spirit.

underscores again the Irenaean principle that God can only be known through God.[35]

The internal relation of the Spirit to the Father and the Son. Thus the doctrine of the Holy Spirit not only completes the Christian (trinitarian) doctrine of God, the including of the Holy Spirit within a triune being of God further specifies that the doctrine of the Spirit must be understood from the *internal* relation of the Spirit to the Father and the Son, *not* from some *external* relation of the Spirit to creaturely reality.[36] Thus Torrance argues that it is more godly and accurate to know the Holy Spirit in the Spirit's internal relations with the Father and the Son, than it is to attempt to know the Spirit through an external relation of the Spirit to creaturely reality.[37]

Torrance is especially adamant that we should not "interiorize" the Spirit in "a concept of psychological inwardness" in human experience or in "a concept of a subjectification of the Spirit in the life of the Church."[38] Reminiscent of Barth, Torrance rejects any and every identification of the Holy Spirit with humanity's natural vitality/spirituality, with humanity's own inward moral/religious nature or with the ecclesiastical spirit as the animating principle of the church.[39] This kind of psychologizing and subjectivizing, Torrance maintains, is singularly absent in the biblical witness, which stresses the transcendence and objectivity of the Holy Spirit who comes to us from the inner trinitarian life and love of the being of God.[40]

In light of his trinitarian approach, Torrance argues that we must think of the Holy Spirit from the Spirit's *enhypostatic* relation in the one triune being of God.[41] From the perspective of the Spirit's enhypostatic relation to and homoousial communion within the Trinity, Torrance understands the Spirit dwelling *within* us and our being *in* the Spirit in a radically *objective* sense. Human though we are, we become partakers of God in the Spirit through Jesus Christ.[42] The Spirit dwells in us not through any re-

---

[35]Torrance, *Trinitarian Faith*, p. 207.

[36]Ibid., pp. 207-8.

[37]Ibid., p. 209. Remember that Torrance follows the Athanasian principle that it is more devout and accurate to know God from the Son and call God Father, than it is to know God from God's work of creation which is external to God. See chapter four above, pp. 127-39.

[38]Torrance, *Christian Doctrine*, p. 148.

[39]See Torrance, *Reconstruction*, pp. 242-45.

[40]Ibid., pp. 242-43.

[41]Torrance, *Trinitarian Faith*, p. 209.

[42]Ibid., p. 208.

ceptivity on our part but always as an "objective inwardness" of the living reality of the Spirit of God who utterly transcends our creaturely existence and can neither be identified with anything human, nor ever come under human control. This is evident in the biblical designation of the Spirit as *Holy*.[43]

The Spirit as the presence and freedom of God. The Holy Spirit then is the living and dynamic reality and presence of God the Almighty, the Lord and Giver of life, to whom we owe our very existence, as well as our new life in Christ, and therefore before whom we cannot but bow down in reverence and adoration.[44] The Holy Spirit, Torrance contends, is the direct *parousia* of the divine *ousia* (being) of God Almighty.[45]

Torrance will also have nothing to do with any separation of God's energies and operations from the immediate presence and activity of God's being. Rather he stresses the utterly astonishing character of what God does in sending the Holy Spirit on the church, for God gives us God's very self so that God himself is the content of God's revelation and reconciliation.[46]

What Torrance finds of ultimate significance here is the *unlimited freedom* of God, freedom not only to become incarnate for our sake in Jesus Christ, but also freedom to impart God's very self to us in the sending of the Holy Spirit. God is infinitely able to do all of this without ever ceasing to be the transcendent Lord God who lives and loves in God's own eternal life and in no way needs us, but nevertheless will not be without us.[47] This is a twofold freedom of God the Holy Spirit who is free to be present to us and actualize God's relation to us, but also free to be with and in us and actualize our relation to God and thereby bring our lives as God's creatures (indeed God's children, Christ's sisters and brothers) to their end in communion with God.[48]

This is what Torrance sees as the real intent of what the Nicene theologians called *theosis* or *theopoiesis*, not the deification or divinization of humanity, but rather the immediate (though always transcendent) presence

---

[43]See ibid., p. 192, and Torrance, *Reconstruction*, pp. 242-43.
[44]Torrance, *Trinitarian Faith*, p. 209.
[45]Torrance, *Christian Doctrine*, p. 149.
[46]Ibid., pp. 149-52, and Torrance, *Trinitarian Faith*, pp. 209-10. This self-giving of the Spirit underscores again that God's being is dynamic, for God's being is always in God's activity and God's activity always inheres in God's being.
[47]Torrance, *Christian Doctrine*, p. 152.
[48]Ibid., p. 152.

of the Holy Spirit through whom we participate in the revealing and saving activity of God in the vicarious humanity of Christ. Through Christ
and in the Holy Spirit, the Lord and Giver of life, we live and move and
have our being in and for God, without in any way doing violence to the
integrity and reality of our creaturely being, as we noted in chapters two,
three and five above.[49]

This openness on the part of God, rooted in the dynamic character of
God's being wherein God is free to be present to us in the Holy Spirit, imparts corollary openness in us as God's creatures in which we are creatively
sustained by the Spirit for union and communion with the triune God.[50] In
Torrance's theology, this created openness in humanity is continuously giv-
en and sustained by the Holy Spirit and is a free relation of grace, not a panentheist continuity in being or inner relation of nature.[51]

Two implications of the Spirit as Lord and giver of life. In light of the
fact that God is Spirit and the Holy Spirit is God, Torrance identifies two
distinctive implications of his pneumatology.[52] The first is that the Holy
Spirit "guards the ultimate mystery and ineffability of God." The Spirit is
not knowable or approachable in his mode of presence with us.[53] As *Spirit*
both in being *(ousia)* and in person *(hypostasis)* in distinction from the Father and the Son, the Spirit does not reveal himself, but remains hidden behind the revelation of the Father in the Son and the Son in the Father which
the Spirit mediates through himself.[54]

The Holy Spirit is the ineffable and invisible Spirit of truth, Torrance argues, who comes to us in the name of Jesus Christ the incarnate Son. The
Spirit does not speak to us of himself, but rather declares the love of the
Father in the grace of Jesus Christ, for the Spirit effaces himself and is invisible in his witness to the Father in the Son.[55] Thus while the Holy Spirit
is *personally* present to us, the Spirit is the transparent *light* who lights up

---

[49]See chapter two, pp. 78-81; chapter three, pp. 117-23; and chapter five, pp. 176-80. Also see
    Torrance, *Reconstruction*, p. 243, and Torrance, *Christian Doctrine* p. 151.
[50]Torrance, *Christian Doctrine*, p. 153.
[51]Ibid., pp. 152-53. From the perspective of theological anthropology, Torrance calls this the
    "transcendental determination" of our being for God (see chapter five above, pp. 176-80).
[52]Torrance, *Trinitarian Faith*, pp. 211-15.
[53]Ibid., p. 211.
[54]Torrance, *Christian Doctrine*, p. 151, and Torrance, *Trinitarian Faith*, p. 211. Torrance notes
    that it is because the Spirit hides himself in his mode of activity that we are apt to con-
    found the Holy Spirit with the human spirit or with the ecclesial spirit (see Torrance,
    Reconstruction, pp. 227, 242.
[55]Torrance, *Christian Doctrine*, p. 151. Also see Torrance, *Trinitarian Faith*, p. 211.

the face of Father in the person of Jesus Christ.[56]

Through this mysterious invisible and ineffable mode of spiritual, personal presence to us, the Holy Spirit confronts us with the sheer mystery and ultimately incomprehensible reality of God the Almighty.[57] We can and do *apprehend* God through Christ in the Spirit, for God does impart *himself* to us within our creaturely condition in the saving and revealing activity of God through Jesus Christ in the Spirit. Yet we cannot *comprehend* God, who remains Lord even in the midst of self-revelation, for the Holy Spirit is the invisible and ineffable *presence* of the Lord God Almighty.[58]

On the other hand, the Holy Spirit is also the pledge that, while God does transcend our comprehension, God is not finally closed to us.[59] God's ineffability, Torrance contends, is positive in that it is an intrinsic intelligibility that transcends our comprehension. The personal presence of the Holy Spirit mediates to us a self-revelation and self-communication of God that is not empty of content, but in fact, full of the Word of God.[60] The Spirit of God and the Word of God coinhere in one another not only in the one *ousia* of God, but also in the *parousia* of the incarnate Son of God and of the Holy Spirit sent from God the Father through the Son.

In Torrance's theology it is because God himself *is* the content of God's self-revelation and self-communication that we cannot comprehend what we apprehend, and thus we know that the God who reveals *himself* to us is infinitely greater than we can ever conceive.[61] God the Holy Spirit is the Spirit of truth who guides us into intrinsic intelligibility of Jesus Christ, the Word of God incarnate, while at the same time preserving the ultimate mystery and ineffability of God.[62]

3. The Mutual Mediation of Jesus Christ and the Holy Spirit

The coming of the Spirit at Pentecost is mediated by Jesus Christ. In this section we are not primarily concerned with Torrance's understanding of

---

[56]Torrance, *Trinitarian Faith*, pp. 194-95, 212. There is only one image *(eidos)* of God from the Father, shining through the Son and visible to us in the Holy Spirit. Also see Torrance, *Christian Doctrine*, p. 151.

[57]Torrance, *Trinitarian Faith*, p. 213, and Torrance, *Christian Doctrine*, p. 151.

[58]Ibid.

[59]Torrance, *Christian Doctrine*, p. 152, and Torrance, *Trinitarian Faith*, p. 214.

[60]Torrance, *Trinitarian Faith*, p. 214.

[61]Ibid., p. 214.

[62]Ibid., p. 215.

the role of the Spirit in creation and its preservation discussed in chapter five, but with the new, more profound and intimate coming of the Spirit at Pentecost.[63] Our receiving of the Holy Spirit, Torrance argues, is rooted in Jesus Christ and his mediation, for while the Son of God was already of one being with the Spirit, Christ received the Holy Spirit into the humanity he assumed from us and was anointed by the Holy Spirit without measure for our sakes.[64] Thus Jesus Christ mediates the Holy Spirit to us through himself.

The Spirit is mediated to us through Christ's vicarious humanity. As both fully God and truly human, Jesus Christ incarnates that "blessed exchange" in which he transfers what belongs to us in our diseased, alienated and dying humanity to himself, while at the same time transferring what is his to our humanity which he assumed from us for our salvation, as we saw in chapter two.[65] Torrance maintains that above all this applies to the gift of the Holy Spirit through whom Christ lived out all of his fully human life. Here in this "union of divine and human natures in the Son," Torrance suggests, "the eternal Spirit of the living God has composed himself, as it were, to dwell with human nature, and human nature has been adapted and become accustomed to receive and bear that same Holy Spirit."[66]

Jesus was born of the Virgin Mary into our humanity by the Holy Spirit. At his baptism Jesus Christ received the Holy Spirit into the humanity Christ assumed from us in the incarnation. While never without the Spirit as the eternal Son, as the Son incarnate for our sake Jesus Christ embraced the presence of the Holy Spirit within his humanity and lived out his entire life and ministry in the power of the Spirit.[67]

The Holy Spirit in his new coming at Pentecost does not simply proceed from the Father, but is mediated through the humanity and earthly life of the incarnate Son. As the Spirit of Jesus, Torrance sees the Holy Spirit not as an "isolated and naked Spirit," but rather "as Spirit charged with all the experience of Jesus as he shared to the full our mortal nature and weakness, and endured its temptation and grief and suffering and

---

[63]Torrance, *Reconstruction*, pp. 245-46.

[64]Torrance, *Christian Doctrine*, p. 148. Torrance emphasizes that Christ freely and completely received the Holy Spirit into his human nature for us.

[65]See chapter two, pp. 92-94.

[66]Torrance, *Reconstruction*, p. 246.

[67]Ibid.

death."[68] The Holy Spirit who proceeds from the Father receives from the incarnate Son and comes as our *Paraclete* so that as Jesus' disciples we are not left as orphans (Jn 14:15-21).

Torrance never spells out all that this receiving from Christ means for the Holy Spirit. Yet he is quite clear that the coinherent relations, the oneness in being and activity, between the Spirit and the incarnate Son include not only Jesus' life, but even his fearful dereliction and passion on Calvary: "The Holy Spirit was afflicted with the affliction of Christ, and suffered with him like the Father in his atoning sacrifice."[69] It is through the Spirit that Jesus Christ offered himself in atoning reconciliation to the Father (Heb 9:14).[70]

In light of all of this, Torrance argues that when we receive the Spirit, it is not a receiving different from or independent of Christ's vicarious reception of the Spirit, but rather a sharing in that reception.[71] Moreover, this means that our reception of the Holy Spirit takes place only through union with Christ and through Christ with God the Father.[72]

The Spirit is mediated to us only after Christ's ascension. Apart from the atoning sacrifice of Jesus Christ on the cross, Torrance argues, the Holy Spirit, who is the immediate presence of the Holy One of Israel, could not be poured out on sinful humanity, for apart from Christ's reconciliation we could never endure the sublime majesty and utter holiness of the Holy Spirit.[73]

Torrance emphasizes the agony it cost Christ to mediate the Holy Spirit to us. We can not begin to fathom the sheer depth of humiliation and passion of our Lord and Savior, for "it was only at infinite cost that Jesus Christ gained for us the gift of the Holy Spirit, receiving him in all his consuming holiness into the human nature which he took from our fallen and alienated condition."[74] Only after Christ sanctified our human nature in

---

[68]Ibid., p. 247. Torrance argues that Jesus faced the temptations in the wilderness in the power of the Spirit. Jesus prayed in the Spirit and proclaimed the kingdom of God in word and deed through the same Spirit. Jesus suffered in the Spirit, bore human evil in the Spirit, offered his humanity (our humanity) to the Father in the Spirit. Jesus died, was raised to life and ascended to the Father all in the presence and power of the Holy Spirit, whom he received vicariously on our behalf (see p. 246).

[69]Thomas F. Torrance, *The Mediation of Christ*, 2d ed. (Colorado Springs: Helmers & Howard, 1992), p. 118.

[70]Ibid.

[71]Torrance, *Christian Doctrine*, p. 148.

[72]Ibid.

[73]Ibid., p. 64.

[74]Torrance, *Reconstruction*, p. 246.

himself; only after his life of perfect obedience in our place; only after his atoning self-sacrifice on the cross; only after the expiation of our guilt; only after the powers of darkness and death itself had been overcome; only after Christ ascended in triumphant glory and presented himself in propitiation in the presence of the Father on our behalf; only then could Christ enter the kingdom of heaven and release at Pentecost the blessing of the Holy Spirit in his renewing and sanctifying power into the world and our hearts and lives.[75]

Pentecost and Calvary are deeply interrelated in Torrance's theology, since the new coming of the Spirit on us and the realization of God's presence within us *fulfills* God's reconciliation of the world to himself in Christ.[76] The Holy Spirit comes on the church *from* Christ's obedience unto death and victory over sin and *in* all of the transforming power of Christ's risen, sanctified, and glorified vicarious humanity. For Torrance the coinherent activity and essentiality of the self-giving of the Son of God and self-giving of the Holy Spirit mean that Jesus Christ mediates the Spirit to us. Yet it also means that it is the Holy Spirit who mediates Jesus Christ to us.

The coming of the Holy Spirit mediates Jesus Christ to us. In Torrance's theology everything that Jesus Christ does vicariously on our behalf throughout his life, death and resurrection is done through the Holy Spirit. Thus the role of the Spirit in mediating Jesus Christ to us begins with Christ's conception and extends through life, death resurrection, and ascension.[77] When the Holy Spirit comes from the Father after the ascension of Christ, the Spirit does so as the Holy Spirit who has already sanctified humanity and realized human knowledge of God in and through the earthly, historical vicarious human life of Christ.[78] It is as the Spirit of Jesus, through whom Christ accomplished our salvation, that the Holy Spirit comes on the church clothed with Christ and his redemptive activity and transforming power as our Savior and Lord.[79]

The Spirit unites us with Christ. We should not think of the Holy Spirit, Torrance argues, as a substitute for Christ, but rather as coming in Christ's name and uniting the church with the risen Christ in Christ's identification

---

[75]Ibid., p. 247.

[76]Torrance, *Christian Doctrine*, p. 64.

[77]Torrance, *Reconstruction*, pp. 222, 227. Also see Torrance, *Christian Doctrine*, p. 62.

[78]Torrance, *Christian Doctrine*, p. 62.

[79]Torrance, *Reconstruction*, p. 148.

with us.[80] The Spirit so unites us with Christ that in the Spirit's coming on the church Christ himself comes again to dwell in the church uniting the church with himself as his body.[81]

The Holy Spirit does not simply actualize within us all that God has done for us in Jesus Christ. Rather, the Spirit opens us up for Christ, so that through union with Christ we draw our life from Christ.[82] In light of this, Torrance argues that we should not think of the Holy Spirit "as acting in the place of, as if in absence of, the exalted Lord, for in his coming and presence Christ himself is with us, acting for us from the side of God toward man but as acting in us from the side of man toward God."[83]

Here Torrance sees a twofold activity of the Holy Spirit (God-humanward and human-Godward) that parallels and answers the twofold work of Christ. The Spirit comes forth from God the Father, receives from the Son, acts from the side of God and unites Christ to us, actualizing Christ's revealing and reconciling activity within us. Yet at the same time the Spirit upholds us from our side and sustains us from within so that we are set free in the Spirit to return through Christ to God and cry "Abba, Father" in faith, obedience, worship and prayer, and thus to be raised up in the Spirit through Christ for communion with the triune God.[84]

This, of course, represents the pneumatological side of *anhypostasis/enhypostasis* couplet and the logic of grace discussed in chapter three above. All of grace means all of humanity, for divine agency in Jesus Christ and in the Holy Spirit does not exclude or override our human agency, but rather brings that human agency to its proper end in relation to God.[85] We will examine the role of the Holy Spirit in mediating revelation and reconciliation to us before dealing with the role of the Holy Spirit in our human response to revelation and reconciliation. The structure of this discussion parallels the christological treatment of these themes in chapters two and three.

The Holy Spirit and revelation. While it is through the vicarious life of Christ that the Spirit is mediated to us, the function of the Holy Spirit is not to bear witness to himself, but to Christ as Savior and Lord. Torrance

[80]Torrance, *Christian Doctrine*, p. 65.
[81]Torrance, *Reconstruction*, pp. 249-50.
[82]Ibid., p. 238.
[83]Ibid., p. 250.
[84]Torrance, *Christian Doctrine*, pp. 148-50, and Torrance, *Reconstruction*, pp. 249-51.
[85]See chapter three above, especially pp. 117-23.

maintains that the Spirit poured out on the church at Pentecost does not focus attention on himself. Nor does the Spirit bring us any knowledge or informational content independent of or other than God's self-revelation in Jesus Christ.[86] It is the mission of the Spirit to glorify Jesus Christ and to guide the disciples into Christ as the way and the truth.

The Holy Spirit is not cognoscible in his own personal mode of being, as noted above, for the Spirit hides himself and effaces himself in his own mode of activity as Spirit, revealing the Father in the Son *through* himself as Holy Spirit.[87] The Spirit directs us through his own transparent presence to the one Word of God, Jesus Christ himself.[88] Torrance argues that this is why there is no kingdom of the Spirit or no body of the Spirit, but only a body and kingdom of Christ, for the presence and activity of Holy Spirit are transparent and self-effacing.[89]

Yet it is only through the presence and activity of the Holy Spirit, Torrance asserts, that we are made free to know, believe and obey God's self-revelation in Jesus Christ. No one comes to Christ simply on the ground of human testimony or argument.[90] This is the soteriological ground of Torrance's rejection of an independent natural theology. God reveals himself through himself, since only God can reveal God and save us.[91]

Thus in Torrance's theology the Holy Spirit acts on both sides of the relation between God and humanity, bringing God's self-revelation in Jesus Christ to bear on us and opening us up to receive and understand that revelation.[92] The Spirit creates within us this relation to himself and the capacity to receive and apprehend God's self-revelation, and thereby reveals himself as *Lord and God*.[93]

Even Jesus' disciples were unable to grasp and were slow to understand

---

[86]Torrance, *Christian Doctrine*, p. 147; Thomas F. Torrance, *Karl Barth: Biblical and Evangelical Theologian* (Edinburgh: T & T Clark, 1990), p. 211; and Thomas F. Torrance, *God and Rationality* (London: Oxford University Press, 1971), pp. 165-92.

[87]Torrance, *Christian Doctrine*, pp. 66, 151.

[88]Ibid., p. 66, and Torrance, *Reconstruction*, p. 252. The Spirit utters Christ the living Word of God, not himself as the Spirit of the Father and the Son.

[89]Torrance, *Reconstruction*, p. 254

[90]Ibid., p. 252, and Torrance, *Christian Doctrine*, p. 62. Also see 1 Corinthians 12:3.

[91]Torrance, *Christian Doctrine*, p. 60.

[92]Ibid., p. 152.

[93]Ibid., pp. 59-60, 147, and Torrance, *Reconstruction*, p. 252. Torrance argues that only if the Holy Spirit is fully and personally God, *homoousios* with the Father and the Son, can we make sense of the Holy Spirit mediating and actualizing within us God's self-revelation in Jesus Christ to us.

who Christ was and is until the Spirit came on them at Pentecost. The Holy Spirit is the "living personal Agent of Christ" sent from the Father to lead the disciples into the truth, to enable them not only to remember all that Jesus said and did, but to create in them faith and understanding and make them witnesses of Christ to the ends of the earth. The Holy Spirit created within the apostles and the apostolic church the matrix within which Jesus Christ continues to be heard and believed as the Word of God.[94]

In the coming of the Holy Spirit, the Spirit of God brings God's self-revelation to its fulfillment, Torrance contends, "for the Spirit is the creative Subject of God's revelation to us and the creative Subject in our reception and understanding of the revelation."[95]

The Holy Spirit and Scripture. It is in light of the coming of the Holy Spirit to mediate and actualize God's self-revelation in Jesus Christ within us that Torrance understands the role of the Holy Spirit in relation to Scripture. Torrance affirms the inspiration of Scripture, but it is an inspiration inseparable from the mediation of revelation that takes place in God's dialogue with Israel through the ages and especially in the vicarious humanity of Christ where the Word of God and the human word are perfectly coordinated within the *hypostatic union*, as we saw in chapters two and three above.[96] The Holy Spirit's inspiration of the New Testament takes place within the matrix of (1) Christ's self-witness, which established a nucleus of relationships with his apostles; (2) Christ's resurrection, which casts new light on all that Jesus had said and done; and (3) the outpouring of Holy Spirit at Pentecost uniting the disciples to Christ and leading them into the truth that Christ is.

When the Holy Spirit came on the apostles, Torrance sees the Spirit as

---

[94]Torrance, *Christian Doctrine*, p. 65, and Torrance, *Reconstruction*, p. 253.

[95]Torrance, *Reconstruction*, p. 253.

[96]Chapter three dealt with the relation between the Word of God and the human word in the vicarious humanity of Christ, in the apostolic foundation of the church and in the genesis of the New Testament (see pp. 102-9). Also see chapter two, pp. 61-69, for the role of Israel in the mediation of revelation, the genesis of the Old Testament and their relation to Jesus Christ. Here we are concerned with the specific role of the Holy Spirit in relation to Scripture in Torrance's theology.

When the inspiration of Scripture is cut off from realities and events of God's self-revelation in Israel, Jesus Christ and the apostolic foundation of the church, the Bible is often viewed as essentially oracular in character. Revelation becomes predominantly propositional, and the words of the text and the Word of God are identical. In this view *God* is not the reality and content of God's revelation. Rather revelation becomes revealed *information* about God. Torrance's view is quite different.

uniting the church to Christ, so that "clothed with the historical facts of the gospel, Jesus Christ now returns to shine with the light of his glory within the apostolic mind and to fulfill in them his own interpretation of himself and his work. This is not any new revelation . . . but the actual unfolding of the mind of the risen Lord within the apostolic Church."[97] The Holy Spirit so reconciled and united the disciples to Christ that the disciples' understanding of and witness to Christ (including their human memories of Jesus) are assumed and molded into oneness with Jesus Christ, the living Word of God. Torrance will even say "that the Apostolic word is the Word of Christ . . . the apostolic revelation of the gospel in which the whole witness of the New Testament is delivered to the Church."[98]

Thus in God's dialogue with Israel and in the incarnation of the Word of God in Jesus Christ, God adapts the creaturely, human structures of thought, language, liturgy and even the lives of the apostles to his self-revelation, while in the mission and presence of the Holy Spirit, Christ uses these creaturely structures as the very means by which the apostles apprehend the mind of Christ. The Spirit assimilated the apostles to that mind, and thereby created as it were the apostolic sphere where Christ continues to be present and proclaimed through the Holy Spirit.[99]

Torrance is much less interested in mechanics of how the Spirit inspired Scripture, than he is in the fact that God "has uniquely and sovereignly coordinated the biblical word with his eternal Word, and adapted the written form and contents of the Bible to his Word, in such a way that the living voice of God is made to resound through the Bible to all who have ears to hear. The Bible is thus constituted by God to be the written Word of God, the holy medium of the very revelation that God himself is."[100]

The Bible, in Torrance's theology, is not simply the "occasion" for God to speak the living Word of God through the Spirit. The relation between God's self-revelation and Scripture, between the divine Word and the human word, is far more complex than this. The mediation of revelation is dynamic, historical and ontological. It involves divine agency and human

---

[97]Torrance, *Reconstruction*, p. 137.

[98]Ibid.

[99]Ibid., p. 253.

[100]Torrance, *Karl Barth*, p. 88. Torrance elsewhere contends that "we have to insist that the creaturely correspondence of Holy Scripture to God's Word is so miraculously assumed and used by divine revelation that even within the perspective of redeemed sinners it is adapted by the Spirit not only to mediate the Holy Word of God but to be the holy expression of that Word in human form" (Torrance, *Reconstruction*, p. 139).

agency in Israel, in the vicarious humanity of Christ, in the eye and ear witness of the disciples, in the early church and in the composition of the documents eventually canonized in the New Testament, as outlined above
and in chapters two and three.

Furthermore, this relation between Word of God and the Bible is a historical, dynamic, ontological relation, Torrance contends, that is not only
freely *established* by God, but is *unceasingly affirmed* and *maintained* through
the presence and activity of the Word of God and the Holy Spirit, for "God
freely and purposely makes himself present in the Scripture he has
brought into being through the activity of his Word" and his Spirit.[101]

Of course, God remains transcendent over Scripture. That the Spirit inspired the Scriptures, Torrance contends, does not mean that there is a static and direct identity between the words of the Bible and the living Word
of God.[102] If God's Word in Jesus Christ is a *self*-revelation, if God's being is
in God's activity and God's activity inheres in God's being, then Torrance
argues that "Holy Scripture cannot be what it is inspired by the Holy Spirit
to be, if its continuing link with God acting and speaking in Person is broken or disregarded."[103] Holy Scripture is and continues to be the written
Word of God by "virtue of the fact that God *continuously coordinates* it with
the active presence of his Word and Spirit" so that there is a *real* relation between Scripture and God's self-communication, one only *God* can and graciously does maintain, not one we can control or create on our own.[104]

We will take up what all of this means for the interpretation of Scripture
in chapter nine when we deal with Torrance's theological method, but
what is at stake here, in Torrance's mind, is the *identity* or *oneness* between
God and the content of God's self-revelation.[105] If we really believe that
God speaks *personally* in Scripture and communicates the living Word of
God to us through Scripture by the Holy Spirit, Torrance thinks our understanding of the Bible and our reading of it will undergo a radical paradigmatic shift in which we pray for and expect the mighty wind of the Spirit
to sweep us "into direct encounter with the wholly other of God who may
be heard only through his own self-witness."[106]

---

[101]Torrance, *Karl Barth*, p. 92.
[102]Ibid., pp. 91-92. Torrance speaks of a dynamic understanding of inspiration.
[103]Ibid., p. 95.
[104]Ibid.
[105]Ibid., p. 98.
[106]Ibid., pp. 87-88.

The Holy Spirit brings God's self-revelation and self-communication through Jesus Christ to fulfillment in the apostles, in Scripture and in our lives today. Part of the reason for this is that revelation and reconciliation are inseparable in Torrance's theology. We cannot know the truth without becoming at-one with the truth. This cannot but involve radical conversion in our lives and reconciliation with God which only God can bring to pass.

The Holy Spirit and reconciliation. While the Holy Spirit is mediated to us through Jesus' vicarious life, death, resurrection and ascension on our behalf, in Torrance's theology, it is the Holy Spirit who mediates Jesus Christ in his reconciling activity to us.[107] The Son of God assumed our sinful and disobedient humanity, reconciled it to God in atoning sacrifice and offered his vicarious humanity to the Father on our behalf and in our place.[108] Torrance argues that we should think of the Holy Spirit sent by Christ from the Father as realizing the reconciling work of Christ in our lives.

Jesus Christ is the one mediator between God and humanity. But the Spirit comes to us through Christ as the Spirit of reconciliation and redemption.[109] The Holy Spirit comes to us from Christ's whole life of obedience and victory in the cross and resurrection as the Spirit clothed with the transforming power of Christ's risen and glorified divine-human reality.[110] In Torrance's pneumatology the Holy Spirit makes the reconciliation of the world to God in Christ efficacious in our lives.[111]

In places Torrance speaks of the Spirit as Christ's *Alter Ego* or *Alter Advocatus* who seals our adoption as children of God in Christ and so unites us to Christ that we come to share by grace in Christ's own filial relationship with the Father realized vicariously within Christ's earthly human life on our behalf.[112] God does not live for himself alone, but has poured out his love for us without reserve in Jesus Christ our Savior and Lord, and sheds the love of God in Christ abroad in our hearts through the Holy Spirit.[113] In and through the living and life-giving Holy Spirit we participate in

---

[107] Torrance, *Reconstruction*, p. 246.
[108] Torrance, *Christian Doctrine*, p. 154
[109] Torrance, *Reconstruction*, p. 248.
[110] Ibid., p. 248.
[111] Torrance, *Christian Doctrine*, p. 64.
[112] See Torrance, *Mediation*, p. 117, and Torrance, *Trinitarian Faith*, p. 249.
[113] Torrance, *Christian Doctrine*, p. 150.

all of God's reconciling and saving activity in Jesus Christ.[114]

Torrance views the Holy Spirit in relation to reconciliation as the freedom of God to actualize our relation to God through Jesus Christ and thereby bring to completion God's loving purpose for our lives so that we participate beyond our own capacity in the communion which the Father, Son and Holy Spirit are in their trinitarian life.[115] The Spirit realizes this relation by going forth from God, activating *God's* relation toward us, and returning to God, activating *our* relation to God and freeing us for faith, obedience, prayer, worship and witness.[116] In so doing the Spirit answers the twofold, God-humanward and human-Godward, mediation of Christ.[117] This brings us to the role of the Holy Spirit in our human response to God's revelation and reconciliation.

The Holy Spirit and our human response. Chapter three dealt with Torrance's conceptualization of our human response to God in relation to the *total substitutionary* character of Christ's vicarious humanity in which Jesus Christ acts on our behalf and in our place at every point in the *ordo salutis* (order of salvation). Torrance develops this theme in such a way that all of Christ and all of grace in no way negate, supplant or undermine the human person and human agency but rather fulfill them within the embrace of God's gracious agency in Christ.[118] Here we will examine the pneumatological side of the relation between divine agency and human agency in our response to God.

In Torrance's perspective, through the Holy Spirit we are united to Christ in Christ's identification with us. The Spirit comes forth from God uniting us to the response, faith, obedience and worship of Jesus Christ in his vicarious humanity, and returns to God, uniting our response, faith, obedience and worship with Christ as our high priest.[119] The Spirit comes in divine freedom and is able to be present to us, sustain our human response to God from below and within, and assimilate us to the self-consecration of Jesus Christ on our behalf in a way that fulfills our personal

---

[114]Torrance, *Reconstruction*, p. 243. Torrance can say that "the Holy Spirit remains the Creative Agent in all God's ways and works" (see p. 254). Torrance maintains that the Spirit personally subsists in all of God's gifts, so that in the Spirit the divine gift and the divine giver are one (see Torrance, *Trinitarian Faith*, p. 225).

[115]Torrance, *Christian Doctrine*, p. 148, and Torrance, *Mediation*, p. 119.

[116]Torrance, *Christian Doctrine*, p. 152, and Torrance, *Reconstruction*, p. 248.

[117]See chapters two and three for the twofold mediation of Christ.

[118]See chapter three, pp. 113-23.

[119]Torrance, *Reconstruction*, p. 250.

being and response in relation to God.

There is imparted to us by the Holy Spirit a freedom and openness to God and others, Torrance contends, that answers and reflects the openness and freedom of God for us rooted in God's own openness and freedom within the trinitarian life that God is, as noted above.[120] This is true across the full spectrum of our human response to God and others.

Consider prayer, for example. In Torrance's perspective, prayer is first and foremost something that Christ does on our behalf in his life and in his death, but also as our ascended Lord and High Priest who intercedes for us in the presence of God the Father.[121] The Holy Spirit sent by the risen Lord unites us with Christ, mediating Christ and his intercession to us in such a way that Christ's prayer echoes in our hearts.[122] Since we do not know how to pray as we ought, Torrance sees the Spirit at work sustaining us from below and within, intervening in our weakness, uniting our unworthy prayer and praise with Christ's own intercession and worship in the presence of the Father.[123]

In the same way, the Spirit of the Son unites us with Christ's filial relation to God, echoes within us that we are daughters and sons of God, sustains our human response of faith in and love for God, and unites it with Christ's own faith and love.[124] This same pattern extends to every aspect of our own human response to the grace of our Lord Jesus Christ, the love of God the Father, and the fellowship of the Holy Spirit.

Therefore, while the Holy Spirit comes to us and is at work within us in the sheer transcendent power of God, Torrance maintains that the Spirit does not overwhelm us in our humanity, for the Spirit's coming is gentle. The presence and activity of the Holy Spirit in our human response is a "kind of quiet but utterly supreme power," for only the Almighty can be so astonishingly gentle.[125]

As with Jesus Christ, Torrance views the activity of the Spirit in our humanity not as overriding or diminishing our humanity and human response, but as personalizing and humanizing us and our response. The indwelling presence of God through Christ and in the Spirit heals, restores

---

[120]Torrance, *Christian Doctrine*, p. 154.
[121]Torrance, *Reconstruction*, p. 249, and Torrance, *Christian Doctrine*, p. 154.
[122]Torrance, *Christian Doctrine*, p. 154.
[123]Torrance, *Reconstruction*, p. 249.
[124]Torrance, *Christian Doctrine*, p. 154.
[125]Torrance, *Trinitarian Faith*, p. 228.

and intensifies our human and personal being and response in relation to God and to others.[126] In all of our human response in faith, obedience, worship, prayer and witness we are upheld by the Holy Spirit on both sides of our relation with God. The Spirit actualizes God's relation with us and activates our relation with God in a way in which the freedom and agency of God interpenetrates, embraces and upholds the freedom and agency of our redeemed humanity through Christ's vicarious humanity to the glory of God.

This personalizing activity of the Holy Spirit in our lives is ultimately rooted in the fully personal character of God who alone is personalizing person. It is because God is a fullness of personal being as Father, Son and Holy Spirit, that God is the author and source of our personal and personalized reality.

4. The Procession of the Holy Spirit

Torrance's understanding of the procession of the Holy Spirit is complex, and his development of it in several publications is lengthy.[127] Essentially, Torrance develops his understanding of the procession of the Spirit based on the work of Athanasius, Epiphanius and Cyril of Alexandria, which Torrance believes provides an alternative to the position of the East and the West in regard to the *filioque* clause.[128]

Following basic ideas drawn from Athanasius, Torrance moves from the *homoousion* of the Son and the Spirit with the Father, and the intensely personal understanding of God implied in the *homoousion*, to the *perichoretic* interrelations of the three persons in the one being (*ousia* with internal relations) of God. The concept of *perichoresis* (and the *homoousion*) leads to a deepening and development of the divine *monarchia* (monarchy) to include not only the Father, but the whole Trinity in Unity, the one Godhead of Fa-

---

[126]Ibid. p. 230.

[127]See ibid., pp. 231-47 and Torrance, *Christian Doctrine*, pp. 168-92. The discussion in *Trinitarian Faith* deals primarily with the debate about the procession of the Spirit in relation to the Nicene-Constantinopolitan Creed, though Torrance's own position is fairly evident. The discussion in *Christian Doctrine* is Torrance's definitive statement.

[128]See Torrance, *Christian Doctrine*, p. 185. The Western "Catholic" Church added the *filioque* clause ("and from the Son") to the Nicene Creed so that the third article of the creed reads "And in the Holy Spirit, the Lord and Giver of life, who proceeds from the Father *and the Son* [emphasis mine]." The West added the clause to affirm the full deity of the Son. The fear was that without the clause, it is possible to view the Son as of lesser deity than the Father, and thereby to open the door for neo-Arian understanding of the Son in relation to the Father.

ther, Son and Holy Spirit. The doctrine of *perichoresis* and this conceptualization of the trinitarian monarchy provide a deeper basis for understanding of
the procession of the Spirit that overcomes the divide between East and West.

We will develop Torrance's understanding of the procession of the
Spirit by following this basic pattern beginning with the *homoousion* and
the intensely personal understanding of God it entails, then dealing with
the concept of *perichoresis*, and the issue of the divine monarchy. The final
subsection will examine Torrance's reformulation of the procession of the
Holy Spirit.

Homoousios and the deity and personhood of the Spirit. The *homoousial*
relation between the incarnate Son and God the Father asserts in the strongest way possible that what God is toward us in God's revealing and saving activity in Jesus Christ, God is in God's own being as God, as
developed in chapter two above.[129] God himself is the content of his Word
and grace in Jesus Christ, for the giver and the gift are identical. The Father
and the Son coinhere in one another, not only in God's activity toward us
in Jesus Christ, but in the one being of God.[130]

It was also the overwhelming conviction of Athanasius, among other
Nicene theologians, that when the Holy Spirit unites us with Christ, reconciles us to God, sanctifies and liberates us, it is *God* who is personally
present to us and who acts personally in our lives in the Spirit, as noted
earlier in this chapter.[131] Since it is *God* who comes in the Holy Spirit in the
name of Christ, Athanasius applied the *homoousion* to the relation of the
Spirit to Christ and through Christ to the Father.[132]

The *homoousion* asserts in the strongest way possible both the divine
and personal character of the Holy Spirit, for what God is in God's illumin-
ing and sanctifying activity toward us in the Holy Spirit, God is in God's
own being (and vice-versa).[133] The Holy Spirit is not external to God, nor
an energy separable from God.[134] The Spirit cannot be any less divine or
less personal than the Son and the Father, for only God can reveal God and
only God can save us from sin and death.[135]

---

[129]Torrance, *Trinitarian Faith*, pp. 215-16, 231-32.
[130]Ibid.
[131]Ibid., pp. 211-22, 232-34.
[132]Ibid., p. 216.
[133]Ibid., p. 233.
[134]Ibid., pp. 217-22.
[135]Ibid., p. 223. Torrance argues that God himself in all the fullness of God's triune being and

In Torrance's theology, the *homoousion* implies not only a oneness of being between the Son, the Father and the Holy Spirit; it also implies distinctions between them, for nothing is *homoousios* with itself. Thus the
application of the *homoousion* to the Son and the Spirit, arising out the
church's evangelical and doxological encounter with God through Jesus
Christ in the Holy Spirit, leads to a radically Christian and trinitarian understanding of the being of God. This means that the *ousia* (being) of God
does not refer to some abstract divine essence, but rather to an intensely
personal concept of being with internal interrelations.[136]

When combined with the fact that God *is* Spirit, as noted earlier in this
chapter, the understanding of the being of God that Torrance sees coming
into view is one in which God's being is essentially spiritual and intrinsically personal, a fullness of interrelational personal being.[137] The Holy
Spirit coinheres with the Father and the Son in the one being of God and
therefore the Spirit belongs to the constitutive internal interrelations of the
Godhead, one being three persons.

Perichoresis and the Holy Spirit. Torrance argues that it was along this
line of development that Nicene theology became convinced that the reciprocal interrelations of the Father, Son and Holy Spirit in God's revealing and reconciling activity through Christ and in the Spirit cannot be
viewed as temporary manifestations of God's nature; they can be viewed
only as intrinsic and coinherent relations in God's own being and trinitarian life.[138] Viewed in this way, the Holy Spirit coinheres or dwells in the inner life and being of the Holy Trinity and shares in the reciprocal knowing
and loving of the Father and the Son.[139]

This is the essence of the theological concept of *perichoresis*, which expresses in our inadequate human understanding and language something
of the astonishing mystery of the oneness and threeness, the Trinity in Unity and Unity in Trinity, of God's triune life revealed in the economic Trinity and traced back to the ontological Trinity through the *homoousion*.[140]

---

trinitarian life is present in all of God's activity in creation, revelation, reconciliation and
  redemption.
[136]See ibid., pp. 241-43; Thomas F. Torrance, *Trinitarian Perspectives: Towards Doctrinal Agreement* (Edinburgh: T & T Clark, 1994), pp. 130-35; and Torrance, *Christian Doctrine*, pp. 155-
  69.
[137]Torrance, *Trinitarian Perspectives*, p. 131.
[138]Torrance, *Trinitarian Faith*, p. 234.
[139]Ibid., p. 232, and Torrance, *Christian Doctrine*, pp. 169-71.
[140]Torrance, *Christian Doctrine*, pp. 168-73.

The distinctions between the persons do not divide, but rather unite them within the one being of God.[141] In Torrance's theology, *perichoresis* refers to the intensely spiritual, personal, dynamic and onto-relational mutual indwelling and coinhering of the three divine persons in the one being of God.[142] Torrance thinks that the perichoretic interrelations of the trinitarian persons completely rule out any notion of subordination within the trinitarian relations.[143]

We will deal with *perichoresis* more fully in chapter eight. What is crucial for this discussion is that the Holy Spirit, in his homoousial relations with the Father and the Son in the one being of God, shares in the knowing and loving of the Father and the Son, and comes to us from the eternal movement of love that God is. The coinherent relations between the persons reciprocally interpenetrate all of their activity.[144] Torrance argues that *perichoresis* is not a speculative concept, but rather expresses the intensely interpersonal and soteriological identity between God's saving activity in Jesus Christ and in the Holy Spirit and what God is inherently and eternally in himself.[145]

Following Epiphanius, Torrance sees the Spirit coming into our midst, proceeding from the being of the Father, receiving from the Son (as developed earlier in this chapter), revealing God to us, uniting us with Christ, and through Christ to the Father so that we participate through the Spirit in the Son's knowing and loving of the Father and therefore in God's self-knowing and communion of love without in any way violating our creaturely reality.[146] There is one divine activity from the Father through the Son and in the Holy Spirit, and in the Holy Spirit through the Son to the Father. Torrance thinks that this cannot but influence how we think about the divine *monarchia*.

The divine monarchy and the Holy Spirit. While the Cappadocian theologians took over the trinitarian pattern from Athanasius, Torrance argues that their emphasis fell sharply on the persons of the Father, Son and Holy Spirit in their differentiation and particular modes of existence.[147] The

---

[141]Ibid., p. 172.

[142]Ibid., p. 171. Torrance says that the first actual use of the term *perichoresis* in extant literature is in the work of an unknown theologian attributed to Cyril of Alexandria (see p. 170).

[143]Torrance, *Trinitarian Perspectives*, p. 112.

[144]Ibid., p. 138

[145]Torrance, *Christian Doctrine*, p. 172.

[146]Torrance, *Trinitarian Faith*, pp. 221-23, 233-25.

[147]Ibid., p. 236, and Torrance, *Christian Doctrine*, pp. 181-82.

Cappadocians affirmed the doctrine that God is "One Being, Three Persons," but Torrance thinks that they were tempted to explain what this threeness and oneness of God means by use of the "dangerous analogy" of three people sharing a common nature.[148]

This, of course, opened up the suspicion that they were really advocating a kind of tritheism (three gods with a common nature), which the Cappadocians rightly and strongly rejected.[149] Torrance maintains that it was at this point that they appealed to the following idea as a way to preserve the oneness of God: that God the Father is the one principle or source (arche) and cause (aitia) of the Son and the Spirit.[150] Despite the qualifications the Cappadocians added—such as that there is no interval of time, space or existence between the Father, and the Son and the Spirit—this way of securing the oneness of the Godhead created what Torrance sees as a damaging distinction between the *uncaused* person of the Father and the *caused* deity and personal nature of the Son and the Spirit.[151]

Torrance notes that this emphasis on the person of the Father as the sole principle (arche) or source of deity tended to weaken "the Athanasian axiom that whatever we say of the Father we say of the Son and the Spirit except 'Father.'"[152] It also undermines the Athanasian and Nicene understanding of the divine *ousia* as being with or in internal relations.[153] The upshot is that it becomes difficult for theology to move from the evangelical acts of God in Jesus Christ and the Holy Spirit to what God is in God's own being. If the Word and Spirit of God do not inhere in God's being, then can we relate what God is toward in Jesus Christ and the Holy Spirit to what God is in God's being?[154]

Here Torrance sees Athanasius taking a rather different path. For Athanasius any notion of the Father alone as the *arche*, principle, cause or origin appeared Arian.[155] Since Athanasius saw the whole Godhead in the Son and in the Spirit, Athanasius held that the Son and the Spirit "must be included with the Father in the one originless Source or *Arche* of the Holy Trinity."[156] Athanasius did not entertain a view of the divine monarchy in

---

[148]Torrance, *Trinitarian Faith*, p. 237, and Torrance, *Christian Doctrine*, pp. 181-82.
[149]Torrance, *Trinitarian Faith*, p. 237.
[150]Ibid. Also see Torrance, *Christian Doctrine*, p. 181.
[151]Torrance, *Trinitarian Faith*, p. 237-42, and Torrance *Christian Doctrine*, p. 181.
[152]Torrance, *Trinitarian Faith*, p. 241. Also see Torrance, *Christian Doctrine*, p. 181.
[153]Torrance, *Trinitarian Faith*, pp. 242, 246.
[154]Ibid., p. 246.
[155]Torrance, *Christian Doctrine*, p. 181.
[156]Ibid., pp. 181, 183.

which the oneness of God is defined by reference to the *person* of the Father alone.[157]

It was Epiphanius, Torrance argues, who prior to the Council of Constantinople "provided the Church with the clearest statements about the Monarchy as the identity of the Trinity in Unity and the Unity in Trinity."[158] Epiphanius developed his position along the line of Athanasius, but applied the *homoousion* not only to each of the persons, but to the inner relations within the Trinity as a whole, and thereby further deepened the concept of the coinhering of the three divine persons in their enhypostatic interrelations.[159] The Father, Son and Holy Spirit and all their enhypostatic interrelations are *homoousios*: the persons are onto-relational and coinhere within the one being of God.

Thus Epiphanius emphasized the full equality, eternity, glory, power and perfection of the Father, and the Son and the Holy Spirit alike, for they coinhere and interpenetrate one another within the *ousia* (being with inner personal relations) of God.[160] In light of this, Epiphanius asserted, "In proclaiming the *Monarchia* we confess the Trinity, Unity in Trinity and Trinity in Unity, One Godhead of the Father, Son and Holy Spirit."[161]

Torrance sees this Athanasian-Epiphanian perspective as clearing away a variety of problems surrounding the doctrine of the Trinity and preparing the way for the ecumenical consensus confessed in the Nicene-Constantinopolitan Creed.[162] This perspective was developed further by Cyril of Alexandria, along with Gregory Nazianzen's trinitarian teaching, and also provided the basis for the doctrinal agreement between Orthodox and Reformed Churches in which Torrance himself played a strategic role.[163] This, of course, could not take place without dealing with the question of the procession of the Spirit.

The procession of the Spirit. Torrance contends that the doctrine of the one monarchy of God (which cannot be restricted to one divine person) together with the doctrine of *perichoresis* (in which the three divine persons

---

[157]Ibid., p. 183.

[158]Torrance, *Trinitarian Perspectives*, p. 138.

[159]Torrance, *Trinitarian Faith*, p. 222.

[160]Torrance, *Trinitarian Perspectives*, p. 139. Also see Torrance, *Christian Doctrine*, p. 184.

[161]Torrance provides this quotation in *Trinitarian Perspectives*, p. 139. Also see Torrance, *Christian Doctrine*, p. 184.

[162]Torrance, *Christian Doctrine*, pp. 184-85.

[163]Ibid., p. 185. See chapter one above, p. 47, for Torrance's important role in the dialogue leading up to the agreed doctrinal statement.

completely interpenetrate and contain one another in the one indivisible being of the holy Trinity) provide the basis for a deeper and more satisfactory account of the procession of the Spirit that cuts behind the division between East and West over the *filioque* clause.[164]

While the Cappadocians (Basil and his brother) rejected the idea that the Spirit is created by God, the idea that the Spirit proceeds from the Father *alone* and from the *person* of the Father, rather than the *being* of the Father, created a serious impasse.[165] The Western church could not but hold, Torrance contends, that the Spirit proceeds not from the Father alone, but from the Father and the Son. If the Spirit proceeds *only* from the Father, the Son could be regarded as subordinate to the Father and not fully God in the same sense as the Father.[166] Thus the West added the *filioque* to the Nicene Creed to guard against any inroad for subordinationism.

The Eastern church, from its perspective, could not but reject any notion that the Spirit proceeds from the Son, as well as the Father, for a double procession from the Father and the Son could not but appear to posit two ultimate divine principles or origins *(archia)* in God.[167] Thus the East rejected the *filioque* clause and affirmed that procession of the Spirit is *from the Father only*.[168]

In contrast to both perspectives, Torrance argues that the triune monarchy of God, and the *perichoretic* or complete interpenetration and coinherent relations of the Father, the Son and the Holy Spirit in the one indivisible being of the Holy Trinity, places the doctrine of the procession of the Spirit on a fully trinitarian basis.[169] Torrance returns to the Athanasian and Nicene *homoousion* in which the Son is from the *being* of the Father, not the *person* of the Father. The application of the *homoousion* to the Spirit has the same effect. The Spirit is one in being and activity with the Father, and the Spirit proceeds from the *being* of the Father, not from the *person* of the Father.[170]

Torrance contends that if we take seriously the perichoretic interrelation and interpenetration of the Father, the Son and the Spirit in one Being,

---

[164]Torrance, *Trinitarian Perspectives*, p. 112, and Torrance, *Christian Doctrine*, pp. 185-86.
[165]Torrance, *Trinitarian Faith*, p. 246, and Torrance, *Christian Doctrine*, p. 186.
[166]Torrance, *Christian Doctrine*, p. 186.
[167]Ibid.
[168]Ibid.
[169]Torrance, *Trinitarian Perspectives*, pp. 112, 141. Also see Torrance, *Christian Doctrine*, pp. 188-91.
[170]Torrance, *Christian Doctrine*, p. 188.

and the monarchy which cannot be limited to the Father, we have to think
of the Spirit proceeding from the Father through the Son.[171] If the Spirit
coinheres in the being of the Father and the Son, and if the Son is inseparable from the being of the Father and the Spirit, then Torrance argues that
we must conceive of the Holy Spirit proceeding from the perichoretic interrelations of the three persons within the one indivisible being of God,
Trinity in Unity and Unity in Trinity.[172]

Strictly speaking, Torrance asserts, "The Holy Spirit proceeds from the
one Monarchy of the Triune God."[173] Thus Torrance thinks that when
properly understood, the ideas that the Spirit proceeds from the Father *and*
the Son, or proceeds from the Father *through* the Son, both mean that the
Spirit proceeds from the communion of the Father and the Son; this is
what the Spirit is—the communion that the Father, the Son and the Holy
Spirit are in their eternal coinherent, perichoretic interrelations with one
another in the one *ousia* (being with inner relations) of God.[174]

Torrance is convinced that the doctrine of *perichoresis*, in which the three
divine persons mutually indwell one another while retaining their distinc-
tives and distinctions in relation to each other, must govern how we formulate the procession of the Spirit. When we think of the procession of the
Spirit from the Father and (or through) the Son, "we must do so in the conviction that the Father and the Son are *with the Spirit* the one identical Being of the Godhead, the Triune Monarchy."[175]

The real problem behind all of the difficulties concerning the procession
of the Spirit lies in the fact, Torrance contends, that we really do not know
what the "procession" of the Spirit actually means, just as we do not know
what the "begetting" of the Son really means.[176] Since this way of speaking
of the divine persons in their relations arises out of God's self-revelation,
Torrance argues that we must respect and utilize these designations, but
always in humility, reverence and care.[177]

---

[171]Ibid., p. 190.
[172]Ibid.
[173]Ibid.
[174]Ibid., p. 192.
[175]Ibid.
[176]Ibid.
[177]Ibid., p. 193. The terms denote ineffable divine realities and relations that we apprehend
    through God's self-revelation in Jesus Christ the incarnate Son of the Father, through
    Jesus' teaching about the Father and the Spirit, and through the outpouring of the Spirit at
    Pentecost. Yet they are divine realities and relations that we cannot comprehend.

When we think of the "begetting" of the Son and the "proceeding" of the Spirit, Torrance says that we are faced with the incomprehensible and inexpressible mystery of the triune God who is more to be worshiped and adored than circumscribed by our thoughts and our words.[178] The wealth of God's glory cannot be captured in the poverty of human conceptualization.[179] In the words of Athanasius, "Thus far human knowledge goes. Here the cherubim spread the covering of their wings."[180]

In all of the Spirit's activity in revelation and reconciliation, the Holy Spirit comes to us from the perichoretic mutual indwelling and communion that the Father, Son and Holy Spirit are in the trinitarian life of the one being of God. The grace of our Lord Jesus Christ and the love of God the Father are actualized in our relationship with God, and with one another, through the communion of the Holy Spirit. "It is then in the Holy Spirit," Torrance contends, "that we have communion or *koinonia* in the mystery of Christ, and are made members of his Body."[181]

The Holy Spirit is God in his freedom to be present to us, to sustain our relationship with God, and to create in our midst this community of reciprocity with Jesus Christ and with one another. In Torrance's theology the church, through the presence and power of the Spirit, the Lord and giver of life, is the body of Christ, the earthly correlate within our creaturely human existence of the trinitarian koinonia that God is in God's very life as one God three persons.[182]

---

[178]Ibid., p. 193. Torrance points out that Athanasius believed that it is irreverent to ask *how* the Spirit proceeds and would not consider the question at all (see p. 188). Also see Torrance, *Trinitarian Faith*, p. 235.

[179]Torrance, *Christian Doctrine*, p. 173.

[180]Ibid., p. 193.

[181]Torrance, *Trinitarian Faith*, p. 250.

[182]Ibid., pp. 250-51.

7

THE CHURCH,
THE BODY OF CHRIST

*The Reality of the Church is the earthly-historical form
of the Existence of Jesus Christ, the one holy catholic and apostolic Church.*
T . F . T O R R A N C E , P A R A P H R A S I N G K A R L B A R T H

I n his two most important essays on ecclesiology Torrance develops the doctrine of the church in the context of his doctrine of the Holy Spirit.[1] The church *is* the body of Christ, since in Jesus Christ, the Son of God

---

[1]See Thomas F. Torrance, *The Trinitarian Faith: The Evangelical Faith of the Ancient Catholic Church* (Edinburgh: T & T Clark, 1988), pp. 9, 250-52. Torrance explicitly associates chapter seven, "The One Church," with chapter six, "The Eternal Spirit." The other crucial essay on the church, "The Foundation of the Church: Union with Christ through the Spirit," appears as the first chapter of part three ("And in the Holy Spirit") in Thomas F. Torrance, *Theology in Reconstruction: Essays Towards Evangelical and Catholic Unity in East and West* (Grand Rapids, Mich.: Eerdmans, 1965), p. 209. The book is trinitarian in the organization of its chapters. Together, these two essays provide the best overview of Torrance's ecclesiology. My chapter draws heavily upon these two sources and also Torrance's book *Theology in Reconciliation* (Grand Rapids, Mich.: Eerdmans, 1975), especially chapters two, three and four which deal respectively with baptism, the Eucharist and worship. In a recent conversation, George Hunsinger told me that he considers Torrance's work on the sacraments to be possibly the most important breakthrough in this area within the Reformed tradition since Calvin.

Much of Torrance's earlier publication in the area of ecclesiology prior to 1960 arose out of his involvement in the ecumenical movement, particularly under the auspices of the World Council of Churches, but in other forms of ecumenical dialogue as well. The majority of the early lectures and essays (and even some book reviews and letters) were published in two volumes titled *Conflict and Agreement in the Church*, vol. 1, *Order and Disorder*, and vol. 2, *The Ministry and the Sacraments of the Gospel* (London: Lutterworth, 1959, 1960). The two volumes have been reprinted recently (Eugene, Ore.: Wipf and Stock, 1996). Since my book deals with Torrance's mature theology and not with the development of his thought, I focus primarily on his later publications.

assumed *our* bodily humanity, and reconciled, healed and redeemed that humanity through his incarnational life, death and resurrection. Christ's vicarious bodily humanity is what Torrance calls the first fruit of the church, the *arche* (beginning) of the new humanity which *is* the church.[2]

The Holy Spirit comes to us from the union and communion of the incarnate Son and the Father and out of the earthly-historical life of Jesus Christ, and unites us to Christ. The Spirit mediates Christ's vicarious humanity to us and creates corporate union and communion between us and Christ, and through Christ with God the Father.[3] The Holy Spirit realizes this corporate union and communion through Christ with God "in the actual structure of our human, personal and social being."[4]

Thus, Torrance understands the church as the "fruit" of the Holy Spirit, the "empirical correlate" of the Holy Spirit's parousia at Pentecost and throughout history.[5] This not only means that Torrance sees ecclesiology as a "function" of pneumatology, but also that the doctrine of the church does not constitute a separate and independent set of beliefs. Rather all that we say about the church has to be developed in integral connection with the gospel, and therefore along christocentric, pneumatological and trinitarian lines, as we will see as this chapter unfolds.[6]

The first section of the chapter deals with the genesis of the church, a genesis that stretches back in time through Pentecost to Jesus Christ's vicarious humanity, yet Jesus Christ *within* the people of Israel and the mediation of revelation and reconciliation in God's covenant relations with Israel. The section develops the interconnections of material from chapters two, three and six with Torrance's ecclesiology, since the church is the result of the mediation of revelation and reconciliation discussed in these earlier chapters.

The second section discusses Torrance's realist doctrine of the church as the *body of Christ*, which he contends is not simply a figurative expression, but rather asserts the ontological reality of the church as the earthly-historical form of Christ's own existence.[7] Everything else that Torrance has to

---

[2]Torrance, *Trinitarian Faith*, pp. 266-67.
[3]Ibid., pp. 9, 252, 266-67.
[4]Ibid., p. 9.
[5]Ibid., p. 252.
[6]Ibid., pp. 252, 253, 263.
[7]Thomas F. Torrance, *Karl Barth: Biblical and Evangelical Theologian* (Edinburgh: T & T Clark, 1990), p. 25.

say about the church flows from this central nexus of relations in which the Holy Spirit unites the church to Christ as his body and through Christ with the Father so that the church as the body of Christ *is* the union and communion of humanity with the triune God, from the Father through the Son and in the Holy Spirit, and in the Spirit through the Son to the Father.[8]

Subsequent sections in the second half of this chapter deal with the marks, the sacraments and the ministry of the church. In all of its reality, life and activity, the church embodies in the power of the Spirit the divine koinonia of the triune God within the earthly-historical conditions of the church's human and temporal existence.[9]

1. The Genesis of the Church

Torrance is adamant that the church is not primarily a human institution with a genesis in the voluntary association of like-minded people around a common moral or spiritual vision.[10] The church does not come into being by itself and for itself. It has its source, its telos, its *raison d'être* in the eternal life, love and koinonia of the triune God who wills not to live alone but creates others with whom God shares the divine love and koinonia that God is in God's own trinitarian life.[11] The church is of divine origin and exists as the object of the grace of our Lord Jesus Christ, the love of God the Father and the communion of the Holy Spirit.

However, the church did not come into existence automatically with the creation of the world, nor all at once in the course of history. Rather, the church has its genesis in history, Torrance contends, "as God called and entered into communion with his people and in and through them embodied and worked out by mighty acts of grace his purpose of love which he brought at last to fulfillment in Jesus Christ."[12]

While Torrance affirms the oneness of the church throughout history, as we will see later when we examine the marks of the church, he sees three stages or phases in the life of the church.[13] Before the incarnation the church took a preparatory form as God elected Israel from among the nations and subjected the people of God under the old covenant to intense

---

[8]Torrance, *Trinitarian Faith*, pp. 252-63.
[9]Ibid., pp. 9-10, 250-51, 252-63.
[10]Ibid., p. 277, and *Reconstruction*, pp. 192-93.
[11]Torrance, *Reconstruction*, p. 192.
[12]Ibid., pp. 192-93.
[13]Ibid., p. 193.

dialogue and interaction with himself. God did this so that Israel might become the appropriate medium, the community of reciprocity, in our human creaturely existence for the mediation of God's final self-revelation
and self-communication to all humanity in Jesus Christ, as we saw in chapters two and three.[14]

In Christ, Torrance argues, the church took on a new and fuller form
within the matrix of Israel. Jesus Christ gathered, fulfilled and transformed the one people of God in *himself* in his life, death, resurrection and
ascension.[15] Torrance can even say that Christ's vicarious humanity *is* the
church, for his vicarious reconciled, redeemed, resurrected and ascended
humanity *is* the new humanity forever united with the love and life of God
in which we participate through the Holy Spirit poured out at Pentecost.[16]

Only when Christ returns at the end of time to judge and renew his creation will the church enter its third phase, fully embody the new creation
that Christ is and share forever in the love and communion of God the Father, Son and Holy Spirit.[17] For now the church lives between the times in
a condition of humiliation and all of the ambiguity of history.

Yet since the Holy Spirit mediates the revelation and reconciliation of
God in Jesus Christ to the church in space and time, the church already
participates in the love and life of God and lives in anticipation of the fullness of God's redemption and new creation in Christ that will be when
Christ returns.[18] The church is the provisional form of the new creation, the
reconciled people of God whose life is hidden with Christ in God. The
church is the sphere in the midst of space-time and human existence/his-
tory, created by God's self-revelation and self-communication where God
is known, worshiped, loved and obeyed. As such the church has a mission
as the servant of Christ to bring the message of the gospel to all the world
in word and deed. The church is sent to call all people to obedience to the
love of God in Jesus Christ so that the Holy Spirit might be poured out on
all flesh, break down every barrier that separates people from God and
one another, and gather all people together to meet the ascended Christ
who comes again in final victory.[19]

---

[14]Ibid.
[15]Ibid.
[16]See Torrance, *Trinitarian Faith*, p. 267.
[17]Torrance, *Reconstruction*, p. 193.
[18]Ibid., p. 193.
[19]Ibid.

The genesis and reality of the church in Torrance's perspective is *in no way separate* from the mediation of revelation and reconciliation that takes place (1) in the life and history of God's covenant relation with Israel; (2) in the atoning life, death and resurrection of Jesus Christ; and (3) in the mutual mediation of Jesus Christ and the Holy Spirit as discussed in chapters two, three and six above.[20] It is the exact same history and activity of God but viewed from the christological perspective (chapters two and three), from the pneumatological perspective (chapter six) and from the ecclesiological perspective (this chapter).

In fact this is also true of chapters four, five and eight which all deal in one way or another with the same unified, yet differentiated reality (form in being). Chapter four deals with the mediation of revelation and reconciliation from the perspective of the doctrine of God the Father, and examines God's almightiness in light of it. Since it is as God the Father Almighty that God is Creator, chapter five deals with what we learn about God the sovereign Creator and the contingent creation (including human creature) from the same history and activity of God. Chapter eight examines the Christian (trinitarian) doctrine of God implicit in this same history and divine activity. And chapter nine explores the actual rigorous scientific theological method by which this differentiated history and activity of God in self-revelation and self-communication come to theological articulation in godly life, thought and worship of the triune God of grace.

What Torrance envisages is interrelated facets of a unified, yet differentiated, dynamic and ontological nexus of continuous divine interaction and human response (involving divine agency and human agency) moving through creaturely space-time (from Israel through Jesus Christ and the church until Christ comes again). This actual pattern of divine interaction in and through our creaturely world of space-time is God's *oikonomia* in history. In this chapter we will develop the ecclesiological facet of God's *oikonomia* discussed in previous chapters.[21]

Israel, the people of God under the old covenant. It is when God called

---

[20]Since redemption presupposes and fulfills creation, the material in chapter four (on God the Father Almighty) and that in chapter five (on creation) are also inseparable.

[21]This is really the essence of Torrance's holism in which we only really understand his position when we grasp the interrelated whole with simultaneous subsidiary attention to the parts. Rather than restate the discussion found in the earlier chapters, I encourage readers to refer back to the those chapters and the treatment of related themes found there. Especially important are chapters two (pp. 61-81), three (pp. 97-123), five (pp. 173-82) and six (pp. 221-33), though all of the chapters are interrelated and qualify one another.

Abraham that Torrance finds the beginning of the church as the sphere of God's redemptive activity leading through history to the fulfillment of God's promise of salvation for all people.[22] With the divine redemption of the people of Israel from bondage in Egypt and the covenant with God at Sinai, Israel became the *ecclesia* or church of God under the old covenant.[23]

Torrance argues that this covenant was sealed with two "sacraments," circumcision and the passover. God also provided the law, which set forth God's will, and the order of sacrifice and worship, which gave the people of Israel a way of cleansing and restoration to fellowship with God, a vicarious covenanted way of response provided by God in God's loving-kindness.[24]

In this way Israel became the people of God entrusted with the oracles of God and the promise of the Messiah, bound to God and God's purpose of revelation and reconciliation, existing in tension and struggle as the preparatory form of the church, unable to be all God intended until after the coming of God's Messiah. God molded and shaped Israel in anticipation of the fulfillment of the covenant, for through Israel God provided the matrix of life and thought within which the new covenant in Jesus Christ and the outpouring of the Spirit of God at Pentecost was and is understood, as we saw in chapters two and three.[25]

Thus Israel was chosen and formed by God to be the servant of God and the bearer of the Messiah, so that Israel therefore is not of human socio-political origin. Despite Israel's ethnic aspirations to be like the other nations, Torrance argues that it was the organic "union of Israel with Christ that constituted it Church and preserved it from extinction throughout all its ordeal of suffering, so that at last when it gave birth to the Messiah its whole historical life was gathered up in him and together with the Church of the Gentiles was constituted one New Man, the Israel of God the universal Body of Christ."[26]

Here in the genesis of the church in Israel in its historical ordeal before the coming of Christ, Torrance finds the basic elements of the church com-

---

[22]Torrance, *Reconstruction*, p. 194. Torrance actually traces the church all the way back to Adam, where communion with God first subsisted. Torrance also says that with the fall of humanity it was not the divine institution, but the constituent members of the church who fell (see pp. 193-94).
[23]Ibid., p. 194.
[24]Ibid., pp. 194-95.
[25]Ibid., pp. 195-96.
[26]Ibid., p. 197.

ing into view: the church is the worshiping people of God called into existence by God's Word; the church is neither a spiritualized, spaceless and timeless reality, nor a juridical or socio-political institution, but rather an earthly-historical reality in real relation to God even though that relation is hidden in the events of history; and as God's creation, the church exists prior to the individuals who are incorporated into the church from generation to generation.[27]

Torrance also argues that the Christian church "must not forget that it has no independent existence, for through Christ it is grafted on to the trunk of Israel, nor must it imagine that God has cast off his ancient people or that the promises made to Israel as a people of divine election and institution have only a spiritualized fulfillment."[28] Rather, in Torrance's perspective Israel and the Gentiles are grafted together into the resurrected body of Christ and form one people of God, the church of Jesus Christ.

Jesus Christ and the genesis of the new form of the church. From the beginning of his public ministry, Jesus proclaimed the kingdom of God, called people to repent and believe the good news and drew people to himself "in his mission to gather and redeem the people of God."[29] Torrance sees the kingdom of God and the people of God as correlative concepts or aspects of the rule of God. The kingdom is ushered in by the coming King, the Messiah who redeems and raises up a people as the constituent members of the kingdom, themselves the community through which the kingdom makes its way into all the world.[30]

This is what happened when Jesus the incarnate Son of God, began his ministry by identifying with Israel and through Israel with all of humanity as the Son of Man. Torrance argues that Jesus Christ, Son of God and Son of Man, recapitulated in himself the chosen people, received the Holy Spirit for our sake and established the new humanity of the future in himself in his vicarious life, death and resurrection. In his ministry leading to the cross and through death to resurrection, Jesus gathered the people of God and raised up the church in its permanent and final form in himself.[31]

---

[27]Ibid., p. 196.
[28]Ibid., p. 198. This is also why Torrance argues that the rift between the Jewish people and Christians "still constitutes the deepest ecumenical problem for the whole Christian Church" (see Torrance, *Reconciliation*, p. 27).
[29]Torrance, *Reconstruction*, p. 199.
[30]Ibid.
[31]Ibid., pp. 199-200.

What is crucial for Torrance's ecclesiology at this point is that the church of Christ "was not just the holy society founded to perpetuate his memory, or to observe his teachings, or to proclaim his gospel."[32] Rather, the church is grounded in the vicarious humanity of the historical Jesus Christ and grows out of the indivisible union of the Messiah and the people of God. The incarnate Son of God came to redeem and raise up the people of God out of the concrete way in which Christ lived his divine life within our human existence as the Son of Man.[33] In Torrance's theology, the genesis of the new form of the church is concurrent with, and the result of, the mediation of the revelation and reconciliation through Jesus Christ in his divine-human reality.[34]

Torrance sees this rebirth of the church in its messianic form as happening in two phases, one before and leading to the crucifixion, and the other after Christ's death, arising out of his resurrection.

The church's genesis in the person and ministry of Jesus.[35] From the beginning of Jesus' ministry, Torrance argues, Jesus gathered disciples around himself, forming the messianic community by his own direct and personal interaction with them. Torrance sees Jesus' historical ministry as an integral part of his atoning reconciliation and therefore absolutely crucial to the formation of the church. Jesus' praying and teaching, his healing the sick and forgiving sin, his preaching and his example, all take place within his vicarious humanity—the broken, sinful, diseased humanity that Christ assumed from us, and which he cleansed, healed, molded and transformed. But Christ's vicarious humanity is neither cut off from Israel, the people of God under the old covenant, nor is that vicarious humanity in any way isolated from Jesus' followers and the nexus of direct and personal interrelations with his disciples.[36]

Of those disciples, Jesus chose the twelve to be the inner nucleus of the new Israel. He trained them and sent them out to participate in his own ministry, preaching the kingdom, healing the sick and baptizing others into the messianic community. They followed Jesus to Jerusalem where he

---

[32]Ibid., p. 201. We will not retrace the details of mediation of Christ from chapters two, three and six here. See chapter two, pp. 65-69; chapter three, pp. 100-113; chapter five, pp. 168-82; and chapter six, pp. 221-25, for the christological, soteriological, anthropological and pneumatological facets of God's *oikonomia*.

[33]Torrance, *Reconstruction*, p. 201.

[34]Ibid., p. 200. Again see chapters two, three and six above.

[35]Torrance, *Trinitarian Faith*, p. 202.

[36]Ibid., pp. 202-3.

inaugurated the Lord's Supper, the new covenant in his body and blood, and incorporated the disciples into a royal priesthood. And then came the crucifixion, the scattering of the disciples, the fulfillment and end of the old economy, and the new beginning of the church in union with Christ in his resurrection.[37]

The rebirth of the church in the risen Jesus.[38] Torrance argues that the genesis of church did not take place in Christ's resurrection or in the outpouring of the Spirit at Pentecost. The resurrection and Pentecost signify not the birth, but the *rebirth*, the *transformation* of the church—under the old covenant and the disciples during Jesus' historical ministry—into the body of the risen Lord and Savior Jesus Christ, indwelt by the Spirit, united to Christ and quickened with new life in him.[39]

With the resurrection and outpouring of the Spirit on the apostles and the whole church, the provisional character of the messianic community in the apostolic nucleus and ministry during Jesus' earthly ministry and life was gathered up, recommissioned and transformed through deepened participation in Christ and his vicarious, resurrected humanity. The Spirit unites the church to Christ, incorporating the faithful from all of history, before and after incarnation, into Christ who is head of the church. The church evermore draws its life and its ministry from Christ through the Spirit in anticipation and manifestation in history of the new creation in Christ awaiting the final consummation of all things in Christ when Christ returns.[40]

Thus in Torrance's theology the Christian church is first and foremost not a human creation, but of divine origin in the earthly and historical mediation of revelation and reconciliation, (1) stretching back in history to the calling of Abraham and the covenant relation with Israel; (2) continuing through the incarnation, vicarious life, death and resurrection of Christ, to the outpouring of the Spirit of the Father and the Son at Pentecost; and (3) pressing forward to Christ's return and the consummation of all things in Christ. The genesis of the church involves the divine agency of Torrance's interactionist God-world relation and the full participation of human agency as Torrance conceptualizes it in his understanding of the logic of grace (see chapter three). The church's genesis and its telos are in the very

---

[37]Ibid., p. 203.
[38]Ibid., p. 204.
[39]Ibid.
[40]Ibid.

life, light and love that God is in God's inner trinitarian koinonia which is
the ontological basis of the trinitarian *oikonomia* out of which the church
arose. The triune God wills to live not for himself alone, but in love unites
himself with us in our fallen and sinful humanity in Jesus Christ, and
unites us with Christ's reconciled and redeemed vicarious humanity as
Christ's body in the sending of the Holy Spirit from the Father through the
Son.

2. The Church as the Body of Christ
It should be clear that in Torrance's theology the church is not merely a
human institution, nor does the church have an independent existence in
and of itself, for it is the earthly historical correlate of the parousia of the
Spirit from the Father through the redemptive activity of Christ. Here Torrance once again follows the early church and especially the Nicene theologians in developing a doctrine of the church that centers on New
Testament teaching about the church as the body of Christ, the Holy Spirit
who creates corporate communion between the church and Christ,
together with baptism in the name of the Father, Son and Holy Spirit.[41]
Torrance's doctrine of the church is thus christocentric, pneumatological
and trinitarian.

The Spirit unites us to Christ and through Christ with the Father, and
thus sustains the life of the church in Christ. The church is the body of
Christ, the community of reciprocity with Christ and one another rooted
in, and a reflection of, the trinitarian relations God *is* as Father, Son and
Holy Spirit.[42]

Torrance's intent here is to develop a rigorous scientific doctrine of the
church (integration of form in knowing) in terms of the intrinsic constitutive structure or the matrix of interrelations (form in being) characteristic
and defining of what the church really is. In the previous section we examined Torrance's understanding of the genesis of the church within the interrelations of God and Israel, Israel and Jesus Christ, and Jesus Christ and
the apostolic community in the mediation of revelation and reconciliation.
In this section the focus is on the doctrine of the church "in terms of its *internal relations* . . . to Jesus Christ, for it is in Christ and his inherent relation
to the Father and the Holy Spirit that the essential nature of the Church is

---

[41]Ibid., pp. 251-77.
[42]Ibid., pp. 250-53.

to be found."[43] We will look at Torrance's understanding of the church as the body of Christ, the church and the deposit of faith, and the church as the correlate of the Trinity.

The church as the body of Christ. Torrance finds the central relations constitutive of the church in the incarnation of the Son of God and the union and communion between God and humanity realized in the incarnate life and reconciling atonement of Jesus Christ as mediator.[44] This union between God and humanity in Christ entails our adoption as daughters and sons of God in Christ, or our participation *(theosis, theopoiesis)* in the communion of God's trinitarian life, light, and love. The church is the body of Christ not because of an external relation of moral resemblance or a mere juridical transaction, but because of a real participation in Christ who is of one being *(homoousios)* with God the Father, but who is also one being with us in his vicarious humanity through the incarnation.[45]

This participation in Christ does not, of course, mean that Torrance conceives of the relation between the church and Christ as exactly the same as the relation the incarnate Son and God the Father. The church's union with Christ is one of grace and adoption through the gift of the Spirit who dwells in us and unites us to Christ and his vicarious humanity through the mutual mediation of Christ and the Spirit.[46] But it does mean that the church as the body of Christ in Torrance's theology is no mere figurative expression, but rather articulates a real ontological relation and participation of the church in Christ through the Holy Spirit.[47]

Furthermore, Torrance argues that since this act of union and communion takes place in Christ, the *incarnate* Son, it incorporates not just a spiritual, but a somatic (bodily) union with Christ.[48] Here Torrance even sees the *bodily* humanity of Jesus Christ as itself "the first fruit of the Church."[49] The Son of God became one in bodily humanity with us, renewing that humanity for us, making it partake of the Holy Spirit, reconciling and sanctifying that humanity in atoning life and death, resurrecting it and uniting it forever through himself with the Godhead. The bodily incarnation is not

---

[43]Ibid., p. 264. See chapter two above, pp. 55-60, for our earlier discussion of the significance of internal relations in Torrance theology.

[44]Torrance, *Trinitarian Faith*, p. 264.

[45]Ibid., p. 265.

[46]See chapter six, pp. 221-33.

[47]Torrance, *Trinitarian Faith*, pp. 10-11.

[48]Ibid., p. 265.

[49]Ibid., p. 266.

a temporary episode in Torrance's perspective, but persists forever as a divine-human reality in the trinitarian life of God.[50]

This consecrated and ascended bodily humanity of Jesus Christ is the "life-giving substance" of the church and "the ground of its continuity and renewal in history."[51] The everlasting character of the soteriological relation between God and humanity embodied in the vicarious humanity of Christ is at the center of Torrance's ecclesiology. The church is the earthly-historical reality of those who are reconciled to God in Christ and united with the risen and ascended Christ in his divine-human reality.[52] The being of the church, in Torrance's theology, is bound up with the bodily character of gospel itself, the torn and bloody flesh of the historical Jesus, the empty tomb and the still nail-scared hands of the risen Lord and Savior, Jesus Christ.

Torrance can even speak of the church as "the *empirical* community of men, women and children called into being through the proclamation of the gospel."[53] The church is the historical manifestation of the saving union of God with us in Jesus Christ. United to Christ through the Holy Spirit, the church is a dynamic and new, even divine, yet fully earthly and historical bodily reality in the world.[54] The church is entrusted with the gospel; it embodies, but does not possess, the *rejuvenating deposit*, as Irenaeus called it, handed on by the apostles. In Torrance's theology the empirical church embodies the gospel and is the body of Christ.

The church and the deposit of faith. Torrance contends that according to the New Testament (particularly Paul and the Pastoral Epistles) and the early church (especially Irenaeus), the church has been "entrusted with a sacred deposit *(paratheke, parakatatheke, depositum)* enshrined in the Apostolic Foundation of the Church laid by Christ himself and livingly empowered through his indwelling Spirit of Truth, which the Church was bound to guard inviolate in contending for the Faith, and for which it had to render an account before God."[55]

Torrance sees this "deposit of faith" as identical with the whole incar-

---

[50]Ibid., pp. 274-75.
[51]See Thomas F. Torrance, "The Deposit of Faith," *Scottish Journal of Theology* 36 (1983): 3. Also see Torrance, *Trinitarian Faith*, p. 267.
[52]Torrance, *Trinitarian Faith*, pp. 266-67, 274-75.
[53]Ibid., p. 253.
[54]Ibid., p. 254.
[55]Torrance, "Deposit," pp. 1-2

nate and living self-communication of God in Jesus Christ and his saving acts. After his resurrection and ascension Christ mediates the deposit of faith in the sending of his Spirit. Through the Spirit, Christ unfolded and fulfilled his living self-communication as Savior and Lord in the apostles (incorporating their historical connection with Jesus) as the inner nucleus of the church.[56] This apostolic community was chosen, molded and commissioned by intimate association with Jesus during his early ministry and indwelt by Christ's Spirit to embody and pass on the deposit of faith "in such a constituting way that the identity and continuity of the church and its teaching in history became inseparably bound up with" the deposit of faith.[57]

In this way Christ clothed with the gospel united himself in the Spirit with the church as his body, so that Christ's person, word and life became embodied in a subsidiary manner in the apostolic nucleus of the church.[58] While this deposit of faith remains *identical* with the *living fact of Christ* himself in the unity of his person, word and life, we have access to that deposit only through the apostolic embodiment of it mediated through the New Testament Scriptures, and through incorporation into Christ and the church as his body where, through the Spirit, Christ and the gospel are present for the salvation of the world.[59]

This also means that Torrance sees the church as *inherently missionary*. Since the church only lives its life in real relation to, and as an embodiment of, the deposit of faith (Christ clothed with the gospel in the power of the Spirit), it cannot but confess its faith in Christ, proclaim the gospel of God's love for the world and embody in itself as the body of Christ the provisional form of the new creation in the midst of the world.[60] The deposit of faith continuously rejuvenates the church and embodies itself in the life of the church. It propels the church to proclaim the gospel, to summon all the nations to believe the good news, to obey it and to break down all barriers and divisions as the one church of the one Lord Jesus Christ.

Thus Torrance sees the deposit of faith as spanning two levels. It is primarily identical with the saving reality of Jesus Christ himself in his vicarious life, death, resurrection and ascension. Yet in a secondary way, the

---

[56]Ibid., p. 2; Torrance, *Trinitarian Faith*, pp. 258-59; and Torrance, *Reconstruction*, p. 205.
[57]Torrance, "Deposit," p. 2. Also see Torrance, *Reconstruction*, p. 206.
[58]Torrance, *Trinitarian Faith*, p. 258.
[59]Ibid., pp. 258-59. Also see Torrance, "Deposit," p. 2.
[60]Torrance, *Reconstruction*, p. 193.

THE CHURCH, THE BODY OF CHRIST

deposit is also identical with the faithful apostolic reception and articulation of Christ and the gospel in the apostolic nucleus which, through the
inspiration of Holy Spirit, comes to expression in the New Testament
Scriptures.[61] In Torrance's theology the two levels are so inseparably coordinated that Christ *himself* continues to be present through the New Testament *kerygma* entrusted to the church as a sacred gift to be guarded and
faithfully transmitted as the source of the church's life and renewal
throughout history.[62]

While the deposit of faith is the regulative source for all theological articulation of Christian truth, it is not a set of propositional truths that can
be abstracted from its embodiment in Jesus Christ himself and the apostolic foundation. In Torrance's theology it is not because the deposit of faith
is devoid of cognitive content that it cannot be resolved into a set of propositions or doctrines. Rather Jesus Christ clothed with the gospel is the *real
substance* of the deposit of faith so replete with the *living Word and truth of
God* that we will never exhaust its content in this life or the next.[63]

The embodied apostolic deposit of faith, alive with the Word and truth
of God, is the source and norm for all explicit formulation of Christian doctrine and for the life of the church. Because the deposit of faith is primarily
identical with the Word and truth of God, Jesus Christ himself, the
church's doctrine, as well as its patterns of life in worship, ministry and organization, have to be seen as *open structures*, always subordinate to the
church's primary constitutive reality as the body of Christ, and always
open to further modulation in light of Christ who is the head of the church.

The primacy of the body of Christ over issues of organization. Torrance's understanding of the bodily character of the incarnation and resurrection, and the embodied notion of the deposit of faith and the church as
the body of Christ, leads to Torrance's criticism of any division between
the church as a mystical body and the church as an external fellowship of
believers, a division which Torrance sees as destructive and characteristic
of the Latin doctrine of the church.[64] Torrance views any kind of distinc-

---

[61]Torrance, *Trinitarian Faith*, p. 259. See Torrance, "Deposit," pp. 14-15. Also see chapter
three, pp. 102-9, and chapter six, pp. 225-30, for Torrance's understanding of Scripture in
relation to the apostles and God's self-revelation in Jesus Christ and the Holy Spirit.

[62]Torrance, "Deposit," p. 3, and Torrance, *Trinitarian Faith*, pp. 259-60.

[63]Torrance, *Trinitarian Faith*. Also see Torrance, "Deposit," pp. 3, 6-7.

[64]Torrance, "Deposit," pp. 16-18. Torrance is equally critical of the idea of the church as a
community of like-minded people formed by voluntary association.

tion between the church as a spiritualized and mystical body, and an empirical church as a juridical society subject to the laws that define human society in this world, as rooted in the same kind of dualisms and gospel of "external" relations discussed in chapter two above. This kind of dualism, Torrance contends, creates a parallel set of entangled problems in ecclesiology, like those that arise in Christology and the doctrine of the atonement (which Torrance collectively calls the "Latin Heresy").[65]

Once again, Torrance finds Nicene theology helpful. It became evident to the Nicene theologians that the same basic issues were at stake in ecclesiology as in the debate about the incarnate Son's *internal* relation (the *homoousion*) to God the Father. The central point in regard to the doctrine of the church on which everything else depends is the church's *internal* relation to Christ, for the church's being and life are rooted in Christ himself as the real substance of the rejuvenating deposit of faith.[66] Through the sanctifying and renewing work of the Holy Spirit, *the church is the body of Christ*, the "earthly-historical form of the Existence of Jesus Christ, the one holy catholic and apostolic Church."[67]

Since the real onto-relational structure constitutive of the church is rooted in Christ himself, the church's relation to Jesus Christ has priority over the patterns of worship, ministry and organization of the church.[68] Torrance maintains that "the coherent and ordered sequences of the Church's life and mission are essentially *open structures*, and more like the scaffolding which is necessary for the erection of a building. . . . Hence we can never identify the patterns of the Church's life in worship or ministry with the real inner forms of its being in the love of God but may regard them only as temporary forms which will fall away when with the advent of Christ the full new humanity of the Church as the Body of Christ will be unveiled."[69] All issues regarding the forms, structure and organization of the

---

[65]See chapter two, pp. 86-88. This opens the door, Torrance contends, for the Roman doctrine of the church "as a divinely instituted society in the world under the universal headship of the bishop of Rome, and with canonically defined structures of unity, continuity and authority" (Torrance, *Trinitarian Faith*, p. 271). Also see Torrance, *Trinitarian Faith*, pp. 269-78, where Torrance traces the problem in Latin ecclesiology to Cyprian, Hilary, Tertullian and Origen.

[66]Ibid., pp. 269-78.

[67]Barth *Church Dogmatics* IV/1:643. Also see Torrance, *Trinitarian Faith*, p. 276.

[68]Torrance, *Trinitarian Faith*, p. 275.

[69]Thomas F. Torrance, *Space, Time and Resurrection* (Grand Rapids, Mich.: Eerdmans, 1976), p. 137.

church, Torrance argues, are subordinate to the living truth of Christ and the church's primary internal relation to Christ as his body.[70]

In Torrance's theology, the church is primarily the community, or *koinonia*, of those who have been united with Christ through baptism and the regenerating gift of the Holy Spirit, and who draw near to the Father through the Son in the Holy Spirit and share in the love, light and life of the triune God.[71] Within this essentially christocentric and trinitarian nature of the church, Torrance thinks that the authority, organization and government of the church should be thought out in terms of koinonia rather than hierarchical structure.[72]

The church as the correlate of the Trinity. Torrance can describe the church as "the place in space and time where knowledge of the Father, Son and the Holy Spirit becomes grounded in humanity and union and communion with the Holy Trinity becomes embodied within the human race."[73] Torrance thinks of the church first and foremost as the soteriological and ontological unification of people in Christ in which God himself dwells through the presence of the Spirit.[74] The church does not live in its own name, for with every baptism in the trinitarian name, the church finds its life beyond itself in the Father, the Son and the Holy Spirit, the transcendent source of the church's existence.[75]

Thus insofar as the church through baptism and faith continues to be one with the apostolic deposit of faith, lives out of its union with Christ in the Holy Spirit and finds its life hid with Christ in God the Father, Torrance contends that the church is bound to see itself as essentially trinitarian, the earthly-historical correlate of the grace of our Lord Jesus Christ, the love of God the Father and the communion of the Holy Spirit.[76]

In Torrance's theology the church is truly the body of Christ when it "dwells in the Holy Trinity and embodies the truth of the gospel in its empirical life and worship."[77] The church of Jesus Christ participates in the koinonia of the Father, the Son and the Spirit, and worships the triune God who is both the source and the telos of the church's existence. This wor-

---

[70]Ibid.
[71]Ibid., pp. 261-62, 274-75.
[72]Ibid., p. 272.
[73]Torrance, *Trinitarian Faith*, p. 256.
[74]Ibid., p. 254.
[75]Ibid., p. 256.
[76]Ibid., pp. 262-63, 268-69.
[77]Ibid., p. 268.

shiping church called into being by the gospel as the body of Christ, Torrance contends, is always evangelical from the Father through the Son in the Spirit, and always doxological in the Spirit through the Son to the Father, the evangelical and doxological correlate of the triunity of God, the one holy catholic and apostolic church.[78]

3. The Marks of the Church

Torrance affirms the classic marks of the church and defines them in light of the church's internal or constitutive relations to Jesus Christ and the triune God. In Torrance's ecclesiology the church as the body of Christ, the earthly correlate of the triune God, is *one*, *holy*, *catholic* and *apostolic*: it is the one church of the one Lord; it is the holy church, the fruit of the Holy Spirit; it is catholic or universal because it is united to the Savior who reconciles and gathers up all things into himself; and it is apostolic for it is grounded through the apostolic nucleus in Jesus Christ himself who is *the* apostle in the absolute sense. These marks are interdependent and inseparable.[79]

The oneness of the church. Torrance argues that it is because we believe in one God who has reconciled the world to himself, in the one Lord Jesus Christ who loved the church and gave himself for it, and in one Holy Spirit poured out on the church uniting the church with Christ, that we also believe in *one* church, the indivisible body of Christ.[80] The church is not the product of human ingenuity, for it is the self-giving of the one God through Christ and in the Holy Spirit which calls the church into existence and sustains it through all the vagaries of history, as intrinsically and essentially the *one* body of Christ.[81]

Furthermore, Torrance argues that it is not the invisible or mystical church, but the "visible or empirical Church" that is one in Christ.[82] The unity of the church in Christ embraces the people of God in all of history, those under the old covenant as well as those under the new, as noted earlier in this chapter. Through its one head, Jesus Christ, who is the alpha and omega, the one church spans the ages from Adam to Christ's return.[83]

---

[78]Ibid., pp. 262-63, 268-69, 275, 278.
[79]Torrance, *Reconciliation*, p. 17.
[80]Torrance, *Conflict*, 1: 263.
[81]Torrance, *Trinitarian Faith*, p. 279.
[82]Ibid., pp. 276, 279.
[83]Ibid., p. 280. Also see Torrance, *Reconciliation*, pp. 17-81, for Torrance's mature and insightful perspective on ecumenicity and the ecumenical movement.

Indwelt by the Spirit who knits us into unity with one another in Christ, the God-given diversity of the members and their diverse gifts of the Spirit do not in any way compromise the unity of the body of Christ.[84] These diversities produce rich variety within the oneness of the church, and not destructive division.

It is "the irrational and awful mystery of iniquity," the force of evil still rampant in creation, Torrance contends, that is the source of sinful division in the church.[85] Because the church lives between the times, the oneness of the church as the body of Christ is a mystery *(mysterium)* that awaits its consummation and full revelation in the return of Christ. Yet since the church is united to Christ in the one Spirit and therefore participates in the new creation in Christ, Torrance argues that the church's disunity and ambiguity does not belong to its essential nature in Christ.[86] While hidden with Christ in God, the oneness of the church as the body of Christ through the ages will be revealed and fulfilled with the glorious return of Christ, the one head who sends the one Spirit and secures, maintains and completes the unity of the one church.[87]

The holiness of the church. Since all knowledge of God entails cognitive union with God, in Torrance's perspective the people of God are called by God out of the world into union and communion with God, the Holy One, whose holy presence in their midst judges and opposes their sin, yet embraces and graciously transforms them into a holy people.[88] Thus the church's holiness is not its own, for it derives not from the moral purity of its members, but rather from the transcendent holiness and glory of God the Father, the Son and the Holy Spirit.[89]

In and through Christ's vicarious humanity, this transcendent and holy God assumes fallen and sinful humanity into union with God and sanctifies our unholy humanity in Christ through the Holy Spirit, and pours out that same Holy Spirit on the church. The Spirit's activity sanctifies the church and makes it holy with the holiness of Christ himself.[90] All of the church's holiness is from Christ, and all of Christ's holiness is for the church.

---

[84]Torrance, *Conflict*, 1:275-79.
[85]Ibid., p. 276.
[86]Ibid., pp. 268-71.
[87]Ibid., p. 268.
[88]Torrance, *Trinitarian Faith*, pp. 280-83.
[89]Ibid., pp. 281-82.
[90]Ibid.

For this reason Torrance says that speaking evil of the church is close to blasphemy against Christ's Holy Spirit, as well as disregard for Christ himself. Yet since the holiness of the church is not its own but is grounded in love of God through the grace of Christ in the communion of the Spirit, the church dares never claim this holiness as its own or assume the authority that belongs to Christ alone. In Torrance's ecclesiology the church is a holy people and a royal priesthood when it finds its life in Christ and lives its life for others. As it does, the people of God reflect the holiness of the Holy One and become the children of light called to shine with the light of Christ in the world.[91]

The catholicity of the church. Torrance sees several interrelated dimensions to the catholicity of the church. Catholicity refers to the universality, the identity and oneness, of the church and its faith throughout the world and history because of its intrinsic relation through the Holy Spirit to its divine origin in Christ. Torrance contends that everywhere, in every time and place, the church "remains one and the same through continuous fidelity to the apostolic foundation of the Church in Jesus Christ, and is therefore the Church which everywhere remains 'orthodox,' that is, 'rightly related' to the truth of the one God, Father, Son and Holy Spirit, common to the universal Church."[92] Here catholicity and apostolicity are closely correlated, for the church that is apostolic is always catholic. Torrance even argues that "apostolic" is not simply one of the marks, but also the norm *(ecclesia apostolica)* for our proper understanding of the other marks as well.[93]

However, catholicity has another dimension which Torrance speaks of as the "deepest level" of catholicity, where it has to do with the universal range of redemption of Christ discussed at the end of chapter two above.[94] This is not a *universalism,* but rather the wholeness and fullness of the gospel of Christ himself, "who reconciles and gathers up all things into himself."[95] Neither the gospel nor the church can be restricted to a spiritual realm or a spiritual elite. Redemption embraces all of creation and all peoples.

Thus in the last analysis Torrance understands catholicity as the "wholeness or essential universality of the Church's existence in Christ"

[91]Ibid., especially p. 30.
[92]Torrance, *Reconciliation,* p. 17.
[93]Ibid.
[94]See chapter two, pp. 94-96.
[95]Torrance, *Reconciliation,* p. 17.

which embraces all aspects of God's people and their existence, which persists in God's people in every age.[96] The church is catholic because it is the
body of Christ, the fullness of Christ who fills all things (Eph 1:22-23).[97]

The apostolicity of the church. In the simplest sense, Torrance views the
apostolicity of the church as referring to the foundation of the church in
the apostles whom Christ commissioned as his witnesses, and to the
church's unswerving fidelity to that apostolic foundation.[98]

As developed in section two above, Jesus Christ himself is the apostle
in the fullest sense. But the peculiar function of the apostles molded by
Christ to be the nucleus of the church is that they form the authoritative
reception and interpretation of the self-witness of Christ clothed with his
gospel. Inspired by Christ's Spirit and integrated with the whole saving
fact of Christ, the apostolic foundation of the church translated Christ
clothed with his gospel into the appropriate form for his continual communication in history out of which the New Testament Scriptures arose.[99]

We will not rehearse the earlier discussion of the deposit of faith, but
what is important here is that Torrance views it as identical with the apostolate and as spanning two levels: (1) the entire saving reality of Christ and
(2) the authoritative embodiment of the saving reality in the apostolic nucleus of the church formed by Christ. The deposit of faith, or apostolate,
therefore constitutes the unrepeatable foundation of the church to which
the church is ever committed and indebted, for it *is* the continuously rejuvenating fount through which the life-giving reality of Christ himself sustains the church through the vicissitudes of its life in history.[100]

Understood in this light, the apostolicity of the church refers to the
church's essential connection to Christ in the *apostolate* through which the
truth of the gospel is transmitted to the ends of the earth throughout history.[101] Thus the church is apostolic when it is constantly renewed as the
body of Christ and bears the imprint of its apostolic origin. Apostolicity refers to the *identity* of the church as the authentic one holy catholic body of
Christ in space and time.[102]

---

[96]Ibid. Also see Torrance, *Trinitarian Faith,* p. 83.
[97]Torrance, *Reconciliation,* p. 17. Also see Torrance, *Trinitarian Faith,* p. 285.
[98]Torrance, *Trinitarian Faith,* p. 285.
[99]Ibid., pp. 285-87.
[100]Ibid., p. 286-87.
[101]Ibid., p. 287.
[102]Ibid.

This brings us back to the point that apostolicity for Torrance is also normative for how we understand the other marks of the church. The oneness, holiness and catholicity of the church are measured by the witness and authority of the apostolate, the apostolic Scriptures and their conjoint witness to Christ.[103] It is always Christ himself who resounds through the apostolic Scriptures, unites the church to himself as his body and therefore defines it as the one holy catholic and apostolic church, thereby distinguishing it from all others.

4. The Sacraments

By now it should be clear that Torrance thinks out every aspect of his ecclesiology in an essentially christocentric, pneumatological and trinitarian manner. It is also along these lines that Torrance develops his theology of the sacraments.

Torrance argues that the sacraments of the gospel have to be understood in terms of their ultimate ground in the incarnation and the vicarious humanity of Christ, the human nature Christ assumed from us and which he reconciled and sanctified in his obedient self-offering to the Father.[104] In light of this, the sacraments have to do with the entire living, historical, redemptive reality of Jesus Christ, for the content, the reality and the power of the sacraments derive not just from God's saving act on us in Christ, but through the reconciling and sanctifying act of God fulfilled in the vicarious humanity of Christ from his birth through his resurrection and ascension.[105]

Understood in this way, Torrance says, "The primary *mysterium* or *sacramentum* is Jesus Christ himself, the incarnate reality of the Son of God who has incorporated himself into our humanity and assimilated the people of God into himself as his own Body, so that the sacraments have to be understood as concerned with our *koinonia* or participation in the mystery of Christ and his Church through the *koinonia* or communion of the Holy Spirit."[106] Baptism and the Eucharist are the divinely provided sacraments of the finished vicarious work of Jesus Christ which have Jesus Christ clothed with the gospel as their content and substance.[107] Torrance also

---

[103]Ibid.
[104]Torrance, *Reconciliation*, p. 83.
[105]Ibid.
[106]Ibid., p. 82.
[107]Thomas F. Torrance, *The Mediation of Christ*, 2nd ed. (Colorado Springs: Helmers & Howard, 1992), p. 90.

sees baptism and the Eucharist in the new covenant as fulfilling and replacing the rites of circumcision and passover under the old covenant.[108]

Torrance sees the two sacraments as essentially enshrining the twofold fact that the church is wholly forgiven and justified in Christ (baptism) yet daily needs cleansing and forgiveness through Christ (Eucharist). Thus he contends that baptism is the sacrament of justification, whereas the Eucharist is the sacrament of sanctification.[109]

The one baptism common to Christ and his church.[110] If Christ's vicarious humanity and our participation in Christ through the Holy Spirit are the basic internal relations (onto-relations) constitutive of the church as the body of Christ, and if the sacraments have to do with our participation in the mystery of Christ and his church, then Torrance thinks that baptism has to be understood in coherence with Jesus Christ and therefore *"in a dimension of depth,"* or a real relation reaching back to the whole saving fact of Jesus Christ. In other words, Torrance thinks that we cannot view baptism as a ritual or ethical act that has its meaning in itself or simply as a response to what God has already done.[111] Baptism entails absolutely real participation in the mystery of Christ.

While ritual and ethical elements have a place within the administration of baptism, Torrance sees baptism itself concentrated essentially in God's saving act embodied in Jesus Christ so that when the church baptizes in the trinitarian name, "it is actually Christ himself who is savingly at work, pouring out his Spirit upon us and drawing us within the power of his vicarious life, death and resurrection."[112] The whole substance of the gospel—the grace of our Lord Jesus Christ, the love of God the Father and the communion of the Holy Spirit—is concentrated in baptism, so that Torrance views it as "the all-embracing sacrament," inseparably linked according to Ephesians 4 with one body, one Spirit, one Lord, one faith, and one God and Father.[113]

---

[108]Ibid., pp. 89-90.

[109]See Torrance, *Conflict*, 1:112, and Torrance, *Resurrection*, p. 150.

[110]This is the title of Torrance's most important essay on baptism and is very revealing. See Torrance, *Reconciliation*, pp. 82-105. Torrance also deals with baptism in the chapter "The One Church" in Torrance, *Trinitarian Faith*, pp. 289-301. This material is essentially a summary of part of the earlier essay. Torrance, *Conflict*, vol. 2, also has a long section on baptism (pp. 93-132), though there is little here that is not also in the later essays.

[111]Torrance, *Reconciliation*, pp. 82-83.

[112]Ibid., p. 83.

[113]Torrance, *Trinitarian Faith*, p. 290.

Since Jesus Christ himself is the content, reality and power of baptism, Torrance sees baptism in the trinitarian name as a participation through the Holy Spirit in the one vicarious baptism of Christ himself, not only in the Jordan River, but throughout his life, death and resurrection. Torrance finds that this objective reality of baptism in Christ is emphasized from the very beginning of the early church.[114]

Torrance argues that the very word for baptism in the New Testament underscores its objective character. Rather than appropriate the common word *baptismos*, which was used in the Greek world for the rite of ablution or ceremonial cleansing, the biblical writers used the term *baptisma*, which regularly refers to the *reality* signified, rather than to the rite itself.[115]

Here Torrance interprets *baptisma* along similar lines as *kerygma*, which refers not simply to proclamation or preaching, but to the *reality* proclaimed—Christ clothed with the gospel. Jesus Christ himself *is* the material content and the active agent of proclamation, for when the church proclaims the gospel, Christ himself is present and active for salvation through the Holy Spirit.[116] Thus both *baptisma* and *kerygma* span two levels: their primary reference is to the whole saving fact of Jesus Christ, whereas their secondary sense refers to the activity of the church baptizing and preaching in Christ's name, as we saw with reference to the deposit of faith earlier in the chapter (*baptisma* and *kerygma* are actually facets of the deposit of faith).[117] While baptism is the act of Christ and the act of the church, its ultimate meaning lies in what *God* has done and continues to do through Christ in the Spirit, not in terms of what the *church* does in Christ's name, though Torrance resists any separation of the two.

Now when we view Christian *baptisma* in this dimension of depth grounded in the whole incarnate reality of Jesus Christ in life, death and resurrection, Torrance contends that we have to think of it "stereoscopically," holding together as a single yet differentiated reality and event: (1) Jesus' vicarious baptism on our behalf in water and the Spirit at the Jordan, (2) Jesus Christ's baptism in blood in his death and resurrection, and (3) the baptism of the church in Christ's Spirit at Pentecost uniting the church

---

[114]Ibid., pp. 292-93, and Torrance, *Reconciliation*, p. 83.

[115]Torrance, *Reconciliation*, p. 83, and Torrance, *Trinitarian Faith*, p. 293. Torrance thinks the church may have coined the word *baptisma*.

[116]Torrance, *Reconciliation*, p. 83.

[117]Ibid., pp. 83-4. Also see Torrance, *Trinitarian Faith*, pp. 293-4.

with Christ in his vicarious baptism (in [1] and [2]) on our behalf.[118]

Torrance sees Jesus' baptism at the Jordan on our behalf, identifying with us as sinners, as pointing back to his birth by the Spirit to be the Savior of the world, and also forward to his suffering and death in atoning reconciliation. Christ's baptism embraces his sacrificial life and death on our behalf in complete solidarity with us as the servant of the Lord and our Savior.[119] When he was anointed by the Holy Spirit at the Jordan, it was into our humanity that Christ received the Spirit in consuming holiness at infinite cost.

Yet the atoning exchange that takes place in Christ's union with us involves not only humiliation and self-sacrifice, but also simultaneous transformation and exaltation.[120] Thus Torrance sees the Spirit coming on Christ at his baptism as also Christ's anointing as king with divine authority, and therefore pointing through Christ's passion to his resurrection, ascension and exaltation to the right hand of the Father with all power in heaven and earth at his disposal. It is in "the exercise of this power that Christ commissioned the Apostles and sent them to make disciples of all nations, baptising and teaching them, and . . . he endowed the Church with power from on high by baptising them with his own Spirit at Pentecost."[121]

Here Torrance finds the coalescence of all three dimensions of baptism, for Christ's commission to the church to baptize in the name of the Father, the Son and the Holy Spirit refers back to Christ's own baptism in the Jordan, a vicarious baptism of humiliation and exaltation on our behalf and in our place. It refers to Christ's baptism of atoning exchange through his life, death and resurrection, but also points forward to the counterpart of Christ's baptism in the baptism of the church with Christ's Spirit at Pentecost.[122]

In this light Torrance's understanding of baptism comes fully into view,

---

[118]Torrance, *Reconciliation*, pp. 84-85, 88-89. Also see Torrance, *Trinitarian Faith*, pp. 92-94. Since we have examined each of these three points in earlier chapters, here we will briefly summarize each and draw out their significance for baptism.

[119]Torrance, *Reconciliation*, p. 85.

[120]See chapter two, pp. 92-94.

[121]Torrance, *Reconciliation*, p. 86.

[122]Ibid., pp. 86-87. In Torrance's words: "What happened to Jesus at his baptism at the hands of John when the Voice of the Father was heard addressing him as the Son and the Spirit came upon him sealing him as the Holy One sent by the Father, was given its counterpart in the Church when the same Holy Spirit sent by the Father in the Name of the Son came down upon the Apostolic Church, sealing it as the people of God redeemed through the blood of Christ, consecrating it to share in the communion of the Father, the Son and the

for in his perspective the whole saving act of God that *is* Jesus Christ (his vicarious life, death, resurrection, ascension) forms the content of Christ's baptism and the church's baptism at Pentecost, making them essentially the *one baptism common to Christ and the church*. For Jesus Christ baptism was his consecration as the Messiah, and for us baptism is our participation in the one vicarious *baptisma* of Christ through his Spirit.[123]

This vicarious baptism, Torrance contends, "is the one baptism common to Christ and his Church which every act of baptism in the Church presupposes and from which it derives its significance and efficacy."[124] Every baptism in the life of the church is grounded *through* the corporate baptism of the church at Pentecost *in* the one vicarious baptism of Christ. While baptism as the act of the church and preeminently the act of Christ himself may be distinguished, Torrance is adamant that they may never be separated.[125] When the church baptizes someone with water in obedience to Christ's commission and in the trinitarian name, it is Christ himself who is present baptizing with his Spirit, blessing the church's action as his own, and fulfilling in the life of the person baptized what Christ has done as the Spirit unites the person with Christ.[126] The reality of baptism is lodged in Jesus Christ himself and all that Christ accomplished within the humanity he assumed from us in the incarnation.

The paschal mystery of Christ and the Eucharist.[127] For Torrance, baptism is the sacrament of our incorporation into Christ as his body and therefore reflects our once-and-for-all union with Christ through his Spirit.[128] The Eucharist, or Lord's Supper, in Torrance's theology reflects and embodies our continuous or ongoing union and communion with Christ,

---

Holy Spirit, and sending it out into the world united to Christ as his Body to engage in the service of the gospel" (p. 86).

[123]Ibid., p. 87.

[124]Ibid.

[125]Ibid. Torrance has a long discussion of what happens when the various elements of baptism break up into separate elements, as he finds happening repeatedly in the Western church due to the influx of dualism from Greco-Roman culture upon the church. Torrance finds Roman Catholic and Protestant forms of this fragmentation of the various aspects of baptism (see pp. 89-99). This is the sacramental dimension of what Torrance calls the Latin Heresy, discussed in chapter two, pp. 81-88.

[126]Torrance, *Reconciliation*, p. 87.

[127]This heading is the title of Torrance's essay on the Eucharist in Torrance, *Reconciliation*, pp. 106-38. For additional essays on the Eucharist, see Torrance, *Conflict*, 1: 122-45; Torrance, *Conflict*, 2: 133-202; and the brief but important statement in Torrance, *Mediation*, pp. 89-92.

[128]Torrance, *Mediation*, p. 90.

and therefore is the sacrament of our continuous participation in all that Jesus Christ is, has done and continues to do in our place and on our behalf so that we live our lives in Christ and Christ lives his life in us as his body.[129]

On the night when Jesus was betrayed and handed over to death, he gathered his disciples into the upper room and celebrated the Passover with them. As he did so, Torrance contends that Jesus linked his passion with the Passover lamb and the people of the old covenant, but also with the inauguration of the new covenant of atoning remission of sins through Christ's sacrificial life, death and resurrection. When Jesus said, "This is my body broken for you" and "This is my blood shed for you," Torrance argues that Christ "constituted himself the mystery of the Supper, and transformed it into the Eucharist of the Church."[130]

The real mystery of the Eucharist, therefore, is not Eucharist itself, but rather "the paschal mystery of Christ which he set forth in the Eucharist for the participation of all who believe in him."[131] Christ shared the loaf and drank the cup actively and vicariously as redeemer, priest and lamb of God, offerer and offering. The disciples ate and drank as the nucleus of the redeemed community, incorporated into Christ, consecrated and presented to the Father through the one self-offering of Christ on their (and our) behalf.[132] Here in relation to the sacrament of the Eucharist we see again Torrance's embodied and holistic understanding of the deposit of faith which spans the level of the whole saving fact of Christ, but also the level of the apostolic reception of that saving fact.

Thereafter all those who believe in Christ through the witness of the apostolic nucleus do so as those who also are incorporated into Christ through the Holy Spirit in baptism and who celebrate the Eucharist in obe-

---

[129]Ibid., p. 91.

[130]Torrance, *Reconciliation*, p. 106.

[131]Ibid.

[132]Ibid. Torrance links this paschal mystery of Christ in sharing of the loaf and drinking of the cup with Jesus' high priestly prayer: "I pray for them . . . Holy Father . . . may they be one, even as we are one. . . . For their sake I sanctify myself, that they also may be sanctified in the Truth. I pray not for these only, but for all those who believe in me through their word, that they may all be one; even as thou, Father, art in me, and I in thee, that they also may be in us, so that the world may believe." This appears to be Torrance's own translation of John 17:9, 11, 19-23, though it is similar to the King James and Revised Standard Versions. Torrance sees Christ's intercession echoing in those who believe in Christ when in the Spirit they cry, "Abba, Father," and are drawn near to the Father in the Spirit through the blood of Christ.

dience to Christ's command, in remembrance (*anamnesis*) of him, in participation in this paschal mystery of Christ. Whenever the church celebrates
the Eucharist, breaks the bread and the drinks the cup in *anamnesis* of Jesus
Christ, who alone is priest and offering, who is himself a new and living
way in the holy presence of God the Father, Torrance thinks that it is
"Christ himself who is really present pouring out his Spirit upon us, drawing us into the power of his vicarious life, in death and resurrection, and
uniting us with his self-oblation and self-presentation before the face of the
Father where he ever lives to make intercession for us."[133] This is the essential and crucial core of Torrance's understanding of the *Lord's* Supper.

Thus, as with baptism, Torrance understands the Eucharist as both the
act of Jesus Christ himself and the act of the church in his name, yet in such
a way that the Eucharist is what it is only in its grounding beyond what
the church does in what Christ himself has done and continues to do for
us in his Spirit.[134] Understood in this way, the Eucharist, done in *anamnesis*
of Jesus Christ himself and his self-giving on our behalf, by its very nature
points beyond itself to its constitutive reality in the paschal mystery of
Christ.[135] The focus falls not on our ritual, religious and ethical activity in
the sacrament but on the internal relations (onto-relations) of the primary
mysterium or *sacramentum*, Jesus Christ himself who has incorporated himself into our humanity, reconciled and renewed that humanity in himself
through the Spirit, and through his resurrection and ascension raises our
humanity to union and communion with the Father.[136] Once again we
have to do with this *dimension of depth* or real participation in Christ
through the Spirit who unites us with the whole saving reality of Jesus
Christ, the incarnate, crucified, risen and ascended Son.[137]

As we saw in chapters two and three above, the saving reality of Christ
includes both his God-humanward activity (the redemptive participation

---

[133]Ibid., p. 107.

[134]Ibid. Torrance thinks that serious problems develop whenever we focus attention upon
the sacramental rite itself rather than on the person of the Mediator, the paschal mystery
of Christ. In the history of the church, when the Eucharist is detached from its reality in
Christ, it is repeatedly interpreted in terms of the performance of the rite itself as a repetition of the sacrifice of Christ or a religious or moral response to the symbolism of the rite
(see p. 108). Also see pp. 112-38, where Torrance discusses examples of problematic conceptualization of the Eucharist, especially in the Western tradition of the church and its
unresolved dualisms particularly in regard to the God-world relation.

[135]Ibid., p. 108.

[136]Ibid., pp. 108-9.

[137]Ibid., p. 109.

THE CHURCH, THE BODY OF CHRIST   269

and passion of God incarnate in our actual human and historical existence) and his human-Godward activity (the redemptive participation of our human nature and reality in the eternal love and life of the triune God).[138] Christ himself is the living content, reality and power of the Eucharist, giving it meaning and efficacy, for when we celebrate it in obedience to Christ, through the Holy Spirit (in the twofold pneumatological activity that parallels Christ's twofold activity), Christ himself is present in his twofold but indivisible activity as mediator, blessing what we do.[139]

The key, then, for understanding the Eucharist, Torrance argues, is the vicarious humanity of Christ whereby Christ acts, (1) as our high priest who in his God-humanward activity receives the things of God for us and thus enables us to receive them through union with him, but also (2) as our high priest who has assumed our humanity and offers that humanity in consecration to God and thus enables us to draw near to God and offer God our sacrifice of praise in union with Christ who gathers up our worship and sanctifies it in union with his self-offering to the Father.[140] Just as the church, in continuous union with Christ through the Spirit, is the body of Christ, the earthly-historical counterpart to Christ's vicarious union with us, so in the Eucharist, the sacrament of our continuous union and communion with Christ, we find a twofold counterpart to the twofold ministry of Christ from God to humanity and from humanity to God.[141] In relation to this twofold counterpart Torrance develops his understanding of the real presence of Christ in the Eucharist and the eucharistic sacrifice.

The God-humanward movement. In the God-humanward movement, the Eucharist is the sacrament of Jesus Christ's reconciling union with us, forgiving our sin and pouring God's love into our hearts. Its sacramental counterpart is Jesus Christ's real and saving presence through the Holy Spirit, who gives us communion with Christ wherein we feed on Christ as the bread of life, receive his life and live our lives in him.[142] The real pres-

---

[138]Ibid.

[139]Ibid.

[140]Ibid., pp. 110-11.

[141]Ibid., p. 118. In Torrance's own words: "To that objective movement of redemptive descent and ascent, *katabasis* and *anabasis*, in Jesus Christ himself the Lord's Supper corresponds as through the Spirit mediated to us by the glorified Christ we participate in the self-giving of God in the incarnate Son which is consummated in his passion and resurrection, and participate in the self-offering of the ascended Son which is grounded in his passion and resurrection."

[142]Torrance, *Mediation*, p. 91.

ence of Christ, or his eucharistic *parousia* as Torrance calls it, is neither the *parousia* of the Lord in the historical form of his thirty-three year life and ministry, nor the glorified *parousia* of Christ at the right hand of the Father. But Torrance argues that it is "nevertheless the real presence *(parousia)* of the whole Christ, not just the presence of his body and blood, not just the presence of his Spirit or Mind, but the presence of the actual Jesus Christ, crucified, risen, ascended, glorified, in his whole living and active reality and in his identity as Gift and Giver."[143] The whole Christ clothed with the gospel is present in the sacrament through the power of the Holy Spirit.[144]

Torrance maintains that we cannot define or explain Christ's real presence in terms of any analogy, causality or spatial relation in our creaturely existence and experience, for Christ is present in a *sui generis* manner *through the Holy Spirit.*[145] Jesus Christ is present "through the same kind of inexplicable creative activity whereby he was born of the Virgin Mary and rose again from the grave."[146] Christ's real presence is explicable only in terms of God's creative activity which transcends any explanation we can construct, and is bound up with Torrance's interactionist God-world relation in which *God acts* directly in the world and is *himself* the content of his action in Jesus Christ and the Holy Spirit, and therefore in the Eucharist.[147]

The human-Godward movement. In the human-Godward movement, the Eucharist is the sacrament of Christ's self-consecration of our humanity which he assumed from us, healed and offers to the Father in obedience and atoning reconciliation on our behalf, lifting us up through himself in resurrection and ascension to the Father.[148] The sacramental counterpart to the human-Godward ministry of Christ is our participation through the Spirit in the self-consecration, the self-offering of Christ to the Father.[149]

Torrance argues that this is really what *anamnesis* means: to do this in *anamnesis* (in remembrance) of Christ is not a mere recollection of what

---

[143]Torrance, *Reconciliation*, p. 119.

[144]Ibid., pp. 120, 132.

[145]Ibid., pp. 126, 129. Torrance says that the only analogy is the hypostatic union of the two natures in Jesus Christ.

[146]Ibid., p. 120.

[147]See ibid., pp. 122-31. Of course, Torrance thinks that the attempt to provide an explanation of "how" Christ is present in the sacrament has created no small amount of problems for, and divisions within, the church, as in the case of the Roman Catholic doctrine of transubstantiation.

[148]Torrance, *Mediation*, p. 91.

[149]Torrance, *Reconciliation*, p. 118.

Christ has done in his death on the cross.[150] Rather, our eucharistic worship, prayer and thanksgiving in the name of Christ which we lift up before God is done in "holy analogue to and in union with" the humanity of Christ and his vicarious human worship, prayer, thanksgiving, self-offering and self-consecration to the Father, as we saw in chapter three in the sections three and four, on our human response and the logic of grace.[151] Torrance views Jesus Christ's obedient worship as a *human being* during his earthly life and in the presence of the Father as an absolutely essential part of his servant ministry and saving activity on our behalf.[152]

Furthermore, through the Spirit, Christ himself is really present to us in the Eucharist, assimilating our worship, prayer and thanksgiving into his own worship and self-offering, sanctifying our worship and making our eucharistic sacrifice of praise and self-offering "the concrete form and expression of his own self-giving and self-offering, assimilating us in mind and will to himself and lifting us up in closest union with himself in the identity of himself as Offerer and Offering to the presence of the Father."[153]

Thus the eucharistic *anamnesis* and sacrifice is something we do in and through the real presence of the whole Christ in the Spirit who so unites us with Christ that "we participate in his self-consecration and self-offering to the Father made on our behalf and in our place, and appear before the Majesty of God in worship, praise and adoration with no other worship or sacrifice than that which is identical with Christ Jesus our Mediator and High Priest."[154] We come to the table with empty hands and receive the elements in union and communion with Jesus Christ through the Spirit. We draw near to God with no other offering, no other worship than Jesus Christ himself, though it is always Jesus Christ in union and communion with us through his Spirit, the Spirit who makes Christ's own self-offering and self-consecration echo with and within us as we give thanks and cry, "Abba, Father." In this way the Eucharist is the sacrament of our continuous participation through the Spirit in Jesus Christ and his twofold activity on our behalf as his body, the church, the earthly historical form

---

[150]Ibid., pp. 118, 136.
[151]Ibid., pp. 113-19, and Torrance, *Mediation*, pp. 91-92.
[152]Torrance, *Reconciliation*, pp. 112-13. Torrance develops his position contra all forms of liturgical Apollinarianism (see p. 116). Also see "The Mind of Christ in Worship: The Problem of Apollinarianism in the Liturgy" (pp. 139-214).
[153]Torrance, *Reconciliation*, p. 118.
[154]Torrance, *Mediation*, p. 92.

25

of his existence until the day that he comes again in final *parousia*.

5. The Royal Priesthood

Like so many areas of his thought, Torrance's theological account of ministry is complex, nuanced and deeply integrated into the overall fabric of his theology. Most of Torrance's reflection on theology of ministry occurred in relation to his ecumenical endeavor[155] and has been published in *Royal Priesthood: A Theology of Ordained Ministry* and in *Conflict and Agreement in the Church*.[156]

Here we will trace the main lines of Torrance's theology of ministry under three headings: (1) Christ's royal priesthood, (2) the royal priesthood of the whole church and (3) the ordained ministry. Since Jesus Christ is the *arche*, the principle or origin of all God's activity—including God's activity in the church and its life and ministry—Torrance's account of the ministry of the church is deeply christological.

Torrance develops his position as a

re-presentation of the biblical and ancient catholic understanding of the royal priesthood of the Church incorporated into Christ as his Body, and of the priesthood of the ordained ministry of the Church in consecrated service to the Lord Jesus Christ our great High Priest who through the atoning sacrifice of himself, offered once for all for the sins of the world, has ascended to the right hand of the Father, where he continues to exercise his heavenly Priesthood in advocacy and intercession on our behalf. That is the Priesthood which is echoed through the Spirit in the corporate ministry of the Church as the Body of Christ and in the particular ministry of those who are called and ordained by Christ to serve him in the proclamation of the Gospel and in the celebration of the Sacraments.[157]

This quotation reveals Torrance's understanding of ministry as primarily the high-priestly ministry of Jesus Christ himself in his life, death and resurrection, and in his ascension to the right hand of the Father where Christ continues to serve as priest on our behalf, in our place and in our stead. The church's ministry (either corporate or particular) is not that of a priesthood endowed with power to act in Christ's place and on his behalf

---

[155]See chapter one, pp. 46-47.

[156]Thomas F. Torrance, *Royal Priesthood: A Theology of Ordained Ministry*, 2nd ed. (Edinburgh: T & T Clark, 1993). There are also some important discussions of ministry in Torrance, *Reconciliation*.

[157]Torrance, *Royal Priesthood*, p. xiv.

in such a way as to extend, prolong or repeat his high-priestly sacrifice in history.

In Torrance's theology, all ministry of the church, whether the corporate ministry of the priesthood of all believers or the ordained ministry of Word and sacrament, is strictly participation in Christ's own high-priestly ministry, in which Christ himself is present to the church through the Spirit, filling the church with his God-humanward activity and human-Godward activity in such a way that the church's obedient activity in the name of Christ is fulfilled and utilized by Christ and *his* ministry to build up the body of Christ and to extend Christ's kingdom. This represents an application to the ministry of the inner *logic of grace* (the relation between divine and human agency which we examined in chapter three), in light of which Torrance asserts, "all the ways and works of God in his interaction with us in space and time may be given careful formulation."[158]

Christ's royal priesthood. Torrance argues that the apostolic church never applied the term *priest* to the ordained ministry; it ascribed the term first and foremost to Jesus Christ himself and then to the church as a whole.[159] In the same way that the church has no existence or life apart from union and communion with Christ in the Spirit, ministry in Christ's name has no power or reality apart from union with Christ and his ministry in the Spirit.

In fact, Torrance maintains that the early church "regarded Christ in the absolute and proper sense, as the only Minister of the Church before God, the only One who was appointed and anointed *(Christos)* for office in the Kingdom of God, the only One endowed with all authority in heaven and on earth."[160] Jesus Christ himself, the firstborn Son of God, alone is our high priest, the anointed and consecrated one.[161]

As Son of God and Son of Man, our great high priest himself fulfills the priesthood of the Old Testament. Torrance finds a double character to the Old Testament priesthood which parallels the bipolarity, or two-way movement, in the mediation of revelation and reconciliation in Israel and in Jesus Christ discussed in chapters two and three. God's self-revelation always incorporates a divinely elicited and sustained human response in thought, speech and life which bears witness to that revelation and be-

---

[158]Torrance, *Karl Barth*, p. 125. Also see chapter three (pp. 117-23).
[159]Torrance, *Royal Priesthood*, p. xv.
[160]Torrance, *Reconciliation*, p. 207.
[161]Torrance, *Conflict and Agreement*, 2:37.

comes the matrix or human vessel for the continuing mediation of that self-revelation in history, so that divine revelation can be anchored and realized within the actual creaturely conditions of our human existence. For Torrance, the true ministry of the church *is* part of the creaturely human vessel for the continuing self-revelation and self-communication of God in history.

Thus, in the Old Testament the priesthood includes both a mediation of the Word of God and the priestly witness to God's revealed Word or will.[162] Torrance sees this represented in the relations between the brother-priests Moses and Aaron. Moses "is priest *par excellence*," the unique mediator who speaks to God face to face and stands in "supreme relation to God's Word."[163] Aaron stands in secondary status to Moses, Torrance contends, "as the liturgical priest who carries out in continual cultic witness the actual mediation [of God's Word] that came through Moses."[164] The cult became the divinely prepared creaturely vessel for the liturgical extension through the history of Israel's life and worship of the once-for-all events of God's revelation and reconciliation that took place in the exodus and on Mount Sinai.

Of course, as in the case of Torrance's account of the mediation of revelation and reconciliation in chapters two and three, this twofold Old Testament priesthood finds its fulfillment in Jesus Christ himself: "Here where the Word of the living God is made flesh, the two aspects of priesthood are combined and fulfilled."[165] Jesus Christ himself is both God's Word and saving action toward humanity, and humanity's perfect response in obedience to God. In Jesus Christ, the Word of God who dwelt (tabernacled) in our midst (Jn 1:14), Torrance finds the ultimate meeting and reconciliation between God and humanity, which the Tent of Meeting in the Old Covenant prefigured.[166]

Furthermore, since the Word of God incarnate as Jesus has real power to forgive sins, Christ and his priesthood have authority over the sabbath and the temple (Mt 9:4-7; 12:6-8). Torrance sees Jesus Christ insisting "on the subordination of priesthood and priestly function to God's initiative and royal grace."[167] In so doing, Jesus presses all human priesthood into its

---

[162]Torrance, *Royal Priesthood*, p. 3.
[163]Ibid.
[164]Ibid., p. 4.
[165]Ibid., p. 7.
[166]Ibid., p. 8.
[167]Ibid.

appropriate role of witness to God's truth in Christ, "of liturgical acknowl-
edgement of what God has done and spoken in His Grace."[168]

In fulfillment of the Mosaic aspect of the priesthood, Christ is the Word
or Son of the Father sent into the world as God's apostle to bear witness for
God and to confess the mercy and grace of God. As Aaronic high priest
Jesus acknowledges this witness, intercedes for humanity and confesses
humanity before the Father.[169]

"In Jesus Christ, as Apostle and High Priest, both aspects of priesthood
are fulfilled," Torrance argues, "but are fulfilled in His Sonship and on the
ground of His Sonship."[170] Jesus Christ is not a priest who bears priestly
witness to something that God has done; Jesus Christ *is* what God has
done, *is* God come down as priest on our behalf in our humanity. Jesus
Christ is God's Word identical with God's kingly act (the Mosaic priesthood), and Jesus Christ's offering is identical with his person, for he offers
himself as our response to the Father (the Aaronic priesthood).[171] Torrance
contends that "this is Royal Priesthood, in the coincidence of Grace and
Omnipotence, in the identity of Person and Work."[172] Jesus Christ as royal
priest, the Son of God incarnate, is both the definitive and final *Offerer* and
the definitive and final *Offering*.

Torrance notes that both aspects of this priesthood are fulfilled *for us*. As
we saw in chapters two and three, Jesus Christ is both the act of God for us
and also our vicarious human response (our obedience, response, witness
and amen), on our behalf and in our stead. Jesus Christ is God's Word to
us and our word to God in his one person. We can offer only what Christ
has already offered in our place and on our behalf. We can minister only
according to what Christ has already ministered in our place and on our
behalf.[173] His offering and his ministry do not perfect or complete our offering and ministry; they replace them, yet in such a way that we may participate in his.

It is as our high priest that Jesus Christ has ascended back to God the Father, offered himself for us through the eternal Spirit and even now and forever lives as our high priest and intercessor (Heb 8:1-3). In and for our

---

[168]Ibid., p. 9.
[169]Ibid., pp. 11-13.
[170]Ibid., p. 14.
[171]Ibid.
[172]Ibid.
[173]Ibid.

humanity, Jesus our brother presents himself in the presence of the Father and presents us with himself to the Father.[174] Christ sends the same Spirit—through whom he offered himself in life, in death and before the Father—to the church with his high-priestly blessing, "fulfilling in the life of His Church on earth what which He has fulfilled on our behalf in the heavenlies."[175]

Jesus Christ is our great high priest who through his atoning life, death and resurrection offered himself once for all for the sins of the world, and who now has ascended to the right hand of the Father, where he exercises his royal priesthood on our behalf, confesses us and intercedes for us before the Father.[176] It is this royal priesthood of Christ that the Spirit echoes in the corporate ministry of the church as the body of Christ, so that the church participates in Christ's ministry in word, deed and life.[177]

The royal priesthood of the whole church. The reconciliation accomplished by Christ on our behalf has been completed once and for all so that by its very nature it cannot be repeated.[178] Thus the ministry of the church can never be viewed, in Torrance's perspective, as a prolongation, repetition or extension of Christ's royal priesthood.

Nevertheless, the reconciliation accomplished by Christ once for all is "given a counterpart in the Church in the form of Eucharistic prayer and praise."[179] In fact, Torrance notes that while "priest" and "royal priesthood" are applied only to Christ, in the plural they are applied "in corporate form, to the Church as a whole."[180] The Spirit echoes Christ's royal priesthood in the corporate ministry of the church.

The church derives the form of its corporate ministry or royal priesthood from the form of Christ, the incarnate Son of God, who considered equality with God not something to be grasped but took the form of a suffering servant, not be served but to serve and to give himself as a ransom for many (Phil 2:1-5; cf. Mt 20:25-28).[181] The church in its corporate reality is baptized with Christ's own baptism (as we saw earlier in this chapter) and therefore baptized into Christ's servant life and ministry.[182]

---

[174]Ibid., pp. 14-15.
[175]Ibid., p. 15.
[176]Ibid., pp. xiv, 12-13.
[177]Ibid., pp. xiv, 22.
[178]Ibid., p. 13.
[179]Ibid.
[180]Ibid., p. xv. Also see pp. 15-18.
[181]Ibid., p. xv.
[182]Ibid.

The crucified, risen and ascended Christ sends the Spirit on the church and thereby creates in the midst of the world, between Christ's first coming and final *parousia*, the body of Christ, in which humanity is opened up from within for the actualization of revelation and reconciliation, a revelation/reconciliation that is inherently missionary and ministerial.[183] The church thus becomes, Torrance contends, the instrument of Christ's saving purpose in the gospel: rooted in the love of God the Father, the church grows to fullness in the grace of Christ and in the communion of the Holy Spirit, and becomes the vessel through which Christ—clothed with the gospel—presses forward toward the fulfillment of a movement to the ends of the earth and the end of the age.[184]

Or to view another facet of the same reality, Jesus Christ is the last Adam, the new man, the head of a new human race incorporating all humanity into himself and drawing that new humanity toward universalization in Christ's resurrection and ascension (Eph 1:10; cf. Rom 5:15-19; 1 Cor 15:21-23).[185] Torrance contends that the church, as the body of Christ indwelt by Christ's Spirit and in accordance with Christ's own life and work, embodies a parallel movement in mission and ministry toward universalization until Christ returns in final victory. The church is the first-fruits of this new humanity, caught up in Christ's own royal priesthood moving forward in mission and ministry in the name of Christ, who fills all things. Torrance calls this a movement from *soma*—the body of Christ—to *pleroma*—the fullness of Christ who fills all things (Eph 1:22-23; cf. 1 Cor 15:22-27).[186]

Torrance means by "the universalization of the gospel" the movement of the love of God the Father, embodied in the grace of Jesus Christ and clothed with the gospel in the communion of the Holy Spirit, to the ends of the earth and the end of the age. This is not a *universalism*. According to Torrance, universalism is another facet of the Latin Heresy, in which grace and the relation between divine and human agency in soteriology is construed in logico-causal categories, as we saw in chapters two and three.[187] Why some people do not believe and instead turn away from Jesus Christ and the gospel is part of the *inexplicable* character of iniquity and evil which, for Torrance, are ultimately *irrational* and *unintelligible*,

---

[183]Ibid., p. 23.
[184]Ibid., pp. 23-24.
[185]Ibid., p. 25.
[186]Ibid., p. 26.
[187]See chapters two (pp. 94-96) and three (pp. 117-23).

and which therefore cannot be explained.

Thus for Torrance, "in this whole movement the being and mission of the Church are inseparable. . . . The Church is . . . rooted in the love of God which has overflowed into the world and embodied itself in our humanity in the Beloved Son, and . . . grounded in the crucifixion and in the resurrection of His Body, so that through union with Him in Spirit and Body the Church participates in the divine nature and engages in Christ's ministry of reconciliation."[188] Here the church's royal priesthood (or corporate ministry) is forever grounded in the church's relation to Christ, in which Christ is pleased to use the church in *his* ministry of reconciliation, renewing the world and extending his kingdom.[189]

Since the church is one body indwelt by Christ's one Spirit, Torrance argues that "the participation of the Church in the ministry of Christ is *primarily corporate*."[190] The one body, of course, is made up of many members who are given diverse gifts of the Spirit for the edification of the church and for its extension into the world and forward in history (Eph 4:11-13; cf. 1 Cor 12:1-31).[191]

Torrance sees the essential movement of the church's ministry as parallel to Christ's whole incarnational movement of *descent (anabasis)* and *ascent (katabasis)*. This is another way of speaking of the God-humanward and human-Godward character of the incarnation and the vicarious humanity of Jesus Christ, as we saw in chapters two and three (and earlier in this chapter in relation to the Eucharist). Torrance maintains that "the ministry of the Church, therefore, is grounded upon a reception of the Christ who descends into the midst and then, on the ground of His substitutionary atonement in which He at once takes our place and unites us to Himself, the motion of ministry is to be described as an oblation of thanksgiving and worship, correlative to Christ' ascension or oblation of Himself in which He present the Church as His own Body to the Father."[192]

This means that there is no relation of *identity* between the ministry of the church and the ministry of Christ. Yet neither is the ministry of the church *another* ministry different or separate from the ministry of Christ.[193]

---

[188]Torrance, *Royal Priesthood*, pp. 28-29.
[189]Ibid., p. 35.
[190]Ibid.
[191]Ibid., p. 36.
[192]Ibid., p. 39.
[193]Ibid., p. 37.

Rather, ministry—like the Christian life in general—is a *participation* in Christ: "It is not one in which . . . we act in Christ's place so that we substitute for him or displace him; rather it is one in which we serve his vicarious Priesthood in accordance with the biblical principle 'not I but Christ' (Gal 2:20)."[194]

This does not mean that Christ's vicarious royal priesthood undermines or destroys the human counterpart, the royal priesthood of the whole church; rather Christ undergirds it and fills it with his own priestly presence and activity (an application of the *logic of grace* to ministry). "The ministry of the Church is related to the ministry of Christ in such a way that in and through the ministry of the Church it is always Christ Himself who is at work, nourishing, sustaining, ordering, and governing His Church on earth. . . . It is Christ Himself who presides as Prophet, Priest, and King, but He summons the Church to engage in *His* ministry by witness, by stewardship, and by service."[195]

The ordained ministry. The royal priesthood of the church, for Torrance, is primarily the ministry of the whole body of Christ. So he argues that Christ's gift to the church of consecration and ordination to special ministry "has its place only within the consecration of the whole membership of Christ's Body, and therefore within the ministry of the whole Body, which it has through sharing in Christ's vicarious Self-consecration."[196] Here within the royal priesthood of the whole body of Christ, this particular priesthood is set apart to edify the whole body until the church reaches its fulfillment in Christ.[197] Ordained ministry serves and edifies the whole body of Christ in order that the church as Christ's own body can fulfill Christ's ministry of reconciliation to the world.[198]

Those called and ordained by Christ and set apart for this institutional ministry or priesthood serve Christ "in the proclamation of the Gospel and in the celebration of the Sacraments."[199] Christ himself intended to establish a community with a form, an order, a leadership and a ministry patterned after his own ministry.[200] This order of ordained ministry (which

---

[194]Ibid., pp. xv-xvi.
[195]Ibid., pp. 38-39.
[196]Torrance, *Conflict and Agreement*, 2:38.
[197]Torrance, *Royal Priesthood*, p. 81.
[198]Ibid.
[199]Ibid., p. xiv.
[200]Torrance, *Reconciliation*, p. 206.

Torrance traces back historically through the apostles to Christ himself) is as crucial to the life of the church and its mission as the Bible or the sacraments.[201] Yet Jesus Christ himself is and remains for all time the one true and original apostle.

This particularized ordained ministry follows the same *servant form of* and *participation in* Christ's own ministry identified in the previous section in relation to the royal priesthood of the whole church. Yet because the goal of this particularized priesthood is the edification of the body until it reaches the fullness of Christ, it has its place in the time between the beginning of the church (Pentecost) and the *parousia* of the Lamb and Christ's final marriage-supper.[202]

Here Torrance argues that while this ordained ministry is as crucial to the church as the sacraments or the Bible, like them "this order of ministry will pass away as the *parousia*, when the real [royal] priesthood of the one Body, as distinct from the institutional priesthood, will be fully revealed."[203] Those ordained are drawn into Christ's own self-consecration, into Christ's ministry, where they share in Christ's consecration and ministry as servants of Christ and Christ's body, fulfilling the ministry of Word and sacrament in Christ's name until Christ returns.[204] When Christ returns, this order of ordained ministry or institutional priesthood, along with the sacraments and the Bible, will pass away like the scaffolding used to erect a building once the building itself is complete.

Since the ordained ministry is a sharing in Christ's self-consecration, Torrance contends, it is Jesus Christ himself who ordains. Yet Christ ordains within the church which Christ founded and through which he continues to act: "It is the risen and ascended Lord who acts directly through His Spirit ordaining His servant to the ministry, but He does that in and through the Church which He has once and for all established in the apostles and bound to the Revelation which He has committed to the Church through the apostles."[205] It is Christ, not the church, who pours the Spirit and the gifts of the Spirit on the ordained ministry, while the laying of hands is the apostolically given sign that attests the obedience of the church to its apostolic origins and bears witness to the presence of the Spirit promised by Christ to the church

---

[201]Torrance, *Royal Priesthood*, p. xv.
[202]Ibid., pp. xv, 81.
[203]Ibid.
[204]Torrance, *Conflict and Agreement*, 2:45.
[205]Ibid., 2:47.

for the fulfillment of this ministry of Word and sacrament.[206]

For Torrance the end of ordination, as mentioned above, is the ministry of Word and sacrament. In fact, he argues that the Word and the sacraments are more important than ordination, so that ordination and the ministry of the Word and sacraments are entirely subordinate or subservient to the Word and sacraments themselves.[207]

Thus ordination does not provide a kind of authority for the minister to exercise over the Word and sacraments, for the minister's authority lies in the Word and sacraments themselves and places the minister in a servant relation to them.[208] This underscores again for Torrance the servant form of ordained ministry which reflects the servant form of Christ's own ministry.

Torrance also argues that in light of the superiority of the Word and sacraments over the minister, "there can in the nature of the case be no higher ministry than that of the ministry of Word and Sacraments, for that would be to suppose that there was a higher authority than that of the Word."[209] This means, Torrance contends, that there can really only be one order of ordained ministry in the proper sense, ordination to the ministry of Word and sacrament. There is therefore no theological ground for a distinction in order between a presbyter and a bishop, though Torrance has no problem with making a distinction in function between them.[210] There can be doctors of the church and bishops who have special functions in teaching and pastoral discipline within a single order of ordained ministry to Word and sacrament.[211]

This understanding of all ministry as participation in Christ's own ongoing ministry contributes substantially to Torrance's unequivocal commitment to women's ordination to the ministry of Word and sacrament. In fact, he states, "there are no intrinsic theological reasons why women should not be ordained to the Holy Ministry of Word and Sacrament."[212] He finds evidence in the early church of women officiating with men in the Eucharist,

---

[206]Ibid., 2:48. Here again we see the same *logic of grace* which Torrance says gives paradigmatic shape to all God's interaction with us in space and time, as we saw in the introduction and in chapter three.

[207]Ibid., 2:50-51.

[208]Ibid., 2:51.

[209]Ibid.

[210]Ibid., 2:51-52.

[211]See Torrance, *Royal Priesthood*, chapter five, "The Corporate Episcopate," for his understanding of "bishops-in-presbytery."

[212]Thomas F. Torrance, *The Ministry of Women* (Edinburgh: Handsel, 1992), p. 12.

and he provides a thorough biblical and theological rationale for women's ordination.[213]

Throughout all of ministry, whether the royal priesthood of the whole church or the particular priesthood of ordained ministry, Torrance is clear that everything goes back to Jesus Christ and his royal priesthood: "That is the Priesthood which is echoed through the Spirit in the corporate ministry of the Church as the Body of Christ, and in the particular ministry of those who are called and ordained by Christ to serve him in the proclamation of the Gospel and in the celebration of the Sacraments."[214] The ministry of the church is true and effective ministry only when it is so related to Christ's high priesthood that Christ himself, through the Spirit, is always at work speaking his Word anew, filling the sacraments with his presence and reality, sustaining, ordering and nourishing the church as his body, and calling the church to carry his gospel to the uttermost ends of the earth and to the end of the age, when he will come again in final victory and fill everything in every way.

[213]Ibid., pp. 1-13.
[214]Torrance, *Royal Priesthood*, p. xiv.

PART IV

THE TRIUNITY OF GOD
& THE CHARACTER
OF THEOLOGY

8

THE TRIUNITY OF GOD,
ONE BEING THREE PERSONS

*No sooner do I consider the One than I am enlightened by the radiance of the Three:
no sooner do I distinguish them than I am carried back to the One.
When I bring any One of the Three before my mind I think of him as a Whole,
and my vision is filled, and the most of the Whole escapes me.
I cannot grasp the greatness of that One in such a way as to attribute more greatness
to the rest. When I contemplate the Three together,
I see but one Torch, and cannot divide or measure out the undivided Light.*
GREGORY NAZIANZEN

Since his retirement as Professor of Christian Dogmatics in 1979,
Torrance has produced an astonishing flood of publications on the Trinity.
The climax to this work on the Trinity is Torrance's book *The Christian
Doctrine of God*, which is really a capstone to his illustrious career as a
theologian and author. This chapter deals with Torrance's doctrine of the
Trinity as developed in *The Christian Doctrine of God*, his most recent and
significant work on this subject.

The opening section of this chapter focuses on that genesis of the doctrine of the Trinity, how it arises out of the incipient trinitarian pattern imprinted on the deposit of faith as embodied in biblical witness. The
doctrine of the Trinity implicit within Scripture comes to explicit articulation, Torrance maintains, in a coordinated set of theological concepts (that
is, *hypostatic union, homoousios, ousia, person* and *perichoresis*) on three interrelated levels. This articulation clarifies and deepens the church's understanding of the Christian doctrine of God inherent in the trinitarian pattern
of God's self-revelation and self-communication in the gospel.

The three subsequent sections of this chapter discuss the content of Torrance's doctrine of the Trinity. The first of these sections deals with the one being *(ousia)* of God, though not apart from the three persons. The focus shifts in the next section to the three persons in their differentiations, and to Torrance's onto-relational concept of person where the inherent interrelations of the three persons are as real as the persons who together are the *one* dynamic being-in-communion of God. The final section concentrates on Trinity in Unity, Unity in Trinity, through use of the concept of *perichoresis* which brings to expression the coinherent way in which the three persons indwell and inexist in one another as the one triune God.

A methodological caution is important at this point: the reader should not view the trajectory and content of this chapter as a new and different movement of thought beyond chapters two through seven above. Rather, this chapter is a refocusing and further development of the trinitarian pattern in the previous discussions so as to further clarify both the content of Torrance's doctrine of the Trinity and how it comes to theological articulation. Thus this chapter brings to light another dimension of the holism of Torrance's scientific trinitarian theology. The first section on the genesis of the doctrine of the Trinity will help clarify the relation of the material from chapters two through seven to the content of the doctrine of the Trinity developed in the last three sections of this chapter.

1. The Genesis of the Doctrine of the Trinity
How the doctrine of the Trinity arises theologically within the life of the church is one of the most difficult subjects in Torrance's theology. It is also one of his most significant contributions not only to trinitarian theology but to theological method.

In the first subsection, we will take note of the evangelical and doxological approach, and the informal undefined mystery of the Trinity that conditions Torrance's scientific account of the formulation of the *doctrine* of the Trinity. The next subsection returns again to the early church and the way in which the *homoousion* brings the trinitarian pattern of God's redemptive activity to articulation. The third and final subsection deals with the stratified conceptual levels that arise in the formulation of the doctrine of the Trinity.

The approach to the formulation of the doctrine of the Trinity. Torrance's development of the doctrine of the Trinity reveals the inherent and incipient trinitarian character of Christian faith. He uncovers the way in which the doctrine of the Trinity is coordinated with the evangelical and doxological life of the church essential to the reality of the church as the body of Christ, the earthly-historical form of Christ's existence.

An evangelical/doxological and rigorous scientific approach. For Torrance, we know God through evangelical (from the Father through the Son in the Spirit) and doxological (in the Spirit through the Son to the Father) participation in the gospel. What is particularly intriguing in Torrance's discussion of how the doctrine of the Trinity arises is the way he deepens our understanding of this evangelical and doxological participation in the gospel by disclosing the trinitarian character and ground of that participation, and therefore how and why all Christian faith and theology is and ought to be aboriginally, intrinsically and comprehensively trinitarian. In Torrance's perspective, the Trinity is both the *ultimate ground* of our salvation and knowledge of God and the *basic grammar* of Christian theology, as we shall see by the end of this chapter.[1]

What Torrance wants to do here, as we have seen throughout the previous chapters, is to clarify the inner constitutive relations embodied in the gospel itself, relations which are fundamentally trinitarian. It is these basic incipient intrinsic relations embedded in God's self-revelation and self-communication that Torrance attempts to uncover, understand and articulate in a way that is as methodologically rigorous as possible, utilizing a few theological concepts developed and deployed in careful connection with the content of that revelation and communication. When theology does this, it is scientific, as we noted in the introduction and chapter two.[2]

This a crucial and insightful point: since we are concerned with God in God's *redemptive self-communication*, the doctrine of the Trinity and a rigorous scientific account of it cannot but be participatory. Torrance argues that the Holy Trinity can only be known evangelically and doxologically, in a transformative encounter with the love of God through the grace of Christ and in the communion of the Holy Spirit which includes personal faith, thanksgiving, worship and prayer, first in the vicarious humanity of Christ and then in us, as we saw in chapter three above on the subject of the mediation of Christ and our human response.[3] So for Torrance there is absolutely no conflict between true theology and true doxology. An evangelical and doxological approach is properly basic to Torrance's rigorous

---

[1]Thomas F. Torrance, *The Ground and Grammar of Theology* (Charlottesville: University Press of Virginia, 1980), pp. 158-59.
[2]See pp. 21-25, 55-60 above.
[3]See chapter three, pp. 113-33.

scientific account of both content and method in theology in light of the reality of God we come to know in the gospel.[4]

The mystery of the Trinity and the necessity of open concepts. In Torrance's theology God is intrinsically knowable, for the Word of God incarnate as Jesus Christ inheres in the being of God. Yet this self-revelation and self-communication of God to us through Jesus Christ and in the Holy Spirit is an astonishing and inexhaustible mystery.[5] The reason this is so, as noted in a number of places above, is that God does not simply reveal propositions about God to which we assent. What the living God gives to us is a *Self*-revelation and *Self*-communication through Jesus Christ and in the Holy Spirit which reconciles us, redeems us from our sin and radically transforms us from unbelieving, self-centered and ungrateful sinners into children of God.

God does all of this only through Jesus Christ and in the Holy Spirit who unites us to Christ in Christ's oneness *(homoousios)* of being, knowing and loving with God the Father so that we share at least in some degree in God's own self-knowing and self-loving.[6] Torrance can describe this as a kind of *ecstatic passion*, for what we know of God is an inexhaustible mystery, *the* inexhaustible mystery of the Trinity so replete in depth and breadth of content that we cannot master and capture it within the confines of our concepts.[7] We come to know far more of God than we can tell.

In all of our theological inquiry into the Trinity, Torrance contends that we have to acknowledge this implicit, informal, inarticulate, inexhaustible element (which is cognitive but not reducible to propositions) of God's self-revelation and self-communication through Jesus Christ and in the Holy Spirit which engenders our faith, love and worship, and which ought always to keep our statements and concepts open to the inexhaustible mystery of the triune God.[8]

It is no coincidence, Torrance maintains, that the early church associated the mystery of godliness or godly worship with thinking of God in a trinitarian manner. In Athanasius, for example, the equation *theologia=eu-*

---

[4]More than a few interpreters of Torrance have been led astray on this point because of a conceptualization of "science" quite different from that of Torrance.

[5]Thomas F. Torrance, *The Christian Doctrine of God: One Being Three Persons* (Edinburgh: T & T Clark, 1998), p. 73.

[6]Torrance, *Ground and Grammar*, pp. 154-55.

[7]See Torrance, *Christian Doctrine*, pp. 73-34, 81-82.

[8]Ibid.

sebia (theology=godliness) "was identified with trinitarian thinking or simply with the worship and doctrine of the Holy Trinity."[9] For Torrance this is the kind of theology that *is* scientific. The inexhaustible mystery of the Trinity, open concepts expressing the doctrine of the Trinity, and godly faith in and worship of the Trinity always belong together.[10]

On the way to Nicaea/Constantinople. This is precisely the kind of approach to formulating the doctrine of Trinity that Torrance finds operative in the early church.[11] The implicit inarticulate mystery of the Trinity is bound up with the original *datum* of God's self-revelation from the Father through the Son and in the Holy Spirit, known in evangelical and doxological participation. The informal, undefined mystery of the Trinity was already embedded implicitly in the deposit of faith within the apostolic church, imprinted on the apostolic mind and inherent in the New Testament Scriptures. The doctrine of Trinity is grounded not simply in the triadic formulae found in Scripture, but even more deeply in the intrinsic order, the trinitarian pattern in the economy *(oiknomia)* of God's redemptive activity in Jesus Christ's life, death and resurrection and in the outpouring of the Holy Spirit on the church at Pentecost.[12]

This implicit mystery of the Trinity, pressing for articulation in explicit form, began to unfold in the early church within the context of meditation on the Scriptures and trinitarian worship of the living God.[13] What Torrance finds happening in the early church, especially from Irenaeus through the Nicene theologians, is the trinitarian heart of the gospel in the implicit trinitarian faith of the church coming to intellectual expression in the incipient confessions of belief in God the Father, Son and Holy Spirit.[14]

As we saw in earlier chapters the primary focus is on Jesus Christ as risen Lord and Savior, for it is in Christ the incarnate Son of the Father that true knowledge of God in accordance with God's nature is possible. This

---

[9]Ibid., p. 74.

[10]Ibid., pp. 74-75.

[11]See Torrance's discussion of this in relation to Irenaeus and the Nicene theologians in ibid., pp. 75-82.

[12]Ibid., pp. 75, 82.

[13]Ibid., pp. 74-75, 82.

[14]Daniel Hardy has Torrance right on this point. See Daniel Hardy, "Thomas F. Torrance," in *The Modern Theologians: An Introduction to Christian Theology in the Twentieth Century,* ed. David Ford (Oxford: Basil Blackwell, 1989) 1:75-6. The editor, David Ford, inexplicably excluded Hardy's insightful essay in the revised edition of the work.

means that in the early church in theologians like Irenaeus and Athanasius (and in Torrance's own theology), the trinitarian understanding of God is thoroughly christocentric and soteriological.[15] In fact, Torrance thinks that the doctrine of the Trinity places the incarnation at the center of faith in God, since it establishes Jesus Christ as the one mediator between God and humanity in the movement of God's trinitarian self-revelation from the Father through the Son and in the Holy Spirit.[16] As we saw in chapter seven on the church, Torrance also sees a corresponding trinitarian movement of faith, worship and devotion in the church, *in* the Holy Spirit *through* the vicarious humanity of the risen Son *to* God the Father.[17] This is why Torrance says that the doctrine of the Trinity is both the *ground* and the *grammar* of all Christian theology and worship.[18]

It is important to note that Torrance sees these creedal formulae taking shape in the early church not as a set of doctrinal propositions deduced from Scripture or even as a speculative system of ideas expressing the religious consciousness of the church. Rather they are coherent convictions in the process of taking definite form in the mind of the church (integration of form in knowing) arising out of and controlled by the trinitarian pattern of implicit relations and structures embedded in the gospel itself (form in being).[19]

These doctrinal formulations arise out of and disclose the organic structure, the inner constitutive relations in God's actual self-revelation and self-communication through Jesus Christ and in the Holy Spirit. They are not *logically* but *ontologically* ordered statements of belief, Torrance contends, which progressively reflect and disclose the objective trinitarian pattern of God's self-revelation, and are therefore open formulations of belief reflecting the transcendent intelligibility of God's self-revelation that exceeds what we can ever bring to explicit understanding and articulate conceptual expression.[20]

As we saw in several chapters above, Torrance thinks that the *homoousion* played an absolutely crucial role in bringing this incipient trinitarian economy of God's redemptive activity in Jesus Christ (or Christian doc-

---

[15]Torrance, *Christian Doctrine*, p. 75.
[16]Ibid., p. 82.
[17]Ibid.
[18]Ibid. Also see Torrance, *Ground and Grammar*, pp. 158-59.
[19]Torrance, *Christian Doctrine*, p. 76.
[20]Ibid., pp. 74-77, 80-82.

trine of God) to articulation. The reason for this is that in the incarnation, the relation of knowing, loving and being between God the Father and God the Son is realized within the vicarious humanity of Christ our Lord, the incarnate Son of God.[21] Since we have already examined this point in detail above, we will not pursue it further here.[22]

The important point, however, is that for Torrance, the *homoousion* signifies that Jesus Christ bridges the chasm "between God's knowing of himself as only God can know himself and man's knowing of God," for real knowledge of God is realized in the vicarious human mind of Jesus Christ.[23] What we know of God in God's immeasurable love for us in God's condescension to us in Jesus Christ is entirely consistent with all that God is in the inexhaustible mystery of ontological Trinity who transcends all that we can know and express, whom we cannot but worship and adore, trust and obey.[24]

Through the application of the *homoousion* to the incarnate Son and later to the Holy Spirit, the essential trinitarian features embedded in the original datum of God's self-revelation come to formal expression in the Niceno-Constantinopolitan Creed. The *homoousion* gives explicit articulation to the decisive substructure of the gospel: the redemptive self-revelation and self-communication of God as Father, Son and Holy Spirit in the economy of salvation is ultimately rooted in and forever sustained by God's own eternal trinitarian reality, nature and life. The *homoousion* is both *evangelical* and *ontological*. It asserts in the strongest possible form that Jesus Christ, the incarnate Son, Savior and Lord, *is* the very heart of the gospel, and that what God is and has done for us in the gospel is ontologically grounded in who God really is and ever will be in God's own eternal being, nature and life.[25] Thus the *homoousion* provides the church with the "theological key," Torrance argues, that unlocks the doctrine of the Trinity implicit in the self-revelation and self-communication of God in the gospel.[26]

Stratified conceptual levels in the doctrine of the Trinity. It is because *God* has become incarnate in Jesus Christ *within* the *creaturely human struc-*

---

[21]Ibid., pp. 77-78.
[22]See chapters two, pp. 73-81; three, pp. 98-113; four, pp. 129-39; and six, pp. 225-33.
[23]Ibid., p. 78.
[24]Ibid., p. 79.
[25]Ibid., p. 80.
[26]Ibid., p. 81.

tures of space and time that the doctrine of the Trinity comes to theological articulation involving several coordinated conceptual levels. These levels deal respectively with (1) God in God's own trinitarian life, (2) the trinitarian economy imprinted on the saving events of God's self-communication in history and (3) our evangelical and doxological apprehension of those events in the gospel.[27] Or to express it the other way around, Torrance's account of the three levels and the cross-level movement of thought they involve illumines the way in which our Christian apprehension of God in the gospel moves *from* the evangelical level of our day-to-day relationship with God in the life of the church *through* what God is and has done for us in God's redemptive activity as Father, Son and Holy Spirit in history (God's *oikonomia* or the economic Trinity) *to* what God is antecedently and eternally in God's own being and life as Father, Son and Holy Spirit (the ontological Trinity).[28] Our apprehension moves from our encounter with God in the gospel through the evangelical Trinity to the theological Trinity.[29]

While this stratified structure of coordinated levels clarifies both the content of the doctrine of the Trinity, as well as how the doctrine of the Trinity arises, there are two extremely important points that we must be clear about before we examine these three levels and the important cross-level movement of thought in more detail. The first is that Torrance's delineation of this stratified structure that arises within the formulation of the doctrine of the Trinity is an *a posteriori* reconstruction of the way in which our apprehension of God takes place. If the multi-level structure of refined theological concepts and relations is *in any way* cut off from the actual saving reality of the gospel, the revealing and redemptive participatory relations in which—through the grace of Christ and in the communion of the Holy Spirit—we really come to know the love of God, the multi-level conceptual structure becomes no more than an empty theoretical construct. Apart from dynamic and cognitive union and communion with God through Christ and in the Spirit, the concepts and cross-level movement of thought they entail would have no validity or objective content and reference.[30]

The second point is that the triune God is a fullness of *personal* being,

---

[27]Ibid., p. 83.
[28]Ibid.
[29]Ibid.
[30]Ibid., pp. 83-84.

and all of God's redemptive activity on our behalf in self-revelation and self-communication is of an intensely personal character. As we saw in chapter three, Torrance sees God as interacting with us in a personalizing or person-constituting manner that includes much more than a movement of thought on our part, for it entails the transformation of our minds and our lives so that we respond in a fully personal manner in faith, worship, obedience and love in the Spirit through the Son to the Father, as noted earlier in this chapter.[31] We cannot know God apart from God's redemptive purpose.

This means that we have to think of the different levels, and the movement between them, in our knowledge of the Trinity and formulation of the doctrine of the Trinity as not simply epistemic but distinctively redemptive and personal as well. What Torrance intends is not a communication of mere ideas or propositions on God's part and some abstract intellectual movement of thought on ours, but rather a redemptive and personal self-communication on God's part and a human response on our part that involves our entire human being. The *doctrine* of the Trinity, in Torrance's theology, cannot be cut off from this redemptive and personal self-communication of God and human response without becoming an abstraction. We are now ready to examine Torrance's understanding of the stratified structure that arises in careful formulation of the doctrine of the Trinity.

The evangelical and doxological level. Torrance describes this first level as "evangelical and doxological" since the focal point is a personal encounter with Jesus Christ and the gospel in which we come to know Christ as Savior and Lord through the communion of the Holy Spirit and respond doxologically in faith, worship and obedience to the love of God. This is not a private religious experience, for it takes place within the day-to-day life and activity of the church where together we encounter God's revealing and saving activity and respond in faith to the proclamation of the gospel and to eucharistic worship.[32]

It is at this evangelical and doxological level, within the fellowship of the church, that we indwell the Scriptures and their evangelical presentation of Christ and of the missionary activity of the early church in the saving power of the cross and the Holy Spirit. As we do so, our thinking and

---

[31]Ibid., p. 88.
[32]Ibid., pp. 88-89. Also see Torrance, *Ground and Grammar*, pp. 156-57.

our worship begin to take on the imprint of the evangelical Trinity, God's threefold self-revelation and self-communication, often tacitly without our even being fully aware of it. This happens, Torrance argues, not through an analytical, logical, speculative or formal process, but in a spontaneous, holistic, informal and undefined manner.[33]

Torrance also calls this the level of "incipient theology" in which form and content, empirical and conceptual, experiential, historical, and theological elements are already and naturally interwoven in what we know (form in being) and in our knowing of it (integration of form in knowing).[34] We learn this within the body of Christ through the transforming presence of God's Word and Spirit in such a profoundly evangelical, personal and transformative manner that we are spiritually, intellectually and ontologically implicated in the patterned personal activity of evangelical Trinity beyond our power to fully understand and explicitly articulate.[35] As a child, by the time she reaches five years old, has spontaneously and informally learned more about the physical world than the child will ever be able to understand even if she becomes a brilliant physicist, so we learn more about the love of God the Father, the grace of our Lord Jesus Christ and the communion of the Holy Spirit within the tradition and living fellowship of the church than we can ever tell.[36]

Torrance argues that at the evangelical and doxological level, in personal union and communion with Christ in the Holy Spirit, we gain the initial anticipatory insights or clues needed for developing theological instruments and concepts that enable us to bring the trinitarian structure of God's self-revelation and self-communication to explicit understanding

---

[33]Torrance, *Christian Doctrine*, p. 89.

[34]This is an important point for it signifies an understanding of the nature and genesis of doctrine in general, and the doctrine of the Trinity in particular, beyond cognitive-propositionalism, experiential-expressive and cultural-linguistic theories outlined by George Lindbeck in his important book, *The Nature of Doctrine* (Philadelphia: Westminster Press, 1984). Also see Elmer M. Colyer, *The Nature of Doctrine in T. F. Torrance's Theology* (Eugene, Ore.: Wipf & Stock, 2001).

[35]Torrance, *Christian Doctrine*, p. 89. We will examine Torrance's account of tacit and informal knowing in greater detail in chapter nine.

[36]Ibid., p. 89. This is an important point, for it enables us to better understand what many pastors and some theologians are already aware of: that there are times when the elderly woman in the back of the church who has long lived in communion with God in prayer, worship, the reading of the Bible and the life of the church knows more about God than the professional theologian who may be extraordinarily adept at manipulating the symbols or concepts of the faith, but for whatever reason has not lived out of evangelical and doxological participation in the gospel.

and conceptual expression.[37] We begin to think of the triune God in ways that are worthy and godly, and therefore appropriate to the mystery of the Holy Trinity who is more to be praised than explored.

This evangelical and doxological level is absolutely essential, Torrance contends, for it is always from the evangelical pattern of God's redeeming activity in Jesus Christ and in the gift of the Holy Spirit that the informational content of God's trinitarian self-revelation as Father, Son and Holy Spirit is mediated. Torrance states emphatically that "this ground level of evangelical experience and apprehension remains the necessary basis, the *sine qua non*, of the other levels of doctrinal formulation developed from it."[38] Without it and apart from it *there could be no trinitarian theology* at all. The other levels of doctrinal formulation arise out of and develop the implicit and intrinsic trinitarian pattern of God's self-revelation in the gospel at the evangelical and doxological level.[39]

The theological level. At the second level (or "theological level," as Torrance calls it) we develop our inquiry into the patterns of interconnection within the basic level of our evangelical apprehension and worship of God and attempt to render explicit and more precise our knowledge of God's self-revelation by forming the appropriate intellectual concepts and relations to express these patterns.[40] As we inquire into the evangelical and doxological field described above, we find a repeated and differentiated threefold pattern in God's revelatory and redemptive activity in Jesus Christ rooted in the love of God the Father realized in the church through the communion of the Holy Spirit. The inchoate apprehension of the Trinity implicit in God's triadic redemptive revelation and latent in the mind, life and worship of the church, as evident in the various triadic formulae in the New Testament documents, begins to come to definite theological formulation. Our thought moves from the incipient evangelical apprehension to explicit understanding and expression in what we call the economic Trinity, the ordered pattern of God's self-revelation and self-communication in redemptive activity in history through Christ and in the Holy Spirit.[41]

---

[37]Ibid., p. 90.
[38]Torrance, *Christian Doctrine*, p. 90. Only within the evangelical and doxological apprehension and shared spiritual insight within the tradition and life of the Church can theologians gain cognitive contact with God through the gospel (see p. 91).
[39]Ibid.
[40]Ibid.
[41]Ibid., p. 92.

In the work of the Nicene theologians, Torrance finds a series of concepts and relations coming to explicit theological articulation so as to provide a deeper and more accurate grasp of the gospel message in the face of challenges and misunderstandings.[42] Forms of ordinary thought and speech, like "Father," "Son" and "Holy Spirit," are taken up by God's self-revelation and radically redefined under the impact or import of the gospel. At times, new terms have to be coined ("Trinity," for example) to articulate the character of the intrinsic relations in our knowledge of God in the gospel that come into view within this second level of inquiry.[43]

As we saw in chapter two, the central issue in the church's attempt to clarify the constitutive relations implicit in the gospel (the meaning of love of God the Father in the grace of our Lord Jesus Christ) was the precise relation of being and agency between God the Father and Jesus Christ. The Nicene theologians gave explicit expression to this relation through the use of a carefully defined theological term, *homoousios*, which affirmed in the strongest way possible that what Jesus Christ is and has done in his life, death and resurrection for the salvation of the world, *God* is and has done for the salvation of the world. As true God from true God, of one being and act with God the Father, Jesus Christ both reveals God to us and is God for us, so that there is no dark inscrutable God behind the back of Jesus Christ on the cross before whom we can only be afraid.[44]

Since we have already discussed the *homoousion* at some length in earlier chapters, we will not restate that material here, but simply note that Torrance views the *homoousion* as a faithful exegetical distillation of not simply the fundamental sense of the New Testament, but an articulation of the basic constitutive relations in the redeeming acts of God in Jesus Christ.[45] The *homoousion* crystallizes the conviction that Jesus Christ is not

---

[42]See chapter two, pp. 73-78.

[43]Torrance, *Christian Doctrine*, p. 93. See chapter four above, pp. 142-46.

[44]Torrance, *Christian Doctrine*, pp. 93-94. It was within the profound evangelical and doxological experience of the gospel, Torrance contends, that the Nicene theologians felt they had to affirm Jesus Christ as *homoousios* with God the Father in order to be true to the implicit constitutive relations embodied in the gospel itself, for it was God that they encountered in Jesus Christ, and it was God the incarnate Son that they worshiped and adored along with the Father in the communion of the Holy Spirit. Thus in their union and communion with Jesus Christ they found themselves in union and communion with God the Father who loved them to the uttermost. If there is no bond in being and activity between Jesus Christ and God, Torrance thinks that the bottom drops out of the gospel, as we noted in chapter two.

[45]Torrance, *Christian Doctrine*, p. 95.

a created intermediary between God and humanity, nor simply some detachable symbol or paradigmatic instance of a panentheist God-world relation, but rather the very Word of God eternal made flesh for us and our salvation.[46] It is in carefully thinking out the astonishing relations and implications of the *homoousion* that the gospel comes to deeper and more explicit articulation, and the fully ontological trinitarian doctrine of God comes into view as well. It is for this reason that Torrance calls the *homoousion* the "ontological and epistemological linchpin of Christian theology."[47]

The *homoousion* thus raises the question concerning the character of the other relation of the incarnation, Jesus Christ's oneness not only with God the Father, but Christ's oneness with us in the depths of our broken, diseased and sinful humanity. The incarnation falls within the life of God, but also within the structures of our spatio-temporal humanity in this world. The ontological and soteriological interconnections of these relations came to theological formulation in the *hypostatic union*, along with Christ's vicarious humanity and atoning reconciliation, as developed in chapters two and three above.

This is also a crucial point for Torrance, since it underscores the fully evangelical as well as ontological character of the *homoousion*, for the incarnation takes place for us and for our salvation. Here Torrance agrees with his teacher, H. R. Mackintosh, that even what we apprehend of the inner life of God through the *homoousion* is "for the sake of redemptive expression, not for the internal analysis of its content."[48]

The *homoousion* is not restricted to the relation between the incarnate Son and God the Father. As we saw in chapter six, it was applied to the Holy Spirit as well, so that at the Council of Constantinople the church confessed its faith "in the Holy Spirit, the Lord and Giver of Life." The *homoousion* is the ground of the mutual mediation of Jesus Christ and the Holy Spirit (see chapter six). The Holy Spirit is also *Lord*, and with the Father and the Son together is worshiped and glorified.[49]

When applied to the incarnate Son and the Holy Spirit, the *homoousion* gives powerful expression to the interrelations implicit in the evangelical

---

[46]Ibid.

[47]Ibid. Also see Torrance, *Ground and Grammar*, pp. 160-61.

[48]H. R. Mackintosh, *The Doctrine of the Person of Jesus Christ* (New York: Charles Scribner's Sons, 1928), p. 526. Also see Torrance, *Christian Doctrine*, p. 91.

[49]Ibid., p. 96.

and doxological level that in Jesus Christ and the Holy Spirit in the gospel we are directly in touch with the ultimate presence and reality of God: *"What Jesus Christ does for us and to us, and what the Holy Spirit does in us, is what God himself does for us, to us, and in us."*[50] The *homoousion* thus deepens and refines our understanding of the self-revelation and self-communication of God in the gospel as Father, Son and Holy Spirit, and it tells us that the incarnation and atoning reconciliation of the Son of God and the mission of the Holy Spirit have a place within the very being and life of God.[51]

By affirming and expressing both the *deity* of the Son and the Spirit, along with the Father, and their oneness of *being*, yet also their distinctive threefold self-revealing and self-giving, the *homoousion* plays a crucial role in the movement of theological reflection from the theological level and the economic Trinity to the higher theological level of the relations in the ontological Trinity.

The *homoousion* also signifies that the theological activity involved here is not a *speculative movement of thought* that leaves the evangelical and doxological experience and life of the church behind. Rather, the *homoousion* gives careful expression to the very core of the gospel in which the faithful know that it is *God* who has loved them to the uttermost in Jesus Christ; and in the fellowship of the Holy Spirit, it is *God* who opens their eyes to the gospel and the Scriptures, and lifts them up in faith, hope and love for God and one another. No cold and lifeless conceptual imposition on the simple gospel, the *homoousion* is a fertile elucidatory insight which evokes and discloses the profound depth of truth in the mystery of the gospel of Jesus Christ, the wisdom and power of God that every believer knows, even though he or she may not be able to fully understand and articulate it.[52]

The higher theological level. This brings us to the third, or "higher," theological level, where we move from God's self-communication in the saving activity of Jesus Christ and the Holy Spirit, and the economic trinitarian relations in all that God is toward us in the gospel, to the trinitarian relations immanent in the Godhead, which are the sustaining basis of economic relations.[53] In the movement from the first to the second level, Torrance ar-

---

[50]Ibid., p. 95. Torrance thinks that this view of the gospel—that what Christ does for us and what the Spirit does in us, *God* does for us and in us—is the real meaning behind the terms *theopoiesis* and *theosis*, as we saw in several chapters above.

[51]Ibid., p. 97.

[52]Ibid., p. 98.

[53]Ibid., pp. 98-99.

gues, "the insight takes the form that what Jesus Christ is toward us in love and grace, in redemption and sanctification, in the mediation of divine life, he is inherently in himself in his own Being—he is not different in himself from what he manifests toward us in his life and work."[54]

In the cross-level movement from the second to the third level, from the economic to the ontological Trinity, the *homoousion* signifies that what *God* is toward us in Jesus Christ and the Holy Spirit, God is antecedently, inherently and eternally in God's own being and life. There is a relation of perfect oneness in being, activity and love between the evangelical and ontological Trinity.[55] This means that our evangelical and doxological knowing of God through Jesus Christ and in the Holy Spirit is grounded in the very being of God; however, the inexhaustible mystery of God stretches far beyond what we can even begin to fathom, so that we cannot but feel somewhat sacrilegious when we speak of the being of God in this way. Thus, we know that awe and adoration are the only appropriate modes of theological inquiry and expression.[56] *Theologia* (scientific theology) and *eusebeia* (godly worship) belong together, especially when we move from the evangelical to the ontological Trinity.[57]

Yet Torrance is quite adamant and clear on the point that we *must* make this movement of thought from the economic to the ontological relations in the formulation of the doctrine of the Trinity, for in Jesus Christ, in the incarnation of God's eternal Word and in the Holy Spirit who unites us to Christ and through Christ with the Father, we really are in touch with *God*, and "with the trinitarian relations of love immanent in God."[58]

In actual reality, of course, this movement of thought from the evangelical to the ontological Trinity on our part is grounded in God's movement in the free outpouring of love in the incarnation and in the coming of the Holy Spirit at Pentecost, who together lift us up to *share in* the divine life and love that God eternally *is* in himself.[59] Torrance thinks that this is "the

---

[54]Torrance, *Ground and Grammar*, p. 161. Also see Torrance, *Christian Doctrine*, p. 99.

[55]Torrance, *Christian Doctrine*, p. 99. What we know of the Father, the Son and the Spirit in their coinherent relations, revealed in God's saving activity through Jesus Christ in the Holy Spirit, are not merely appearances. They are ultimately sustained by and grounded in the reciprocal and intrinsic relations that God *is* in God's trinitarian being and life (p. 102).

[56]Torrance, *Ground and Grammar*, pp. 166-67.

[57]Torrance, *Christian Doctrine*, p. 74.

[58]Ibid., p. 107.

[59]Ibid., p. 99.

inner core of the Christian faith which the *homoousion* expresses so succinctly and decisively."[60] To say any less, from Torrance's perspective, is
not true theological humility, but rather unfaithfulness to the "utterly staggering" (one of Torrance's favorite expressions) good news of the gospel:
God loves us to the uttermost, even more than God loves himself, and God
loves us with the very love that God is.[61]

As our theological reflection moves from the second (economic) level to
the third level of the ontological Trinity, Torrance finds that we have to develop further concepts beyond the *hypostatic union* and the *homoousion* in
order to understand and articulate what we know and only imperfectly
understand of the trinitarian persons and relations in the one being of
God. Since we will develop the material content of these concepts in the
subsequent sections of this chapter, we will only briefly note them here.

Torrance appropriates and develops the term *perichoresis* to articulate the
mutual indwelling and coinhering of the three divine persons in the one being of God.[62] This refined concept of *perichoresis*, when utilized to express the
intra-trinitarian relations in God, is intimately related to Torrance's *onto-relational* concept of "divine person" in which the ontic relations between the
persons belong to what the persons *are* as persons. The communion between
the persons is as real as the persons themselves.[63]

These new relational and personal forms of thought deeply and radically altered the concept of *being (ousia)* which the Nicene theologians appropriated from Greek philosophical sources, as we developed in chapter
four. When used to speak of the one *being* of the ontological Trinity, *ousia*
becomes intensely personalized so that the one *ousia* of God is as profoundly personal as the trinitarian persons. God is a fullness of personal
being in himself, a communion of persons in which being and communion
are finally one.[64]

Torrance argues that all theological concepts and statements "fall short
of the God to whom they refer."[65] However, he sees this as serving a posi-

---

[60]Ibid.
[61]Ibid., p. 108. "It cannot be sufficiently emphasized, that the theological or ontological Trinity remains *evangelical*, not only because it is coordinated with the evangelical revelation of
God as Father, Son and Holy Spirit, but because it is essentially and intrinsically evangelical."
[62]Ibid., p. 102.
[63]Ibid., pp. 102-3.
[64]Ibid., pp. 103-4.
[65]Ibid., pp. 105, 110-11.

tive purpose, even part of their truth and precision, for the fragility and inadequacy of all theological concepts and statements underscore their
semantic reference to the truth of God that can never be captured in human
thought and concepts.[66] This does not mean that when theological activity
moves from the economic to the ontological Trinity that it breaks off into
some form of apophatic contemplation *via negativa* (the attempt to contemplate God by asserting that God is unlike any characteristic of mundane reality). Though God is more to be adored than expressed, Torrance
maintains that "the ultimate Rationality, as well as the sheer Majesty of
God's Self-revelation, and above all the Love of God, will not allow us to
desist."[67] The inadequacy of our concepts reminds us that God is always
greater *(Deus semper maior)*. In godly reflection and exultant adoration we
know that we know more than we can tell, and we know that what we
know is only a faint reflection of what lies ahead.

The human concepts that arise in the course of human knowledge of
God are really part of the fact that God establishes reciprocal relations with
us within our creaturely existence in space-time. The God-humanward relation and activity of God sustains a human-Godward relation as well, as
we saw particularly in relation to the vicarious humanity of Jesus Christ.
God's self-revelation (form in being) embodies itself in a human coefficient
which is part of its concrete actualization within creaturely human life and
understanding (integration of form in knowing). Whatever difficulties this
may create for theological formulation, it is viewed by Torrance as part of
the astonishing character of the gospel, that we, human beings though we
are, can really know God and have communion with God because God
condescended to us in Jesus Christ and lifts us in the communion of the
Spirit into union with Christ and through Christ with God the Father so
that we share in God's own life and love.[68]

2. Being as Communion: One Being, Three Persons

In his most significant elucidation of the doctrine of the Trinity, Torrance

---

[66]Ibid. Of course, as noted in the chapter on the Holy Spirit, the *homoousion* does not allow us
to read back into God in an indiscriminate way what is human and finite in Jesus Christ.
That God is *Spirit* means that we must think of God's being, and God's trinitarian relations
and life, in a wholly spiritual way. Torrance argues that we must hold together in all our
thinking of God the unity between the economic activity of the Son and the Spirit so as not
to read any material or creaturely images back into God (see chapter six above, pp. 216-21).
[67]Torrance, *Christian Doctrine*, pp. 110-11.
[68]Ibid., pp. 103-6.

develops his position under three headings: "One Being, Three Persons"; "Three Persons, One Being"; and "Trinity in Unity and Unity in Trinity."[69] I will adopt this pattern in my analysis and commentary in the remainder of this chapter, though with an important caveat: Torrance is adamant that there can be no division or separation between the one being and the three persons, the three persons and the one being, for the Holy Trinity is an inseparable and indivisible Trinity in unity and unity in Trinity.[70] The exposition of Torrance's doctrine of the Trinity in the following sections will clarify this point.

The approach. This unitary approach to the Trinity also means that Torrance (following Barth and Karl Rahner) is self-consciously setting aside the Augustinian-Western conception of the Trinity (Rahner's expression), which first discusses the divine essence of the one God and only afterwards takes up the discussion of the three persons.[71] Torrance emphasizes the indivisible wholeness of the divine Triunity where the one being, three persons, and the three persons, one being are the obverse of one another.[72] Our apprehension of the self-revelation of the triune God is holistic: in the one gospel of the one Lord God we implicitly know the love of the Father through the grace of Christ in the communion of the Spirit simultaneously in the differentiated wholeness of God. It is in the course of bringing what is implicit to explicit formulation that the *doctrine* of the Trinity arises, as we saw in the previous section.[73]

Thus in the same way that we do not approach Jesus Christ from below (beginning with his humanity) or from above (starting with his deity), from any kind of disjunction between Christ's humanity and deity, but from the undivided wholeness of Christ's divine-human reality, so also Torrance argues, we approach the doctrine of the Trinity conjunctively, thinking together the economic Trinity and the ontological Trinity, and also God's unity in Trinity and Trinity in unity.[74] In light of this unitary perspective Torrance develops his understanding of the one being, three persons of the triune God.[75]

---

[69]See ibid., pp. 112, 136, 168.

[70]Ibid., p. 113.

[71]Ibid., p. 122.

[72]Ibid., pp. 112-13.

[73]The doctrine of the Trinity, Torrance contends, is not a conclusion to a logical argument or even an inductive movement of thought.

[74]Ibid., pp. 116-17.

[75]Ibid., p. 115.

As in so many areas of his theology, here again Torrance unfolds his doctrine of the Trinity in dialogue with the great Nicene theologians. He contends that while the Greek fathers used the term *ousia* to designate the one "being" of God—a term that had a significant history in various strands of Greek philosophy—in the Christian use and development of it, *ousia* undergoes a thorough adaptation and transformation.[76] Under the impact of God's self-revelation and self-communication in the Old and New Testaments, *ousia* sheds it static, metaphysical meaning, as found in Aristotle's *Metaphysics*, for example, and becomes living, speaking, personal being, rather than static and mute being: "Being in communion, Being for others," rather than solitary being.[77]

Torrance wants to draw the meaning of *ousia* from within the trajectory of the redemptive activity (the *oikonomia*) of the ever-living God who has spoken (and continues to speak) to us in an intensely personal, living and dynamic way in God's covenantal relation with Israel and preeminently in Jesus Christ,[78] as we have noted throughout the previous chapters of this book. This is not a speculative notion of being, but one derived from God's actual self-revelation and self-communication through Jesus Christ and in the Holy Spirit.[79]

The "I am" of Yahweh. Drawing on Athanasius, Torrance develops the meaning of the being of God in light of the self-naming of God in God's revelatory and redeeming covenant relationship with Israel. Torrance sees God's answer to Moses' question regarding God's name (Ex 3:14) as of crucial significance: "Say to the people of Israel 'I am who I am.' "[80] Torrance argues that the Hebrew equally means "I will be who I will be," and Torrance finds a rather fuller and deeper significance in this self-naming of God than a cursory reading of the text may disclose.

---

[76]Ibid., pp. 116-17.

[77]Ibid., pp. 116, 131-34. Torrance notes that Athanasius preferred verbs to nouns when speaking of the living, dynamic reality of God (see p. 117).

[78]Ibid., pp. 116-17.

[79]Ibid., p. 116. This is another way of stating Torrance's *semantic principle* that terms are not prior to realities, though this does not mean that our experience of reality is prior to language and a form of life, since all human beings are embedded in a culture, language and form of life from birth (see p. 117). What it does mean is that Torrance gives priority to objective reality (as tendentious as this may sound in a postmodern context) over language, even though language is crucial to knowing and articulating reality, as we will see in the final chapter on Torrance's theological method. It is the careful distinction between reality and our language and form of life that makes Torrance's realism critical.

[80]Ibid., p. 118.

In a sense, Torrance sees the whole Old Testament as concentrated in this self-naming of *Yahweh* as the dynamic divine "I am who I am/I will be who I will be," for the early Exodus narrative subsumes under this *I am/I will be* all that the living God has done for Israel from the calling of Abraham to the exodus, and all that the living God will do for his people in delivering them from bondage.[81] The primal constitutive event defining God's relation to Israel and Israel's relation to God is not the creation narrative, but rather the exodus event and God's covenant purpose in God's saving activity on Israel's behalf.[82] *Yahweh* defines who he is as the "I am who I am/I will be who I will be" by delivering Israel from bondage as Savior and Redeemer beside whom there is no other God. In so doing, Torrance argues, God's being is revealed in the pattern of God's saving and redemptive activity in Israel's history.[83]

Torrance finds it instructive that God's self-naming and self-revelation as "I am who I am/I will be who I will be" is spoken by *Yahweh* in the first person singular. It signifies that *Yahweh* is the Lord God, the transcendent subject *(Kurios)* and "the sole Subject of all he is and will be, and of all his ways and works."[84] Yet the Lord of Israel is the God of steadfast love who in the freedom of grace establishes so intimate a covenant relation with Israel in holy fellowship that God adopts Israel as God's firstborn child. Thus Israel's very existence bears the imprint of God's personal, revealing and saving, fellowship-seeking and communion-creating activity. Israel becomes *Yahweh's* people formed by God's name and self-giving, and indwelt by God's presence, indelibly marked as the people of *Yahweh*, the divine "I am who I am."[85]

Already in the Old Testament, even apart from the "I am" of Jesus Christ, Torrance finds a dynamic and intensely personal understanding of the being *(ousia)* of God developing.[86] Under this old covenant, the being of God is only known through the fellowship that the living God creates through God's self-naming and self-giving to the people of Israel, and *this*

---

[81]Ibid., p. 120. See Exodus 1—6, especially chapter 3 and 5:22—6:8.

[82]God delivers Israel from bondage and prepares Israel to be the immediate earthly-historical context within which God's self-communication in Jesus Christ and the Holy Spirit takes place, as developed in chapter two above.

[83]Torrance, *Christian Doctrine*, p. 120.

[84]Ibid.

[85]Ibid., p. 122.

[86]Ibid., p. 123. It is a concept of being very different from the static metaphysical conceptualizations of being or substance in the various strands of the Greek philosophical tradition.

being of God is the living, dynamic and personal being of God in redeeming presence and activity for Israel. Torrance finds in the Old Testament a free self-determining "being of God for others," even while this being is the self-grounded "I am Who I am" of God.[87]

The "I am" of Jesus and God's trinitarian being. Of course, for Torrance, it is in the relation of the "I am" of God and the "I am" statements of Jesus Christ that the whole biblical, Christian and trinitarian understanding of the being of God comes into view. Torrance sees Jesus and the early church appropriating this dynamic self-revealing and self-naming of God in the Old Testament as "I am who I am," and connecting it with the various "I am" statements that the New Testament attributes to Jesus.[88]

In the doctrinal development in the early church, the various "I am" statements (along with many other texts) in the New Testament played an important role in clarifying the relation between Jesus Christ the incarnate Son and God the Father, and therefore an important role in the genesis of the *homoousion*. Once the *homoousion* came to expression, however, it served as an exegetical instrument that clarified the import of the New Testament "I am" sayings of Christ in relation to the "I am" of God in the Old Testaments witness.[89] When viewed in this light, Torrance contends that, Jesus' "I am" in the New Testament underscores the personal character of the "I am who I am" of *Yahweh*, whereas the "I am who I am" of *Yahweh* reveals the ultimate ground of the "I am" of Christ in God.[90]

Torrance argues that these "I am" sayings together with the *homoousion*, the *oneness in being* between the incarnate Son and God the Father, enabled the early church to think out the nature of God's *ousia* with greater faithfulness and precision as stated in Athanasius' memorable aphorism, "It is more godly and more accurate to signify God from the Son and call him

---

[87]Ibid.

[88]Ibid., p. 124.

[89]Ibid. Torrance thinks that the various "I am" sayings of Jesus must be understood in terms of the *homoousion*, Christ's oneness of being with God (see p. 119). Torrance finds Jesus' words to his disciples "I am in the Father and the Father is in me" (Jn 14:10) as especially significant here, for Torrance argues that it indicates that Jesus' own "I am" statements are grounded in the mutual indwelling of the Son and the Father in one another within the eternal communion or inner life of God (see p. 124).

[90]Ibid., p. 119. It was the christological and trinitarian development of this line of thought that generated the concept of person and the personal.

Father, than to name him from his works and call him Unoriginate,"[91] as we saw in chapter four.

This is the epistemological significance of the incarnation: God provides real knowledge of himself, as God is in himself, in Jesus Christ the incarnate Son within the matrix of Israel. Thus Jesus Christ is both the revelation of the Father and the human reception of that revelation in Christ's vicarious human knowing of the Father. When combined with the coming of the Spirit at Pentecost from the Father in the name of the Son, the Spirit who is the Lord and the giver of life, in whom we participate in personal union and communion through Christ with the Father, Torrance discerns an onto-relational and fully personal understanding of the being of God coming into view.[92]

God's soteriological relations with us in the evangelical (economic) Trinity are grounded in the internal relations of the theological (ontological) Trinity, as we saw in the first section of this chapter on how the doctrine of the Trinity arises. This also discloses the absolutely essential place of the Trinity in Torrance's Christian understanding of the being of God.[93] God is not, in the end, ontically different in God's eternal being than the personal and personalizing Father, the Son and the Holy Spirit we encounter and come to know in the gospel through the biblical witness.[94] The intensely personal and profoundly ontological interrelation between the economic (evangelical) Trinity and the ontological (theological) Trinity given precise and succinct expression in the *homoousion* tells us that God's being is *being-in-communion*.

Thus we come to see that the communion-constituting activity of God's *ousia* in God's covenant making and self naming in Israel in the Old Testament, and in the love of God the Father that we know through the grace of Christ in the communion of the Spirit in the New Testament, has its source in the mutual indwelling, coinhering and inexisting of the Son and the Father and the Holy Spirit in the internal differentiations of the inner life of God.[95] We must now deal more precisely with the relation of the one being to the three persons of God.

---

[91]Thomas F. Torrance, *Trinitarian Perspectives: Towards Doctrinal Agreement* (Edinburgh: T & T Clark, 1994), p. 8.

[92]Torrance, *Christian Doctrine*, p. 124

[93]Ibid., p. 117.

[94]Ibid., pp. 119, 121.

[95]Ibid., pp. 124-25.

The relation of God's one being to the three divine persons. This is one of the more difficult elements of Torrance's doctrine of the Trinity, and readers will want to consult Torrance's own intricate development of it in dialogue with the evolution of post-Nicene trinitarian theological reflection.[96] Torrance wants to guard against not only tritheist and modalist heresies, but also the subtle danger of viewing *ousia* as abstract and impersonal, a problem that developed in the sharp Cappadocian distinction between *ousia* (being) and *hypostasis* (person).[97]

Here, once again, Torrance finds the *homoousion* revolutionary and decisive, for it articulates the fundamental evangelical truth that what God is and what God does in our midst, embodying the love of the Father through the grace of Christ in the communion of the Spirit for our salvation, God really *is* in himself *"in the internal relations and personal properties of his transcendent Being as the Holy Trinity . . . and ever will be,"*[98] and, of course, vice versa. The ultimate ground of the fellowship-seeking, communion-constituting activity of the Father, the Son and the Holy Spirit on our behalf in the *parousia* of Jesus Christ (the incarnate Son whom the Father gave up for us all) and the sending of Holy Spirit (who unites with Christ and through Christ with the Father) is the *koinonia* (communion) of the *ousia* (being) of God. God's being *is* being-in-communion. This is implied in the *homoousion* itself which underscores both the oneness and differentiation within the Godhead.

God's being for others in the Father, the Son and the Holy Spirit in God's *oikonomia* (economy) in history reveals, and is grounded in, the everliving, intrinsic being-in-communion that the *ousia* of God is.[99] God's being, Torrance asserts, is "inherently altruistic, *Being for others, Being who loves,"*[100] not out of any kind of necessity, but in freedom, for God is already Being in and for Others in the innermost nature of God's reality.

This means, Torrance contends, that the one indivisible *ousia* of God cannot be less personal, less loving, less dynamic, less active, less communal than God is in each trinitarian person who is true God of true God.[101] Rather, the one being *(ousia)* of God is intensely and intrinsically personal,

---

[96]See ibid., pp. 128-35.
[97]Ibid., p. 129.
[98]Ibid., p. 130.
[99]Ibid., pp. 130-32.
[100]Ibid., p. 131.
[101]Ibid., pp. 129, 133.

dynamic, active, loving being.[102] The one *ousia* of God *is* communion (*koinonia*), the personal self-communication of love shared between the trinitarian persons.[103] Torrance maintains that "the three divine Persons in their Communion with one another *are* the Triune Being of God."[104] This personal triunity of internal relations and eternal distinctions *is* the one being three persons of God.[105]

Once again, it is important to reiterate at this point before we move on to the next section, "Three Persons, One Being," that in Torrance's theology we do not come to know the one being of God by an abstract, speculative or logico-deductive movement of thought, but rather by way of participation, through cognitive union and personal communion with God through Jesus Christ in the Holy Spirit in which our lives as well as our minds are transformed by the power and presence of Christ clothed with his gospel.[106] Our knowledge of God's being in communion, as well as our knowledge of God at every level, can never be more than a clarification and amplification of our basic knowledge of God at the evangelical and doxological level.

3. Persons in Relations: Three Persons, One Being

In this section we turn our attention to Torrance's understanding of the three divine persons in communion, who in their perichoretic interrelations *are* the one *ousia* of God.[107] Of course, it is through the grace of Christ that we come to know the love of God the Father in the communion of the Holy Spirit, and therein come to know something of the trinitarian persons in their interrelations, for *God* is the content of God's self-revelation and self-communication. The *homoousion* expresses the fact that the Father, the Son and the Holy Spirit are not different in their personal interrelations in the theological Trinity than they are in the economic pattern of personal relations in the evangelical Trinity.[108]

An onto-relation concept of person. Torrance views "Father," "Son"

---

[102]Ibid., pp. 132-33.
[103]Ibid., p. 133.
[104]Ibid., p. 124. "The theological concept of the Being of God . . . is not to be understood as referring to three Persons *in* God's Being as if the three Persons were other than and not identical with the one Being of God, but precisely as the One Being of God" (p. 104).
[105]Ibid., p. 125.
[106]Ibid., p. 128.
[107]Ibid., p. 136.
[108]Ibid.

and "Holy Spirit" as proper names which designate the three persons (*hypostases*) who are distinct and therefore not interchangeable, even though they are of the one being of God.[109] All three persons are equally and fully Lord and God, though there are not three Lords or Gods, but one Lord God. Indeed, Torrance asserts, "The Holy Trinity of three divine Persons is thus perfectly homogeneous and unitary, both in the threeness and oneness of God's personal activity, and in the threeness and oneness of his eternal unchangeable personal Being."[110]

While Torrance does not find an explicit and developed concept of "person" in the biblical witness itself, he discerns in the use of the Word, the name, the glory, the face of God a kind of differentiation in reference to God that is "quasi-hypostatic."[111] The incarnation of the Son of God in Christ, the linking of the "I am" statements of Jesus with the "I am" of *Yahweh* and the threefold pattern of God's self-manifestation as Father, Son and Holy Spirit all forced the early church to unfold the implicit trinitarian self-communication of God that generates a fully theological concept of person.[112] We cannot trace the details of Torrance's analysis of how the concept of (divine) person developed, but simply note several crucial points before summarizing his own understanding of person.

The Greek word *hypostasis,* used in Hebrews 1:3 in reference to Christ as the Son of God ("the express image of his [God's] being [*hypostasis*]"), was the term appropriated by the early theologians and molded into a fully developed concept of person.[113] *Hypostasis* was utilized first to speak of the self-revelation of God in the incarnate Son in whom the living God confronts us with his incarnate "I am."

However, Torrance argues that only when the early church fathers further adapted *hypostasis* in relation to the trinitarian self-communication of God as the Father, the Son and the Holy Spirit did a fully onto-relational

---

[109]Ibid., p. 155. Because earlier chapters developed Torrance's understanding of each of the persons, we will not recapitulate that material here. For the earlier discussions on Jesus Christ, the incarnate Son, see chapter two, pp. 70-81 ("The Inner Relation of Christ to God"); on God the Father, see chapter four, pp. 139-51 ("The Person, Love and Being of God the Father"); and on the Holy Spirit see chapter six, pp. 216-21 ("God Is Spirit and the Holy Spirit Is God"), and pp. 233-41 ("The Procession of the Holy Spirit").

[110]Torrance, *Christian Doctrine*, p. 155.

[111]Ibid.

[112]Ibid., pp. 155-56.

[113]Ibid., p. 156.

concept of *person* come to articulation within the theological context of the interpersonal relations of the trinitarian God.[114] Thus when the early theologians carefully thought out "the homoousial and hypostatic interrelations of the three divine Persons *(hypostases)* within the one Being *(ousia* understood in its internal relations) or Communion *(koinonia)* of the Holy Trinity, it became clear to them that the ontic relations between the divine Persons belong to what they are as Persons."[115] The divine persons are what they are only in distinction from *and* in essential relation to one another within the one being of God where each of the persons is whole God.

In other words the differentiating characteristics of the Father, the Son and the Holy Spirit, rather than dividing them, hypostatically interrelate the persons with one another and are constitutive of their unity as well as their differentiation. The interrelations between the persons are ontic, dynamic, holistic and constitutive of what and who the persons are in the one being of God. Torrance utilizes the term "onto-relation" to express the substantive character of the constitutive relations between the persons.[116]

Torrance finds the essential elements of this onto-relational concept of person as constitutive interrelations in Gregory Nazianzen, who adapted the Greek concept of *pros ti* to articulate the eternal and essential "for to" interrelations between the trinitarian persons in contrast to the concept of "mode of being" *(tropos hyparxeos)* deployed by the other Cappadocians.[117] The relations between the persons are not, Torrance contends, simply modes of being, but rather hypostatic coinherent relations that are absolutely real and intrinsic, and in fact belong to what the divine persons actually are as persons.[118]

The ontic, dynamic and holistic character of the relations helps clarify what we mean when we speak of God as Father, Son and Holy Spirit. Torrance is unequivocal that Father and Son in reference to God are absolutely *not* forms of analogical predication where we begin with human experience of father and son, posit their perfections, and then apply these terms to God by means of this *via eminentiae*.[119]

---

[114]Ibid. Once again Torrance finds here a term taken over from Greek thought, radically transformed by God's self-revelation, and utilized to express what the early theologians believed they had to say in order to remain faithful to the threefold self-communication of God from the Father, through the Son and in the Holy Spirit for the salvation of the world.
[115]Ibid., pp. 156-57.
[116]Ibid., p. 157.
[117]Ibid.
[118]Ibid.
[119]Ibid., pp. 157-60.

Torrance maintains that "Father" and "Son" when applied to God are radically altered and "point utterly beyond what we mean by 'father' and 'son' . . . and thus utterly beyond all sexist connotations and implications,"[120] as we saw in chapter four. All analogies are set aside and the terms refer to the divine persons in an imageless, spiritual and ineffable manner in light of God's self-revelation from which the terms derive their meaning.

The same pattern holds true for the derivation of an onto-relational concept of person. We must not begin with a preconceived notion of person.[121] When used in reference to the Trinity, person has to be understood in light of God's self-communication in the economy of salvation out of which the concept had its genesis. "Person" may be applied to human beings made in the image of God, but the meaning of the term changes. As we saw in chapters three and five, Torrance argues that we should think of God as "personalizing person" and ourselves as "personalized persons."[122]

It is preeminently in Jesus Christ that we find an acute personalization of God's relationship with humanity and our relationship with God. Here Torrance again points to the *anhypostasis/enhypostasis* couplet, which underscores that—while there was no independent human hypostasis in the incarnation—there was still a real and fully human hypostasis *enhypostatic* in the incarnate Son or Word of God.[123]

In Christ's vicarious humanity we find our humanity intensely personalized and humanized in relation to God, and brought into intimate union and communion with God, the communion that God is as three onto-relational persons who are what and who they are in the differentiating characteristics that unite them hypostatically as Father, Son and Holy Spirit.[124] Torrance contends that we must think of Jesus Christ "as embodying within our human life the onto-interrelations which obtain not only between him and the Father but between the three divine Per-

---

[120]Ibid., p. 157.

[121]Once the concept of "person" entered the stream of human ideas from its genesis in Christian faith, it has taken on a life of its own and a range of meanings in various cultures, often in conflict with the Christian view of person, as in modern Western culture with its vision of a human person as a discrete autonomous individual (not unlike a Newtonian atom).

[122]Torrance, *Christian Doctrine*, 160. Also see chapter three above, pp. 117-23, and chapter five, pp. 178-80.

[123]Torrance, *Christian Doctrine*, pp. 160-61.

[124]Ibid., p. 161.

sons in their undivided Communion with One Another."[125]

It is, therefore, in God's personalizing us in Jesus Christ and the Holy Spirit, and in the communion between the Father, the Son and the Spirit revealed in the evangelical Trinity in the gospel, that we come to know something of the interrelations and homoousial communion which the Father, the Son and the Holy Spirit are in their inner life in one another which is identical with the one being of God.[126] This means, Torrance argues, that we "think of the one God as a fullness of personal Being in himself"; not that the one God is a *person* in the interrelational sense of the trinitarian persons, but in the sense that "God is a Communion of personal Being in himself, a Trinity in Unity and a Unity in Trinity."[127]

Being for others: mutual loving and indwelling. The personalizing activity of God on our behalf in the mission of the evangelical Trinity has to be understood in terms of the outgoing movement of God's eternal love embodied in our midst in the incarnation of God's beloved Son in order to reconcile us with God so that we may share in the communion of love that God is in God's trinitarian life. As we noted in chapter two, Torrance argues that the whole undivided Trinity is present and active in the incarnate reality of the Son in Jesus Christ; not that the Father or the Spirit became incarnate, but rather that the trinitarian persons in their homoousial and hypostatic onto-relations are all present and active in the realization of God's love for humanity in Jesus Christ, though in the distinctive

---

[125]Ibid.

[126]Ibid. If there is a form of analogical predication in Torrance's theology, here is where we see what it means. The divine trinitarian persons are who they are in their ontic, dynamic and holistic relations. Human persons are truly who they are when they are *personalized* by God in union and communion with God and with others. The relations between human persons and God are constitutive of who the human persons are, though *not* vice versa, for if God were constituted by God's relations with the world, we would have a form of panentheism like what we find in process theology, which Torrance rejects. The relations between human persons, however, do also entail constitutive elements.

While these various relations are ontic, dynamic and constitutive, they are far from being identical because we are dealing with radically different realities—God and creaturely human beings. One could say that there is an analogical relation involved, but it operates in the opposite direction. We do not begin with human persons, posit their perfection and apply this concept of person to God. Rather we begin with the trinitarian onto-relational concept of person. We find the perfect human analogue to this divine concept of person in Jesus Christ in his relation with God and Christ's relations with other human persons. Then we allow this concept of person as we find it embodied in Jesus Christ to judge and critique our own faulty and often sub-personal *concepts* of the human person, and also judge our actual and sinful sub-personal human existence.

[127]Ibid.

characteristics that unite the persons with one another.[128]

Here in the sending of God's Son out of love to live and to die in atoning reconciliation for us all, and in pouring out the Holy Spirit who spreads the love of God in our midst and in our hearts, Torrance points out that God loves us with the very love that God is. In other words the self-giving love for others, the communion of love with others, the freedom of love to others manifested through Christ and in the Holy Spirit for us in the activity of the evangelical Trinity flow from and correspond to the self-giving, communion-creating, free-flowing love of the Father, the Son and the Holy Spirit for one another, the eternal love that God is. Torrance asserts that this is, in fact, "what the doctrine of the Holy Trinity supremely means, that God himself is Love."[129]

This is a dynamic kind of love in freedom which the Father, the Son and the Holy Spirit *are* in their ceaseless love of each other. Torrance describes this as a "Being for One Another" in which the trinitarian persons love one another, dwell in, give to and receive from one another, and therefore are the communion of love of the triune God.[130] Of course, as noted in earlier chapters, it is the free overflowing of this love of God that is the ground both of our creation and our redemption. And it is this free overflowing love of the Father (giving up the Son), the self-giving of the Son (even to death for our sins) and the self-giving of the Spirit (through whom Christ offered himself as a sacrifice for sin) that reveals what the love of God really is.

Thus we come to know that God does not withhold the love that God is from us, but rather loves us to the uttermost, without reserve, and even "more, astonishingly," Torrance says, "than he loves himself."[131] This, then, is both the real meaning of God's "being for others," and also a revelation of at least something of the inmost nature of God's being as love. The dynamic and ontic reciprocal indwelling and loving, giving and receiving, between the Father, the Son and the Holy Spirit are the onto-relations which belong to what the trinitarian persons are as persons in homoousial and hypostatic relations, which Torrance describes as a "sort of ontological communication between them," a Trinity in Unity and Unity in Trinity, three persons, one being.[132]

---

[128]Ibid., p. 162.
[129]Ibid.
[130]Ibid., p. 163.
[131]Ibid., p. 166.
[132]Ibid.

4. Perichoresis: Trinity in Unity and Unity in Trinity

The concept of perichoresis. Torrance finds *perichoresis* to be an extremely helpful concept for deepening and clarifying the onto-relations between
the trinitarian persons within the unity of the Trinity.[133] Though Athanasius never utilized the term *perichoresis*, Torrance maintains that Athanasius' elucidation of the mutual indwelling of Father and the Son in light of
the oneness (the *homoousion*) in being and activity between them expressed
the essential content of *perichoresis*.[134]

The *homoousion* itself articulates not only the oneness in being and activity between the incarnate Son and the Father, and the real distinctions between them, but also the coinhering of the three divine persons in the one
being of God.[135] Athanasuis also demonstrated, Torrance contends, that
this mutual indwelling and coinhering applies to the homoousial interrelations of the Holy Spirit and the Father and the Son, and therefore to the
whole Trinity.[136]

Only God can reveal God, and only God can save humanity. Only if the
Holy Spirit is *homoousios* with the Father and the Son, can the Spirit mediate to us what the love of the Father in the grace of Jesus Christ has accomplished for us. It was very clear to Athanasius that the Nicene faith of the
Christian church depends on the soteriological and ontological interconnection between the being and activity of the Father, of the Son and of the
Holy Spirit in the economy of salvation.[137]

As developed by other Nicene theologians, *perichoresis* refers to the reciprocal relations between the Father, the Son and the Holy Spirit in
which they mutually indwell, coinhere, inexist and wholly contain one
another without in any way diminishing the persons and their real distinctions.[138] This, of course, is unintelligible, Torrance grants, with regard
to creaturely objects and human persons. But it is quite different with
God who can contain all things without being contained by anything.[139]
The divine persons have their being in one another and coinhere and inexist within one another without commingling or compromising the in-

---

[133]Ibid., p. 168.
[134]Ibid., pp. 168-69.
[135]Ibid., p. 169.
[136]Ibid.
[137]Ibid.
[138]Ibid., pp. 169-71. Torrance develops the doctrine of *perichoresis* in dialogue with Gregory
Nazianzen and Epiphanius, among others.
[139]Ibid., p. 171.

tegrity of the persons and their distinctions.[140]

Torrance argues that *perichoresis* has to be understood as dynamic, rather than static, in order to express the living, relational character of the homoousial communion between the trinitarian persons. Indeed, if God is Spirit, if God is personal and if God is love, *perichoresis* has to be conceived "in a wholly spiritual and intensely personal way," Torrance contends, "as the eternal movement of Love or the Communion of Love which the Holy Trinity ever is within himself, and in his active relations toward us."[141] *Perichoresis* expresses the "immanent in-each-otherness" of the three divine persons whose incommunicable characteristics do not divide, but rather unite them in their mutual and personal indwelling of one another in the communion of the inner life of God.[142] *Perichoresis* refers to that eternal, dynamic, inexhaustible movement of love between the Father and the Son and the Holy Spirit, a love which is the source of the entire universe and of the entire outworking of God's purpose in the economy of salvation to reconcile, renew and redeem a world tarnished by sin, but loved by God to the uttermost.[143]

Perichoretic wholeness, a circle of reciprocal relations. Following his *Doktorvater*, Karl Barth, Torrance sees God's self-revelation as a self-enclosed *novum* in which we only know God through God and as God, in our knowing of God the Father through the incarnate Son in the communion of the Spirit.[144] Or to say it another way, we only know God as we share through the Holy Spirit in the mutual knowing and loving of the Father and the Son realized in the vicarious humanity of Jesus Christ the incarnate Son of God, as noted throughout previous chapters and this one too.

It is impossible, in Torrance's mind, for us to know and to speak of the whole Trinity without an implicit awareness of the three divine persons, or to know and speak of any one of the persons without subsidiary knowledge of the whole Trinity, for God is only God as a Trinity in Unity and a Unity in Trinity.[145] This is, in fact, what Torrance contends *peri-choresis* really means: God can only be known and rightly understood in a "circle of reciprocal relations."[146]

---

[140]Ibid., pp. 170-71.
[141]Ibid., p. 171.
[142]Ibid., p. 172.
[143]Ibid.
[144]Ibid., pp. 173-74.
[145]Ibid.
[146]Ibid., p. 174.

The rationale for the holism and circularity of our knowledge of the Trinity of God is linked once again to the *homoousial* onto-relations of the trinitarian persons which the doctrine of *perichoresis* deepens and establishes ever more firmly, for the three divine persons are what and who they are, even in their distinctions, only as they so mutually indwell, interpenetrate and contain one another in such a way that each person is whole God of whole God. Thus Torrance concludes that "the Holy Trinity is revealed and is known only as an indivisible Whole, in Trinity and Unity, Unity and Trinity."[147]

Perichoresis and distinctions within the Trinity. Yet at the same time, *perichoresis* deepens and confirms the hypostatic distinctions of the three divine persons within the indivisible triune whole. *Perichoresis* does so by showing that the reciprocal interrelations between the Father, the Son and the Holy Spirit are what they are in virtue of the individual incommunicable properties of the persons, in the same way that the distinctions between the trinitarian persons are rooted in the distinctive onto-relations between the divine persons in communion.[148]

Of course, *perichoresis* stresses the equality of the trinitarian persons, as is also evident, Torrance notes, in the variation of order in which the New Testament mentions the persons and in the fact that the New Testament refers to each of the persons as Lord and therefore true God and whole God.[149] Torrance sees the doctrine of *perichoresis* strengthening this equality by stressing the distinctive properties and interrelations, but also emphatically asserting, not only the oneness in being of the three divine persons, but "their identity in will, authority, judgement, energy, power or any other divine attribute."[150] The Father, Son and Holy Spirit share fully and equally everything except the individual characteristics that differentiate them from one another in their distinctive interrelations.

Perichoresis, with its emphasis on the mutual indwelling, coinhering, inexisting of the three divine persons, rules out any "before" or "after," any degrees of deity, any notion of causality, priority or superiority in deity between the trinitarian persons, which we find in the Cappadocians brothers, Basil and Gregory. Torrance argues that Basil and Gregory viewed the relations between the divine persons as a kind of causal chain in which the

---

[147]Ibid.
[148]Ibid., p. 175.
[149]Ibid.
[150]Ibid.

person of the Father causes, personalizes, even deifies the Son and the Spirit.[151] Torrance contends that *perichoresis* keeps the doctrine of the Trinity on the Athanasian basis of the *homoousion*, which affirms the oneness of being and undivided wholeness in which each divine person is whole God of whole God, yet in such a way that the real hypostatic distinctions between the three fully coequal persons are fully affirmed within the "perichoretic togetherness and in-each-otherness" of the Father, the Son and the Holy Spirit.[152]

This distinction between the trinitarian persons in their *perichoretic* togetherness allows Torrance to reconceive the divine *monarchia* of the Father and the procession of the Spirit in a way that cuts behind the impasse between the Eastern church and the Western church, as we saw in chapter six.[153] It is no coincidence that the doctrine of *perichoresis* played a significant role in the "Agreed Statement on the Holy Trinity" reached between Orthodox and Reformed churches in 1991.[154]

Perichoretic coactivity of the Trinity. One of Torrance's repeated concerns is the danger that using technical terms such as *homoousion, hypostasis* and *perichoresis* easily leads us into merely thinking *concepts* and conceptual relations rather than the *realities* to which concepts refer, and then into thinking in static modes of thought.[155] Theological terms by their very semantic character can develop an independent character and force in our thinking over the very realities they intend.[156] Especially in theology, Torrance thinks that our concepts are only used rightly "when we do not think the concepts themselves, thereby identifying them with the truth," but rather think through the concepts about the realities or truths that the concepts are designed to disclose.[157]

This is particularly true as we move from the evangelical and doxolog-

---

[151]Ibid., pp. 176, 179. Torrance has an extremely helpful discussion of the way in which the doctrine of *perichoresis* resolves many of the problems in the relations between the divine persons in the Cappadocian theology of Basil and Gregory (see pp. 176-80).

[152]Ibid., pp. 179-80.

[153]See chapter six, pp. 233-41.

[154]See chapter one, p. 47.

[155]Torrance, *Christian Doctrine*, p. 194.

[156]By "semantic," Torrance means that theological terms have a referential function. They are not identical with the referent to which they refer. Torrance also argues that there is no logical bridge between concepts and the realities they intend. We will examine Torrance's understanding of language in the next chapter dealing with theological method.

[157]Ibid.

ical level through the evangelical Trinity to the divine persons and relations of the theological Trinity where we use highly refined theological
concepts and relations in order to express what we discern of the trinitarian mystery of God revealed through Jesus Christ in the communion of the
Holy Spirit. While we utilize *perichoresis* to aid our reflection on what God
has revealed to us in God's self-communication in the evangelical Trinity,
which we cannot but interconnect through the *homoousion* with the ontological Trinity, in Torrance's perspective we must repeatedly remind ourselves of the danger of allowing our thinking and our concepts to take on
an independent life of their own apart from the divine realities they intend. We do this so as to keep our concepts (as well as our minds, our
hearts and our lives) open to the living God who has loved us to the uttermost, who has condescended to redeem us in Jesus Christ and who in the
Spirit unites us to Christ so that we may share in the *perichoretic* love and
life of the triune God.

Therefore, when we utilize the concept of *perichoresis* in the appropriate
manner, Torrance argues, we are referring to "real objective onto-relations
in the eternal movement of Love in the Communion of the Holy Trinity as
they have been disclosed to us in the incarnate economy of God's revealing and saving acts in Jesus Christ and the Holy Spirit."[158]

Earlier in this chapter we saw how Torrance understands the being (*ousia*) of God in light of the linking of the "I am" of God in the Old Testament
and the "I am" statements of Jesus, especially in John's gospel. When this
is combined with the *homoousion*—the oneness in being and act between
the incarnate Son of God and the Father, a oneness in being and act that
includes the Holy Spirit—it leads, Torrance believes, to a concrete, dynamic and intensely personal understanding of the *ousia* of God.[159]

In light of this theological development, Torrance conceives of God's
triune being in terms of God's being-in-act and God's act-in-being, reminiscent of Karl Barth's doctrine of God that Torrance heard in lecture form
during his study with Barth in Basel in 1937. Here Torrance finds Athanasius' concept of *enousios energia* (activity inherent in God's being) in relation to the *homoousion* to be especially fruitful, for it implies mutual
indwelling, coinhering and inexisting of the trinitarian persons not simply
in their *being*, but also in *all of their activity*.[160]

---

[158]Ibid.
[159]Ibid.

Torrance finds the biblical root of this *coactivity* of the three divine persons in their *perichoretic* reciprocal indwelling and mutual coinhering, especially in John's gospel with all that it has to say about the intense and profound interrelations between the incarnate Son and the Father, but also with the Holy Spirit who is "another Advocate" for the disciples.[161] In the biblical witness, Torrance finds a "coordination and unity of Being *(ousia)* and Activity *(energia)* in the Holy Trinity, *from* the Father, *through* the Son and *in* the Holy Spirit, although the distinctive mode of operation by each of the three divine Persons is maintained."[162]

The concept of *perichoresis* fruitfully deepens and reinforces this unity of being and coactivity of the divine persons, Torrance argues, because it helps us to see not simply "a one-way set of relations" but a "dynamic three-way reciprocity."[163] Thus the Triunity of the Father, the Son and the Holy Spirit, Torrance contends, is not simply a mutual indwelling and coinhering of the three persons, but also the mutual interrelation and interpenetration of the distinctive activities of the three persons.[164] In the same way that we conceive of the distinctive incommunicable characteristics of the trinitarian persons as uniting them in communion and contributing to their inseparable inner life together without in any way detracting from their distinctive properties, so also we conceive of the distinctive activities of the three divine persons as uniting them in a dynamic oneness of activity with one another without in any way detracting from the differences in their coactivity.

---

[160]Ibid.

[161]See, for example, John 5, 14 and 17, and Jesus' statements that he is in the Father and the Father is in him. But what Torrance finds of particular importance in this context is the interconnection of the activity or works of the Father and the Son, as in John 5:19 where Jesus says that "whatever the Father does the Son does likewise" and in John 14:10 where Jesus states that "it is the Father who dwells in me who does his works." This text is especially significant for Torrance on the subject of the coactivity of the Trinity because the immediate subsequent context is Jesus' promise to send the Spirit to the disciples. Jesus himself will come to disciples through the Spirit, and on that day the disciples will know the indwelling between Jesus and the Father, and between the disciples and Jesus himself (see Jn 14:15-21).

What Torrance finds in the biblical witness and its development in the Nicene theologians is a threefold coactivity of God manifested in the evangelical Trinity and disclosed to us in the saving activity of God in the whole life and ministry of Jesus Christ and actualized among us in the Holy Spirit, who comes to us on the ground of what Christ has accomplished for us (see Torrance, *Christian Doctrine*, pp. 195-96).

[162]Ibid., p. 196.

[163]Ibid., p. 197.

[164]Ibid.

In other words, as Torrance states it, "Perichoretic relations characterize both the hypostatic subsistencies and the hypostatic activities of the three divine Persons, so that they are not only Triune in Being but are Triune in Activity."[165] In all their coactivity in creation and redemption, the Father, Son and Holy Spirit act completely together in such a way that their distinctive activities and incommunicable properties as three divine persons are not only maintained, but actually contribute to their inseparable communion in being and activity.[166] This is what Torrance calls "the perichoretic coactivity of the Holy Trinity."[167]

Torrance notes that it is not possible for us to delineate sharply between the distinctive activities of the trinitarian persons, for the coactivity of the persons perichoretically contain and interpenetrate one another and even pass over into each other, while of course maintaining the distinctive character of their respective activities.[168] Only in light of the incarnate reality of God's saving self-revelation to us, Torrance argues, can we think and say anything about this, for we must say that it was the Word or Son of God who became incarnate, suffered, died and rose again from the dead, and *not* the Spirit or the Father, even though, as we noted earlier in this chapter and previous ones as well, the Father and the Spirit are integrally and intimately present and active in accordance with the distinctive properties of their persons and coactivity from Jesus' birth, throughout his life and death, to his resurrection, ascension and high-priestly ministry.[169] Only in the activity of the evangelical Trinity are we able to discern something of the activity of the ontological Trinity, for the economic pattern of coactivity of the divine persons is inseparable from, and a reflection of, the coactivity of the Father, the Son and the Holy Spirit in the Godhead.[170]

A final point of significance before we bring this chapter to a close has to do with the so-called "law of appropriations" utilized in Latin theology to overcome the unbalanced approach to the doctrine of the Trinity (Tor-

---

[165]Ibid.
[166]Ibid., p. 198.
[167]Ibid.
[168]Ibid.
[169]Ibid. There, behind the veil, Christ's ascended, incarnate reality and the coactivity of the divine persons persist as the first-fruits of all that the triune God, Trinity in Unity and Unity in Trinity, has accomplished for our salvation and that of the entire universe. Torrance argues that the Father and the Spirit will participate in the consummation of all things in Christ at the final resurrection in a pattern of perichoretic coactivity.
[170]Ibid.

rance maintains) which begins with the one divine essence of God as a whole and only afterwards deals with the three persons.[171] The principle of appropriations allows certain attributes and activities of the whole Trinity to be "appropriated" or assigned to one of the three persons as a way to disclose the distinctive character of that particular divine person.[172]

In light of the perichoretic coactivity of the Trinity in which the three divine persons and their distinctive activities completely interpenetrate one another, Torrance argues that this "law of appropriations" falls "completely away as an idea that is both otiose and damaging."[173] The Triunity of God so profoundly articulated in this concept of perichoretic coactivity tells us that all of God's activities are acts of God who is a Trinity in Unity and Unity in Trinity in which each person, who is whole God from whole God, acts in a way appropriate to that person's distinctive nature and activity, yet always in union and communion in being and activity with the other divine persons in every activity of the one God. Here the difficulties that the "appropriations" were designed to resolve never arise in the first place within the kind of homoousial interconnections between the trinitarian persons in the evangelical Trinity and ontological Trinity, which cannot be separated in Torrance's theology.

*   *   *

There is One eternal Godhead in Trinity, and this is one Glory of the Holy Trinity. . . . If theological truth is now perfect in Trinity, then this is the true and only divine worship, and this is its beauty and truth, it must always have been so.

As it always was, so it is even now; and as it is now, so it always was and is the Trinity, and in him Father, Son and Holy Spirit. (Athanasius)[174]

---

[171]Ibid., p. 200.
[172]Ibid.
[173]Ibid.
[174]See Torrance, *Trinitarian Perspectives*, pp. 117, 137.

9

THE INTEGRATION OF
FORM IN THEOLOGY

*Theology is the unique science devoted to knowledge of God,
differing from other sciences by the uniqueness of its object which can be apprehended
only on its own terms and from within the actual situation
it has created in our existence in making itself known.*
T. F. TORRANCE

1. The Fundamental Axiom of Torrance's Theology

The fundamental axiom that runs through all of Thomas F. Torrance's many publications on theological method is that the nature of the object or subject-matter in question defines the methods employed in investigating it, the mode of rationality used in conceptualizing what is discovered, and the form of verification consonant with it.[1] Torrance describes his theology "as a dogmatic, or positive and independent, science operating on its own ground and in accordance with the inner law of its own being, developing distinctive modes of inquiry and its essential forms of thought under the determination of its given subject-matter."[2]

The fact that method must be apposite to the nature of the reality under investigation means that method can be distinguished, but never separated, from content. This is the reason for Torrance's rigorous attention to *scientific* methodology *and* theological content throughout his career. This is also why questions of content and method are interrelated throughout the previous chapters of this book, even though the primary focus has been on

---

[1]Thomas F. Torrance, *Theological Science* (Oxford: Oxford University Press, 1969), p. xii.
[2]Ibid., p. 281.

content. Ontology and epistemology ought to unfold together.[3]

Thus we cannot lay down the conditions on which valid knowledge is possible in detachment from the actual knowing relation intrinsic to the reality or subject-matter, for to do so is to risk allowing habits of mind acquired within some other frame of reference or field of inquiry to adversely influence the apprehension and expression of the reality in question.[4] This accounts for the critical element in Torrance's epistemology.

This is really another way of stating (1) Torrance's concern to investigate realities in their interrelations and intrinsic structures (form in being) and (2) his affirmation of the *potential* or *possible* (not *inherent* or *automatic*) correlation or isomorphism between the human mind/thought and reality (integration of form in knowing), as we saw at the beginning of chapter two. Throughout our theological investigation Torrance contends that we need to "operate with an *open* epistemology in which we allow the way of our knowing to be clarified and modified *pari passu* [at equal rate] with advance in deeper and fuller knowledge of the object."[5]

Torrance is well aware of the problems posed for a critical realist epistemology by the way in which Hume and then Kant among others demonstrated that the act of knowing conditions our knowledge of the real. Yet Torrance also maintains that it is possible, though far from inevitable, to devise and refine methods and cognitive structures that serve the disclosure of realities in their interconnections and remain open to revision in light of them.[6]

Reality is, in some sense, capable of rational apprehension and semantic designation. This is an assumption that Torrance believes is continually operative in ordinary experience and in every scientific field of inquiry,[7]

---

[3]For a fuller discussion of Torrance's understanding of the integration of form in relation to the nature of doctrine, see Elmer M. Colyer, *The Nature of Doctrine in T. F. Torrance's Theology* (Eugene, Ore.: Wipf & Stock, 2001).

[4]Ibid. Thus critical questions about the possibility of knowledge cannot be raised *in abstracto*, but only *in concreto*, not *a priori* but only *a posteriori* (see, p. 1).

[5]Ibid., p. 10.

[6]Ibid., p. xii.

[7]See ibid., pp. 3, 10, 286. See Thomas F. Torrance, *Reality and Scientific Theology* (Edinburgh: Scottish Academic Press, 1985), pp. 46-54, and Thomas F. Torrance, "Theological Realism," in *The Philosophical Frontiers of Christian Theology*, ed. B. Hebblethwaite and S. Sutherland (Cambridge: Cambridge University Press, 1982), pp. 169-96.

Torrance accepts the fact at the center of historical consciousness, as expressed by James Brown, that "we are inevitably and inseparably inside the knowledge relation, from the start to the end, and so cannot step outside of ourselves to an indifferent standpoint from

despite the serious issues raised by modernity's turn to the subjective pole of the knowing relation, and the postmodern rejection of foundationalist epistemologies that attempt to render the conditions for knowledge entirely explicit. In fact, for Torrance scientific knowledge—natural and theological—is "a rigorous and disciplined extension" of ordinary ways of knowing.[8]

In light of these convictions, it should be clear that Torrance is a realist, but only in a qualified sense.[9] If realism suggests a *necessary* correspondence between reality and thought, as in a static analogy of being, then Torrance is not a realist.[10] However, in another sense he is a realist, for he maintains, as Hardy points out, that there can be "an *actual* correspondence between reality and thought or language *if* the thinker is conformed to the mode of rationality afforded by reality."[11] When this happens, there is genuine knowing and a transparence between reality and thought or language.[12]

Torrance maintains that it is the struggle to overcome our "artificiality" (that is, the mind's propensity to impose preconceived forms on the real), to develop appropriate methods and apposite modes of speech, that leads

---

which to view and adjust the relations of thought and being" (James Brown, *Subject and Object in Modern Theology* [New York: Macmillan, 1955], p. 170). Also see Torrance, *Theological Science*, p. 1. Yet Torrance is equally convinced that this does not necessarily lead to the kind of skepticism and nihilism we hear in the voices of people like Frank Kermode, who thinks, "World and book are hopelessly plural, endlessly disappointing. . . . Our sole hope and pleasure is in the perception of a momentary radiance, before the door of disappointment is finally shut on us." This quotation is cited by Ronald Thiemann in his chapter in Garret Green, ed., *Scriptural Authority and Narrative Interpretation* (Philadelphia: Fortress Press, 1987), p. 21.

[8]Thomas F. Torrance, *God and Rationality* (New York: Oxford University Press, 1971), pp. 9-10, 91. Also see Thomas F. Torrance, *The Ground and Grammar of Theology* (Charlottesville: University of Virginia Press, 1980), p. 8.

[9]Thomas F. Torrance, *Space, Time and Resurrection* (Grand Rapids, Mich.: Eerdmans, 1976), p. 6. Also see Thomas F. Torrance, *Divine and Contingent Order* (New York: Oxford University Press, 1981). Hardy indicates the need for caution when using the term "realist" to describe Torrance's epistemology. See Daniel Hardy, "Thomas F. Torrance," *The Modern Theologians: An Introduction to Christian Theology in the Twentieth Century* ed. David Ford (Oxford: Basil Blackwell, 1989), 1:77.

One puzzling aspect of Alister McGrath's outstanding book *Thomas F. Torrance: An Intellectual Biography* (Edinburgh: T & T Clark, 1999), is that it contains no analysis of Torrance's place within the Scottish realist tradition, even though Torrance seems to see himself as standing within it (see Torrance, *Divine and Contingent*, p. x).

[10]Hardy, "Thomas F. Torrance," p. 77.

[11]Ibid.

[12]Ibid.

to "the proper adaptation of the human subject to the object of his knowledge, whether it be God or the world of nature or man."[13] The age-old issue at stake here is the relationship between the discovery of form or
intelligibility and the creation of it in human rational activity in philosophy, science and theology.

In order to grasp Torrance's reformulation regarding how form ought
to be integrated (how concepts are derived or how appropriate categories
are generated) it is helpful to understand his analysis of the shift in the integration of form from Newton through Hume and Kant to Einstein and
Polanyi, for Torrance argues that the legacy of modern philosophy, science
and theology is the struggle of the human subject for fidelity, "for the appropriate adaptation of the human subject to the object of knowledge."
Somehow the more the modern human subject "comes to know, the more
masterful he tries to be and the more he imposes himself upon reality, the
more he gets in the way of his own progress."[14] In delineating Torrance's
critical realist epistemology (how we integrate form in human knowing)
by locating it in relation to a narrative on modern epistemology, I am *not*
implying that Torrance developed his perspective from within his analysis
of modern epistemology. I simply find this to be a helpful way to explain
Torrance's position.[15]

2. The Integration of Form from Descartes Through Kant
According to Torrance, René Descartes (1596-1650) and Isaac Newton
(1642-1727), in different but complementary ways, both operated with an
epistemological dualism between subject and object on the one hand, and
a cosmological dualism between God and the world on the other.[16] The

---

[13] Torrance, *Theological Science*, p. xiii.
[14] Ibid.
[15] Torrance maintains that he developed his theological position in terms of content and epistemology in dialogue with the Greek fathers (and Karl Barth) before he deliberately set out
to define his epistemological position by taking issue with modern critical philosophy and
the history of modern epistemology which he analyzes in various places in his later publications. See Thomas F. Torrance, *Divine Meaning: Studies in Patristic Hermeneutics* (Edinburgh: T & T Clark, 1995), p. 3. Much work needs to be done here regarding the sources of
Torrance's basic epistemology and methodological assumptions, especially in relation to
Scottish realism, Clerk Maxwell, Thomas Reid and the theologians H. R. Mackintosh and
Karl Barth.
[16] See chapter two, pp. 57-60, for Torrance's understanding of dualism. Also see Thomas F.
Torrance, *Transformation and Convergence in the Frame of Knowledge: Explorations in the Inter-
relations of Scientific and Theological Enterprise* (Grand Rapids, Mich.: Eerdmans, 1984), p. 6.

hiatus between subject and object tended to reduce the human subject to "inner states of consciousness over against a determinate nature as object."[17] This led to a notion of "representative perception" in which subjective representations (sense data *between* the independent immaterial human mind and the material reality or matter of nature) control the relation between the human subject and the object of knowledge.

This kind of representative perception generated the modern turn *to* the human subject's inner consciousness and mental processes, and *away from* the intrinsic and constitutive interrelations in objective reality (nature).[18] The goal of the modern analysis of the mental processes and the consciousness of the human subject was to provide an adequate account (a foundation) of how the immaterial human mind is able to achieve or generate knowledge of the material world through the sense data that mediate between the subject and object or between mind and matter. This led to the prodigious modern quest for (and eventually critique of) an epistemology in which the conditions for indubitable knowledge are rendered entirely explicit.

Isaac Newton. Torrance argues that Newton accepted Cartesian dualism with its doctrine of "subjective representations" between the mind of the observer and the objective structure of nature, including the sharp distinction between the realms of mind and of matter. Newton thought that these representations were somehow related to the immaterial mind through a particular part of the brain called the "sensorium." But Newton had a much stronger belief than Descartes that these notorious "secondary qualities" that "arise in the sensorium are in some sense properties of nature, for they are sensations of motions or dispositions in the external world."[19]

While the emphasis in Newton is still on the *discovery* of form and a close relation between scientific concepts and sense experience, Torrance maintains that Newton unfortunately built Descartes' fundamental dualisms (epistemological and cosmological) into the structure of Western science.[20] Torrance argues that Newton's conception of the *manner* in which form is integrated (how concepts are derived) also created epistemological problems for modern natural science and philosophy.

---

[17]Ibid.
[18]Ibid.
[19]Ibid., pp. 13-14.
[20]Ibid., p. 14.

Newton conceived of natural science as an inquiry into the causal inter-relations between material realities in terms of "manifest principles" and their expression in scientific concepts that are *deduced* from phenomena or *derived by way of abstraction* from observation.[21] Thus, Newton made his fa-mous statement, "I frame no hypotheses," for "whatever is not deduced from phenomena, is to be called an hypothesis; and hypotheses, whether metaphysical or physical, whether occult qualities or mechanical, have no place in experimental philosophy. In this philosophy particular proposi-tions are inferred from the phenomena, and afterward rendered general by induction."[22]

Science, therefore, becomes a discipline that yields *indubitable truth* about the interaction of the natural world expressed in terms of natural laws (deduced from phenomena) that state the mathematical characteris-tics of nature (motion and gravity, for example). Everything else is *unsci-entific*.[23]

This, of course, means that the human subject plays a minimal role in the integration of form (generation of concepts) which is conceived prima-rily in terms of discovery, rather than imaginative creation. In this regard, Einstein noted that the material world was like an "open book" to Newton, for the concepts "he used to reduce the material of experience to order seemed to flow spontaneously from experience itself, from the beautiful experiments which he ranged in order like playthings and describes with affectionate wealth of detail."[24]

The problem, however, which Hume soon uncovered, is that this was not, in fact, how Newton carried out his scientific endeavor. Newton was aware of the problem, for he did not—and could not—derive the theoret-ical components of absolute space and time so important for his under-standing of laws of motion from observation or experience. Newton admitted, "It is a matter of great difficulty to discover and effectually to distinguish the true motions of particular bodies from the apparent, be-cause the parts of that immovable space in which those motions are per-

---

[21]Ibid.

[22]Isaac Newton, *Philosophiae Naturalis Principia Mathematica*, rev. and ed. Florian Cajori, trans. Andrew Motte (1729) (Chicago: Encyclopedia Britannica, 1955), p. 547. See Torrance, *Transformation*, p. 17. However, it is true that Newton did in fact advance speculative hypotheses, as Torrance points out.

[23]See Torrance, *Transformation*, p. 18.

[24]See Albert Einstein's foreword to Isaac Newton, *Opticks*, 4th ed. (New York: Dover, 1952), p. vii. Also see Torrance, *Transformation*, p. 16.

formed do by no means come under the observation of our senses."[25]

Torrance argues that at this important juncture, Newton was forced to bring in theoretical components that he was unable to derive by abstraction from observation in order to do justice to the empirical world. In the end, Newton really proceeded on the basis of his implicit and profound belief in the uniformity and simplicity of order in the natural universe. In light of this ultimate belief, Newton developed and deployed the concepts of absolute time and space (which are independent of the natural relations and events that unfold within them) as the most efficacious way of articulating the intricate facets of nature in a logically coherent and comprehensive explanation of the natural world.[26]

Furthermore, it was Newton's astonishing success in providing a uniform and exact explanation of motion that seemed to justify the theoretical basis that he had developed. This is an extremely important point, Torrance contends, because it misled Newton's successors into thinking that all scientific concepts can and must be *deduced* from phenomena or *abstracted* from sense experience.[27]

The issue at stake here is *how* these concepts are generated and integrated with the empirical world of sense experience. On this point Newton's actual practice did not conform to his stated methodology.

David Hume. David Hume (1711-1776), who had accepted the account of passive perception and active reason which he received from empiricists like Locke, astutely exposed this problem in Newton's notion of the integration of form by showing that important theoretical elements like time, space and causality are not "given" in sense experience. Hume's critique revealed, Torrance notes, that there is no real relation between one immediately observed fact and another in an account grounded *solely* in sense perception.[28] In Hume's words: "Objects have no discoverable con-

---

[25]Newton, *Principia Mathematica*, p. 12. See Torrance, *Transformation*, p. 22. Thus Einstein points out that "we can see indeed from Newton's formulation of it that the concept of absolute space, which comprised that of absolute rest, made him feel uncomfortable; he realized that there seemed to be nothing in experience corresponding to this last concept" (Albert Einstein, *The World as I See It*, trans. Alan Harris [London: John Lane, 1935], p. 135). Also see Torrance, *Transformation*, p. 52.

[26]Torrance, *Transformation*, pp. 22-23.

[27]Ibid., p. 23. This does not mean that scientific concepts derived in ways other than abstraction and deduction are necessarily false, though absolute time and space have proved problematic for science and theology, and have been displaced by Einstein's work on relativity (see pp. 24-31).

[28]Ibid., p. 35.

nexion together; nor is it from any other principle but custom operating upon imagination, that we can draw inference from the appearance of one to the existence of another."[29]

When we see a stone shatter a window what we really perceive is a series of sensory impressions. We say that the stone is the "cause" of the window's breaking. But what the senses provide is only a sequence of impressions of the stone and the window; no cause is observed in strict analysis of sense perception.[30] Thus Hume defines cause as "an object followed by another, and whose appearance always conveys the thought to that other."[31]

Despite the fact that it seemed to contradict so much of everyday human experience, Hume's analysis created a serious impasse for the empirical approach to knowledge, for as Torrance points out, "If no intrinsic or necessary connection is perceivable between one observed factor and another, then some of the most important components of scientific knowledge, e.g. in Newton's system of the world, such as substance, relation, causality, are not reached through sense experience, and cannot be employed in inductive operations from phenomena."[32] This was the shock that awakened the great Enlightenment philosopher Immanuel Kant from his "dogmatic slumber," revealing the inadequacy of a purely empirical approach to knowledge.

Immanuel Kant. At this point, Torrance argues, Kant (1724-1804), who was a mathematician and astronomer himself, realized that a new and more adequate account had to be given concerning the way in which form is integrated so that theoretical or conceptual factors, not observationally derived, could again play a role along with empirical elements in ordinary experience and in scientific inquiry. Kant's ingenious contribution to the development of Western thought lies in his construction of an epistemology that combines the empirical approach of Newton, Locke and Hume with the rationalist orientation of Descartes and Leibniz—an epistemology that synthesizes an *a posteriori* (derived from experience) empirical ingredient with the *a priori* (independent of experience) categorical structures of the mind. The empirical and categorical ingredients function inseparably

---

[29]David Hume, *A Treatise of Human Nature* (London: Longmans, Green, 1909), I.iii.8, pp. 403-4. Also see Torrance, *Transformation*, p. 35. Torrance also points out that Hume's position was not as skeptical as it appears.

[30]This illustration is found in Colin Gunton, *Enlightenment and Alienation: An Essay Towards a Trinitarian Theology* (Grand Rapids, Mich.: Eerdmans, 1985), p. 22.

[31]David Hume, *An Enquiry Concerning Human Understanding*, ed. L. A. Selby-Biggs (Oxford: Clarendon, 1962), 7.2, p. 77. Also see Gunton, *Enlightenment*, p. 22.

[32]Torrance, *Transformation*, p. 36.

in all human knowing from everyday experience to the formulation of scientific concepts.[33]

Since these *a priori* categories and structures of the mind are the necessary condition for the possibility of intelligible experience, we cannot know the thing-in-itself (*Ding-an-sich*), but only how it appears to us through our cognitive grid, the categories and structures of the mind. Since these categories are unchanging, they are beyond the possibility of criticism or modification by the empirical component.[34]

Here, Torrance argues, the emphasis is no longer on the *discovery* of form, as it had been in the case of Newton. Rather, intelligibility and the theoretical element of knowledge are transferred to the human pole of the knowing relation where the human mind organizes the raw data or empirical ingredient provided by the senses, rendering it intelligible. This, in turn, leads to the idea that humanity can only understand that which it creates.[35] This represents an "inversion of the knowing relation" away from the intrinsic intelligibility of nature or reality to the mental processes and categories of the human mind. It leads to "a constructivist mentality" in which the mind can only *impose* form on experience and everything it attempts to know, an orientation characteristic of what Torrance calls "the modern mind."[36]

Thus in his *Critique of Pure Reason*, Kant makes a famous assertion: "Hitherto it has been assumed that all our knowledge must conform to objects. . . . We must . . . make trial whether we may not have more success in the tasks of metaphysics, if we suppose that objects must conform to our knowledge."[37] Torrance notes that the idea of the inherent intelligibility of the universe inevitably began to fade as well, for Kant was forced to admit

---

[33]Ibid., p. 36.

[34]See ibid., pp. 38-40.

[35]In hermeneutics, this mentality has worked itself out in the idea that the Bible does not portray a "followable world" or in the direction of a "reader-response" hermeneutic where readers *make* sense out of the text. This can take a decidedly "individualistic" turn, as in the case of Edgar McKnight and his *The Post-Modern Use of the Bible: The Emergence of a Reader-Oriented Criticism* (Nashville: Abingdon, 1988), p. 159. However, thus far this trend seems more often to lead to a "community of hermeneutical privilege" that can properly construe the meaning of the biblical text. But with both there is a diminution of the intrinsic intelligibility (perspicuity) of the biblical text that parallels the loss of the intrinsic intelligibility of nature latent in Kant's synthetic *a priori*.

[36]See Torrance, *Transformation*, p. 37.

[37]Immanuel Kant, *Critique of Pure Reason*, trans. by N. Kemp Smith (London: Macmillan, 1933), p. 22.

that the *human mind is the origin* of the laws and uniformity of nature.[38]

This signals an astonishing epistemological shift from the perspective of Newton to Kant; from the *discovery* of form to the *imposition* of form in everyday life and in formal science; and from the *intrinsic* intelligibility of the universe to the synthesizing and *constructive* power of the human mind which reads rational structure into nature. When Kant's categories of the mind are historicized, as they have been for many since the rise of historical consciousness, enlightened humanity's noetic pretensions are radically challenged, and the modern quest for an epistemological foundation yielding indubitable knowledge (by rendering the conditions for knowledge entirely explicit) becomes a highly questionable endeavor.[39]

3. The Integration of Form in Einstein and Polanyi

Torrance finds deep and unresolved difficulties in the way these important modern thinkers from Descartes through Kant construed basic epistemological issues. Or to put the issue more positively, Torrance sees Newton, with his emphasis on the discovery of form, and Kant, with his emphasis on the imposition of form or the constant coordination of theoretical and empirical ingredients, as both partly right and partly wrong. According to Torrance, Kant made a significant contribution to our understanding of the integration of form by showing that Newton had, in fact, operated with a constant coordination of empirical and theoretical components of knowledge in which the theoretical was not directly deduced from phenomena.[40]

Where Kant went wrong was in his conception of the *manner* in which these components are combined, for he construed this relation in terms of *necessary* and legislative structures *imposed* on the world in all our experience of it.[41] Torrance grants that there is "a profound element of truth

---

[38]See Torrance, *Transformation*, p. 38.

[39]The emphasis ends up almost entirely on the cultural creation and imposition of form in human "knowing." Torrance traces the deep problems this "modern mind" created for Protestant theology and for natural science in the nineteenth and early twentieth centuries in natural science. See ibid., pp. 61-71; Torrance, *Ground and Grammar*, pp. 15-43; and Thomas F. Torrance, *Reality and Scientific Theology* (Edinburgh: Scottish Academic Press, 1985), pp. 15-28.

[40]See Torrance, *Transformation*, p. 41.

[41]Thus Kant could say of the geometer, "The true method was not to inspect what he discerned in the figure, or in the bare concept of it, and from this, as it were, to read off its properties; but to bring out what was necessarily implied in the construction by which he

here," in that "in all our knowing there is a real interplay between what we know and our knowing of it," and in that "we do not apprehend things apart from a theoretic structure."[42] However, Torrance notes that if the mind's categorical structures determine our apprehension of reality, then objective reality and its intrinsic relations play no formative role in human knowledge which, in turn, must be construed as primarily *constructive* or *subjective.*[43]

On this point Torrance maintains that Newton was correct that form must be grounded in the intelligibility of that which we seek to know.[44] But Newton failed to fully appreciate the fact that theoretical elements play a fundamental role in our apprehension of things and that these elements are not directly deduced from phenomena.[45]

Torrance argues, "The one way out of that impasse requires a theoretic structure which, while affecting our knowledge, is derived from the intrinsic intelligibility of what we seek to know, and is open to constant revision through reference to the inner determinations of things as they come to view in the process of inquiry."[46] In order to grasp Torrance's formulation of how form is integrated (his epistemology) it is helpful to view it in relation to Albert Einstein and Michael Polanyi, though this does not mean that Torrance developed in theological epistemic convictions in dialogue with them or that Torrance builds his theology on an Einsteinian or Polanyian epistemology.[47]

Albert Einstein. According to Torrance, it was Einstein (1879-1955) who

---

[41]presented it to himself. If he is to know anything with a priori certainty he must not ascribe to the figure anything save what follows from what he himself set into it in accordance with his concept" (quoted by Torrance in ibid., p. 41).

[42]Ibid., p. 42.

[43]Ibid.

[44]See ibid., pp. 22-28.

[45]Ibid.

[46]Ibid., p. 42.

[47]A careful reading of Torrance's work on the integration of the positive content and method in his theology reveals that it is just plain foolish to say that Torrance builds his theology on an epistemology borrowed from Einstein or Polanyi, from natural science or empirical philosophy. See Thomas F. Torrance, *The Mediation of Christ,* 2nd ed. (Colorado Springs: Helmers & Howard, 1992), chaps. 1, 2; *The Trinitarian Faith: The Evangelical Theology of the Ancient Catholic Church* (Edinburgh: T & T Clark), chaps. 1, 2, 4, 6; and especially *The Christian Doctrine of God: One Being Three Persons* (Edinburgh: T & T Clark, 1996), chaps. 2-4.

Alister McGrath has Torrance right on this point. See McGrath's astute analysis of Torrance's relation to Polanyi and McGrath's effective criticism of Colin Weightman's caricature of Torrance as heavily dependent upon Polanyi. See Colin Weightman, *Theology in a Polanyian Universe: The Theology of Thomas F. Torrance* (New York: Peter Lang, 1994);

perceived the essential problem regarding the real epistemic character of scientific activity, the notion discussed above in relation to Newton that concepts and theories in natural science are *deduced or derived from sense experience by logical inference or abstraction.*[48] Yet for Einstein, scientific concepts are also not *a priori* categories imposed on data in scientific inquiry as with Kant. Einstein's work has put an end to both of these notions of the integration of form, Torrance argues, not just by his criticism of them, but by Einstein's actual achievements in developing scientific knowledge of the universe in an astonishing manner.[49]

However, Torrance points out that Einstein indicated that "nothing can be said concerning the manner in which concepts are to be made and connected, and how we are to coordinate them with experience."[50] Thus, while actively engaged in the process of inquiry, the knower in another sense is, in Einstein's own words, "helpless . . . until principles he can make the basis of deductive reasoning have revealed themselves to him."[51] Nevertheless, Torrance suggests that Einstein provided some indication of how he proceeded.

McGrath, *Thomas F. Torrance*, pp. 228-32. A careful reading of Torrance's early writings reveals that his basic realist theological commitments were in place long before his encounter with Polanyi.

In examining modern science and philosophy of science, what Torrance actually discovered is that Christian theology (as renewed through the work of Karl Barth) and natural science (as in Faraday, Maxwell, Einstein and Polanyi) were both struggling with similar sets of epistemological problems embedded in the received dualist framework of thought (see Torrance, *Transformation*, p. xii).

[48]Torrance, *Scientific Theology*, p. 73.

[49]Ibid., p. 77. Of course, Torrance has in mind Einstein's theories of relativity. Torrance argues that quantum theory and relativity theory not only dramatically modified Newton's laws of motion, but demonstrated that theories and concepts are not deduced from experience or abstracted from sense data by any logical means. What Einstein's work disclosed is that the relation between experience or the empirical component and the theoretical ingredient (concepts or theories) in human knowing is far more complex than this. Yet there is real congruence between the theoretical and the empirical, as in Einstein's theories of relativity, for example (see p. 66).

Einstein said with reference to the idea that scientific theories are directly derived from experience that "a clear recognition of the erroneousness of this notion really only came with the general theory of relativity, which showed that one could take account of a wider range of empirical facts, and that too in a more satisfactory and complete manner, on a foundation quite different from the Newtonian than was possible with it" (Einstein, *World*, p. 135). Also see Torrance, *Transformation*, p. 76.

[50]See Albert Einstein, *Out of My Later Years* (New York: Philosophical Library, 1950), p. 61. Also see Torrance in *Transformation*, p. 77.

[51]Einstein, *World*, p. 138. See Torrance, *Transformation*, p. 115.

While Einstein could also describe the ideas he developed as "free creations" and "freely chosen conventions," Torrance argues that Einstein did not mean that his theories of relativity, for example, were simply fictions or subjective fantasies, for they arose out of years of detailed and intimate scientific inquiry within an ultimate belief that the universe is intelligible and can be comprehended at least to a degree by scientific inquiry.[52]

Thus, the theories that Einstein developed were in one sense freely chosen (integration of form in knowing). Yet nevertheless, in another sense, they arise out of, are controlled by, experiential and experimental contact with reality in its intrinsic structures and relations (form in being), and are tested and confirmed by applicability to that reality.[53] This means that Einstein sees a significant harmony between scientific concepts and reality. Yet Torrance states that "it is easier to speak of this harmony negatively . . . since we are not concerned with a logical but a trans-logical or an extra-logical relation between concepts and experience."[54] This last point is extremely important, for it underscores one of Torrance's most significant epistemological convictions: there is no logical bridge between the human mind, including language, and reality and experience of it.

Despite the fact that he agrees with Einstein's refutation of earlier notions of how form is integrated, Torrance maintains that we have to go beyond Einstein at this point.[55] Here Torrance finds Michael Polanyi's work in science to be helpful.[56]

Michael Polanyi. More than any other philosopher of science, it has been Michael Polanyi (1891-1976), Torrance believes, who clarified the process of natural scientific inquiry and the integration of form (the formulation of concepts/theories and the coordination of ideas and experience) and "has shown us that creative scientific discovery of this kind is *unformalisable.*"[57]

---

[52]Torrance, *Scientific Theology*, pp. 77, 79.

[53]Ibid.

[54]Thomas F. Torrance, "The Integration of Form in Natural and in Theological Science," *Science, Medicine and Man* 1 (1973): 153. This essay is reprinted in Torrance, *Transformation*, pp. 61-106.

[55]Torrance, *Scientific Theology*, p. 132.

[56]See Hardy, "Thomas F. Torrance," p. 78.

[57]See Torrance, *Scientific Theology*, p. 77. Also see Thomas F. Torrance, "The Place of Michael Polanyi in the Modern Philosophy of Science," *Ethics in Science and Medicine* 7 (1980): 57-95. Torrance's article was republished in Torrance, *Transformation*, pp. 107-73.

The tacit dimension. Central to Polanyi's position (and Torrance's), is his claim that "we know more than we can tell," for in Torrance's words, "in addition to our 'focal awareness' and the explicit knowledge to which it gives rise, we always operate with a 'subsidiary awareness' and an implicit knowledge on which we rely in all our explicit operations."[58] This is what Polanyi calls the "tacit dimension" of the human mind, which enables it to discern *Gestalten* or patterns of coherence previously undetected in a given field through a heuristic leap from the parts to the whole.[59]

Torrance clarifies some of what is entailed in this tacit dimension when he notes that "much of our basic knowledge on which we rely throughout life is gained in our earliest years, as we learn to speak and adapt ourselves to the physical and social world around us."[60] We know more physics by the age of five than we will be able to understand even if we became great scientists. This implicit informal knowing plays a formative role in all explicit understanding and conceptualization. It is by relying on this tacit dimension, Torrance contends, that all scientific inquiry, natural or theological, proceeds,[61] though the tacit dimension in theology develops at the evangelical and doxological level within the church as the body of Christ, as we saw in the opening section of chapter eight on how the doctrine of the Trinity arises.

This implicit knowledge or tacit dimension, Torrance maintains, is influenced by the tradition, community, language and culture we inhabit, an influence which can further, but also inhibit, explicit understanding and scientific inquiry.[62] This calls for a critical inhabiting of tradition, community and culture.[63] We will return to the place of community and tradition in Torrance's theological method in a later section of this chapter. What is of significance here is that for Polanyi and Torrance, the tacit dimension, in general and in any field of scientific inquiry, is informal, undefined and in large measure inarticulate, yet still of critical significance in explicit thought and conceptual formulation.

If explicit concepts, theories and statements are related to reality through the tacit dimension or coefficient associated with them, Torrance

---

[58] Torrance, "Polanyi," p. 60.
[59] Torrance, *Transformation*, p. 116.
[60] See Thomas Torrance, *Christian Theology and Scientific Culture* (New York: Oxford University Press, 1980), p. 13.
[61] Ibid.
[62] Ibid.
[63] Ibid.

argues that this demands "a significant modification in what we under-stand by knowledge, for knowledge cannot then be defined merely in terms of what is explicit, and also in what we understand by reality, for correspondingly, reality cannot be defined in terms of what is only corre-lated with explicit concepts and statements."[64]

Indwelling the field of inquiry. On the basis of this "tacit knowing," form is integrated in everyday experience and in science.[65] Thus in scientific en-deavor, the kind of integration of form that Polanyi and Torrance advocate entails *indwelling* the particular field of investigation and the intrinsic in-terrelations of that field.[66] Indwelling is a holistic, significantly informal, integrative and heuristic process of investigating a field of inquiry. As this inquiry develops, our minds begin to assimilate the internal constitutive relations embodied in what we seek to know.[67]

This process of *tacit inference* leads to an anticipatory insight, an intui-tive foreknowledge, into the intelligibility of the field or the constitutive relations of the reality under investigation.[68] For Polanyi and Torrance form is properly integrated on the basis of a tacit foreknowledge, an intu-itive insight, what Torrance also calls a *prolepsis*, which "takes shape in our understanding under the imprint of the internal structure of that into which we inquire, and develops within the structural kinship that arises between our knowing and what we know as we make ourselves dwell in

---

[64]See Torrance, "Polanyi," p. 60. This point parallels Torrance's contention that in our knowledge of God through Christ and in the Spirit we know more than we can bring to explicit articulation, and that the reality of God is greater than all of our theological formu-lations.

[65]Torrance, *Transformation*, pp. 114, 122.

[66]Ibid., p. 78. Indwelling is more holistic and less formal than beginning with discrete partic-ulars and then connecting them through an inductive process. A significant part of the rea-son for this is that there are no *discrete particulars*, for particulars are what they are through their *interrelations*, as in the case of the electro-magnetic field.

[67]Ibid., p. 114.

[68]Ibid., p. 78.

[69]Torrance, "Polanyi," p. 61. Torrance also describes this process of tacit foreknowledge in this way:

Whether in natural science or theology, we find that progress in knowledge is neces-sarily circular. We develop a form of inquiry in which we allow some field of reality to disclose itself to us in the complex of its internal relations. . . . As we do that we come up with a significant clue in light of which all evidence is then re-examined and reinterpreted and found to fall into a coherent pattern or order. . . . In a scientific inquiry the fundamental insight we have discovered may have to be revised as all the pieces of evidence come together and throw light upon each other, but nevertheless it is under the direction of that insight that the discovery is made. . . . Once the insight

it and gain access to its meaning."[69]

How is it that we enter any new field of inquiry? For instance, how can we gain an integrated view of Torrance's theology from the discussions of various aspects of his position found in his diverse publications? Adopting Polanyi's and Torrance's perspective, we "indwell" the corpus of Torrance's writings until we gain an insight into the intrinsic structure, the internal relations of his theology, which we then test and refine through our continued research. This entails an irreducible element of creative imagination, but an imagination controlled from beyond by the field under investigation—Torrance's theology in his publications.

The integration of form. Contra Kant, the *prolepsis* and structural kinship that develops between our knowing and what we indwell is not an *a priori* (independent of experience) cognitive structure or *innate* conceptual counterpart to the intrinsic intelligibility of the field or reality under investigation. It is rather an anticipatory intimation of a pattern of order that arises dynamically out of heuristic indwelling and the informal tacit dimension.

Contra Newton, this intuitive insight or new conceptualization is not deduced or abstracted from sense perception or phenomena, for the heuristic process of indwelling and the element of tacit inference entail an extra-logical (*not* illogical) relation between the human mind and the intelligible relations constitutive of the reality under investigation. Within the heuristic activity of the human mind a cognitive kinship develops between human knowing and the reality known, a kinship that is neither *inherent* in the mind, nor a *necessary* inference deduced or abstracted from phenomena, but *contingent* on the all-important dynamic, integrative interaction between the knower and the known.[70]

Furthermore, as Hardy points out, for Polanyi and Torrance "this is a *personal* and *informal* integrative process . . . [which is] not limited to the initial moment of discovery, but persists in scientific work and—through its alternation with analytic and deductive procedures—produces a deepening awareness of the object."[71] This is not to depreciate the importance of analytic and deductive operations that help us test the coherence of a

---

has put us on the track of that discovery, something irreversible has taken place in our understanding: a pattern of truth has been built into our minds on which we cannot go back, and which we cannot rationally deny. (Torrance, *Mediation*, pp. 13-14)
[70]See Torrance, *Transformation*, p. 78.
[71]Hardy, "Thomas F. Torrance," p. 78

theory or develop its implications.[72] But for Polanyi and Torrance the integrative element predominates.[73] No matter how successful a theoretical construction may be at mediating insight into the inherent organization or intelligibility of any field, Torrance argues that there is still *no logical bridge* between the human mind, including the concepts and theories it develops, and the objective structures or intrinsic relations or form that is inherent in objective reality.[74]

Perceptual integration as a model. Polanyi uses the *logic of perceptual integration* as a model in order to clarify this integrative activity of the mind that cannot be reduced to inferential or analytical processes.[75] Visual perception operates with two kinds of awareness, *focal* and *subsidiary*. As Torrance notes, "They operate conjointly in such a way that we are subsidiarily aware of the marginal elements with a functional bearing on the object we know focally. This functional relation is a product of an integration carried out tacitly . . . linking the subsidiary elements to the focal centre in such a way that our apprehension of the clues is transformed into an apprehension of the objective reality to which they point."[76]

An example of focal and subsidiary awareness is the popular *Magic Eye* pictures which at first look like a jumble of tiny detailed figures. However, if one holds the picture close to one's face and then gradually moves the picture away from one's eyes without focusing on the details, suddenly an astonishing three-dimensional image comes into view. What happens is that the mind integrates the subsidiary clues to the matrix of intrinsic *interrelations* between the parts that constitute the three-dimensional whole (which the creators of the *Magic Eye* in a sense hide amidst what first appears to be a chaotic collection of tiny figures). As the mind integrates the clues, the 3-D image that creators of the *Magic Eye* build into the picture comes into view.[77]

---

[72]Torrance, *Transformation*, p. 80.

[73]It is this integrative element that Polanyi spells out, in the words of Torrance, "as far as he finds possible, without allowing it to disintegrate in, and be replaced by, an analytic and discursive movement of thought operating only with explicit, formal connections" (Torrance, "Polanyi," p. 63). Behind the explicit hypothetico-deductive processes arising out of hunches, guesses, intuitions, in the heuristic process of discovery in science is the human *mind* engaged in tacit integrative activity (as described in the previous sections on the tacit dimension and indwelling, pp. 335-37).

[74]Torrance, *Transformation*, p. 80.

[75]Ibid., pp. 117-18.

[76]Torrance, "Polanyi," p. 63.

[77]Robert K. Martin also sees the way the *Magic Eye* prints help illustrate the integrative activity of the human mind. See his excellent book *The Incarnate Ground of Christian Faith:*

Notice that the form or 3-D image is intrinsic to the *interrelations* of the detail of the *Magic Eye* (form inheres in being). Yet the mind has to assimilate and integrate these particulars *in their intrinsic interrelations* in order to see the 3-D image (form has to be integrated with the sense "data" or empirical element in human perception).

The difficulty of visual perception and the integration it involves (a perception that we take for granted) is also revealed in the experiments using inverting spectacles.[78] When a person puts on inverting spectacles in which one sees things upside-down, or reversed from right to left, such a person is thrown into a state of disorientation. It takes about eight painful days before the person can see "properly" again. What happens during those eight days is a process of tacit learning, as well as active experimentation, much like that through which a child passes when first coordinating vision with her surroundings. In the case of the inverting spectacles, which alters the visual image, it is the conceptual image or mental integration of form that has to—and does—change in those eight painful days.[79]

Yet the very fact that it does change, Torrance argues, "reveals how the visual and the conceptual images operate inseparably together in our orientation to the objective structure of the world around us,"[80] and does so not simply on the basis of active experimentation, but through tacit learning. Or to put it another way, the conceptual image is neither deduced from, nor imposed on, the visual image, but rather is integrated with it in a complex and holistic manner that defies expression in entirely explicit terms; though in significant measure *tacit*, the integration that results is none the less *real*. Thus, Torrance asserts that the shift in the integration of the conceptual image illumines the fact that the perceptual image and the conceptual image operate together in a way that the empirical and theoretical (the perceptual and conceptual) are realigned in our knowing (integration of form in knowing) and reflect the fusion of form and being that

---

Toward a Christian Theological Epistemology for the Educational Ministry of the Church (Lanham, Md.: University of America Press, 1998), pp. 160-64.

[78] See ibid., p. 118.

[79] See Torrance, *Scientific Theology*, p. 43. Visual perception is really an astonishing feat, one that a child learns only gradually, with great difficulty, and some bumps and bruises. Form and being are integrated in the physical world that the child inhabits, and form and being have to be integrated in the child's perception in order to judge distances, to identify food and place it in her mouth, or to avoid being run over by a car.

[80] Torrance, "Polanyi," p. 64.

inhere in one another in the world around us.[81]

Polanyi and Torrance see the integration of form in scientific inquiry following a similar pattern: we indwell (somewhat like the informal eight-day
process when wearing inverting spectacles) the field of inquiry until a
"structural kinship" arises (somewhat like the 3-D image we perceive in the
Magic Eye) between our knowing and what we know. This dynamic structural kinship in scientific inquiry takes the form of an insight or *prolepsis* (a
concept or theory—integration of form in knowing), which we develop, test
and refine until we are convinced that it is an accurate conceptual instrument that discloses the intrinsic intelligibility of the field (form in being) that
we seek to know. But this structural kinship that arises between our knowing and what we know is not *inherent* or *necessary*, but contingent on the all-
important *dynamic, integrative interaction* between the knower and the
known (as revealed in the inverting spectacles experiment or the *Magic Eye*).

Fusion of form and being, integration of form in knowing.[82] The integration
of empirical and theoretical ingredients in reality (form in being or the intrinsic interrelations of nature), and the need for the integration of empirical and theoretical factors in our knowledge of reality is one of the basic
elements of Torrance's rejection of epistemological dualism and one of the
most important aspects of his epistemology. It is this fusion of form and
being in nature that requires an integrative kind of knowing beyond analyzing discrete particulars and deducing "knowledge" from them, in a
similar way in which we cannot perceive the three-dimensional image in
the *Magic Eye* by analyzing the tiny figures in the picture and then trying
to fit them together into the 3-D image (or in which we cannot reorient the
conceptual image by analytic and deductive procedures so that it reflects
the visual image distorted by the inverting spectacles).[83]

A similar kind of epistemological issue is at stake in Clerk Maxwell's
struggle to conceptualize the electromagnetic field and also in Einstein's dis-

---

[81]See ibid. and Torrance, *Scientific Theology*, p. 43.

[82]Torrance argues, "It is this fusion of the rational and ontological elements in nature, and of
the empirical and theoretical elements in our apprehension of it, that Polanyi took pains to
establish in the opening chapter of his Gifford Lectures of 1951-2, by showing that twenti-
eth-century physics, and Einstein's discovery of relativity in particular, demonstrate the
power of science to make contact with reality in nature by recognizing what is rational in
nature" (Torrance, "Polanyi," p. 64).

[83]Torrance, *Transformation*, p. 119. The *subsidiary fusion of the clues* imbedded in the *Magic Eye*
picture yielding the focal apprehension of the 3-D image is neither analytic nor deductive,
but rather integrative.

covery and formulation of relativity. If form and being are in fact fused together in nature, as in the case of the electromagnetic field, we must grasp them together, Torrance argues, in our apprehension and articulation.[84] This is what Maxwell did in developing his field theory, which has led to an immense revolution not simply in terms of our *knowledge* of the natural world, but also with reference to *epistemology* in science (how we integrate form), the equally astonishing *dynamic* power of the human mind to heuristically respond to reality and expand its conceptualization of reality, as reality comes more fully into view in the course of scientific inquiry. (Einstein saw this clearly after forming the general theory of relativity.)[85]

This is why Polanyi and Torrance argue that scientific discovery involves an epistemic process that is essentially *integrative*, not primarily analytic, deductive or abstractive,[86] even though analytic and deductive activities have important roles to play in scientific endeavor. Polanyi and Torrance are skeptical regarding the possibility of construing the integration of form in terms of wholly explicit procedures, for that would fail to account for the dynamic and creative nature of this integration, the mind's ability to expand and take in what is genuinely new through the informal process of indwelling, and the extralogical relation this involves.[87]

If there is an ineradicable informal, tacit dimension and an extra-logical

---

[84]Ibid., p. 119. For an excellent discussion of the relational character of reality (form in being) in Maxwell and Einstein in natural science and Torrance in theology, see W. Jim Neidhardt's introductory essay "Key Themes in Thomas F. Torrance's Integration of Judeo-Christian Theology and Natural Science," in Thomas F. Torrance, *The Christian Frame of Mind: Reason, Order, and Openness in Theology and Natural Science* (Colorado Springs: Helmers & Howard, 1989), pp. xi-xli. Neidhardt's essay is a fine introduction to Torrance's work in the area indicated in the essay's title.

[85]If form and being are fused together in reality, whether in an electromagnetic field or the indivisible space-time continuum or in the *Magic Eye*, they have to be grasped together in our apprehension of them. Hardy has Torrance right on this point as well. Hardy also astutely notes that the kind of integration of form that Torrance (and Polanyi) advocates, and the resulting conceptual frameworks that arise (including ultimate beliefs), are not like Kant's unalterable categories or even Bernard Lonergan's structures of consciousness. Torrance's understanding of the integrative powers of the mind are "far less consciousness-centered, and far less bound by the limits of rational accounts of the conscious mind" (see Hardy, "Thomas F. Torrance," p. 81). Hardy is dealing with Torrance's understanding of fiduciary frameworks, but Torrance's account of the character of belief parallels his account of the integration of form (see p. 79). Both are responses of the human person to the boundless objectivity of reality.

[86]Ibid., p. 119.

[87]Ibid. Torrance argues here that this is why Polanyi resisted the predominance of analytic philosophy and the undue emphasis of explicit deductivism.

relation in the integration of form in scientific discovery, then Polanyi argues that "any critical verification of a scientific statement requires the same powers for recognizing rationality in nature as does the process of scientific discovery."[88] The actual application of scientific theories to the natural world, which for Torrance is the crucial test, is not all that different from the way the scientist discovered the theory in the first place.[89] In the end, Torrance contends, the "meaning, the success and the validity of a scientific theory depend on its *ontological import*, i.e., its *power of objective reference* to point to and reveal the hidden structure in the world to which it is correlated, and which determines its cognitive and heuristic values."[90] The significance of theoretical formalizations lies in their ability to disclose reality in its intrinsic relations (form in being) through the dynamic integrative adaptation of our knowing (integration of form in knowing) to the intrinsic structure of what we seek to know.[91]

Personal knowledge. This kind of epistemic activity entails *personal* knowledge and *personal* judgement, though for Polanyi, and emphatically(!) for Torrance, personal knowledge and judgement are not purely subjective, for they arise (or should arise) out of the process of indwelling the field of inquiry. Personal knowledge and judgement are therefore made (or should be made) in light of the objective intrinsic relations that come into view in the course of inquiry and provide an objective pole for

---

[88]See Michael Polanyi, *Personal Knowledge: Towards a Post-Critical Philosophy* (Chicago: University of Chicago Press, 1958), p. 13; Torrance, *Transformation*, p. 120.

[89]See Torrance, *Scientific Theology*, pp. 76-77. Also see Torrance, *Theological Science*, pp. 161-203, 222-80, where Torrance distinguishes between "existence-statements" and "coherence-statements" and the logic of both. Here Torrance clarifies many of the important functions of the logico-deductive processes in natural and theological science that we cannot deal with in an introduction like this one.

[90]Torrance, "Integration," p. 155. Torrance also asserts:

> Hence, just as it was not through any logical nexus that the basic concepts (out of which the theory was built) were derived from experiences, so likewise there is at the conclusion no logical nexus by means of which it can be demonstrated or verified: the all-important connection at the end must be just as empirical and intuitive as it was at the start. . . . No direct comparison between scientific concepts or statements and empirical facts is involved . . . but what is involved is an *analogical* reference in which an indirect comparison is in place, between 'empirical facts' imported by the theory and an actual set of empirical facts.

He also maintains that human knowledge in any field of inquiry originates in actual experience and terminates in experience even while it entails complex intellectual operations throughout.

[91]See Torrance, *Transformation*, pp. 135-42, 145, and Torrance, *Scientific Theology*, p. 80.

personal knowledge and judgment.[92]

Torrance maintains that "only persons are capable of distinguishing what they know from their knowing of it, and of engaging in sustained self-critical operations in the interest of objectivity and consistency."[93] Thus the personal element is not eliminated, but rather controlled by constant reference back to the reality under investigation.[94] This also means that there is an ineradicable moral dimension to all human knowing, for personal knowledge requires *openness* toward reality, *honesty* and *self-criticism*, which curtail the illegitimate imposition of form, the imposition of our subjective states and preconceptions onto the reality we are investigating.[95] For Torrance (and Polanyi) personal agency in knowing cannot be placed in contra-position to genuine objectivity, for personal being, Torrance contends, is the *bearer of objectivity*.[96]

Thus, it is *personal participation*, through the process of indwelling, that keeps personal knowledge and judgement from being purely subjective, for it is through interactive participation that the structural kinship develops between human knowing and what is known.[97] At precisely this point

---

[92]Torrance, *Transformation*, p. 123. Torrance disagrees with Polanyi on the details of this point, seeing a certain "phenomenalist" tendency in Polanyi's thought stemming from the influence of existentialist and phenomenalist thinkers (see Torrance, *Scientific Theology*, pp. 133-35). For Torrance, the final judge of the truth or falsity of our concepts and theories is reality itself, a point we will take up in the final section of this chapter (see Torrance, *Transformation*, p. 123).

[93]Torrance, "Polanyi," p. 72.

[94]Here Torrance speaks of an *epistemological inversion* in which, though we begin where we are within our socially shaped personal frame of thought, we pose our questions and proceed with our inquiry in such a way that we allow the reality we seek to know to question us and mold our thinking. We reformulate our questions so that we invert the formative factor in our ongoing inquiry *from* ourselves *to* the intrinsic constitutive relations of reality (form in being) we seek to know (see Torrance, *Scientific Theology*, p. 26).

[95]Ibid., p. 27.

[96]Ibid., p. 133-34. This last point—that personal being is the bearer of objectivity—brings us back to what Torrance calls the most startling feature of the new science, the *anthropic principle* discussed in chapter five, the astonishing fact that humanity cannot be separated from the structure of the universe of which humanity is a constituent element. Humanity is the highest level or boundary point through which the astonishing intelligibility of the created universe comes to articulation in praise of its Creator (see Torrance, *Transformation*, p. 84). Here Torrance sees scientific inquiry moving in a deep and convincing circle from the ultimate belief in the contingent intelligibility of the universe (a belief of Judeo-Christian origin), through manifold scientific inquiry, to the astonishing dynamic harmony between the contingent intelligible universe and human knowing, and its cry for a sufficient reason, which points toward the active agency of God.

[97]Ibid., p. 135. Thus, if the tacit dimension constitutes an epistemological "foundation," it is a foundation affected by one's cultural-linguistic framework and therefore by all the

we see why Torrance argues that theological science can never be built on natural science or vice versa. The two fields entail significantly *different kinds of personal participation*, for each develops its *own distinctive methods and conceptualities* in harmony with the *nature* of the different realities each investigates, the space-time universe or the triune God.

---

problems of sociology of knowledge. Furthermore, it is clear that for Torrance the tacit dimension is open to critical modification as inquiry proceeds. Torrance explicitly rejects the Greek notion of science "where the stress is upon unchanging foundations of knowledge." In its place he upholds personal knowledge, which is possible but not inevitable (see Torrance, *Transformation*, p. 65).

However, Torrance is certainly not the kind of foundationalist Ronald Thiemann contends that he is (see Thiemann, *Revelation and Theology: The Gospel as Narrated Promise* [University of Notre Dame Press, 1985], pp. 32-42). According to Thiemann, Torrance is a foundationalist, for "Torrance uses the term *intuition* to signify the indubitability and incorrigibility of this *causally imposed knowledge*" (see p. 40). Yet Torrance repeatedly asserts that "no rational knowledge is merely *per modum causalitatis* . . . [for] even though I think rationally as I am compelled to think . . . I am free and not a puppet." (Torrance, *Rationality*, p. 198).

Furthermore, in rejecting the "mechanization of knowledge," Torrance argues that history, human knowing and reality at all levels of the created universe are "found to be much too subtle and flexible . . . to be open to explanation or understanding within the old framework of 'necessity and chance'" (see Torrance, *Christian Frame*, pp. 43-46, 48-50). Torrance also maintains that "if beliefs were causally imposed on our minds. . . that would eliminate freedom to believe or not to believe as we judge we must and so relieve us of personal responsibility for our belief. . . . If beliefs were causally imposed on us, that would also eliminate the possibility of error" (see Thomas F. Torrance, ed., *Belief in Science and in Christian Life: The Relevance of Michael Polanyi's Thought for Christian Faith and Life* [Edinburgh: Handsel Press, 1980], p. 14).

It seems that Thiemann himself has not moved all that far beyond the problematic dichotomy of chance and necessity, for he presents the reader with an all too similar disjunction: either foundationalism, with its appeal to non-inferential, causally imposed intuitive apprehension of the real, *or* a "narrated promise" awaiting an "eschatological justification" and a "person-specific act" of faith "with reasons and causes related to that person's individual history" (One cannot help but think of Feuerbach!), the explanation of which "lies beyond theology's descriptive competence" (see Thiemann, *Authority and Revelation*, pp. 94 and 147-48).

Thiemann's misreading of Torrance's theology is partly rooted in his highly selective encounter with Torrance's work, engaging just three of Torrance's books. This kind of selective approach is simply inadequate to the character of Torrance's publications, which requires a significantly broader acquaintance with Torrance's diverse literature on epistemology and method.

The other source of Thiemann's misunderstanding of Torrance is that he reads Torrance in light of the foundationalist-antifoundational debate, rather than in light of the Greek fathers' concept of *prolepsis*, and in light of Einstein and Polanyi. The irony is that Torrance actually agrees with Thiemann that the conditions for knowledge cannot be rendered fully explicit. But Torrance rejects Thiemann's alternative for its failure to develop an adequate way to control the personal element that cannot be eliminated from human knowledge. Thiemann has been beguiled by the antinomies of the limited categories he utilizes in thinking through basic epistemological questions.

4. Scripture and the Integration of Form in Theology

The scientific status of theology. As we saw in the introduction and in chapter four, Torrance wants to develop a rigorous, scientific account of theology. This does not mean that theology conforms to the presuppositions/procedures of a universal science or even other special sciences like natural science. Each special science must conform its inquiry to the nature of its object. Theology can be scientific *if* God is knowable and *when* theology proceeds in accordance with the nature of God in God's knowability (self-revelation).

In Torrance's theology this means we direct our attention to the central realities of the Christian faith, Jesus Christ and the gospel, and attempt to understand Christ within the actual matrix of interrelations where we find him within the history and people of Israel, and also in light of the intrinsic structure of who Christ is in himself in relation to God and to sinful humanity. Torrance argues that as theology investigates and articulates these relations (integration of form in knowing) it enables us to grasp the organic structure (form in being) of our knowledge of God and God's relation to us in redemption and creation.

While there are certain formal similarities between natural and theological science, Torrance does not attempt to ground his *scientific* theology on an epistemology arising within natural science.[98] What Torrance has discovered, however, is that theology and natural science over the past hundred years have had to face similar problems because of the received framework of thought with its <u>epistemological and cosmological dual</u>isms. Theology and natural science can learn from one another because of their mutual struggle to develop more adequate ways to integrate form in their special areas of inquiry.[99]

Dualism in modern theology and biblical studies.[100] Torrance finds

---

[98]Torrance finds the kind of natural science encountered in Einstein, Polanyi and others to be rather helpful in his attempt to *expound* Christian theology (including theological method) in modern culture and in his goal to *transform* the received framework of thought in light of the gospel.

[99]Torrance, *Transformation*, pp. viii-xiv.

[100]Those interested in Torrance's critique of modern historical-critical biblical studies and theology should examine Torrance, *Resurrection*, pp. 1-21, 159-93; *Preaching Christ Today: The Gospel and Scientific Thinking* (Grand Rapids, Mich.: Eerdmans, 1994), pp. 1-11; and "The Historical Jesus: From the Perspective of a Theologian," in *The New Testament Age: Essays in Honor of Bo Reicke*, ed. William C. Weinrich (Macon, Ga.: Mercer University Press, 1984), 2:511-26.

that often modern theology and historical-critical biblical studies have also been adversely influenced by the same received framework of thought that has troubled natural science, a frame of reference character-ized by epistemological and cosmological dualisms, and inadequate ac-counts of how form is integrated in knowing in relation to the way form is intrinsic to being. Torrance finds similar analytic, deductive, abstract and mechanistic patterns of thought applied to the Bible, as Torrance finds in the history of natural science and philosophy from Newton to Kant.

Newton viewed science as an inquiry into the causal relations between material realities, and his idea that concepts as deduced from phenomena or sense data led to a kind of scientific method that first focuses on isolat-ing data or observing phenomena. Then on the basis of the "empirical da-ta" that results, science deduces or abstracts its concepts or natural laws.[101] The problem with this approach is not only that Newton did not (could not) *deduce* or *abstract* theoretical elements (like absolute time and space) from observed data, as Hume revealed, but also that the analytic isolation of "empirical data" tends to break up the natural cohesion (form in being) of the electromagnetic field, for example, (or the space-time continuum) into discrete particles (externally related to one another), which effaces the intrinsic interrelations that are constitutive, defining or characteristic of what realities are.[102]

In a similar way, Torrance thinks that streams of modern historical-crit-ical biblical studies and theology operate with methods of inquiry in rela-tion to the Bible which attempt to penetrate through the biblical witness as

---

[101]See Torrance, *Preaching Christ*, pp. 5-8.

[102]This kind of scientific method that isolates data and attempts to deduce concepts and laws that state the causal and necessary relations between realities is even more destruc-tive to the subtle kind of order in higher forms of life, like human beings, which are sim-ply too complex and open-structured for this kind of reductionist explanation. Einstein's work demonstrated not only that form can be integrated in a much more dynamic and holistic manner; his work also revealed the equally important interrelatedness of reality. There are intrinsic relations in reality. What we find in reality are not discrete particulars (related through external causal relations) that are observed as empirical facts and events from which we then deduce concepts or laws explaining their relations. An electro-mag-netic field, the behavior of light, Einstein's space-time continuum, all call for a different epistemology (integration of form in knowing) because they reveal a different ontology in which reality is characterized by dynamic intrinsic interrelatedness (form inheres in being). The result of this radical change is that now scientists, Torrance contends, "think from beginning to end in terms of the integration of empirical and theoretical factors, both in nature and in our knowledge of it" (Torrance, *Preaching Christ*, p. 42).

it stands and isolate the various textual and pre-textual sources so as to arrive at authentic (probable) historical data on which to construct an accurate historical or theological portrayal of Jesus, for example. But Torrance
thinks that various versions of this kind of approach tend to tear the natural cohesion of Scripture (form in being) by severing the New Testament
from the Old, breaking up the gospels into various fragmentary sources
and separating various books within the New Testament from one another
in light of their "conflicting" theologies. This analytic isolation of data effaces the intrinsic interrelations defining or characteristic of Jesus Christ
and the gospel, as we saw in chapter two, for example, in reference to
Christ's relation to Israel and the Old Testament.

In modern constructivist epistemology, the human mind *imposes* form
(either a priori, as in Kant, though now more often *cultural-linguistic* form,
the culturally acquired categories and activities of the mind) on experience
and everything it seeks to know.[103] Torrance finds a similar pattern in segments of modern biblical studies and theology that explain the natural
theological cohesion of the Gospels, of the New Testament as a whole, and
between the two testaments in terms of the early church imposing its theological framework on earlier sources.[104] Modern scholars attempt to cut
through the later *theological* accretions that overlay the earlier materials so
as to unearth the "historical" sources (empirical data) which in some sense
more accurately depict the *real* historical Jesus. The result is often an "his-

---

[103]See chapter two, pp. 57-60, for Torrance's rejection of epistemological and cosmological
dualisms.

[104]For example, two of the texts that played a key role in the development of Nicene theology are Matthew 11:27 (and Lk 10) where Jesus says, "No one knows the Son except the
Father, and no one knows the Father except the Son and anyone to whom the Son chooses
to reveal him"; and Matthew 28:16-20 where the risen Jesus tells his followers to make disciples and baptize in the trinitarian name. Torrance says that biblical scholars "argue that
Jesus could not have said that, for in accordance with their preconceptions . . . those
reported sayings of Jesus have a theological ingredient which cannot 'scientifically' be
accepted as part of the empirical data relating to the historical Jesus. . . . They cut out theological elements from the Gospels and attribute them to the activity of the Christian Community" (Torrance, *Preaching Christ*, p. 8).

At this point epistemic and cosmological dualisms often coalesce and operate together
(see note 10 of chapter two, pp. 58-59). Modern cosmological dualisms (and panentheisms) reject the kind of "interactionist" God-world relation that Torrance finds in Scripture, and therefore interpret what the Bible says about God's activity in the world in Jesus
Christ (the incarnation or resurrection, for instance) in terms of the mythopoetic or apocalyptic imagery of first-century Christian faith historically distant from modern-postmodern readers/communities, or as evidence of the *imposition* of later theological elements on
the original source material.

torical" Jesus who bears little resemblance to the Jesus Christ of the early church.[105]

Torrance thinks that it is no coincidence that segments of modern theology and historical-critical biblical studies end up in a very different place theologically than classic, ecumenical Christian theology as it comes to expression in the Nicene-Constantinopolitan Creed. The real problem, as Torrance sees it, is the presuppositions and methods that break up the biblical witness and efface the very intrinsic interrelations that have to be integrated in order to grasp God's *oikonomia* (the divine realities and saving events in God's interaction with Israel, in Jesus Christ, and in the apostolic church) which generated the biblical witness in the first place, as we discussed in chapters two, three and six.[106]

In order to better understand some of what Torrance has in mind, think of the Bible as a giant literary *Magic Eye* which has clues to a three-dimensional image imbedded amidst the massive detail. If we break the Bible up and examine the detail separately, it is impossible to grasp God's *oikonomia*, the intrinsic relations imprinted on the saving events to which the Old and New Testaments together bear witness, in a similar way in which merely analyzing the detail of the *Magic Eye* picture inhibits one's ability to integrate the distinctive interrelations of the detail and perceive the 3-D image embedded in the picture.[107] God's *oikonomia* only comes into view by way of an *integrative* perception in which we indwell the conjoint witness of Scripture (Old and New Testaments) until we assimilate it, and through it grasp the pattern of God's self-revelation and self-communication, somewhat like the way we utilize a subsidiary awareness of marginal elements or clues with a functional bearing on the 3-D image imprinted on the *Magic Eye* that we see in our focal awareness.[108]

Despite the limitations of this comparison, it points to the fact that Tor-

---

[105]Torrance, *Preaching Christ*, p. 8. Torrance thinks that it is at this point that another theology, more compatible with the modern interpreter, is utilized to link together what is "really" authentic to the historical Jesus in the New Testament documents once the later theology is removed (see p. 10).

[106]See chapter two, pp. 57-70, 73-78; chapter three, pp. 102-9; and chapter six, pp. 224-30.

[107]After decades of historical-critical investigation which so very seldom ever leads to a robust doctrine of the Trinity—*the* distinctive Christian doctrine of God—Torrance thinks that we have to raise serious questions about the adequacy of the presuppositions and methodologies of this kind of approach to the Bible.

[108]What would happen if we broke up the *Magic Eye* and only examined it in terms of the tiny figures that make it up? One would, of course, learn a lot about the detail, color, kind

rance views theological inquiry in relation to the Bible as a predominantly *integrative* activity that has to engage the Bible holistically in its witness to God and God's *oikonomia*.[109] Any presuppositions or methods that rule out a holistic, integrative and theological approach to the interpretation of Scripture are suspect in Torrance's perspective on several levels.

They all too often yield results that are incompatible with, or fall short of, the kind of trinitarian theology that comes to expression in ecumenical Christian consensus in the Nicene-Constantinopolitan Creed. Furthermore, presuppositions or methods like these have been radically undermined and set aside in the kind of scientific advance that we find in Einstein, Polanyi and others in natural science. Should we not be suspicious, Torrance queries, of applying similar presuppositions or methods to the field of theological science?[110]

Toward a holistic, integrative, theological approach. This does not

---

of ink and paper, etc., that make up the picture, all of which is has its appropriate place, for they all have something to contribute to understanding the *Magic Eye*. But if one stops there and only focuses on the disconnected and isolated parts of the picture, one effaces or erases the very clues embedded in the *interrelations* in the detailed figures needed to discern the *Magic Eye*, so that it never comes into view.

This is what Torrance thinks can happen to Scripture when the Testaments are disconnected, and books are isolated, analyzed and broken up into textual and pretextual components. Torrance argues that it is impossible to develop an authentic theology on the basis of the disconnected components of the Bible, anymore than it is possible to discern the three-dimensional image in the *Magic Eye* by reconnecting the various tiny figures once they have been torn out of their intrinsic interrelations that provide clues that the mind tacitly integrates so as to discern the 3-D image. The theological whole is significantly greater than the sum of the isolated constitutive parts that comprise the biblical witness. The essential interconnection and intrinsic relations in God's *oikonomia*, out of which Scripture arose and to which Scripture bears witness, cannot be grasped within a dualist framework or by analytic, deductive or other modes of thought that by their very character efface the very interconnections (the form in being) needed to grasp God's self-revelation.

The 3-D *Magic Eye* image is also participatory. You either see it, or you don't. We can help others by telling them not to focus on the detail, to place the picture close to their face and gradually move it away. But in the end, it is a *participatory integration* of subsidiary clues yielding a focal awareness of the 3-D image.

[109]For instance, we cannot abstract Jesus Christ from the matrix of Christ's relations to Israel and the Old Testament. Nor can we dispense with the theological elements in the Gospels or disregard the way in which the overarching narratives depict the identity of Jesus Christ, or only examine elements of the Gospels apart from the matrix within which they are embedded in the entire gospel account, or only interpret the various books of the New Testament independent of one another.

[110]In Torrance's perspective, if the complex kind of interconnected order (form in being) that we find in the natural world—like an electromagnetic field, for example—requires a sophisticated integrative cognitive activity (indwelling) in order for the mind to develop a

mean that Torrance is opposed to form, source and redaction criticism, or opposed to acknowledging the inconsistencies between the Gospels or the distinctive theological perspectives of the various books that make up the Old and New Testament. In fact, it is often the distinctive elements, even in apparent irreconcilable tension, that are the very clues to deeper intrinsic interrelations and intelligibility.[111]

Yet what interests Torrance most as a theologian is not just the Bible as a collection of historical documents with complex textual and pre-textual histories, which Torrance grants that the Bible is. What interests Torrance is the living God to whom the various biblical documents bear witness, and God's *oikonomia*, that distinctive (trinitarian) pattern of God's revealing and saving activity in Israel and Jesus Christ imprinted on the series of events proclaimed in the biblical witness out of which Scripture arose.[112] We cannot *deduce* or *abstract* the incarnation or the Trinity (intrinsic form in the divine realities and saving events) from the "data" concerning the historical Jesus, for these doctrines arise out of a much more complex integrative theological activity concerned with the conjoint witness of Scripture to God's *oikonomia*.[113]

It is important for the reader to keep in mind Torrance's account of God's molding and shaping of Israel to be the appropriate matrix of forms of thought, speech and life within which Jesus Christ and the gospel were understood and ought to be understood today. It is this embodied and pat-

---

dynamic structural kinship (integration of form in knowing) that enables us to apprehend this kind of complex onto-relational order (form in being), why should we think that the even more complex and subtle order (form in being) that theology investigates is amenable to predominately analytic, deductive and similar modes of inquiry that in one way or another tear apart the fabric of the biblical witness?

Torrance thinks that it is not enough simply to trace the sources of the text of Scripture, to determine which sayings of Jesus in the Gospels for instance are authentic, or to decide the *Sitz im Leben* of particular texts and what they meant for the first communities to which they were addressed. As important and interesting as all these questions are, they only bring us up to the point where we ask what are the realities to which these various texts bear witness? What are the essential interrelations and intrinsic constitutive structures of the gospel? Who is Jesus Christ? What is Christ's relation to Israel and to God? And so forth.

Torrance thinks that these questions can only be adequately answered by a holistic, participatory and theological approach to Scripture that integrates the manifold conjoint focus of the various strata of the biblical witness to God's self-revelation in Jesus Christ and the gospel.

[111]Torrance, *Resurrection*, pp. 2-15.

[112]Ibid., and Torrance, *Christian Doctrine*, p. 82.

[113]See Torrance, *Resurrection*, pp. 1-26.

terned understanding of revelation (form in being), its progressive actualization (integration of form in knowing) within the history of Israel
(mirrored in the Old Testament), and its final actualization in Jesus Christ
and the apostolic community (reflected in the New Testament which arose
within this community) that demands a predominately holistic, integrative, participatory and theological approach to the interpretation of the Bible.[114] In Torrance's theological perspective, content, method and doctrinal
form are inseparable and arise together in theological inquiry.

Thus Torrance contends that there is no logical, analytical, deductive or
abstractive way to enter the ordered field of dynamic relations with which
Christian theology is concerned (important as those procedures are in theology), because these procedures are inadequate to the relations and patterns inherent in the divine realities and saving events (complex intrinsic
form in being) to which the biblical texts witness.[115] Torrance argues that
because we are concerned with the living God in self-revelation and self-
communication, theological interpretation of the Bible requires a holistic
form of knowing that integrates the empirical and theoretical, the historical and theological, and includes profound cognitive and personal participation (integration of form in knowing) in the divine realities and saving
events, and their intrinsic interrelations.

The integration of form in theology. According to Torrance, the first
step to be taken in the approach that he advocates is similar in form to
what we find in Einstein and Polanyi: we *indwell* the field of inquiry, in this
case the biblical witness, until a structural kinship arises between the human mind (integration of form in knowing) and the interrelations and intrinsic structures in the realities (form in being) to which Scripture bears
witness.[116] Because the order with which theology is concerned is of such
a character that it must be grasped holistically (we have to view Jesus

---

[114]Indeed, for Torrance, the biblical witness itself is an instance of effective integration of
form (at primarily the evangelical and doxological level) in which there is a structural kinship between human and creaturely forms of thought and speech in the manifold and
diverse character of the biblical documents and God's *oikonomia* out of which the biblical
documents arose. This, of course, is what makes Scripture the suitable and inspired
medium for God's continuing self-revelation and self-communication, as we outlined in
chapters two, three and six.

[115]In fact, Torrance is convinced that dualist epistemological and cosmological presuppositions combined with predominately analytical, deductive and mechanistic methods and
modes of thinking render virtually impossible the kind of integrative participatory theological activity he envisages.

[116]Torrance, *Scientific Theology,* pp. 83-84.

Christ and the gospel within Israel, for example), the method employed must be integrative so that it enables us to enter the complex and interrelated character of that order.[117] Indwelling is an informal integrative movement of thought that enables our minds to expand, so to speak, so that we can attend to all that the field entails and holistically assimilate it until we gain the clues or insights which, in turn, enable us to begin to apprehend and articulate the intrinsic order of the field in question.

The fusion of form (intrinsic interrelations) in the realities and saving events in God's *oikonomia* (Jesus Christ's life, death and resurrection and the outpouring of the Holy Spirit within the matrix of Israel) requires an integrative kind of knowing beyond analyzing empirical/historical data and deducing theoretical elements from it. But since the structural kinship that arises between our knowing and what we know is not inherent or necessary (contra Kant), it requires a dynamic indwelling and participation in order to assimilate and integrate form in knowing in a way that reflects and discloses the fusion of form (or intrinsic relations) in being.

What is significantly different in theological inquiry (compared to natural science) is that theology is concerned with the biblical witness to the living God, a God who has come to us in a redemptive self-revelation and self-communication and therefore calls for a kind of participation beyond what is called for in natural science. The clues in theological inquiry arise only out of an ongoing, intimate and participatory contact with God's *oikonomia* through the conjoint witness of Scripture.[118] Torrance suggests that this is the sort of clue that Clement of Alexandria called a *prolepsis*, the forward leap of the mind to a hitherto unknown aspect of reality.[119] Only the great theologians who were childlike in spirit, Torrance notes, have succeeded in coming up with this kind of basic insight that has significantly advanced theological understanding.[120]

The role of the church in theology. Furthermore, Torrance contends that the place where we have access to the set of conditions within which we find the kind of order theology investigates, the place where we can ind-

---

[117]Thomas F. Torrance, *Reality and Evangelical Theology* (Philadelphia: Westminster Press, 1982), p. 45.

[118]Remember Torrance's account of the way Scripture arises out of God's interaction with our world of space and time in Israel, Jesus Christ and the apostolic foundations in chapters two (pp. 61-82), three (pp. 98-113) and six (pp. 221-33).

[119]Torrance, *Scientific Theology*, p. 84.

[120]Ibid.

well this order and come up with these anticipatory conceptions or clues, is within the church, the worshipping community of the people of God and its fellowship and service of the gospel: "It is through religious experience, in the context of tradition in the continuity of the life of the Church where learning through others, meditation upon the message of Holy Scripture, prayer and worship regularly take place, that these basic convictions and primary concepts take their rise."[121]

Of course, the reason for this is that the Bible is more than simply an account of a particular religious history: it is the medium through which the living God continues to speak and to draw us into participation in the gospel to which it bears witness. Torrance suggests that as a child learns more about physics by the age of five than she will ever be able to fully understand even as a brilliant physicist, so within the church which participates in the gospel, we come to know more of God than we can ever fully articulate.[122]

In fact all scientific pursuits, according to Torrance, are related to the structures and paradigms of the community in which we think and express ourselves.[123] Those structures and paradigms embodied in group habits of life and thought in the church and in society influence theological inquiry and doctrine. There is a personal and social coefficient in all knowledge, including knowledge of God and doctrine.[124] This is simply an implication of Torrance's contention that we are always already within the

---

[121]Thomas F. Torrance, "The Integration of Form in Natural and in Theological Science," *Science, Medicine and Man* 1 (1973): 164. Furthermore, this is not all that different from natural science, where the scientific community and its tradition also play a major role in the cultivation of the proper mind-set and skills necessary for the student to become a full-fledged scientist. See Alexander Thomson's discussion of this in his important book, *Tradition and Authority in Science and Theology* (Edinburgh: Scottish Academic Press, 1987).

[122]Torrance, *Evangelical Theology*, p. 48. "Knowing more than we can tell" is what Torrance means by "theological instinct."

[123]Torrance, *Scientific Theology*, p. xv.

[124]This is also one of the fascinating elements of Torrance's theological method, for he concedes not a little to sociology of knowledge, yet also argues for a critical epistemic realism. Virtually all of Torrance's discussions of the social coefficient in knowledge of God and doctrine occur within the matrix of other subject matter. To my knowledge, the only place where Torrance devotes an entire chapter or essay to this subject is in chapter four ("The Social Coefficient of Knowledge") of his important book *Reality and Scientific Theology*. What Torrance has written is highly suggestive, and deserves further attention.

Within the social coefficient the human mind and imagination find their orientation toward the world and acquire the ability to recognize patterns of intelligibility and meaning in the world or a particular field of inquiry. This provides the matrix for our basic informal relation to reality (the tacit dimension), which is the source of the essential clues

knowing relation, that there are no final categories in the Kantian sense, and that we do not apprehend anything without a socio-personal and conceptual framework.

Torrance's view of God's relation to humanity is not that of a mathematical point or simply an event, but rather a *community of reciprocity* in relation to God moving through space-time and progressively adapted by God to God's self-revelation. This happens first in the nation of Israel, then in Jesus Christ (within Israel) and in the apostolic nucleus Christ drew to himself, and now in the church as the body of Christ gathered and commissioned to carry the gospel forward in history, as we saw in chapters two, three and seven.[125]

The church embodies (or should embody) the all-important social coefficient of knowledge of God, providing "the semantic focus," a milieu within which people's relation with the reality of God is established and

---

that are of critical importance for all scientific inquiry (see Torrance, *Scientific Theology*, p. 104). The social coefficient includes the full gamut of what a society or particular community entails in shaping its inhabitants, including institutions, language, tradition, education and so forth.

A genuine social coefficient of knowledge, as Torrance understands it, has no meaning or validity on its own when abstracted from what is known, for it does not generate knowledge, but rather predisposes us toward explicit apprehension of the intelligibility of what we seek to know (see pp. 102, 114).

However, while our thinking is implicitly shaped by the social coefficient, Torrance argues that, "this does not imply that we must operate uncritically within the knowledge or wisdom accumulated in our cultural tradition, just because we are unable to extricate ourselves from involvement in it. On the contrary, it is because our thought is so powerfully influenced by culture that we must bring its latent assumptions out into the open and put them to the test. . . . Hence if theology is not to be swamped by cultural relativism but is to retain its integrity, it must put all cultural assumptions rigorously to the test before the compelling claims of its own proper subject-matter and its objective evidential grounds" (see Torrance, *Scientific Culture*, pp. 13-14). For a further discussion of this see Colyer, *Nature of Doctrine*, chap. three.

What Torrance envisages is a free society of persons with open structures of thought and life correlated to the depth and range of the intrinsic intelligibility of reality, contingent and divine—an intelligibility only partially grasped and therefore pursued unfettered by closed ideologies, yielding a notion of science and society open to transformation in light of further disclosures of reality (see Torrance, *Scientific Theology*, pp. 108-9). Here we see some of the political overtones of Torrance's perspective on the way in which a proper social coefficient of knowledge ought to function.

[125]See Torrance, *Rationality*, p. 17. He also says that Christ "does come to us directly but not apart from His coming personally and historically through the Word communicated by other historical persons. Christ communicates Himself to us personally in and through the historical Church where the Word is mediated to us in temporal acts . . . from generation to generation, within the Church as the . . . Body of Christ" (Torrance, *Theological Science*, pp. 210-11).

nurtured, and their understanding of God deepens.[126] For Torrance theology is always faith seeking understanding within the church in an attitude of prayer and thanksgiving, though not without disciplined and rigorous mental activity.[127]

---

[126]Torrance, *Scientific Theology*, p. 106. Torrance is adamant that this is not an independent openness or readiness for God traceable to something immanent in humanity or the church's social being apart from a relation to the living God. Rather this social coefficient embodied in the church arises in reciprocity with God's self-revelation, for God's self-revelation creatively evoked Israel's and the apostolic church's corporate responses and utilizes those responses in God's continuing self-revelation to humanity, as we saw in chapters two and three (see Torrance, *Scientific Theology*, p. 105). Furthermore, Torrance notes that this coefficient cannot be abstracted out of that relation of reciprocity between God and Israel/the church, and treated as an autonomous structure or epistemological *a priori*, anymore than there are innate *a priori* human cognitional structures in the Kantian sense. Rather Torrance characterizes the social coefficient of knowledge of God embodied in Israel and the church as a modification of human life and thought that arises within the Creator-creature relationship that may not be abstracted out of the relation of reciprocity with God and treated as an *autonomous* structure (see p. 106). Underlying this whole discussion is Torrance's understanding of the "contingent" nature of humanity in a relation to God that entails humanity's dependence on, yet utter difference from, God, and an element of human independence. See Torrance, *Theological Science*, pp. 55-105, and all of Torrance, *Divine and Contingent Order*.

Theology cannot be abstracted from its appropriate matrix within the church, which provides the initial and ongoing orientation for theological activity. This is something Torrance believes that evangelical churches have missed, for "in the general development of the Evangelical Churches . . . there has been a failure to appreciate adequately the living embodiment of faith and truth in the corporate life and structure of the Church" (see Thomas F. Torrance, *Theological Dialogue between Orthodox and Reformed Churches* [Scottish Academic Press, 1985], p. 107).

[127]Torrance, *Scientific Theology*, p. 118. Here we see once again that in Torrance's perspective, scientific theology and the evangelical and doxological life of the church are inseparable. As a Reformed theologian, Torrance argues that "the Reformed Church sought from the very beginning to allow the dogmatic and ecclesiastical forms of the Church's life and ministry to interpenetrate each other in obedience to the Word of God. . . . Liturgy and theology go hand in hand. . . . Such is the integration of doctrine and discipline, of faith and order, of worship and theology so characteristic of the Calvinistic Reformation" (see Thomas F. Torrance, "Our Witness Through Doctrine," in *Conflict and Agreement in the Church* [London: Lutterworth, 1959], 1:94).

Thomas Langford has criticized Torrance as having "an extremely rationalistic or intellectualistic understanding of faith" (see Thomas Langford, "T. F. Torrance's Theological Science: A Reaction," *Scottish Journal of Theology* 25 [May 1972]: 158). But this criticism is difficult to sustain when one considers the role of Christian life and community in Torrance's theology. Torrance explicitly states that "we cannot undertake these tasks [theology and doctrinal formulation] without a living, personal experience of the Truth, and without constant prayer that we may be given illumination to understand and ability to speak of the Truth which by its very nature is utterly beyond us" (Torrance, *Evangelical Theology*, p. 136). Similar assertions are found in *Theological Science*: theological statements "are at their very root statements of inquiry, prayer and praise to God made in the Name

Scientific theology. Thus the basic insights or fundamental clues that theology utilizes to grasp and express the intrinsic relations in God's self-revelation arise out of the evangelical and doxological life of the church in response to the gospel as the church indwells the Scriptures.[128] According to Torrance, scientific theology is always a refinement and development of knowledge of God in God's self-revelation and self-communication through Jesus Christ and in the Holy Spirit that arises at the evangelical and doxological level described in the previous chapter.[129]

The specific tasks of theology are to refine, extend, correct and unify such knowledge, and, of course, test the church's proclamation and life in light of it. This entails a return to the Scriptural witness with those primary convictions or clues that have taken shape in the theologian's mind within the evangelical and liturgical life of the church as it meditates on Scripture. The theologian "indwells" the conjoint semantic focus of the various strata of the Old Testament and New Testament witness in their reference to God's self-revelation in Jesus Christ; then the basic clues or convictions mentioned above are tested, refined, extended, or possibly questioned and significantly revised.[130]

Torrance maintains that this demands a *theological* exegesis and interpretation of the biblical text, a movement of thought in which we try to discern and articulate the intrinsic interrelations within God's *oikonomia* out of which Scripture arose and to which Scripture bears witness.[131] Now

---

of Jesus" (Torrance, *Theological Science*, p. 160). Also Torrance, *Theological Science*, pp. 39, 41, 135, 163, 200, 210, 212-14, 282.

This common criticism of Torrance arises out of a failure to discern the way theological activity and formulation are related to God's self-revelation through *participatory knowing at the evangelical and doxological level*. Once detached from that matrix, theology and doctrine become abstract conceptual activity/structures, and we are left thinking concepts instead of divine realities through concepts, something Torrance repeatedly warns against.

[128]Torrance, *Transformation*, p. 94.
[129]See chapter eight, pp. 286-301. Also see Torrance, *Scientific Theology*, p. 85.
[130]Torrance, *Resurrection*, p. 10.
[131]Torrance, *Evangelical Theology*, p. 42. Elsewhere Torrance writes, "Evangelical theology is built up not through systematic construction out of biblical propositions, but through such a cognitive indwelling of theologians in the Holy Scriptures that the objective truths of divine revelation become steadily imprinted upon their minds. It is then on the ground of those truths and their inner connections to which the Scriptures refer, and under the guidance of the theological instinct they generate, that theologians must think it all out for themselves and bring it to coherent expression" (Thomas F. Torrance, "The Distinctive Character of the Reformed Tradition," in *Incarnational Ministry: The Presence of Christ in the Church*, ed. C. D. Kettler and T. H. Speidell, [Colorado Springs: Helmers & Howard, 1990], pp. 13-14).

Torrance never spells out all that this "indwelling" entails—indeed, there is a real sense in which it cannot be made fully explicit because it is an integrative activity that is rooted in the personal participation and the tacit dimension. However, the process of indwelling involves all of the normal hermeneutical apparatus, including the historical-critical method which Torrance maintains is "scientifically obligatory," despite its limitations as already noted.[132]

Through this interpretive process of indwelling the biblical witness, the theologian's mind "becomes assimilated to the *integration* of the different strata [of the biblical texts] in their bearing upon the objective events and realities they intend, and . . . there arises a structural kinship between his knowing and what he seeks to know."[133] For Torrance—and this is a point of critical significance in understanding his theological method, particularly his position regarding hermeneutics and his resultant formulation of the nature of doctrine—this entails an integration of form "which operates at a profounder level than any formal deduction . . . and which cannot be reproduced or replaced by any explicit processes of a logical or inferential kind,"[134] important as they may be in other aspects of theological inquiry, as they are in natural science, as we noted above.

Torrance's formulation of the integration of form in biblical and theological inquiry is of a profoundly *personal* (on the divine and human poles of the knowing relation), though not *subjective*, character. In fact, Torrance argues that personal participation is radically accentuated in Christian theology, since we are concerned with a personal self-communication of God through Jesus Christ in the Spirit—a communication in which we are intimately and intensely personalized in our being and knowing of God.[135] Knowledge of God cannot be separated from the mediation of reconciliation, for knowing God entails a cognitive union with God in which God's

---

[132]Torrance, "Distinctive Character," p. 9. Torrance has written nearly twenty articles and books dealing with hermeneutics, including articles on Aquinas, Reuchlin, Erasmus and Schleiermacher, and a book devoted to the hermeneutics of early patristic writers (Thomas F. Torrance, *Divine Meaning: Studies in Patristic Hermeneutics* [Edinburgh: T & T Clark, 1995]) and another to Calvin's hermeneutics (Thomas F. Torrance, *The Hermeneutics of John Calvin* [Edinburgh: Scottish Academic Press, 1988]). For the primary places where Torrance discusses his own position in some depth see the "Reader's Guide" for chapter nine, pp. 385-86.

[133]Torrance, *Resurrection*, p. 11.

[134]Ibid., pp. 11-12.

[135]Torrance, *Evangelical Theology*, p. 46.

love and holiness affects everything in our lives.[136]

There is an appropriate circularity to this theological activity in which exegesis and interpretation of Holy Scripture proceed with, and are

---

[136]Torrance, *Mediation*, pp. 35-36. At this point we need to examine what I consider to be the most serious criticism of Torrance's theological position to date. Daniel Hardy argues that the obscurity of Torrance's theology is not simply due to Torrance's complex style of writing or even to the difficulty of the subject-matter. Rather it is "the nature of the position he adopts," Hardy contends, "which verges on the private and publicly inexpressible" (Hardy, "Thomas F. Torrance," p. 86). For Torrance it is impossible to verify the correlation between the knower and what is known outside of the participatory relation. All that those in the knowing relation can do is speak or write in a way that will help others "see" the reality in question, somewhat like trying to help another person see the 3-D image in the *Magic Eye*.

Hardy identifies three difficulties with Torrance's position: (1) the privileged position of those in the knowing relation, (2) the "occasionalist" character of that position and (3) the "exclusivist" claims for the knowledge thus attained (see Hardy, "Thomas F. Torrance," pp. 87-88).

Hardy's critique is as serious as it is pointed and deserves sober consideration. The charges of "occasionalism" and "actualism" have become standard criticisms of theologians who, like Torrance, are Barthian-oriented. How far are these valid objections to Torrance's position?

First of all, it must be pointed out that the "occurrence" of the integration of form, for Torrance, is not a "bare" occurrence, but part of a process of "indwelling" a particular field of inquiry. It does not *just* occur for those to whom it occurs, but occurs as one attends to all that the field embraces, until the basic clues or insights arise which then serve to guide further investigation of the field. That those insights arise in a extralogical or nonabstractive manner—on the basis of tacit knowing and personal participation, which cannot be rendered completely explicit or displaced by analytic or deductive methods—certainly implies the importance of the "occurrence" of those clues or insights. But what Torrance has in mind is not nearly as bare as Hardy depicts it, and therefore, not nearly as private and publicly inexpressible as Hardy suggests. In fact, for Torrance there is a decidedly communal element to all of this, as we have noted at various points in this chapter.

Second, for Torrance the integration of form does not just "occur" and then disappear. To be sure, Torrance speaks of the importance of "reliving the event," and "ending in experience." But he also says that, once successful integration of form occurs in human inquiry, it continues manifesting itself, not unlike once one has solved a puzzle, one can no longer approach the puzzle as if one does not know the solution. Another example is the *Magic Eye*. Once you have seen the 3-D image, you can no longer forget its presence and it becomes even easier to "relive" the participatory event of seeing that 3-D image.

In Torrance's epistemology the integration of form entails a rational counterpart to what we know, often expressed in terms of a concept or a theory. The *homoousion* is a good example; it is a counterpart firm enough to merit the kind of analysis Torrance has developed and which I have tried to summarize throughout this chapter and at other points in the book.

It is also at this point that Torrance has consciously moved beyond Barth, as is clear from Torrance's questioning of Barth at precisely this point: "How far did Barth appreciate this and how far did he really get to grips with it [the need for a rational counterpart in our knowing of God]?" See Thomas F. Torrance, *Karl Barth: Biblical and Evangelical Theologian* (Edinburgh: T & T Clark, 1990), p. 155. Torrance sees Barth as very close to restricting the

guided by, a theological understanding of the truths and realities they mediate. Yet at the same time the theological understanding of those truths
and realities is itself controlled by the ongoing exegesis and interpretation
of the biblical texts.[137]

Furthermore, in Torrance's mind, this "inevitably has the effect of allot-
ting to the Scriptures a subsidiary status" to the realities they intend.[138]
This is why Torrance is willing to grant the difficulties and even contradictions in the New Testament accounts of the resurrection for example,[139]
and yet not be terribly concerned by them.

This does not diminish the importance of Scripture in Torrance's theology, for "without all that the Scriptures in the saving purpose of God have
come to embody, we would not be able to know God or to have intelligible
communion with him within our continuing human and historical existence."[140] Rather for Torrance this has meant a profound rethinking of the
doctrine of Scripture in relation to God's self-revelation, as we have seen
in chapters two, three and six.[141]

The role of tradition in theology. Torrance finds the kind of theological
inquiry described here in the classical conciliar theology that came to ex-

---

relation between God and humanity to the event of grace without working out the ontology and nature of the epistemological structures (form in knowing) that arise in theological inquiry into God's dynamic self-revelation and self-communication (see pp. 156-59).

A third qualification of Hardy's criticism is the formidable body of arguments and docu-
mentation that Torrance (and Polanyi) offer in support of the fact that both the process
leading up to the "occurrence" and the "occurrence" itself (with the qualifications regarding its character just offered) are, *due to their very nature,* not fully formalizable, which
seems to be the real point of Hardy's criticism. If this is the case, then what Hardy seems to
be calling for is a return to some form of foundationalism in which the conditions of
knowledge are rendered completely explicit, an ideal that has been something of a holy
grail for modern philosophy and theology, at least until recently when many have been
giving up the quest for indubitable foundations.

Finally, Torrance does not advocate simply remaining at the level of occurrence, but
rather going as far as one can toward rendering the occurrence explicit, while acknowledging that there are limits because of the finite and historical character of human existence, and because of the informal, participatory character of the tacit dimension and extra-
logical relation it entails.

[137]Torrance, *Evangelical Theology,* p. 42. Also see Torrance, *Resurrection.*

[138]Torrance, *Resurrection,* p. 12. Also see Torrance, *Evangelical Theology,* pp. 13, 17-19, 46-48,
105-9, 119-20, 122-24.

[139]Torrance, *Resurrection,* p. 4.

[140]Ibid., pp. 12-13.

[141]See above chapters two, pp. 61-82; three, pp. 98-113; and six, pp. 221-33. Also see Thomas
F. Torrance, "My Interaction with Karl Barth," in *How Karl Barth Changed My Mind,* ed.
Donald K. McKim (Grand Rapids, Mich.: Eerdmans, 1986), p. 53.

pression in the early church in the Niceno-Constantinopolitan Creed, which has been so beneficial to Torrance's own theological work.[142]

Torrance believes that a real grasp of the basic interrelations and intrinsic structures of the realities of the Christian faith is not only possible, but has actually taken place in certain crucial periods in history, like Nicaea-Constantinople and the Reformation. Though not uncritical of tradition, Torrance carries on a substantive dialogue with the history of theology in developing his own theological perspective. This is an important element in Torrance's theological method that Daniel Hardy has correctly identified, for Torrance utilizes what he learns from this dialogue in order to discriminate what is a genuine advance from the various distortions of the gospel that have occurred in the history of the church.[143]

Thus Torrance subtly interweaves his own positive position and his historical research. This is no naive circularity, but a sympathetic and critical assimilation between truth in the past and truth of the present, which Hardy notes reinforces Torrance's critical realist methodology and "provides a powerful argument for the normalcy—as against alternatives—of both the content and the method which he [Torrance] advocates."[144] Tradition plays an essential and positive role in Torrance's theology and theological method, though always in service of Torrance's scientific intent of allowing theology's subject-matter, God in God's self-revelation, to be the determining factor in content and method.

Examples of the integration of form in theology. Torrance finds an example of the kind of integration of form described throughout this section taking place again and again in the life and history of the church as "something like the doctrine of the hypostatic union . . . keeps on forcing itself upon our minds and we are convinced that here we have penetrated deeply into the inner logic of the evangelical material."[145]

Another example of what Torrance has in mind, of course, is the *homoousion.* Torrance sees the *homoousion* as an effective integration of form, a faithful theological concept that is neither deduced from Scripture, nor imposed on Scripture, nor even a conclusion to an inductive process of examining all the texts that speak of Christ's relation to God.[146] The *homoou-*

[142]Torrance, *Evangelical Theology,* p. 49.
[143]Hardy, "Thomas F. Torrance," pp. 73-75.
[144]Ibid., p. 74.
[145]Torrance, "Integration," p. 165.
[146]See chapter two, pp. 70-81, and chapter eight, pp. 286-301.

sion articulates the basic constitutive relations in the revealing and redeeming acts of God in Jesus Christ. The *homoousion* crystallizes the evangelical conviction that it is *God* who is present in Jesus Christ for our salvation; and in the fellowship of the Holy Spirit, it is *God* who opens our eyes to the gospel and the Scriptures, and lifts us to share in the love which God is as Father, Son and Holy Spirit.[147] The *homoousion* gives "compressed expression in exact and equivalent language, not so much to the biblical terms themselves but to the objective meaning or reality they were designed to point out and convey."[148] As such, it has continued to serve as a guide to further interpretation of the Holy Scriptures, though in Torrance's mind always in a manner subordinate to, and revisable in light of, the reality of God's self-revelation mediated through Scripture.

Moreover, as we saw in the last chapter, Torrance also points out that when this kind of theological activity, and the integration of form it entails, is carried a stage further, "we find that we penetrate into a higher level of unity and simplicity [the Trinity] which gives coherent order to the whole stratified structure of our theological concepts."[149] While the *doctrine* of the Trinity, Torrance contends, is an apprehension of God that falls short of reality of the Trinity, it represents what we must think and say of God in light of God's self-revelation and self-communication as Father, Son and Holy Spirit, and as such the Trinity constitutes the ground and grammar of Christian faith and thought.

The *doctrine* of the Trinity is an example par excellence of the kind of interpretation of Scripture and integration of form in theology that Torrance advocates. This means that Torrance's account of how the doctrine of the Trinity arises and the actual content of his doctrine of the Trinity is the example par excellence of the fundamental axiom of his scientific theology:

---

[147]Torrance, *Evangelical Theology*, p. 112. Torrance elsewhere argues that "here the historical Jesus Christ and the theological Jesus Christ are found to be fused not only in a dimension of spatio-temporal depth but in a dimension of divine-human depth, for the *energeia* and the *logos* intrinsic to him are found to be intrinsic to the *being* of God itself. It is that fusion which makes the fact of Jesus Christ the creative, self-interpreting reality he is in our worshipping experience and interpreted understanding of him. Once we have come to know Jesus Christ in this way, we cannot return to the Gospels and read them in such a way as to obliterate this understanding of him from our minds, any more than, on quite a different level, we can try to fit together a second or third time the scattered pieces of a jigsaw puzzle in pretended ignorance of the picture that emerged when we completed it the first time" (Torrance, "Historical Jesus," p. 524).

[148]Torrance, *Evangelical Theology*, p. 112.

[149]Also see Torrance, "Integration," p. 165, and chapter eight above, pp. 286-301.

the rigorous development of material content and theological method together in light of the intrinsic interrelations in the subject-matter theology
investigates, God in God's trinitarian self-revelation and self-communication.

Torrance maintains (he believes in ecumenical harmony with the trinitarian faith and evangelical theology of the ancient catholic church) that
the doctrines of the hypostatic union (including the *anhypostasis/enhyposta-
sis* couplet), the vicarious humanity of Christ, the *homoousion*, the christocentric creation, and the Trinity together enable us to enter the inner
cohesion of the biblical witness so that we discern something of the intelligible pattern in God's *oikonomia*.[150] Such doctrinal formulations arise out
of the integrative theological activity described throughout this chapter
and disclose the intrinsic interrelations of God's self-revelation and self-
communication.[151]

The nature of doctrine.[152] Torrance's scientific theology, as we have
seen, is not developed by logical deduction from fixed premises taken
from Scripture or from the "data" regarding the historical Jesus that are
unearthed by historical-critical exegesis. Rather it is the kind of theology
that operates with a profounder integration of form. In this kind of scientific theological inquiry or theological science, Torrance contends that the
basic clues arise out of a participatory process of indwelling the biblical
witness within the evangelical and doxological life of the church.

We organize those clues into a model, a set of concepts or doctrines that
enable us to grasp and articulate the intrinsic interconnections in God's
self-revelation and self-communication.[153] Such a "model" is a flexible and
revisable conceptual instrument utilized in the forward movement of
theological inquiry. If this model enables us to probe deeply into the cohesion and pattern of God's revelation, Torrance says that we then proceed
to develop a higher-level "disclosure model," such as the doctrine of the

---

[150]Torrance, "Integration," pp. 165-66.

[151]If the historical-critical method is unable to arrive at these clues that are developed into
refined theoretical components (doctrines) in our knowledge of God (the hypostatic
union, *homoousion*, and the Trinity), it is because the analytic and abstractive tendencies of
the historical-critical method hinder it from entering the all-important *integrative* process
that enables theological science to attend to all that the biblical texts embrace in their witness to God's self-revelation and grasp at least something of the complex of relations
underlying the biblical message.

[152]For an in-depth treatment of the nature of doctrine in the theology of Thomas F. Torrance
see Colyer, *Nature of Doctrine*.

[153]Torrance, *Scientific Theology*, p. 85.

Trinity (and the three levels of interrelated concepts it entails), in order to clarify and simplify the whole structure of our knowledge of God, as we saw in the previous chapter.[154]

Thus doctrines, for Torrance, are not simply propositions corresponding to objective realities (evangelical rationalism), for that is a misunderstanding of how thought is related to reality. Nor are doctrines non-discursive symbols of inner pre-conceptual experiences (the experiential-expressivism characteristic of so much of modern theology). Neither are doctrines second-order rules governing first-order discourse (the cultural-linguistic paradigm of George Lindbeck).[155] According to Torrance, doctrines are disclosure models. When properly developed as integrations of form arising out of the kind of theological and hermeneutical activity described, they are theoretical formulations that can progressively disclose the realities they signify, but always in a manner subordinate to, revisable in light of and relativized by those realities. Though imperfect and creaturely, doctrines bring to expression something of the ineluctable order and relations constitutive of the realities to which theological inquiry is directed.

5. The Nature of Truth

The relation of language to being in theology. Theological formulation occurs as convictions and concepts arise not by deduction, abstraction or even induction but out of indwelling the Scriptures and participatory knowing at the evangelical and doxological level that is personal and informal, though nonetheless rational.[156] This includes real self-revelation and self-communication on the part of God through the creaturely medium that revelation called into contrapuntal relation for the continuing mediation of God's self-communication. Theology also entails real human cognitive activity yielding creaturely conceptual structures that arise first as clues and then as even more carefully formulated doctrines like the *homoousion* or the doctrine of the Trinity. This kind of knowing is dynamic *and* ontological on the divine *and* human poles of the knowing relation.

The significance of this discussion for the relation between language and being is that Torrance is adamant that there "is not and cannot be any

---

[154]Ibid., p. 86. See chapter eight (pp. 286-301) above.
[155]See George Lindbeck, *The Nature of Doctrine* (Philadelphia: Westminster Press, 1984).
[156]See Torrance, *Ground and Grammar*, pp. 92-96, and Torrance, *Scientific Theology*, pp. 72-86.

logical bridge between concepts and experience."[157] There is no logical
bridge between doctrines and the realities they intend. Rather, doctrines
are correlated with the realities they intend through indwelling, participatory knowing, and the tacit coefficient at the evangelical and doxological
level out of which doctrines arise.[158]

What is of importance is the *disclosive* relation that obtains between doctrines and the realities they intend. Doctrines do not arise by deduction,
abstraction or induction from the Scripture or from data concerning the
historical Jesus or propositional statements distilled from the Bible. Thus,
the application of doctrines to the realities they intend requires unformal-
izable integrative acts of recognition or spiritual discernment not all that
different from those out of which the doctrines arose, for it is a *relation* between our concepts and reality that cannot be resolved into the relations
that obtain between ideas.

This is why Torrance argues that "dogmatic structures [doctrines] . . .
cannot be complete in themselves if they are to be meaningful and consistent."[159] Doctrines are empty of material content and empirically irrelevant
if cut off from the participatory level, tacit dimension and extra-logical relation to God they entail.[160] This extra-logical relation is critical in all doctrinal formulation, though it is a relation that cannot, itself, be formalized.[161]

Yet, the significance of the kind of doctrinal disclosure model (the three
coordinated levels of concepts examined in the previous chapter) that Torrance advocates is that it clarifies and simplifies our knowledge of God. It
does this by enabling us to relate the evangelical and doxological level to the
economic (evangelical) Trinity and the ontological Trinity in such a way that
the actual informational content of God's self-revelation and self-communication comes to precise theological articulation, doing so without in any way
detracting from the participatory evangelical and doxological level.[162]

---

[157]Torrance, *Scientific Theology*, p. 76.

[158]This is why Torrance calls for a modification in how we define knowledge, since knowledge cannot be construed simply in terms of what is explicit (we know more of the mystery of God than we can tell). Thus reality cannot be defined simply in terms of what can
be correlated with explicit concepts and statements. Torrance's convictions regarding the
relation between language and being deeply influences his understanding of truth and
authority in theology (see Torrance, *Transformation*, pp. 112-13).

[159]Torrance, *Scientific Theology*, p. 93.

[160]Ibid., p. 85.

[161]Ibid., p. 123.

[162]Ibid., p. 86.

This is what brings theological order into our everyday experience and faith in God, promoting further and deeper understanding of God, as we saw in the previous chapter regarding the way in which our evangelical and doxological knowledge of God ultimately rests on inner trinitarian relations between the Father, the Son and the Holy Spirit in which we participate through Christ and in the Holy Spirit.[163] Doctrines like the hypostatic union, the *homoousion* and the Trinity enable us to integrate the enormous complexity within the Scripture and its conjoint witness to the realities and events of God's *oikonomia*.[164] This, I believe, is one of Torrance's greatest theological contributions to the church.

We need cognitive instruments in order to grasp and express the relations inherent in the gospel of the Christian faith. Doctrines serve that function. As such they are, of course, always subject to revision in light of God's self-revelation out of which they arose and which they bring to explicit formulation.[165]

The nature of truth. Christians, however, do not always agree in their interpretations of Scripture or in their theological understanding and doctrinal formulation. How are interpretations and doctrinal formulations put to the test in the kind of approach Torrance advocates? How does he understand truth and the truth claims of doctrine? This is particularly significant in light of the fact that disagreements are not always overcome by an appeal to Scripture.[166]

Drawing on the work of Anselm, Torrance develops several distinctions in order to elucidate his understanding of truth in theology. He outlines a stratification of truth comprising several levels that clarifies the character of truth and the truth-claims of doctrine.[167]

---

[163]Ibid., p. 85.

[164]The stratified structure of our knowledge of God, which arises in our thought as we probe into the intrinsic intelligible relations of the realities and events of God's self-revelation and our evangelical and doxological experience of them, would finally "be no more than a pyramid of speculative constructs, if it did not throw any light on that subject matter and could not be evidentially and epistemically correlated with it in such a way that . . . [it] is opened up in its power of ontological reference, so that our experience is considerably deepened" (Torrance, "Integration," pp. 165-66).

[165]Torrance, *Scientific Theology*, p. 81.

[166]Torrance, *Evangelical Theology*, p. 122. Torrance argues that we have to allow the truth of God to retain its priority over all our interpretations and theological formulations (see pp. 122-23). Torrance finds this kind of approach in John Calvin's preface to the *Institutes* of 1536 in which Calvin defended the doctrine that he outlined in it by an appeal not simply to biblical citation or ecclesiastical authority, but to the "Truth of God."

[167]See Colyer, *Nature of Doctrine*, chapter five, for a more detailed treatment of the nature of

On the first level there are *two truths of statement:*[168] (1) a syntactical element whereby a statement functions in a consistent and coherent manner
with other words and (2) a semantic function in which a statement refers
to a state of affairs beyond itself.[169] Strictly speaking, a statement is truthful
only when it is true in both of these ways.[170] Torrance calls this the "truth
of signification," in which the syntactical element and the semantic element operate together in such a way as to disclose the truth of being (form
in being) in the reality signified.[171]

However, since truth is dependent on the nature of the reality signified (form in being must condition the integration of form in knowing),
the truth of signification is not located strictly in the statement, for the
truth of being is always prior to the truth of statement which is dependent on the truth of being for its content. This content is assimilated and
integrated by the human knower through participatory interaction with
the reality known (there are no *a priori* categories), as we have seen
throughout this chapter.[172] Thus the truths of statement and signification

---

truth in Torrance's theology.

[168]Torrance, *Scientific Theology*, p. 144.

[169]See ibid., p. 144, and Torrance, *Evangelical Theology*, p. 128.

[170]Torrance, *Scientific Theology*, p. 144. Also see Torrance, *Evangelical Theology*, p. 128, and Torrance's lengthy discussion of the nature of truth and problems of logic, in Torrance, *Theological Science*, pp. 141-280.

[171]Torrance, *Scientific Theology*, p. 144.

[172]Ibid. Even though it is impossible to articulate in a statement how statements are related
to reality, this does not mean that the truth of a statement has no real relation to the truth
of being (see p. 143). While there is no logical bridge between language and being, statements serve the truth of being by directing our minds to reality so that the reality itself
shows through. This is the ground of Torrance's suspicion of correspondence and coherence theories of truth, for he asserts that when we attempt to develop an account of epistemology as an abstractive process it seems to repeatedly generate a kind of correspondence
view of truth as a way of relating form to being. But when form assumes its own independent status, then a coherence theory of truth gains acceptance (see p. 49). Torrance argues
that no consistent theory of truth can be developed within the epistemological dualism
presupposed by each of these theories. See Thomas F. Torrance, "Theological Realism" in
The Philosophical Frontiers of Christian Theology, ed. Brian Hebblethwaite and Stewart Sun-
derland (Cambridge: Cambridge University Press, 1982), pp. 169-73. Also see Torrance,
Evangelical Theology, p. 59, and Torrance, "Theological Realism," pp. 169-76, for a detailed
discussion.

Mark Achtemeier suggests that "Torrance clearly operates with some sort of notion of
correspondence between thought and reality . . . but that correspondence is a complex
one" (see P. Mark Achtemeier, "The Truth of Tradition: Critical Realism in the Thought of
Alasdair MacIntyre and T. F. Torrance," *Scottish Journal of Theology* 47, no. 3 [1994]: 365).
Achtemeier's article is a careful and extremely thoughtful comparison of Torrance and
MacIntyre on tradition, truth and the process of rational inquiry. What is missing in Achtemeier's account of Torrance's perspective on these themes, is Torrance's understanding

presuppose the *truth of being* which is reality in its intrinsic relations (form in being).[173]

Yet the truth of created being is not a self-subsistent truth, for it is a contingent truth dependent on the supreme truth of God for its existence. This is why Torrance thinks that the truth of creaturely being already has a mute reference beyond itself, though a subtle reference, as we saw in chapter five in relation to Torrance's reconceived natural theology.[174]

The ultimate level of truth, of course, is the *supreme truth* of the self-existent being of God. Here there is a difference between the truth of God and all other truths, for while the other truths are true only by reference beyond themselves, the truth of God is what it is without any reference to anything beyond itself.[175]

Torrance points out that his account of the stratification of truth is an *a posteriori* reconstruction that prescinds from the actual heuristic process of human knowing or integration of form that we discussed earlier in this chapter.[176] Yet Torrance finds this stratification of truth of great significance, for it clarifies the fact that since the truth of a statement lies in its referring beyond itself, a true statement cannot be reduced "simply to its truth-function in discourse and it discloses the objective depth that a true statement must have beyond itself."[177]

Furthermore, this stratification of truth reveals, Torrance contends, that we cannot define truth purely in relation to the human subject, since the truth of reality signified remains whether it is signified falsely or not sig-

---

gration of form that arises out of indwelling, the tacit dimension and participatory knowing, as outlined throughout this chapter. A discussion of Torrance on the integration of form would clarify Torrance's understanding of truth and the role of tradition, especially in relation to MacIntyre.

My suspicion is that it is precisely at the point of the relation between tradition and Torrance's holistic, integrative, participatory, critical realist epistemology, that Torrance and MacIntyre are the furthest apart. I believe that Torrance would view MacIntyre's emphasis on tradition and community as only a partial answer in response to enlightenment liberals and their modern foundationalist epistemologies based in universal reason untainted by tradition. I think Torrance would see MacIntyre's movement back into tradition and community as a way to answer modernity, but also to cope with the fundamental epistemological dualism mediated through the Aristotelian-Thomistic tradition which MacIntyre inhabits, as Achtemeier points out in his insightful article (see Achtemeier, "Truth of Tradition," pp. 372-73).

[173]Torrance, *Scientific Theology*, p. 145. Also see Torrance, *Evangelical Theology*, pp. 128-29.

[174]Torrance, *Scientific Theology*, p. 145. Also see Torrance, *Evangelical Theology*, pp. 128-29.

[175]Torrance, *Scientific Theology*, p. 145. Also see Torrance, *Evangelical Theology*, pp. 129-130.

[176]Torrance, *Scientific Theology*, p. 146.

[177]Torrance, *Evangelical Theology*, p. 130.

nified at all.[178] There is thus an "irreversible relation" between the truth of statement and the truth of the reality stated, for the truth of our statements is the consequence of the existence of things, and not vice versa.[179]

In light of the stratified structure of truth, Torrance contends that doctrinal formulations are properly made only as we seek to penetrate through the created speech and truth of the biblical witness (which arose in the course of the events and realities of God's self-revelation and self-communication in space and time) to the "solid ground of the Truth, Speech, and Rationality of God" on which the biblical witness rests. We must do this so "that everything may be understood and expounded directly in the light of the Truth that God himself is." The real content of God's self-revelation "is not the signifying truths of the Scriptures but the Truth of God revealed in and through them."[180]

While the Holy Scriptures are the mediate source of doctrine, doctrinal formulations—when they are true—are objectively grounded in God's own self-revelation that resounds through Scripture as God continues to address us anew.[181] In this way theology does greater justice to the Holy Scriptures, Torrance contends, for it seeks to establish its doctrinal formulation not simply in the signifying truth of the biblical statements but in the solid truth of God which the Holy Scriptures serve.[182]

Justification and authority in theology. As noted throughout this book, Torrance contends that in Jesus Christ, God communicates not simply truths about himself, but the supreme truth of his very self. This, in turn, implies that theological formulations, insofar as they are true, are relativized by this truth and indicate far more than they express. Torrance thinks that this is epistemologically consistent with the proper, realist function of words and statements within his understanding of the way in which form is integrated in the day-to-day life of Christian faith and in scientific theology.[183]

---

[178]Torrance, *Scientific Theology*, p. 146. Torrance contrasts this with Kant's view of truth (see p. 159).

[179]Torrance, *Evangelical Theology*, p. 130.

[180]Ibid., p. 135.

[181]Ibid., pp. 134-35.

[182]Ibid. Of course, for Torrance, knowing the truth of God is quite impossible apart from God's condescension to be one with us in our creaturely conditions and therefore to sustain our knowing and our doctrinal formulation that arise out of a real relation to God through God's self-revelation (see p. 136.) This is what God has done in the incarnation of his truth within our contingent creaturely existence in Jesus Christ within the matrix of Israel, and in the outpouring of the Holy Spirit upon the apostolic community.

[183]Torrance, *Scientific Theology*, p. 144.

In other words, Torrance thinks that "theological concepts and statements have their justification through the Grace of God alone."[184] Doctrines do not have their proper truth by a process of verification that we enact, for we cannot force God to be the truth of our thoughts and our statements about God.[185]

Of course, out of respect for the truth of God revealed in Jesus Christ, the church is called to think and speak faithfully and correctly about God through its doctrinal formulations. Torrance thinks that this is the essential meaning of orthodoxy and humility before God.[186] The verification of our theological formulations requires the same kind of participatory relation to the divine realities that occurs in the genesis of theological concepts at the evangelical and doxological level.[187] This is in keeping with Torrance's dynamic *and* ontological understanding of revelation, in which *God* is the content of revelation.

Yet God's self-revelation and self-communication is one in which God has created a profound reciprocity with us and a corporate medium of relations and structures of thought and life (for example, Israel, Christ's vicarious humanity, apostolic witness and the Scriptures that arose out of it) that God has called into contrapuntal relation to God's self-revelation as the continuing creaturely instrumentality through which God's self-communication still meets us.

Since God honors this creaturely medium of structures of thought and life, Torrance argues that we must acknowledge "secondary authorities or delegated authorities whose function it is to serve his [God's] supreme Authority . . . in such a way as not to obscure it but let it appear in all God's Prerogative and Majesty."[188] The Holy Scriptures are certainly authoritative for doctrinal formulation, though Torrance accords primacy to God's self-revelation that resounds through Scripture,[189] as noted above.

Furthermore, while the ultimate authority for doctrinal formulation

---

[184]Ibid., p. 148.

[185]Ibid. Torrance maintains that justification by the grace of God in Jesus Christ has an *epistemological* application as well as an ethical one, for it calls into question all our attempts at epistemic self-verification. To attempt such self-verification, in Torrance's mind, is to falsify the gospel at its very root.

[186]Ibid., p. 149.

[187]Torrance, *Theological Science*, p. 198

[188]Torrance, *Evangelical Theology*, p. 154.

[189]Ibid., p. 96.

and verification is the *autousia* and *autoexousia* (the self-being and self-authority) of God through Scripture, when this authority is given its rightful place, the church and its tradition also carry authority, so long as the church's structures and doctrines remain open through Scripture to the objective truth and authority of God's self-revelation and self-communication through Christ and in the Holy Spirit.[190]

However, the church often allows the cultural divisions and ideological passions present in the world to cut back into its own existence, so that the church comes to reflect the fragmentation and pluralism of secular culture.[191] Torrance thinks that this has led to an inappropriate multiplicity of beliefs and doctrines that derive from unending questions posed by different cultural ages and contexts, rather than "the deep invariances in our human relation to God."[192] Torrance sees this as one of the causes of church division, for instead of serving as a reconciling force in human society, overcoming the divisions that arise in a world impacted by sin, the church has all too often allowed the tensions in the world to cut back into

---

[190]Torrance, "Theological Realism," pp. 180-81.

[191]Torrance, *Scientific Theology,* p. 151. The fluidity of human life and thought allows social coefficients from different fields of inquiry to influence one another, creating the potential for structures of meaning or systems of ideas conditioned by other frames of reference to influence the church's life and thought in a negative manner (see Torrance, *Theological Science*, p. 221, and Torrance, *Scientific Theology,* p. 105). Torrance also states, "Theology can never operate outside the historical situation and therefore cannot but be conditioned by the notions and tools which it uses from age to age" (see Torrance, *Rationality,* p. 4).

Here Torrance also notes, "Sociologists tell us that the theology of every generation is conditioned by the culture through which it passes—and of course they are right. But whereas the sociologists are professedly indifferent to whether such a state of affairs is right or wrong, a scientific theology cannot remain indifferent" (Thomas F. Torrance, *Theology in Reconciliation: Essays Towards Evangelical and Catholic Unity in East and West* [Grand Rapids, Mich.: Eerdmans, 1975], p. 273).

All of this becomes immensely complex when one considers Torrance's admission that there is not *a* social coefficient of knowledge, rather social coefficients that arise in symbiosis not simply between society and the world of intelligible reality, but in particular communities (scientific, religious, etc.) and their individual fields of interest, coefficients which are not sharply cut off from one another (see Torrance, *Scientific Theology,* pp. 102, 105). The complexity and difficulty created by this admission, not to mention conflict between competing social coefficients, leads Torrance to admit the difficulty of genuine knowledge and the need for humility (see p. 115). Thus the corporate relation toward God in and through the church, including the tradition this generates, can become distorted by nontheological factors arising out of the changing cultures within which the church finds itself, so that differing interpretations of divine revelation develop, yielding conflicting patterns of faith and practice (see, pp. 105, 119-20, 151).

[192]Torrance, *Scientific Theology,* p. 152.

its own life and thought with schismatic results.[193]

Doctrinal criticism. In light of this, Torrance believes that a recovery of the stratified structure of truth and authority, described in this section, could have a purifying effect through the discipline of doctrinal criticism, opening the way for significant clarification and simplification of the church's doctrinal heritage.[194] Theology must be a critical science, for it must constantly "examine historical doctrines with a view to distinguishing in them what is proper to the authentic substance of the faith and what is foreign to it but which has understandably been merged with it from the paradigms of contemporary society."[195] This kind of theological science and doctrinal criticism must "engage the Church in repentant rethinking of all its interpretation, preaching, and teaching."[196]

This demand for repentance *(metanoia)* in which the church is progressively liberated from the ideological twist of the prevailing social consciousness, inevitably entails a renewal of the church's whole interpersonal life and mission, since doctrine and life are not sharply separated in Torrance's theology.[197] This is, in fact, part of Torrance's motivation for developing a rigorous scientific theology that tries to identify the central theological concepts and relations through which knowledge of God can be organized into various levels of thought with fewer and more natural concepts or doctrines having wider applicability.[198]

Torrance thinks that this kind of theological activity cannot but serve an

---

[193]Ibid., p. 120, and Torrance, *Reconciliation*, p. 8. Torrance finds this particularly troubling today because of the pluralistic fragmentation of society that he sees as infecting Western culture, which the church has come to reflect (see Torrance, *Scientific Theology*, pp. 120, 151-52). One of the reasons that this is a problem for the church is that the church must communicate the message of the reconciling love of God in Jesus Christ in the idiom of the culture. This can lead to the temptation to adapt the interpretation of that message to prevailing paradigms of the social consciousness of secular life. Yet the struggle is not only with the structures of secular life, but with popular religion in the church that also adversely influences knowledge of God and doctrinal formulation (see Torrance, *Scientific Theology*, p. 120). Also see Torrance, *Rationality*, p. 118, and Torrance, *Theological Science*, p. 277.

[194]Torrance, *Scientific Theology*, pp. 152-53.

[195]See Torrance, *Reconciliation*, p. 273.

[196]Torrance, *Evangelical Theology*, p. 47.

[196]Torrance, *Evangelical Theology*, p. 47.

[197]See Torrance, *Rationality*, pp. 116-20; Torrance, *Scientific Theology*, pp. 40-48; and Torrance, *Theological Science*, p. 221. Torrance even speaks of reconstruction of the psycho-social patterns of communities we inhabit, indeed repentant reconstruction of ourselves. Also see Torrance, *Reconciliation*, pp. 272-75.

[198]Torrance, *Scientific Theology*, p. 154.

ecumenical function, for it is possible to attack the divisions within the church from behind by starting from the consensual theological center of Christian faith and utilizing a rigorous scientific approach to liberate the church from entrenched divisions of ideological origin.[199] For this reason, Torrance argues that the scientific theology he advocates, with its criticism and reformulation of doctrine, "becomes the *sine qua non* of ecumenism in which we come to grips with the psychological and sociological condition-ing even of our most profound theological concepts."[200]

In fact, according to Torrance, theology ought to so lift the mind and life of the church above that of the current sociocultural milieu that the church is set free to "play a similar role in relation to the world."[201] There is not space here to discuss the details of this further, but what is important to note here is that Torrance sees himself as a theological evangelist who thinks that theology should not only transform the church, but change hu-man culture as well.[202]

This brings us full circle in our investigation of how to read the scientific theology of T. F. Torrance. Born on the mission field, Torrance is a theolo-gian who never ceased to be an evangelist. He has always been concerned with the theological renewal of the church and the need to evangelize the foundations of scientific culture so that the gospel can take root and trans-form the world to the praise and glory of the triune God. Torrance sees no conflict between a rigorous scientific theology and a participatory evan-gelical theology in which every area of our life and thought is affected by the love of God the Father through the grace of our Lord Jesus Christ in the communion of the Holy Spirit.

Jesus Christ, the way, the truth and the life. This kind of evangelical and doxological, scientific trinitarian theology will always keep Jesus Christ, who is the way, the truth and the life, at the center of all of its activ-ity. As the way, Jesus Christ is not just a teacher, for he himself is the way

[199]See Torrance, *Scientific Theology*, pp. 154-56. Also see Torrance, *Reconciliation*, pp. 8-9. It is in this light that we must understand Torrance's work at the center of the dialogue between the Orthodox and Reformed churches leading to the "Agreed Statement on the Holy Trinity."

[200]See Torrance, *Rationality*, p. 118. Torrance, drawing on a passage from one of the church fathers, even argues that through the reformation of its life and doctrine, the church should be viewed not as growing older, but as getting younger and younger (see Thomas F. Torrance, "Our Witness Through Doctrine," in *Conflict and Agreement in the Church* [Lon-don: Lutterworth, 1959], 1:96).

[201]Torrance, *Scientific Theology*, p. 120.

[202]See Torrance, *Transformation*, pp. vii-xiv, and Torrance, *Theological Science*, p. 278.

in his own personal being.[203] Torrance thinks that this has the effect of prohibiting theology from straying into "timeless and spaceless generalities or abstract possibilities" and demands doctrinal formulations to be correlated with Christ's personal being.[204]

In Christ and his majestic "I am," Torrance argues that we meet the ultimate truth of God face to face. This means that all of the levels of truth from the truth of signification through the truth of created being to the ultimate truth of God are indivisibly united in the oneness of Jesus Christ's divine-human person.[205] As such, Christ is the truth of God to humanity and the truth of humanity to God, the self-revelation and self-communication of God to humanity and the perfect human response in thought, word and deed, and therefore the standard and norm for the all Christian doctrine concerning God and God's relation to the world and all Christian mission in the world.[206] As *the truth,* Jesus Christ is the decisive embodiment of God's truth and thus the *authoritative judge* to whom doctrinal formulations and all aspects of the life and ministry of the church must submit.[207]

Since it is the very truth and Word of God that we encounter in Jesus Christ, theological formulations are true only as they arise out of and refer to the truth of God embodied in the divine-human reality of Jesus Christ himself.[208] Doctrines must refer away from themselves as truths of signification through the truth of Christ's human and creaturely being to the supreme truth of God revealed in and through Christ. We use doctrines correctly and truthfully when we think realities through doctrines.[209]

---

[203]Torrance, *Evangelical Theology,* p. 137.

[204]Ibid., p. 138.

[205]Ibid., p. 137.

[206]Ibid.

[207]Ibid., p. 138. This admission that Jesus Christ is the truth also entails the intense personalization of the truth (see p. 139). This is truth in the form of personalizing being, Torrance argues, which not only radically transforms the subjective pole of our knowing relation, but also retains essential mystery even in self-revelation (see pp. 140-41).

The revelation of the truth of God in Jesus Christ is not, however, an unintelligible mystery, for though it reaches out beyond our comprehension, it is a truth that we may apprehend, and as we do so it illumines ever-wider areas of our knowledge and our lives. Insofar as doctrinal statements are true, they will manifest a persistent fertility in their openness to the truth embodied in Jesus Christ, as in the case of the Nicene-Constantinopolitan Creed, which has played such an important role in the history of Christian faith. See Torrance, *Trinitarian Faith;* this whole book is a demonstration of this point.

[208]Torrance, *Evangelical Theology,* p. 142.

[209]Ibid., pp. 146-47.

Jesus Christ is also the life, the actualization of the creative life of God among humankind and, as such, the sole source of life and salvation. Torrance thinks that this demands a "living theology" in which thinking is embodied in a way of living in relation to the life-giving acts of Christ mediated to us through the Spirit of Christ, as we have seen throughout the previous chapters.[210]

This is really the core of what Athanasius, Calvin and Torrance mean by *Eusebeia*: godly living, godly worship, godly thinking, all first embodied in the primal *datum*, the mystery *(mysterion)* of God's trinitarian self-revelation in Jesus Christ and the relation of *his* vicarious humanity *to* God the Father *in* the Holy Spirit. *Eusebeia*, in Torrance's theology, is first and foremost Jesus Christ himself. The one true theology is the bodily resurrected vicarious human mind of Christ himself where *Theologia* is *Eusebeia*. "Great beyond all question is the mystery of godliness *(to tas eusebias mysterion)*, he who was manifested in the flesh, vindicated in Spirit, seen by angels, proclaimed among the nations, believed on throughout the world, raised to glory."[211]

Yet we may participate in this *Eusebeia* (which is identical with Jesus Christ) in the communion of the Spirit who unites us to Christ's vicarious humanity and through Christ with the Father so that we come to know the love that God is, and live life in union and communion with God who is love.[212] To know God in this evangelical and doxological, christocentric and trinitarian manner is to know God *kata physin* (according to God's nature), and therefore in a rigorous scientific manner (in strict accordance with God's nature, the intrinsic trinitarian interrelations, the being-in-communion, one being three persons of God who loves us to the uttermost). *Theologia* (trinitarian and scientific theology developed in strict accordance with God's triune nature) *is Eusebia* (godly living, worship and thinking that comes about through evangelical and doxological participation in the gospel from the Father through the Son in the Spirit, in the Spirit through the Son to the Father). *Theologia* is *Eusebia*. If you understand this point, you know something about how to read T. F. Torrance.

> It is more godly and accurate to signify God from the Son and call him Father, than to name him from his works and call him Unoriginate. (Athanasius)

---

[210]Ibid., p. 138.
[211]1 Timothy 3:16. This is Torrance's translation. See Torrance, *Christian Doctrine*, p. 73.
[212]See Ephesians 3:19.

Selected Bibliography of Thomas F. Torrance's Major Publications

The following selected bibliography, arranged chronologically in each category, includes nearly all of Torrance's books published since 1965 and his many important articles since 1970. For the most complete and accurate bibliography of Torrance's publications see Alister E. McGrath, *T. F. Torrance: An Intellectual Biography* (Edinburgh: T & T Clark, 1999), pp. 249-96.

Books
Theology in Reconstruction. London: SCM Press, 1965. Reprint, Eugene, Ore.: Wipf & Stock, 1997.

Space, Time and Incarnation. London: Oxford University Press, 1969. Reprint, Edinburgh: T & T Clark, 1997.

Theological Science. London: Oxford University Press, 1969. Reprint, Edinburgh: T & T Clark, 1996.

God and Rationality. London: Oxford University Press, 1971. Reprint, Eugene, Ore.: Wipf & Stock, 1997.

Theology in Reconciliation: Essays towards Evangelical and Catholic Unity in East and West. London: Geoffrey Chapman, 1975. Reprint. Eugene, Ore.: Wipf & Stock, 1997.

Space, Time and Resurrection. Edinburgh: Handsel, 1976.

Christian Theology and Scientific Culture. New York: Oxford University Press, 1980.

The Ground and Grammar of Theology. Charlottesville: University of Virginia Press, 1980.

Divine and Contingent Order. New York: Oxford University Press, 1981. Reprint, Edinburgh: T & T Clark, 1998.

Juridical Law and Physical Law: Toward a Realist Foundation for Human Law. Edinburgh: Scottish Academic Press, 1982.

Reality and Evangelical Theology. Philadelphia: Westminster Press, 1982. Reprint, Downers Grove, Ill.: InterVarsity Press, 1999.

Transformation and Convergence in the Frame of Knowledge: Explorations in the Interrelations of Scientific and Theological Enterprise. Grand Rapids, Mich.: Eerdmans, 1984.

Reality and Scientific Theology. Edinburgh: Scottish Academic Press, 1985.

The Hermeneutics of John Calvin. Edinburgh: Scottish Academic Press, 1988.

The Trinitarian Faith: The Evangelical Theology of the Ancient Catholic Church. Edinburgh: T & T Clark, 1988.

The Christian Frame of Mind: Reason, Order, and Openness in Theology and Natural Science. New enlarged edition. Colorado Springs: Helmers & Howard, 1989.

Karl Barth: Biblical and Evangelical Theologian. Edinburgh: T & T Clark, 1990.

The Mediation of Christ. New enlarged edition. Edinburgh: T & T Clark, 1992.

Preaching Christ Today: The Gospel and Scientific Thinking. Grand Rapids, Mich.: Eerdmans, 1994.

Divine Meaning: Studies in Patristic Hermeneutics. Edinburgh: T & T Clark, 1995.

The Uniqueness of Divine Revelation and the Authority of the Scriptures. Edinburgh: Rutherford House, 1995.

The Christian Doctrine of God: One Being Three Persons. Edinburgh: T & T Clark, 1996.

Articles

"The Place of Word and Truth in Theological Inquiry According to St. Anselm." In *Studia medievalia et mariologica: P. Carolo Balic OFM septuagesimum explenti annum dicata.* Edited by R. Zavalloni, 131-60. Rome: Editrice Antonianum, 1971.

"The Framework of Belief." In *Belief in Science and in Christian Life: The Relevance of Michael Polanyi's Thought for Christian Faith and Life.* Edited by Thomas F. Torrance, 1-27. Edinburgh: Handsel, 1980.

"The Place of Michael Polanyi in the Modern Philosophy of Science." *Ethics in Science and Medicine* 7 (1980): 57-95.

"Ultimate Beliefs and the Scientific Revolution." *Cross Currents* 30, no. 2 (1980): 129-49.

"Theological Realism." In *The Philosophical Frontiers of Christian Theology: Essays Presented to D. M. MacKinnon.* Edited by B. Hebblethwaite and S. Sutherland, 169-96. Cambridge: Cambridge University Press, 1982.

"The Deposit of Faith." *Scottish Journal of Theology* 36, no. 1 (1983): 1-28.

"The Substance of the Faith: A Clarification of the Concept in the Church of Scotland." *Scottish Journal of Theology* 36, no. 3 (1983): 327-38.

"The Historical Jesus: From the Perspective of a Theologian." In *The New Testament Age: Essays in Honor of Bo Reicke*. Edited by William C. Weinrich, 2 vols., 2:511-26. Macon, Ga.: Mercer University Press, 1984.

"A Pilgrimage in the School of Faith: An Interview with T. F. Torrance," by John I. Hesselink. *Reformed Review* 38, no. 1 (1984): 49-64.

"Karl Barth and the Latin Heresy." *Scottish Journal of Theology* 39, no. 4 (1986): 461-82.

"Karl Barth and Patristic Theology." In *Theology Beyond Christendom: Essays on the Centenary of the Birth of Karl Barth*. Edited by John Thomson, 215-39. Allison Park, Penn.: Pickwick, 1986.

"The Legacy of Karl Barth (1886-1986)." *Scottish Journal of Theology* 39, no. 3 (1986): 289-308.

"My Interaction with Karl Barth." In *How Karl Barth Changed My Mind*. Edited by Donald K. McKim, 52-64. Grand Rapids, Mich.: Eerdmans, 1986.

"The Reconciliation of Mind." *TSF Bulletin* 10, no. 3 (1987): 4-7.

"The Goodness and Dignity of Man in the Christian Tradition." *Modern Theology* 4 (1988): 309-22.

"Interview with Professor Thomas F. Torrance." In *Different Gospels*. Edited by Andrew Walker, 42-54. London: Hodder & Stoughton, 1988.

"The Soul and Person in Theological Perspective." In *Religion, Reason and the Self: Essays in Honour of Hywel D. Lewis*. Edited by Stewart R. Sutherland and T. A. Roberts, 103-18. Cardiff: University of Wales Press, 1989.

"The Christian Apprehension of God the Father." In *Speaking the Christian God: The Holy Trinity and the Challenge of Feminism*. Edited by Alvin F. Kimel Jr., 120-43. Grand Rapids, Mich.: Eerdmans, 1992.

"Incarnation and Atonement: Theosis and Henosis in the Light of Modern Scientific Rejection of Dualism," *Society of Ordained Scientists*, Bulletin no. 7, Edgware, Middlesex (spring 1992): 8-20.

"The Atonement. The Singularity of Christ and the Finality of the Cross: The Atonement and the Moral Order." In *Universalism and the Doctrine of Hell*. Edited by Nigel M. de S. Cameron, 225-56. Exeter: Paternoster Press, 1992; Grand Rapids, Mich.: Baker, 1993.

"Ultimate and Penultimate Beliefs in Science." In *Facets of Faith and Science, vol. 1: Historiography and Modes of Interaction*. Edited by Jitse van der Meer, 151-76. Lanham, Md.: University Press of America; New York: Pascal Centre for

Advanced Studies in Faith and Science, 1996.

"Einstein and God." *Reflections* 1. Princeton, N.J.: Center for Theological Inquiry (spring 1998): 2-15.

Selected Secondary Works
Books

E. L. Mascall. *Theology and the Gospel of Christ*. London: SPCK, 1977, pp. 46-50.

Ronald F. Thiemann. *Revelation and Theology: The Gospel as Narrated Promise.* Notre Dame, Ind.: University of Notre Dame Press, 1985, esp. pp. 32-43.

Christian D. Kettler. *The Vicarious Humanity of Christ and the Reality of Salvation.* New York: University of America Press, 1986, esp. pp. 121-55.

Alan G. Marley. *T. F. Torrance: The Rejection of Dualism.* Edinburgh: Handsel, 1992.

Colin Weightman. *Theology in a Polanyian Universe: The Theology of Thomas Torrance.* New York: Peter Lang, 1994.

Roland Spjuth. *Creation, Contingency and Divine Presence in the Theologies of Thomas F. Torrance and Eberhard Jungel.* In Studia Theologica Lundensia Series. Lund, Sweden: Lund University Press, 1995.

John Douglas Morrison. *Knowledge of the Self-Revealing God in the Thought of Thomas Forsyth Torrance.* Vol. 2, Issues in Systematic Theology. New York: Peter Lang, 1997.

Robert K. Martin. *The Incarnate Ground of Christian Faith: Toward a Christian Theological Epistemology for the Educational Ministry of the Church.* Lanham, Md.: University Press of America, 1998.

Alister McGrath. *T. F. Torrance: An Intellectual Biography.* Edinburgh: T & T Clark, 1999.

Elmer M. Colyer. *The Nature of Doctrine in T. F. Torrance's Theology.* Eugene, Ore.: Wipf & Stock, 2001.

Elmer M. Colyer. *The Promise of Trinitarian Theology: Theologians in Dialogue with T. F. Torrance.* Lanham, Md.: Rowman & Littlefield, forthcoming.

Articles

Thomas A. Langford. "T. F. Torrance's Theological Science: A Reaction." *Scottish Journal of Theology* 25, no. 2 (1972): 155-70.

Bryan J. Gray. "Towards Better Ways of Reading the Bible." *Scottish Journal of Theology* 33, no. 4 (1980): 301-15.

Robert J. Palma. "Thomas F. Torrance's Reformed Theology." *Reformed Review* 38, no. 1 (August 1984): 2-46.

Frank D. Schubert. "Thomas F. Torrance: the Case for a Theological Science." *Encounter* 45, no. 2 (spring 1984): 123-37.

Edward O. De Barry. "Review Article." *Saint Luke's Journal of Theology* 27, no. 3 (1984): 209-13.

Frederick W. Norris. "Mathematics, Physics and Religion: A Need for Candor and Rigor." *Scottish Journal of Theology* 37, no. 4 (1984): 457-70.

Walter R. Thorson. "Scientific Objectivity and the Listening Attitude." In *Objective Knowledge: A Christian Perspective*. Edited by Paul Helm, 59-83. Leicester, England: Inter-Varsity Press, 1987.

Walter Jim Neidhardt. "Thomas F. Torrance's Integration of Judeo-Christian Theology and Natural Science Some Key Themes." *Perspectives on Science and Christian Faith* 41, no. 2 (1989): 87-98.

Daniel W. Hardy. "Thomas F. Torrance." In *The Modern Theologians: An Introduction to Christian Theology in the Twentieth Century*, 2 vols. Edited by David Ford, 1:71-91. Oxford: Basil Blackwell, 1989.

C. Baxter Kruger. "The Doctrine of the Knowledge of God in the Theology of T. F. Torrance: Sharing in the Son's Communion with the Father in the Spirit." *Scottish Journal of Theology* 43, no. 3 (1990): 366-89.

Richard A. Muller. "The Barth Legacy: New Athanasius or Origen Redivivus? A Response to T. F. Torrance." *Thomist* 54 (1990): 673-704.

David F. Siemens Jr. "Two Problems with Torrance (reply to W. J. Neidhardt) 41 (1989): 87-98." *Perspectives on Science and Christian Faith* 43, no. 1 (1991): 112-13.

Kang Phee Seng. "The Epistemological Significance of *Homoousion* in the Theology of Thomas F. Torrance." *Scottish Journal of Theology* 45, no. 3 (1992): 341-66.

Stephen D. Wigley. "Karl Barth on St. Anselm: The Influence of Anselm's Theological Scheme on T. F. Torrance and Eberhard Jungel." *Scottish Journal of Theology* 46, no. 1 (1993): 79-97.

P. Mark Achtemeier, "The Truth of Tradition: Critical Realism in the Thought of Alasdair MacIntyre and T. F. Torrance." *Scottish Journal of Theology* 47, no. 3 (1996): 355-74.

John D. Morrison. "Thomas Forsyth Torrance's Critique of Evangelical (Protestant) Orthodoxy." *Evangelical Quarterly* 67, no. 1 (1995): 53-69.

Elmer M. Colyer. "Thomas F. Torrance." In *A New Handbook of Christian Theologians*. Edited by Donald W. Musser and Joseph L. Price, 460-68. Nashville, Tenn.: Abingdon, 1996.

John D. Morrison. "Heidegger, Correspondence, Truth and the Realist Theology of T. F. Torrance." *Evangelical Quarterly* 69 (1997): 139-55.

Paul D. Molnar. "God's Self-Communication in Christ: A Comparison of Thomas F. Torrance and Karl Rahner." *Scottish Journal of Theology* 50, no. 3 (1997): 288-320.

Reader's Guide

The following bibliography provides a guide concerning where to begin reading Torrance's mature theology on the themes covered in this book. The order of bibliographic entries under each chapter represents my suggested sequence for reading Torrance's work on the theological topics covered in that chapter. I privilege Torrance's later publications, and monographs over articles. For some chapters (chapter five on creation, and chapter nine on theological method), the range of Torrance's publication is so vast that only a sampling of his work can be included here. I also provide chapter titles from the books listed so that the reader can have a better idea of the content in particular bibliographic entries. The full bibliographic information appears only in the first citation. Unless otherwise indicated, Torrance is the author of the work.

Chapter 1: Torrance's Life & Achievement
John I. Hesselink. "A Pilgrimage in the School of Faith: An Interview with T. F. Torrance." *Reformed Review* 38, no. 1 (1984): 49-64.
"My Interaction with Karl Barth." In *How Karl Barth Changed My Mind*. Edited by Donald K. McKim, 52-64. Grand Rapids, Mich.: Eerdmans, 1986.
David W. Torrance. "Thomas Forsyth Torrance: Minister of the Gospel, Pastor and Evangelical Theologian." In *The Promise of Trinitarian Theology: Theologians in Dialogue with T. F. Torrance*. Edited by Elmer M. Colyer. Lanham, Md.: Rowman & Littlefield, forthcoming.
Alister McGrath. *T. F. Torrance: An Intellectual Biography*. Edinburgh: T & T Clark, 1999.

Chapter 2: The Mediation of Christ: *Homoousios*, Hypostatic Union, Atonement
The Mediation of Christ. Edinburgh: T & T Clark, 1992. Colorado Springs: Helmers & Howard, 1989.

Chapter 1: The Mediation of Revelation
Chapter 2: The Mediation of Reconciliation
Chapter 3: The Person of the Mediator
Chapter 5: The Atonement and the Trinity
The Trinitarian Faith: The Evangelical Theology of the Ancient Catholic Church. Edinburgh: T & T Clark, 1988.
Chapter 4: God of God, Light of Light
Chapter 5: The Incarnate Saviour
Preaching Christ Today: The Gospel and Scientific Thinking. Grand Rapids, Mich.: Eerdmans, 1994.
Chapter 1: Preaching Christ Today
Chapter 2: Incarnation and Atonement in the Light of the Modern Scientific Rejection of Dualism
Reality and Evangelical Theology. Philadelphia: Westminster Press, 1982. Reprint, Downers Grove, Ill.: InterVarsity Press, 1999.
Chapter 3: A Realist Interpretation of God's Self-Revelation
"The Deposit of Faith." *Scottish Journal of Theology* 36, no. 1 (1983): 1-2.
"The Atonement. The Singularity of Christ and the Finality of the Cross: The Atonement and the Moral Order." In *Universalism and the Doctrine of Hell*. Edited by Nigel M. de S. Cameron, 225-56. Exeter: Paternoster, 1992; Grand Rapids, Mich.: Baker, 1993.

Chapter 3: The Mediation of Christ: Christ's Vicarious Humanity
Mediation of Christ.
Preface
Chapter 4: The Mediation of Christ in our Human Response
Evangelical Theology.
Chapter 3: A Realist Interpretation of God's Self-Revelation
God and Rationality. London: Oxford University Press, 1971. Reprint, Eugene, Ore.: Wipf & Stock, 1997.
Chapter 6: The Word of God and the Response of Man
Space, Time and Resurrection. Edinburgh: Handsel, 1976.
Introduction
Chapter 8: The Lord of Space and Time
"The Deposit of Faith."

Chapter 4: The Love of God the Father Almighty
Trinitarian Faith.

Chapter 2: Access to the Father

Chapter 3: The Almighty Creator

"The Christian Apprehension of God the Father." In *Speaking the Christian God: The Holy Trinity and the Challenge of Feminism*. Edited by Alvin F. Kimel Jr., 120-43. Grand Rapids, Mich.: Eerdmans, 1992.

The Christian Doctrine of God: One Being Three Persons. Edinburgh: T & T Clark, 1996, pp. 55-59, 137-41, 203-7.

Chapter 5: Sovereign Creator, Contingent Creation

1. The Sovereign Creator; and 2. The Contingent Creation

Trinitarian Faith.

Chapter 3: The Almighty Creator

Christian Doctrine of God.

Chapter 8: The Sovereign Creator

The Ground and Grammar of Theology. Charlottesville: University of Virginia Press, 1980.

Chapter 3: Creation and Science

3. The Human Creature

"The Goodness and Dignity of Man in the Christian Tradition." *Modern Theology* 4 (1988): 309-22.

"The Soul and Person in Theological Perspective." In *Religion, Reason and the Self: Essays in Honour of Hywel D. Lewis*. Edited by Stewart R. Sutherland and T. A. Roberts, 103-18. Cardiff: University of Wales Press, 1989.

Ground and Grammar.

Chapter 1: Man, Priest of Creation

The Christian Frame of Mind: Reason, Order, and Openness in Theology and Natural Science. New enlarged edition. Colorado Springs: Helmers & Howard, 1989.

Chapter 3: Man, Mediator of Order

4. Natural Science and Theological Science

Christian Frame of Mind.

Chapter 2: The Concept of Order in Theology and Science

Chapter 4: Theological and Scientific Inquiry

Chapter 5: Fundamental Issues in Theology and Science

Chapter 6: Realism and Openness in Scientific Inquiry

Divine and Contingent Order. New York: Oxford University Press, 1981. Reprint, Edinburgh: T & T Clark, 1998.

Chapter 1: Determinism and Creation

Chapter 2: God and the Contingent Universe

Chapter 3: Theological and Scientific World-Views

Chapter 4: Contingence and Disorder

Transformation and Convergence in the Frame of Knowledge: Explorations in the Interrelations of Scientific and Theological Enterprise. Grand Rapids, Mich.: Eerdmans, 1984.

Chapter 7: Christian Theology in the Context of Scientific Change

Chapter 8: Newton, Einstein and Scientific Theology

5. A Reformulated Natural Theology

Karl Barth: Biblical and Evangelical Theologian. Edinburgh: T & T Clark, 1990.

Chapter 5: Natural Theology in the Thought of Karl Barth

Ground and Grammar.

Chapter 4: The Transformation of Natural Theology

Evangelical Theology.

Chapter 1: The Bounds of Christian Theology

Reality and Scientific Theology. Edinburgh: Scottish Academic Press, 1985.

Chapter 2: The Status of Natural Theology

Chapter 6: The Holy Spirit

Theology in Reconstruction. London: SCM Press, 1965. Reprint, Eugene, Ore.: Wipf & Stock, 1997.

Chapter 14: Come, Creator Spirit, for the Renewal of Worship and Witness

Trinitarian Faith.

Chapter 6: The Eternal Spirit

Christian Doctrine of God

pp. 59-67, 147-55, 180-94.

Chapter 7: The Church, the Body of Christ

Reconstruction.

Chapter 11: The Foundation of the Church: Union with Christ Through the Spirit

Trinitarian Faith.

Chapter 7: The One Church

"The Deposit of Faith"

Theology in Reconciliation: Essays Towards Evangelical and Catholic Unity in East and West. London: Geoffrey Chapman, 1975. Reprint, Eugene, Ore.: Wipf & Stock, 1997.

Chapter 1: Ecumenism

Chapter 2: The One Baptism Common to Christ and His Church

Chapter 3: The Pascal Mystery of Christ and the Eucharist

Chapter 6: The Church In the New Era of Scientific and Cosmological Change

Chapter 8: The Triunity of God, One Being Three Persons
Mediation of Christ.

Chapter 5: The Atonement and the Holy Trinity

Trinitarian Faith.

Chapter 8: The Triunity of God

Ground and Grammar.

Chapter 6: The Basic Grammar of Theology

Scientific Theology.

Chapter 6: The Trinitarian Structure of Theology

The Christian Doctrine of God.

Chapter 9: The Integration of Form in Theology
2. The Integration of Form From Descartes Through Polanyi

Ground and Grammar.

Chapter 2: Emerging from the Cultural Split

Scientific Theology.

Chapter 1: Classical and Modern Attitudes of Mind

Transformation and Convergence.

Preface

Chapter 1: The Making of the "Modern" from Descartes and Newton to Kant

Chapter 3: The Place of Michael Polanyi in Modern Philosophy of Science

Chapter 5: Ultimate Beliefs and the Scientific Revolution

4. Scripture and the Integration of Form in Theology

Transformation and Convergence.

Chapter 2: The Integration of Form in Natural Science and Theological Science

Ground and Grammar.

Chapter 5: Theological Science

Scientific Theology.

Chapter 3: The Science of God

Chapter 4: The Social Coefficient of Knowledge
Space, Time and Resurrection.
Introduction
Chapter 8: The Lord of Space and Time
Evangelical Theology.
Chapter 2: Theological Questions to Biblical Scholars
Chapter 3: A Realist Interpretation of God's Self-Revelation
"The Historical Jesus: From the Perspective of a Theologian." *The New Testament Age: Essays in Honor of Bo Reicke.* Edited by William C. Weinrich, 2 vols., 2:511-26. Macon, Ga.: Mercer University Press, 1984.
"The Deposit of Faith"
"Theological Realism." In *The Philosophical Frontiers of Christian Theology: Essays Presented to D. M. MacKinnon.* Edited by B. Hebblethwaite and S. Sutherland, 169-96. Cambridge: Cambridge University Press, 1982.
Christian Doctrine.
Chapter 2: The Christian Perspective
Chapter 3: The Biblical Frame
Chapter 4: The Trinitarian Mind
Theological Science. London: Oxford University Press, 1969. Reprint, Edinburgh: T & T Clark, 1996.
5. The Nature of Truth
Evangelical Theology.
Chapter 4: Truth and Justification in Doctrinal Formulation
Scientific Theology.
Chapter 5: The Stratification of Truth

Name Index

Achtemeier, Mark, 366-67
Adam, Karl, 197
Anderson, Ray S., 201
Anselm, 365
Aquinas, Thomas, 130-32, 186, 194, 357
Aristotle, 303
Arius, 70, 72, 188
Athanasius, 20, 29, 31, 45, 73, 75-77, 95, 104, 127-28, 134, 145, 149, 156, 159, 188, 193, 215, 217, 233, 234, 236-38, 241, 289, 303, 305, 314, 318, 321, 374
Baillie, John, 40, 44
Barth, Karl, 20-25, 38, 39-40, 43-45, 48-51, 55, 74, 75, 80, 86, 88, 93, 94, 102, 111, 118, 130-32, 156, 160, 165, 192-94, 197, 201, 205-6, 211, 218, 302, 315, 325, 333, 358
Basil the Great, 239, 316-18
Bauman, Michael, 16, 36, 40, 43-45
Blane, A., 187
Bloesch, Donald G., 120, 197
Boethius, 186
Bromiley, Geoffrey, 44
Brown, James, 323-24
Brunner, Emil, 41, 43
Bultmann, Rudolf, 39, 190

Butzer, Martin, 45
Cajori, Florian, 327
Calvin, John, 20, 40, 43, 44-45, 75, 93, 103, 163, 186, 242, 357, 365, 374
Cameron, Nigel M. des, 86
Campbell, John McLeod, 45, 118, 132
Clement of Alexandria, 352
Colyer, Elmer M., 37, 59, 120, 187, 294, 323, 365
Comte, Auguste, 186
Cullmann, Oscar, 44
Cyprian, 256
Cyril of Alexandria, 233
Descartes, René, 17, 33, 148, 325, 326, 329, 331
Dockx, Stanislav, 46
Einstein, Albert, 16, 20, 33, 48, 55, 56, 133, 184-88, 192, 193, 196, 198, 202, 325, 327-28, 331-34, 340-41, 344-46, 349, 351
Epiphanius, 31, 215, 233, 236, 238, 314
Erasmus, 357
Fackre, Gabriel, 63
Faraday, Michael, 333
Feuerbach, Ludwig, 344
Ford, David, 16, 20, 60, 289, 324
Gossip, A. J., 43
Green, Theodore, 41
Green, Garret, 324
Gregory of Nyssa, 111, 316-17
Gunton, Colin, 59, 329
Hardy, Daniel, 16-17, 60, 289, 324, 334, 337,

341, 358-60
Harris, Alan, 328
Hebblewaite, Brian, 75, 365
Heidegger, Martin, 17
Hesselink, John I., 16, 21, 23-24, 36, 37, 39-47, 50-51, 192
Hilary of Poitiers, 138, 256
Houston, James, 167
Hume, David, 17, 33, 38, 48, 196, 323, 325, 327-29, 346
Hunsinger, George, 22, 24, 242
Irenaeus, 253, 289
Kant, Immanuel, 17, 33, 38, 48, 58, 111, 196, 323, 325, 329-31, 333, 337, 341, 346-47, 352, 368
Katsir, B., 184
Kennedy, H. A. A., 24
Kermode, Frank, 324
Kernohan, R. D., 15, 24
Kettler, Christian D., 117-18, 356
Knox, John, 45, 118, 132
Langford, Thomas, 355
Lamont, Daniel, 38
Leibniz, Gottfried Wilhelm, 329
Lewis, Hywel D., 174
Lindbeck, George, 294, 363
Locke, John, 186, 195, 328-29
Lonergan, Bernard, 131, 341
Lovell, Bernard, 40, 187
Luther, Martin, 45, 88
Mackintosh, Hugh

p 70
p 144